SOCIAL PSYCHOLOGY AT THE CROSSROADS

Under the Editorship of GARDNER MURPHY

SOCIAL
PSYCHOLOGY
AT
THE CROSSROADS

THE UNIVERSITY OF OKLAHOMA LECTURES IN SOCIAL PSYCHOLOGY

Edited by JOHN H. ROHRER, Director, Urban Life
Research Institute, Tulane University (Formerly of
the University of Oklahoma)

and MUZAFER SHERIF, University of Oklahoma

HARPER & BROTHERS, Publishers, NEW YORK

SOCIAL PSYCHOLOGY AT THE CROSSROADS
Copyright, 1951, by Harper & Brothers
Printed in the United States of America

CONTENTS

PREFACE

The chapters of this volume are made up of papers which were presented at the conference on *Social Psychology at Crossroads* sponsored by the University of Oklahoma and held on its campus April 6–11, 1950. The sheer magnitude of the momentous events and complications of modern life are necessarily beginning to focus attention of men within the field of social sciences—as well as in other fields—on the problems created by man himself in his relations with other human beings and groups in an ever increasingly complex world. The various aspects of human problems, both on individual and group levels, are being studied by independent research workers in biology, psychology, anthropology, sociology, and other social sciences. The findings in any one of these fields do not always coincide with the findings in the related fields. Unless the findings in the related areas are synthesized by viewing them in a common perspective, by comparing notes and by considering together the implications of the results of each of them in relation to others, they are doomed to remain rather discrete pieces of knowledge no matter how valuable they may be in themselves. Social psychology, with its concern with the experience and behavior of the *individual* on one side and, on the other side, its concern with *group relations* and effects of *culture,* is becoming more and more such a meeting ground for these related fields. It was felt by the University of Oklahoma that it would be a profitable step toward an integrative synthesis of the sciences of man if a group of research men who were engaged in working on the frontiers of the sciences of man were brought together for a week to provide them with an opportunity to present their latest notions concerning their own special area and to have those notions discussed by the other scientists in attendance at the conference.

In organizing the conference topics an attempt was made to select topics which are of major importance to and understanding of why men act as they do. These topics were given to the participant speakers far enough in advance of the conference date to enable them to have sufficient time to organize their presentation. The general excellence of the papers included herein is evidence that the speakers made effective use of the time allowed. We are indeed grateful to them, not only for the excellent quality of their papers, but for the intense and stimulating task-oriented discussion which followed the presentation of each paper.

Credit for the realization of the plans for the conference, and this volume, is directly attributable to Mr. Ward Merrick of Ardmore, Oklahoma. Mr. Merrick is more than a great and good friend to the University of Oklahoma. His deep sense of social responsibility marks him as a great and good friend to all his fellow men. His faith and belief that our conference might ultimately contribute something to a better understanding of men (and hence provide a sound base for developing ways in which men can live more congenially with their fellow men) led him to provide for the cost of holding the conference.

As with any coöperative project undertaken, there are always real, generous contributions made by a number of people. From its inception, the conference had the fullest support of Dr. George L. Cross, President of the University, Dr. L. H. Snyder, Dean of the Graduate College, Dr. E. D. Meacham, Dean of the College of Arts and Sciences, Dr. M. O. Wilson, Chairman of the Psychology Department, Mr. B. Gunning, Executive Secretary of the University of Oklahoma Foundation and Mr. Merrick's fellow members of the Foundation's Board of Directors. Much help was given, especially in the preliminary planning by Dr. T. J. White and Mr. J. B. Freeman of the staff of the Extension Division of the University. Mr. M. Baker of the Extension Study Center was responsible for the flawless arrangements for conference rooms, and sleeping, dining and transportation facilities.

J. Paxton, J. Y. Ruth, W. Simpson, A. Smykal, and D. Swanders— all graduate students in the Department of Psychology at the University of Oklahoma, contributed much to the success of the conference through the effective accomplishment of unforeseen tasks which arose as the conference progressed.

The effective help of Miss Virginia Strickland and Mrs. Lu Hudson in preparing the manuscripts for publication materially shortened the time of putting together the various chapters of the volume.

Norman, Oklahoma   JOHN H. ROHRER
July 22, 1950   MUZAFER SHERIF

SOCIAL PSYCHOLOGY AT THE CROSSROADS

CHAPTER 1

Introduction

MUZAFER SHERIF
University of Oklahoma

In spite of the impressive achievements of the natural sciences and the technological developments which bring the means of living, communication, and transportation within the reach of human comfort and convenience, human relations today are fraught with confusion, uneasiness, and anxiety. As a consequence of this confusing state in human relations, more and more people today are turning for solutions and even prescriptions, to social psychology, whose main concern is the study of reciprocal relations between men and groups.

Social psychology is, as yet, in no position to write easy prescriptions. It is still groping its way at the crossroads. Groping at the crossroads may be taken as a sign of vitality. A few decades ago, conditions were not ripe even for serious groping.

From the perspective of the crossroads, we see the dead ends of individualistic "psychological" approaches to social psychology on one side. On the opposite side, we see the dead ends of the rival socio-cultural approaches to social psychology. Each of these dichotomous approaches, "individual" vs. "socio-cultural," branches off into little intricate blind alleys. When we survey the blind alleys of both approaches, we find refined material which can be utilized advantageously in the construction of the thoroughfare which we are bound to take some day.

The so-called "individual" approach is full of formulations which attempt to derive the products of human interaction—social structures, institutions, technology, values, and norms—simply by extrapolating the picture formed of individuals under given circumstances

1

and time, or from the operation of a sovereign instinct or list of them (e.g., MacDougall and Freud). The rival approach of culture apologists or exponents of various sorts of sociologisms is full of formulations almost obliterating the individual—making him well-nigh an empty vase into which culture and social prescriptions are poured (e.g., Durkheim). The result is obvious—fruitless controversy, without any prospects of resolution, over the adequacy of either an "individual" or "social" approach. Thus, both parties run in circles which constitute an intellectual heritage of the dichotomies still prevalent in so many areas of vital concern (e.g., secular vs. spiritual in education, individual rights vs. state rights in politics).

In recent years the state of helplessness has forced both parties to borrow from each other. It is becoming clear that mere juxtaposition of little segments from each other is not the way out; nor is there the possibility of laying down the two approaches along the same continuum. For the problem involved is not how much we can get along with one and how much more is needed of the other to complete the picture.

It is rather a matter of *levels*. If we are working on the psychological level, our unit of study is the single individual, and, hence, must be in terms of his psychological functioning—in such concepts as his motivation, his perception, his learning, and his reacting—in short, in psychological concepts. If we are working on the sociological or cultural level, our concepts of study are in terms of social organization, institutions, kinship system, status system, value system, language, art forms, technology—all the accumulated products of human interaction.

To be sure, if there were no human beings to interact, there would be no cultural or social products, social organization, status system, value system, or technology, etc. But once such products come into existence and accumulate, they take their appropriate places as stimulus conditions setting certain limits, certain perspectives for the very human beings who were originally responsible for them. It is man who made machines; we can also say machines, in turn, make man. It is man who created social organization; we can also say it is social organization that recasts man. Man is in the beginning of things, but his products are not man himself. His products (social organization, technology, language, etc.) become subject matters of new disciplines—which can be, and are, studied on their own level in a meaningful way without reference to single individuals. Thus, economics is a discipline in its own right, and so is ethnology, philology, fine arts, or music. To think otherwise would lead us to the absurd position of saying that everything is psychology—including physics and chemistry.

If we are working on the psychological level, no matter how overwhelming the effects of social and cultural conditions may be, the concepts and their functional relations have to be in psychological terms —viz., in terms of perception, learning, motivation, etc. If we can think of an individual whose conformity to his group is complete, and who is perfectly happy in his conformity, even in this case it would be a mistake, if we are psychologists, to explain him in any terms other than psychological—his motives, his temperament, his perceptions, his learning, his ego, etc. Of course, all these concepts have no meaning in vacuum; they have meaning only in their functional relationship to stimulus conditions. Perception is perception in relation to its stimulus conditions, and learning is learning of something. Demands of motives are in relation to the objects, things, and people in the surroundings.

Now let us take the case of the most ardent nonconformist. Even though he may be violently rebelling against everything in his society, his psychological accounting will be pitifully inadequate if his development is not traced in relation to so many settings of his life circumstances. Our analysis will fall pitifully short if it is restricted to a few items which we make sovereign in accounting for everything. It is becoming more and more evident in psychology in general, not only in its social brand, that reactions of any sort acquire their full significance only in relation to the whole framework of factors or determinants operating at a given time. Hence, man's experience and behavior take place in relation to a setting. Understanding of that setting becomes imperative. An adequate understanding of the setting derives from the study of sociology, ethnology, and other social sciences. Improvised notions concerning the nature of the social setting in fanciful quasi-psychological language have kept us in an imaginary world concerning the social stimulus conditions.

If we have the conception of levels clearly in mind, the controversy over individual vs. cultural approaches to social psychology becomes a meaningless controversy. The absurdity of two kinds of social psychology ("individual" as opposed to "social") becomes obvious. There emerges one unified conception of social psychology, the principles of which stem from general psychology only, whatever the rounded structure of these principles ultimately may prove to be. In rounding out itself, this unified social psychology does not have to neglect any factor or determinant coming from the individual himself; nor need it neglect any factors coming from the social stimulus conditions which are external in relation to the individual at birth. The *reductionism* so prevalently practiced by psychologists in regard to social stimulus conditions has been one of the most effective perpetuators of the fruitless dichotomy. Surrounding social stimulus conditions are not haphazard affairs. The family and other units of social organization, the furniture, the language, the social norms, the tools, etc., are patterned realities of the stimulus field, which are, we repeat, studied as such by sociologists, ethnologists, and others working on the social level. Such reductionism, so prevalent among the exponents of the so-called "individual" approach, has caused several authors interested in concrete social behavior of man to improvise the equally objectionable socio-cultural psychology as opposed to experimental psychology (e.g., Spranger, Durkheim). To save himself from the destruction of reductionism, the psychologist is waking up to the realization that he cannot simply improvise his notions about social stimulus conditions—about family organization, kinship system, language, status and role systems, and about the value or norm system. He is becoming aware of the necessity of learning these socio-cultural stimulus conditions from the social scientists who study them at their appropriate meaningful level.

Such a unified social psychology, which deals with individuals in relation to social stimulus conditions, uses only psychological concepts in its functional analysis. This functional analysis implies a well-rounded knowledge of the social stimulus conditions, which can be learned only from social scientists. To account for the patterning of the individual experience and behavior at any given moment, all the factors or determinants coming from the individual—his motivation, intelligence, temperament, his life history as it particularly relates to the situation at hand—must be brought into the picture simultaneously. For perception is the product of the external and internal factors operating at the given time—the totality of which constitutes the *frame of reference* of the functional relations of various items. That all the factors coming from the external field of stimulation and the factors coming from the individual influence each other in an interdependent way imposes upon us a very difficult task. The task is to go beyond the general statement that everything is related to everything else within the frame of reference and laboriously to vary this factor now, that factor later, with the ultimate aim of finding the relative *weights* for each and finally, expressing the relations in short-cut expressions.

Newcomb addresses himself to the crucial problem of the necessity of a unified social psychology (Chapter 2). First, he expresses his dissatisfaction with the present dichotomous state of social psychology. He rightly points his finger at the confusion caused by the existence of two social psychologies—one espoused by the "psychological approach," the other upheld by the "sociological approach." The major inadequacy of the "psychological approach" is that "it has never really faced the implications of the psychologists' claim to study the 'organism in environment,'" because it has been a "bit naïve concerning the full conditions of group life under which individual's perceptions of social behavior occur." On the other hand, social psychology represented by the "sociological approach" is equally defective. It has never really faced the well-established fact of biologically and otherwise determined *selectivity* of the organism. It has taken human organisms as "virtually empty receptacles into which culture is simply poured."

Newcomb insists on building a unified "social psychology which takes full account of the realities of psychological processes as well as the realities of social organization." Of course, the realities of social organization in relation to which the individual interacts as an active agent with certain motives, attitudes, frustrations, and gratifications of his life history cannot be accounted for merely by improvised notions concerning their nature.

On the side of psychological processes, Newcomb takes *perception* as the starting point, in line with the major development in social psychology of the last two decades. From here we can profitably extend ourselves to shared "frames of reference" of the group and its standardized products, viz. *social norms*. The social norms, in turn, constitute the matrix on which the *social attitudes* of the individual are formed in the process of *interaction*. With such a basic approach, we can effectively move to the interaction between individuals and the social norms, group structures, the established roles within them. The distinction that Newcomb makes between more or less socially established roles and the particular individual perception of them resulting in particular *role behavior,* which may vary from individual to individual, is a much needed distinction.

Another valuable point stressed by Newcomb is that norms, which are products of group interaction initially, are not dead entities. Norms develop about anything and everything which are of shared interest to two or more people who interact with each other. With the rise of new situations, new norms arise which in time become common property of the group.

Newcomb further elaborates on these major points, ending his chapter with concrete proposals for crucial research areas to be investigated within such a unified scheme of social psychology. Newcomb's incisive contribution should serve as a healthy corrective to those who are still cloistered as partisans of "psychological" or "sociological" approaches. The unified social psychological approach herein proposed, we repeat, takes full account of the realities of all the psychological factors and the realities of social organization which are initially on the side of the stimulus conditions. Our task then is the study of the interaction process between the two sets of factors and the reciprocal effects or products of the interaction.

This conception of social psychology does not neglect any factor coming from the individual—his biological endowment, his motives, his special thresholds in perception, learning, etc., the state he is in at the time as a consequence of the frustrations and gratifications of his particular life history, including the particular shadings of his affectivity. Likewise, it takes full account of the realities of culture and group structures without falling into the mutilating trap of reductionism. It can be easily demonstrated by concrete evidence that it is a mistake to state that in the interaction between internal factors and external social factors, the one or the other set is invariably the most weighty determinant of the psychological product. There are cases of interaction in which the external social factors play the dominant role in a lawful way; and there are cases in which factors coming from the individual are the weighty factors in determining the psychological product.

A unified scheme of social psychology will be achieved, then, by the full recognition of the factors coming from the individual himself and the factors coming from his socio-cultural surroundings. Accordingly, some of the most representative topics on biological, psychological, and socio-cultural levels are chosen for this book. Each one of these topics, and the underlying basic principles, are presented by men who are in the research frontiers of their particular area.

In any attempt to evaluate the various factors which may significantly influence the socio-psychological behavior of the individual, appropriate consideration must, of course, be given to the individual's biological inheritance. David and Snyder's review of some of the major concepts of classical genetics emphasizes the essentially heuristic nature of the concept of the gene as an isolable entity; at the same time, it shatters pre-formationist views of individual development which, although long since obsolete among geneticists, are still commonly attributed to them by laymen (Chapter 3). Even on levels of physiological activity, it is seen that the course of individual development cannot be described in terms of the genotype alone; interactions of environmental factors must be taken into account all along the line. At the psycho-social level, environmental influences impinge upon and interact with the developmental processes concerned in the formation of behavioral patterns at so many points that the role of genotypic differences as determinants of socio-psychological differences becomes negligible.

Consideration of the probable nature of evolutionary processes in the light of modern genetic theory leaves no vestige of scientific support for racist theories which pretend that there are genetic distinctions among ethnic groups which differentiate them in respect to temperament, mental capacity, or other characteristics of socio-psychological significance. The dominant selective forces which appear to have been operative throughout human evolutionary history, in all geographic regions and in all societies, are those which favor the evolution of *plasticity,* rather than of tendencies toward stereotyped response; plasticity is reflected, for example, in extraordinary capacity for the modification of behavior through learning. Purposeful modifiability of behavioral response is present in man so universally, and to such a unique degree, that it is properly to be regarded as a species-specific possession of *Homo sapiens.*

The contrast between social evolution and biological evolution in regard to the rate and facility with which these processes may occur exposes clearly the naïveté and futility inherent in ideas of improving the human species through *eugenic* programs. Significant changes in human population through biological evolution may be expected to occur over time intervals measured in hundreds or thousands of millennia; time intervals requisite for significant change through social evolution can be measured in generations or even decades.

On the basis of the above considerations, David and Snyder conclude their definitive treatment of genetic variability and human behavior with the significant statement that ". . . if mankind goes to the dogs within the next ten or twenty centuries, it is far more likely to do so as a result of inexcusable bungling in the management of human relations than as a consequence of genetic deterioration."

In view of the increasing attempts to carry over the generalizations reached on the basis of the study of lower animals to the explanation of the social relations of man, the discussion of the principles underlying social organization along the phylogenetic scale is a timely one. Schneirla performs this task in his well-documented chapter on "the 'levels' concept in the study of social organization of animals" (Chapter 4).

As a criterion of levels in animal capacity, complexity of process is far less significant than is aptitude for behavioral changes under new and variable environmental emergencies. Thus learning in some social insects is at times fairly complex, but is stereotyped and psychologically limited as compared with that in higher vertebrates. An important similarity among various levels of organized group behavior in animals is characterized by an extension of Wheeler's "trophallaxis" concept to include all types of reciprocal stimulation underlying approach responses in the social situation. A realistic theory is thereby obtained in place of vague "gregarious instincts." Thus the properties of group unity may be understood on different levels by investigating evolved species' organic characters promoting group reactivity, in relation to capacities (e.g., learning) which influence group pattern through ontogeny and group experience. In social insects, for example, a simple conditioning or habituation learning promotes a stereotyped affiliation of individual with group situation and group members, in contrast with the more extensive and plastic group affiliations introduced through advanced learning capacities in the higher mammals.

Once the basis of group unity has been clarified, conditions such as "dominance hierarchies" may be studied as factors modifying or opposing individual approach reactions to group situation and group members. A concept must be obtained which is not restricted to the implications of aggression-dominance relations, but which also subsumes ascendancy and other types of priority in group organization. A close comparison of different social levels suggests the need for a sharper differentiation of intra-group communication processes, as might be represented by the terms bio-social for insects and psycho-social for higher mammals—the latter being capable of social "signal" functions and in advanced cases, of symbolic interchanges.

In Chapter 5, Harlow discusses various aspects of animal social behavior with special emphasis on learning. He gives a survey of representative studies carried out on a single great biological order—the order of primates, which includes monkeys, apes, and man among its members. The first part of the chapter is devoted to a summary of studies on primate social behavior by Maslow, Carpenter, Zuckerman, Nissen, and Harlow and Yudin. Among these, of course, Carpenter's extensive field studies dealing with social organization and relations of howling monkeys, Rhesus monkeys, orang-utans, and gibbons are particularly noteworthy for the student of comparative social psychology. Harlow devotes the second part of his chapter to a discussion of the "role of learning in primate social behavior and personality," and suggests a number of experiments designed to rear various groups of primates (whose life histories are controlled) "under a variety of social environments, and test the effect of these diverse environments on personal-social traits." These suggestions are in line with the already existing studies and explorations of Carpenter, Stone, Louttit, Hunt, and others. The last part of the chapter deals with the promise of animal studies for the central problems of stress (neurosis), language, motivation, and learning. Harlow ends the chapter with a brief introduction of his "learning set" theory presented first in some detail in the *Psychological Review* in 1949.

Harlow is of the opinion that the study of learning and social behavior of lower animals will effectively help our understanding of human social psychology. From a methodological point of view no one can deny this possibility, as it is feasible to experiment on lower animals with the scientifically desirable controls and precision. It seems that there is a serious drawback to extending the generalizations reached on lower animals to human social behavior. Without exception, every aspect of social behavior of the human individual is affected, and even transformed, by his having a culture, no matter how primitive his particular grouping may be. The emergence of culture, as Harlow mentions in his chapter, is unique to the human species. For example, the accumulated system of language—just one aspect of culture—becomes such a vehicle in the ontogeny of human development that the acquisition of social attitudes, which constitutes perhaps the characteristic feature of human personality, is unthinkable without it. It might be well to ponder the fact that it takes highly trained university personnel to teach an anthropoid ape to utter merely three words of a *codified* language system; whereas even the most primitive, illiterate human grouping, without such scholarly assistance, possesses a *codified* language system consisting of words and structure which is transmitted, and at times expanded, by each succeeding generation. Until these points are clarified, it might be preferable to utilize the findings from subhuman species as valuable data of comparative psychology, and not overgeneralize to highly complex human relations. In this connection, perhaps the cautious scientific attitude may be to give due regard to the notion of *levels* along the phylogenetic scale in line with the discussion by Schneirla.

Now let us turn to two chapters which are specifically concerned with the major aspects of the functional relationship between the experience and behavior of the individual and his culture. In Chapter 6, Herskovits presents a sophisticated discussion of "cultural and psychological reality," based on his recent book, *Man and His Works: Science of Cultural Anthropology* (1948).[1] Herskovits devotes the major portion of his chapter to methodological aspects of the subject, turning at the end to various problems raised by the notion of "cultural relativism." The author starts by pointing out the importance that the concept of culture acquired during the first half of the 20th century. Culture, which may be defined in short as "the man made part of the environment" is a peculiarly *human* phenomenon which exhibits regularities of structure and process. In this chapter we find a clear statement of the author's views of the relationship between concepts of culture, society and behavior. The concept of *"enculturation,"* which is one of the key concepts in the systematic view pre-

---

[1] The more detailed statement of the elaborated position of Herskovits concerning man, society, and culture is fortunately available in his book mentioned above, especially pages 625–641.

sented by Herskovits, deserves particular emphasis and elaboration.

One of the primary contributions of ethnology has been the implications of cross-cultural data in formulating generalizations concerning the human species. It was mainly through the eye-opening impact of cross-cultural data that psychologists finally realized the provincialism of their notions about so many psychological phenomena among which their ethnocentric concepts of "human nature" and various brands of instinct theories may be cited as representative examples.

Chapter 7 by Hallowell, entitled "Cultural Factors in the Structuralization of Perception," takes us down to the solid meeting ground in recent years of psychologists and the investigators in sociology and ethnology toward building a unified structure of social psychology. In recent years, perceptual reactions have become the prototype of all psychological reactions for social psychologists in singling out the effects of socio-cultural influences on the one hand and biological and strictly personal factors on the other. It is this conception of the patterning of perception by both personal and socio-cultural factors that has made a closer rapprochement between anthropologists and psychologists possible in recent years (p. 165). Society and culture do not get into the psychological make-up of the individual as devilish or angel-like entities in their own right; nor do they flow into him through his sense organs in discrete quantities. In so many concrete situations, they come in as factors (through his sense organs) which participate in the patterning of his perceptions along with other factors stemming from within himself. Hallowell, in this chapter, first presents a summary statement of the rapidly accumulating facts of cultural factors in structuring perception—a topic to which he has been contributing richly for over a decade. In addition to the statement of general facts of the contribution of cultural factors in perceiving, he gives fascinating illustrations of two specific kinds of cultural phenomena as factors in the structuring of perception—viz. language and art forms. The special point of symbolic factors is a much needed and timely one, inasmuch as symbolic factors have not yet been systematically brought into this emerging unified scheme. Linguistic symbols or labels come in as factors in structuring and categorizing individual experience in relation to stimulus situations. When stimulus objects are classified in one class rather than another, under a symbol or label, they are perceived as members of one group rather than the other. The functional significance, the value of these objects to the individual, follows these lines of categorization on the whole. If some berries, which are not harmful in themselves, are put under a tabued category in a culture, they are perceived as nonedible berries, of course, as fixated through learning. Likewise, if some women are classified in the kinship system of a society under a sexually tabued category and other women under a sexually sanctioned category, the perceptual selectivity and thresholds are modified in relation to the two respective groups of women. In short, linguistic symbols or labels come in as categorizing factors in the structuring of perception. This in turn brings about shifts in the functional relationship of the individual to the stimuli in question. It is only under artificial and deliberately mutilated conditions that perceiving is a mere cognitive process.

The same socio-cultural factors do not produce *exactly* the same psychological effects on the members of the same social group. Strictly *personal* or *idiosyncratic* factors take part in the structuring of perception. Thus perceptions of the different members of the same social group in relation to the same socio-cultural stimuli are not identical; they vary within limits of a scale peculiar to the group.

In Chapter 8, two psychologists, Barker and Wright, present an approach to the problem of concretely studying and defining the specific stimulus conditions in relation to which interaction takes place. So long as social psychologists must make guesses concerning the social stimulus situations, their theorizing is of necessity highly tentative. For, as the authors state, "we do not know with precision for different cultures and different conditions of life the degree of occurrence of the factors thought to be of importance for social behavior and psychosocial development." It is therefore fitting that social psychologists study such *ecological* problems, defining the particular social stimulus conditions in different life situations.

Necessarily such ecological problems involve work on different levels of study. If we claim to take all the factors influencing behavior and their due weights into consideration, the lines of study delineating the various social sciences must be crossed and recrossed. Barker and Wright correctly start with the *non-psychological milieu,* which includes the natural surroundings, the material surroundings, the economy, social structure, and social products, such as the ideology or value system. This non-psychological milieu provides concrete "behavior settings" and objects in relation to which behavior takes place. The existent behavior settings include not only the physical objects, but their *value* aspects as well. In relation to each, a definable sort of behavior is standardized as "appropriate," whereas other sorts of behavior would in this situation be "inappropriate" or "wrong." In most cases, there is a socially standardized *range* of behavior in which " 'fully right' behavior is modal and the 'clearly wrong' behavior least frequent."

On the basis of the study of the non-psychological milieu and the specific behavior settings and objects, a naturalistic examination of the "psychological habitat" becomes possible. At the University of Kansas, Barker and Wright and their colleagues have been conducting such field studies with the aim of developing methods for describing the psychological environment of children in their natural settings. Excerpts from a sample "specimen record" are therein reported. This specimen record was obtained by detailed recording of one child's behavior and the settings in which it occurred from the time he awakened in the morning until he was asleep at night. The investigators are somewhat critical of this method. Its obvious disadvantage, of course, is that the presence of an adult observer may considerably alter the psychological environment. However, the method yields detailed and interesting data which have the advantage of being complete and covering successive events over a time span.

In the following three chapters (Chapters 9, 10, and 11), MacLeod, Postman, and Volkmann discuss fundamental psychological processes, viz. judgment, perception, memory, and, partly, motivation, which are at the bases of any adequate treatment of the indispensable concepts of social psychology, such as attitudes, ego or self, and differential effects of group situations. From the point of view of psychological analysis, these three chapters probably constitute the core of fundamental functional relationships which are applied in most of the other chapters. The concepts discussed in these three chapters are organically related to the more concrete problems of social psychology presented by Newcomb, Sargent, Hartley, and Sherif.

In Chapter 9, MacLeod presents a systematic treatment of the "place of phenomenological analysis in social psychology." In the way of introduction to the main topic, discussion starts with a brief characterization of psychology in general, its relation to social psychology and brief historical summaries of four of the major theoretical settings of social psychology. At the very beginning MacLeod stresses the fact that social psychology, the principles it relies on, are part and parcel of psychology in general. "One of our tasks today is to break down the barriers which segregate it from the rest of psychology, and to develop a unifying point of view from which all experience and behavior can be understood as regulated by the same set of fundamental laws." The first of the four historically significant theoretical backgrounds the author mentions is the social psychological approach which is primarily concerned with the study of the structural properties of groups. Various types of "group mind" theories exemplify this approach in its initial crude form. The second main approach discussed is the instinct-oriented approach as exemplified by the systems of MacDougall and Freud. The learning-oriented theories represent the third major approach, which maintains that the primary explanatory principles of social psychology are the "laws" of learning. The fourth and most recent theoretical orientation is represented by the growing attempts "to find in the psychology of perception the basis for an understanding of social behavior and experience." This general orientation, represented in the most clear-cut way by Gestalt psychology, is the phenomenological approach. The historical sketch of the phenomenological approach, which had its beginnings long before the appearance of Gestalt psychology, serves to broaden the perspective of the recent enthusiasts of phenomenology who proclaim it to be a new frame of reference in psychology.

The rest of the chapter is devoted to the clarification of the phenomenological point of view in psychology, especially through the specific treatment of the central topics of perception, social perception, and ego as illustrative material. There is "a growing belief that if we are to understand social behavior we must have an understanding of the processes of perception"—"the direct and immediate datum of experience in relation to a concrete world of meaningful objects." The problems of *social perception* are not separate problems; their essential properties are included in the problems of perception in general. The exception MacLeod takes to the fashionable notion of *projection* is illuminating. It is assumed that perceiving the stimulus objects, especially when they are not well structured, in terms of our desires, "complexes," etc., is projection to those stimuli of what is really in us. In short, "we do not project the meaning into an object any more than we project the redness or the squareness into it."

The essential point in MacLeod's chapter is, of course, his characterization of the nature of psychological phenomenology. Phenomenology "is not a school or a system, but an approach. A phenomenon is by definition an appearance." Phenomenology in itself is not psychology; it is "sheer description." Psychology, which aims to be a science, must go beyond the stage of sheer description. It has to use concepts and explanatory principles which are not given in immediate perception or experience. But the main emphasis in the phenomenological approach is the insistence upon starting with immediate, "naïve," and (as Koffka and others also maintained) "unbiased" experience in relation to the objects of a concrete and meaningful world. As such, phenomenological observation should occur prior to the adoption of explanatory principles or a systematic theory. But phenomenological analysis must be used with discipline on the part of the investigator, if it is to serve us in formulating significant problems. If we let ourselves loose in phenomenological intricacies, we are bound to fall into a "private" world of subjectivisms, exemplified by various philosophical tendencies and certain recent trends in psychotherapy which come to the verge of saying that the world is merely what I have in my perception—my private psychological world. As MacLeod states, "beyond phenomenology there is always the lure of epistemology and metaphysics."

Traditionally, social psychology worked out by socio-culturally oriented writers was *artificially* posed against the "individual" oriented approach. During the last two decades, serious attempts have been made to work out a unified social psychology, based on experimentally verified generalizations, which embody at the same time the inescapable facts of culture and social organization. So far, the two most noteworthy attempts in America in this direction have been in terms of (1) of perceptual (cognitive) conceptualizations and (2) of "learning theory" based primarily on recent elaborations of the conditioning process. At present, at least, the majority of social psychologists seem to be proceeding along the perceptual (cognitive) approach. Postman's chapter constitutes a systematic contribution along this line of development (Chapter 10). Inasmuch as Postman makes a rather successful attempt to support his systematic propositions by factual evidence from experimental literature as well as studies carried out by himself and his associates during recent years, the chapter should prove to be highly useful to those who are interested in perceptual (cognitive) approach to social psychology.

It has become evident that perception, which is taken as the prototype of all cognitive processes, is not an additive build-up. It is not a mere intellectual affair. Perceptions are organized or structured products. And organization or structuring is a *bipolar* affair which is jointly determined by both external stimulus factors and internal or directive factors. The fact of bipolar determination of perception was stressed by Köhler in 1929 (4),[2] by Koffka in 1935 (3). This central fact was made the starting point of his social psychology by Sherif in 1935–1936 (12, 13). A series of significant experiments were carried out at the City College of New York by Gardner Murphy and his associates in the early '40's, each designed to determine the relative weights of external stimulus conditions and internal directive factors, respectively, which jointly determine the bipolar organization of the perception or memory in question (6, 7, 8, 10, 11). Since 1945, Postman, who was one of the contributors of the City College group, and his associates at Harvard have pushed forward this perceptual (cognitive) approach considerably (1, 2, 9). More recently, Krech and Crutchfield made the fact of bipolar organization of perception (cognition) one of the key points of their social psychology (5).

Before getting to the positive statement of a unified cognitive theory as the sound basis for an adequate social psychology, Postman rightly calls attention to the one-sidedness of *formalists,* whose main concern is almost exclusively on the stimulus side, and of *instrumentalists,* whose main concern is primarily with the adaptation and adjustment of the organism. The accumulating facts concerning bipolar organization of perception, which cannot be adequately understood without

---

[2] The following excerpts quoted from Köhler (*Gestalt Psychology,* 1929) are representative: "We may even say that, apart from drowsiness and similar states of low vitality, the organization of the total field will almost always have just that bipolar character, the self being directed to something else or away from it." (p. 323) . . . "Evidently it is not only the external situation which in a great many cases has to be considered, but the internal situation of the organism as well." (p. 325) . . . "This is the case, indeed, for, in the total field including the self, we find grouping dependent upon those directed attitudes." (p. 327)

full recognition of all external stimulus conditions and internal directive factors jointly operating at a given moment, make the one-sided emphases of both formalists and instrumentalists factually inadequate. There are conditions, lawfully studied, which render the relative weight of external (stimulus) factors more dominant. On the other hand, there are conditions in which internal (directive) factors come in as more weighty factors in the process of bipolar organization. Then our specific task is to vary systematically the properties of external stimulus factors and internal motivational factors, respectively, and to determine their exact relationship in so many possible cases of joint determination of perceiving and other cognitive processes. Probably the most valuable aspect of Postman's contribution is a number of propositions he formulates to this end, and the experimental evidence he presents in their support. An equally valuable aspect of Postman's chapter is his treatment of memory in concepts which are "continuous with the propositions on perceptual organization."

Postman prefers to use special terminology in referring to external stimulus factors and internal directive factors which jointly determine the perceptual organization. *Hypotheses* is the word he chooses to refer to *internal factors* (motives, attitudes, etc.) in a generic way. In his own words: "By hypotheses we mean, in the most general sense, expectancies or predispositions of the organisms which serve to select, organize and transform the stimulus information that comes from the environment" (p. 249). In short, the meaning of the word hypothesis is stretched to include all the topics covered under the psychology of motivation—hunger, sex, attitude, set, interest, etc. If the word "hypothesis" were a meaningless or neutral word to start with, it might not be so difficult to use it in this broad generic sense. Also, Postman prefers to refer to external factors with the word *"information,"* and to structured and unstructured stimulus situations with the expressions "appropriate information" and "absence of appropriate information." Since the characteristic that counts here in giving greater or lesser weight to external stimulus factors is not necessarily the amount of physical energy, but rather the structural relationship of the whole external stimulus field, it may be more parsimonious to refer to them in terms of structured-unstructured and gradations thereof. Since we already know something about properties of the external stimulus field in their being conducive or not conducive to perceptual grouping or organization on the basis of the studies of Wertheimer and others, a new set of terminology may not be in the interests of a unified theory on which Postman so rightly insists.

During the last two decades, an ever-increasing number of social psychologists have realized the almost direct implications of findings in the general psychology of perception for a host of their central problems. The implications of firmly established findings in the general psychology of judgment are not yet widely grasped. When the possibilities of this area of research are grasped, we shall advance a long way in establishing social psychology on firmer grounds methodologically. The great advantage of judgmental work is that it necessarily leads us to formulate our research designs in terms of precise dimensional analysis. Volkmann's authoritative chapter, which is significantly entitled "Scales of Judgment and Their Implications for Social Psychology," will help many of us to see new research areas in terms of more clear-cut formulations (Chapter 11).

It has become almost a truism that our reactions are not determined by the physical properties of external stimulus situations alone. Reaction is the consequence of the way we perceive, judge, and appriase situations. In this process, the persons we are at the moment—with all our past experience, present tensions, attitudes, etc.—come into the picture. The recent findings on perception led several contemporary authors to unwarranted extreme positions. They almost come to the point of saying that perception of things is what the individual makes of it. Against such an extreme subjectivistic position, the psychology of judgmental scales along the lines presented by Volkmann can serve as an effective corrective. Social psychology can utilize certain aspects of culture, in any society, for this purpose. Culture and social organization are not chaotic entities. Their main features consist of certain regularities, certain value scales with more or less definite beginning and end points, certain poverty-riches range, certain magnitudes and routines in use in everyday life. Many attitudes, many standards of reaction of the individual members of any culture are formed in relation to such scales of values, riches, magnitudes, and routines. The individual member's evaluations, appraisals, take place in terms of such scale values, of course subject to variations due to his particular status, role in the group and, within limits, to personal characteristics. Volkmann gives us the fundamentals of the relationship between stimulus values and psychological scales which is at the basis of the *perspective* the individual develops in relation to his environment. In the light of basic experimental findings, the major portion of which comes from his own work and the studies of his associates, Volkmann gives a critical evaluation of the current educational attempts at broadening the perspective of the new generation.

His discussion of anchoring effects, up to what point new anchoring factors can be effective, beyond what point they fail, should be of particular interest to the student of social psychology. These laboratory findings are full of implications for the student of attitudes and public opinion.

Volkmann notes as a fact demonstrated in one of his own experiments that "anchoring can be achieved by appropriate verbal instructions, without the use of anchoring stimuli." A good many scales of judgment used by individuals in their personal and group relations are thus derived. Much of the work dealing with standards and scales of judgment in social psychology has necessarily been with the verbally established ones. A series of judgmental experiments studying the relationship between reference scales established through exposure to actual stimulus series and through verbal dictums lacking such anchorings in various degrees may be basic to the clarification of the relationship between verbal factors and actual contact factors in the functioning of attitudes.

The next series of chapters (Chapters 12–14) is devoted to group structures and the functioning of individual members within them. As we noted before, psychologists' approach to the study of group problems has been largely by way of extrapolations from the characteristics of the individual in more or less isolated situations. Even those who insisted on dealing in terms of group structure improvised their notions of group organization and did not bother much to assimilate the wealth of concrete empirical data already collected by sociologists. It is fortunate, therefore, to have the contributions of Whyte, Hughes, and Arensberg in this vital area. These three sociologists have been engaged for a good many years in exploring the complex problems of social organization, status, and role problems created by membership in various groups.

The tremendous influence of group membership on the experience and behavior of individuals is now beyond the point of controversy.

Yet social psychologists are still too prone to study the reactions of the individual within the confines of experimental or observational groups as if the group in question embodied in itself all the factors that go to influence the individuals comprising it. Whyte starts his lucid discussion of "Small Groups and Large Organizations" by taking issue with this short-sightedness so prevalent today among a good many experimental social psychologists (Chapter 12). Small groups, Whyte points out, "need to be placed in a perspective of larger organizational structures." For small groups do not function in a vacuum. They are related to and, in many cases, parts of larger organizations. As such, the functions of the small groups and their individual members have little meaning apart from their relation to other groups to which they are organically tied. This main stand of the chapter is supported by concrete illustrations revealing the interdependent nature of different groups which are all parts of the modern industrial structure. It becomes clear, therefore, that instead of losing sight of weighty factors by overconcentration on the confines of in-group relations alone, we should broaden our perspective to the larger framework of *"mutually dependent sets of relations."* This realistic orientation of Whyte makes us feel that his advice to us is well taken: "The social psychologists interested in small groups must be fully aware of the work going on in the larger structures." The practical implication of this realistic orientation is clear. "Then, if we wish to modify behavior within the group, we will recognize that it will sometimes be necessary, in order to effect significant modifications, to first make changes in the over-all structure of the organization *first*" (p. 312).

Whyte confines his illustrations to the cases of large industrial formations in America. If the perspective he suggests is utilized in the study of inter-group relations, it would be easier to realize fully the inadequate and wasteful nature of many current prejudice studies. The prejudice studies, which lay overdue emphasis on individual experiences with only a few lip-service remarks to the influence of actual group structures, and which extrapolate the generalizations derived from the confines of in-group relations to inter-group relations, without any serious stress on the nature of inter-group relations themselves, are certainly good illustrations of theoretically inadequate and practically wasteful approaches.

Whyte presents a clear discussion of methods for studying groups.

Group structure, in the final analysis, boils down to the reciprocal relations or roles between members occupying hierarchical positions in it.
This is studied by the way of leader-follower relations. It seems to me
that Whyte clarifies considerably the concept of "leadership." "Quite
different phenomena are often lumped together" under the term leadership. If the word leadership is to be used consistently in any functional sense, it should be used in the sense of operational leadership,
in which the main criterion is the fact of initiation of action in which
group members, including the leader, participate. With this criterion,
leadership should be distinguished from popularity, "the assumed representative," and prominent or talented individuals. Another particularly noteworthy point of Whyte's chapter is his insistence on *time
dimension* in the study of group relations. In the study of groups, the
time sequence of interactions is crucial in understanding the true significance of overall results.

In a closely related chapter (Chapter 14), Arensberg presents a co-
ordinated survey of the major aspects of "human relations" studies
carried out over the past twenty years by men close to industry, by
sociologists, anthropologists, and psychologists. His survey of the field,
in which he is one of the leading authorities, is not a compendium of
summaries of so many studies. He discusses the concepts and methodology used by each of them, appraises them critically, and relates them to
each other, noting the lines of convergence as well as divergence. As
such, it should serve as a systematic introduction for the student of
social psychology to the general problems of "behavior and organization" in this area of human relations in the Western world today.

One overall fact that emerges from this survey of the experience and
behavior of individuals working in units of industrial plants is full of
indications for social psychology. This overall fact is that the most
effective determinant in the production and shifts of attitudes and,
hence, behavior is the pattern of *interaction* in one's group situation.
By whatever name the particular investigators call themselves—sociologist, anthropologist, or psychologist—no matter with what kind of
theoretical orientations they start ("cultural," "psychological," "clinical," etc.), and whether or not they play up or down the implications
in this regard in the final write-up of their studies, this general overall
fact is almost always there. The incorporation of some of the most re-
current factual evidence from these industrial studies to the main body

of social psychological writing will be one of the best correctives in broadening our rather provincial view of group studies.

Yet most of these studies have been carried out as studies of small groups without sufficient emphasis on the forces impinging on the group unit under study—forces from other related units, from the overall organization of which all these units are parts, and from other groups of the general structure of which the overall organization is in turn a part. For small groups, especially today, are not closed systems. Their very functioning is related to the functioning of other groups in a social setting of definite structural properties. Arensberg untiringly insists on this important consideration throughout his chapter. In fact, he starts his chapter by calling attention to it. "The evidence from the study of industrial behavior and industrial relations seems to indicate that building theory upon research concentration on the small group may be mistaken, however experimentally justifiable as an object of research the small group may be."

What Arensberg really means here by "small group" is the small group taken as a closed system more or less in isolation. In actual observation and experimentation, the unit of study necessarily has to be the small group and its individual members, no matter how comprehensive our perspective of larger organizational ties may be. The objectionable thing, therefore, is not the study of small groups *per se,* for there is no way of getting out of it. The adequate approach, as Arensberg himself later points out, is to study small groups in their functional ties with groups to which they are organically related. Arensberg makes a plea for such a necessary broadening of perspective in the interests of an adequate theory of small groups. In this plea, he is voicing at the same time the opinion of his colleagues who comprise the last group ("subgroup") of the students of small group behavior in industry which he discusses at some length in the last part of the chapter. The facts and views advanced by this group, which can be "best identified as the group of persons associated in the Society for Applied Anthropology," are among the useful ones in breaking away from our provincialisms as social psychologists. This praiseworthy plea to study small groups without losing sight of their ties with other groups and the general setting is, we believe Arensberg and his colleagues will agree, still in programmatic form, rather than a body of accumulated research. The social psychologist interested in the whirlwind of socio-economic forces will be eager to see how far this group of applied anthropologists can manage to go in this direction in the practice of their investigations.

It becomes evident, then, that an adequate study of small groups implies the study of at least a minimum degree of inter-group relations. At times, the in-group relations and properties simply become unintelligible without a consideration of the general setting in which they operate. Even the very composition of modern in-groups at the present time is tied up with certain inter-group problems which have a bearing on the participation of the particular member in question within the in-group as well as on the consistency or inconsistency of in-group effects in other situations in a time perspective. For in-group members of a plant today are members of other groups at the same time—the union, the religious group, probably a political party, etc.—which have their claims on the constituent members in this or that direction.

It is not just coincidence that a mounting number of industrial studies happened to be carried out during the last twenty years or so. One learns from Arensberg's chapter that this is not due merely to the refinement of research techniques of the investigators. The studies are products of the concern over mounting "labor unrest" and the desire to do something about it. In view of this fact, the necessity for broadening the small group studies from within the narrow formulations of their own confines and placing them in their general setting and in their *historical* time perspective becomes so much more urgent. However, just saying that all historical influences are embodied in the actual factors under study is no way out. The tracing of the influences of so many factors under study in a longitudinal way certainly makes us more intelligent in understanding the nature of and dependencies among these factors.

In Chapter 13, the sociologist Hughes presents findings concerning the demands and conflicts of certain statuses and roles to exemplify the need and possibility for joint work by psychologists and sociologists. His aim has been, in the author's terms, to raise problems rather than to work out any one systematically. The area chosen is *work,* for, says Hughes, "a man's work is one of the more important parts of his social identity, of his self, indeed, of his fate, in the one life he has to live." Here is a lesson in methodology which social science must learn if it is to move forward. In the area of work relationships, Hughes points out, the problems are often obscured because they are approached with concepts deriving from the point of view of certain groups within the social structure and with their attendant "value-loading" and "pretentiousness." The plea is not for "neutrality" in social science—no doubt an impossibility—but for "a point of view and concepts which will enable us to make comparisons between the junk peddler and the professor without intent to debunk the one and patronize the other." In short, the concepts must be valid in relation to any work situation. With this aim, Hughes illustrates some common properties of work situations derived from study of occupations traditionally low in status in this society.

Finally, the last part of the book is devoted to central topics of social psychology at the present time (Chapters 15–17). Three social psychologists, Sargent, Hartley, and Sherif, discuss these topics. First, the *interaction* between the individual and social situations is discussed in terms of role and ego concepts. Then, the much neglected, yet currently inescapable, topic of multiple group memberships and the effects on the individual of the demands in various directions thus produced is presented with convincing concrete illustrations. In this connection again, the necessity of the systematic clarification of the concept of ego or self is indicated. In the last chapter, a theoretical approach to the study of inter-group relations is outlined and the approach is illustrated with an actual experimental study.

As social psychologists have reëxamined old paths and explored new, the futility of going ahead without the aid of social scientists working on different levels has become increasingly evident. In Chapter 15, Sargent illustrates the gains which may be obtained through interdisciplinary study, with special emphasis on the concept of *role*. With such an aim in mind, Sargent gives a concise survey of the concept as used by anthropologists, sociologists, and psychologists. He then proposes the following definition as a useful tool in social psychology: *"A person's role is a pattern or type of social behavior which seems situationally appropriate to him in terms of the demands and expectations of those in his group"* (p. 360; italics in original).

The evidence of sociologists, anthropologists, and psychologists clearly negates accounts of behavior in group situations conceived solely in terms of individual factors—personality traits, drives, or the like. In the case of existing, definitely structured groups, the individual's behavior is to an important extent determined by the *position* in which he finds himself or which he attains in the group structure and the expectations, responsibilities, privileges attending that position. Sargent points out that in such instances the psychologist must give due weight to such structural properties of the group as part of a stimulus situation which the individual *perceives* and *learns*. Accordingly, his behavior in such social situations becomes harmonious with that prescribed by his *role* and, in this sense, may be spoken of as *role behavior*. In this process, individual factors contribute in such a way that the behavior of two individuals in the same objective roles is not exactly alike.

However, says Sargent, a conception of roles taken as existent, static prescriptions of behavior is inadequate for social psychology. When the social situation in which individuals interact is new, strange, or otherwise unstructured—such as a chance meeting of strangers—certain roles emerge in the course of interaction. In such situations, individual factors come into fuller play. Roles then are initially products of interaction in groups of any size. Social situations seldom remain chaotic for long, but assume some sort of structure. Since individuals ordinarily move in many established groupings and in many interactional situations, each learns, attains, participates in the creation of many roles of a lasting or transitory nature. The individual's conception of himself, his ego, is in large part derived from these roles, especially those relating to lasting or recurring group situations. Small wonder that objective conflict in the demands of these various roles results in confusion, conflict, anxiety for the individual.

The analysis of such conflicts stemming from contradictory roles and statuses is illuminated by Hartley in his discussion of "Psychological Problems of Multiple Group Membership" (Chapter 16). Since roles and statuses "stem from a functional differentiation of position within a social group," Hartley correctly reasons, the problems of contradictory roles and statuses "must refer back to the different reference groups from which these roles and statuses have come." The analysis of these problems on a psychological level is clarified by a genetic or developmental approach, viz. the study of the child's gradual awareness and identification with groups of which he is a member. In the complex societies of today, every individual is a member of many groups. Starting with the family, the child acquires symbolization of his group membership in diverse groupings long before their social significance is appreciated. Such affectively charged symbols or attitudes come to constitute in large part the child's concept of self. The understanding of the functional relatedness of such symbols or attitudes (which constellation may be termed ego or self) can, Hartley suggests, be greatly improved through developmental study.

When the individual's behavior is seen as occurring in terms of the norms of various and often contradictory reference groups, a number of confusing problems are approached with a common perspective. For example, Hartley notes that in much social conflict today, individuals may react ethnocentrically, i.e., solely and uncritically in terms of a dominant reference group, at the expense of the goals and norms of a larger group of which both parties in the conflict are members and, perhaps, refer to in other situations. The urgent need here is the study of how identifications with the norms of the larger, common group can be increased to the extent that they become dominant in cases of potential conflict. "If behavior is referred to group norms," concludes Hartley, "if the individual has many group memberships, if the regnant norms may be that of a social group not physically present, I would search in such dimensions to account for changes in social behavior."

In short, by making a systematic issue of the problems of multiple group memberships, Hartley brings into focus for social psychologists one of the most basic and timely topics in the inter-personal and inter-group relations of our day. Probably this problem underlies many of the inconsistencies in the individual's behavior in his group relations and the uneasy plight of modern man struggling to keep an even keel in the midst of conflicting currents.

In Chapter 17, Sherif presents a report of a preliminary experiment on inter-group relations conducted in the summer of 1949. The first part of the report is concerned with the theoretical approaches to the study. The main point is that it is erroneous to extrapolate uncritically the nature of in-group relations to inter-group relations and try to resolve inter-group problems by such extrapolations. Likewise, the understanding of inter-group relations has been retarded by the extensions based on generalizations from the gratifications and frustrations in the life histories of single individuals. Groups stand in certain definite functional relationships *as groups* to each other. The functional relationship between any two or more groups *as groups* may or may *not* be in line with the characteristics of in-group relations. For example, even a high degree of harmony and coöperativeness within the in-group does not necessarily imply harmony and coöperativeness with an out-group. The experiment is presented as a demonstration of this point.

In the preceding pages, an evaluative summary statement of the sixteen chapters constituting the main body of this book is presented. The discerning reader will take note of some basic converging lines running through the biological, socio-cultural and psychological levels of reality represented in the various parts of the book. He will notice, at the same time, some representative lines of divergence. This is as it should be. The host of material utilized from biology, anthropology, sociology, and from general psychology itself still reflect these convergences and divergences, as well as selective use of them. Only time will prove which choice of concepts and selectivity have been with the general run of the nature of things in question.

REFERENCES

1. Bruner, J. S., and Postman, L.   Emotional selectivity in perception and reaction, *J. Personal.*, 1947, **16**, 69–77.
2. Bruner, J. S., and Postman, L.   Symbolic value as an organizing factor in perception, *J. soc. Psychol.*, 1948, **27**, 203–208.
3. Koffka, K.   *Principles of Gestalt Psychology*, N. Y.: Harcourt, Brace, 1935.
4. Köhler, W.   *Gestalt Psychology*, N. Y.: Liveright, 1929, especially pp. 319–329.
5. Krech, D., and Crutchfield, R. S.   *Theory and Problems of Social Psychology*, N. Y.: McGraw-Hill, 1948.
6. Levine, J., and Murphy, G.   The learning and forgetting of controversial material, *J. abn. & soc. Psychol.*, 1943, **37**, 507–517.
7. Levine, R., Chein, I., and Murphy, G.   The relation of the intensity of a need to the amount of perceptual distortion, A preliminary report, *J. Psychol.*, 1942, **13**, 283–293.
8. Postman, L., and Murphy, G.   The factor of attitude in associative memory, *J. exper. Psychol.*, 1943, **33**, 228–238.
9. Postman, L., Bruner, J. S., and McGinnies, E.   Personal values as selective factors in perception, *J. abn. & soc. Psychol.*, 1948, **43**, 142–154.

10. Proshansky, H., and Murphy, G.   The effects of reward and punishment in perception, *J. Psychol.*, 1942, **13**, 293–305.
11. Schafer, R., and Murphy, G.   The role of autism in a visual figure-ground relationship, *J. exper. Psychol.*, 1943, **32**, 335–343.
12. Sherif, M.   A Study of Some Social Factors in Perception, *Arch. Psychol.* No. 187, 1935.
13. Sherif, M.   *The Psychology of Social Norms*, N. Y.: Harper, 1936.
14. Sherif, M.   An experimental approach to the study of attitudes, *Sociometry*, 1937, **1**, 90–98.

Part One

Social Psychology: Integrating Individual and Social Approaches

CHAPTER 2

Social Psychological Theory

Intregrating Individual and Social Approaches

THEODORE M. NEWCOMB
University of Michigan

I am dissatisfied with the present state of social psychology. There are, of course, reasons for satisfaction and even for pride. I suppose we are entitled to do some gloating over the fact that there are more and more students who wish to do graduate work in our field, that several universities now offer the doctor's degree in social psychology, and that there are more job openings than competent people to fill them. Perhaps we can even become a profession. Perhaps the flood of new texts in this area is an index of the rapid growth of the field, though I am not sure that I consider this a happy omen. Our growth and quasi-public recognition bears some of the marks of too rapid inflation; I fear that it is based upon expectations which are greater than anything which we can deliver in the near future.

Quite apart from these superficial signs of stirring in our field, my dissatisfactions have to do with the state of theory and research in social psychology. In particular I want to discuss what seems to me the unfortunate circumstance that there are two social psychologies thriving in the land—not one. Since I am dissatisfied with both of them, you can understand my misanthropic state.

Take first what may be labelled the psychological approach to social psychology. (At the moment there are probably more graduate students in psychology than in sociology departments in most universities, and probably a majority of people who call themselves social psychologists have had primarily psychological training.) My basic dissatisfaction with psychological social psychology is that it has never really faced the implications of the psychologist's claim to study the "organism *in environment.*" The day has happily long since passed when psychologists claimed to be studying psychological processes isolated from the world with which organisms interact, and yet most social psychologists of primarily psychological persuasion take no systematic account of the facts of the social environment in which human organisms live. More specifically, they minimize or even ignore the nature of the social structure of which their subjects are members. They often speak and write as if the differences between the human and non-human environments could be ignored. The result of this comes perilously close to being a human social psychology without people. I suppose that we would all agree with Professor MacLeod in asserting that "every percept is a function of the field conditions" under which it occurs. Too many of us who have been psychologically trained are, I fear, a bit naïve concerning the field conditions of group life under which individual's perceptions of social behavior occur.

Psychological social psychologists—at least those who take their theory seriously—quite rightly insist that the same *basic* principles of behavior must be applied to human beings in social or in non-social situations. They decry the all-too-prevalent tendency to devise special principles to account for special forms of social behavior; much of the mythology of crowd behavior is of exactly this nature. All of this I can only applaud, but within the limits where these basic principles apply there is still room for much better refinement of the specifically human conditions in the environment which serve to determine the nature of human behavior. I shall have more to say later about what seems to me to be the fallacy of assuming that a human environment introduces no new problems into the study of psychological processes.

The sociologically trained social psychologists have, with few exceptions, made different but no less serious errors. They have never come to terms with the biological and psychological conditions under which human organisms *selectively* participate in their environment. Their fallacy—if I may state it in its most extreme form—has been that of assuming that human organisms are virtually empty receptacles into which culture is simply poured. Too many of them have seemed to assume that, for social psychological purposes, not only may the receptacles be regarded as more or less equivalent but the nature of the process by which they get filled can more or less be taken for granted. This stricture by no means applies to all social psychologists whose training has been primarily sociological. It does, however, tend to be the occupational danger to which such people are most prone.

To summarize my reasons for dissatisfaction with the present state of our two social psychologies, then, the situation seems to me something like this. You can take your choice between the study of intra-individual processes, allegedly related, by way of social behavior to the facts of social organization; and, as the other alternative, the study of social organization, allegedly related to the processes by which individuals learn and become socialized.

I should like to outline what seems to me to be the possibility of developing a social psychology which takes full account of the realities of psychological processes as well as the realities of social organization. Such a social psychology would, of course, accept the most adequate available theories concerning the organization of individual behavior and also concerning the organization of groups and societies. Such a social psychology would deny nothing which has been verified concerning either kind of organization; it would not be concerned to deny anything which even seemed plausible, but it would insist upon knowing how psychological processes function under the field conditions of group life. In fact I should like to offer this as what seems to me to be the desirable goal of social psychology within the next decade or two— that is, to clarify and systematize our knowledge of how psychological processes function under the field conditions of group life.

With such an objective, social psychologists would plan research programs at levels which test hypotheses concerning psychological processes under such conditions. By this I mean that they would not merely hypothesize concerning psychological processes as related to social behavior, nor merely test hypotheses concerning overt behavior under various conditions of group life. Rather they would so plan their research *programs* (though not necessarily each single investigation) that observable behavior can be related simultaneously to both kinds of variables.

Let me outline what seem to me to be a few necessary postulates of a theory upon which such a research program would be based. Because my time is brief I shall necessarily seem somewhat dogmatic in outlining these postulates.

1. Any observable behavior is not only a response (on the part of a subject) which is to be treated as a dependent variable; it is also a stimulus to be perceived by others with whom the subject interacts, and thus to be treated as an independent variable. (It would be an oversimplification to say that psychologists have in general treated social behavior on the part of individuals as a dependent variable while sociologists have in general treated it as an independent variable; nevertheless such an oversimplification points to some characteristic differences between these two approaches to the same phenomena.)

2. There is a most remarkable correspondence between the psychological processes on the part of the overtly behaving individual and on the part of the individual who perceives and responds to him. Social psychologists have, with rare exceptions, paid little attention to this correspondence. It is, of course, not a correspondence of identity but one of sufficient similarity so that everyday communication is carried on with remarkably little misunderstanding. This correspondence can be explained only by the assumption that interacting individuals are parts of some more inclusive system—groups or whole societies.

3. The relations among the parts (i.e., individuals) of such systems (i.e., groups) are quite different from the relations of individuals to sticks and stones and other inanimate objects. That is, while the same basic psychological principles apply to the interaction of organisms with the non-human and with the human environment, there are also orderly conditions of interaction with the human environment which do not apply to interaction with the non-human environment. These additional orderly processes correspond to laws and principles which, in my judgment, should be the special province of the social psychologist.

Thus the directions which I should like to see social psychology take in the next few years are those of concentrating on the variable conditions, the variable processes, and the variable consequences of interaction among group members.

Such being the territory which I should like to stake out for social psychology, let me now point to some conceptual and theoretical possibilities of such an approach. First, although we have rarely made the attempt, the ineluctable facts about group life can and must be treated in terms accessible to psychologists. The conceptual tools with which this may be done have been laid down with singular clarity by Professor Muzafer Sherif of the University of Oklahoma. His experimental work and conceptual outlining of the importance of social norms have many revolutionary implications for the kind of social psychology in which I am interested. It is to Sherif's eternal credit that he has had the wisdom to formulate the problem of social norms in terms of perceptual processes. The tremendous fact about social norms, which in the main we social psychologists have failed to exploit, is that they represent shared ways of perceiving things or, more exactly perhaps, shared frames of reference within which things are perceived. It is the elementary fact of perceiving things in shared ways which gives us our major foothold for the study of social behavior as simultaneously related to psychological processes and to social organization.

If social psychology is to take as its special province the study of interaction, it must make a special place for those kinds of interaction which presuppose shared frames of reference, and by which shared frames of reference are acquired. This special kind of interaction I shall refer to as communication.

The processes of norm-building and of communication are circularly related to each other. Norms arise through communication, which in turn is made possible because norms already exist. Every child is born into a society whose members already make use of shared ways of perceiving things. He comes to take their frames of reference as his own simply because he finds motive satisfaction of a thousand kinds in doing so. The more important the things concerning which he wants to communicate with others, the more poignant his disappointments until he learns to perceive them in terms shared with others.

Norms, then, are developed about anything and everything which is of shared interest to two or more people who interact with each other. Of all the things, however, concerning which norms may be developed, nothing compares in importance with other people. As the sociologists never tire of pointing out, the basic fact of human interdependence— not only in infancy but throughout life—makes this inevitable. And so we find in all known societies, and in somewhat different ways in all continuing groups, sets of norms according to which people are differentiated and perceived in shared ways. The best way of taking account of this fact, for social psychological purposes, is in terms of positions (or statuses, as some anthropologists and sociologists like to term them) and roles.

One of the things which disappoints me in most of the social-psychological literature with which I am familiar is that the fact of shared norms concerning people rarely receives systematic treatment. The term "role" is still used by most social psychologists in a common-sense, figure-of-speech manner. Perhaps there are better terms than "role" for those sets of behavior which are associated with occupants of specified positions and which are perceived in shared ways. If so, let us find and use the better term. If "role," however, is for the present the best term to apply to this phenomenon—and no other term has so far been proposed, I believe—then let us use the term in its strict and technical sense and abandon its dramatic and literary usage.

A role, as I think the term should be used by social psychologists, thus consists of a limited set of behaviors "tied together" by a common understanding of the functions of a position. Not all of these behaviors will be performed by every occupant of the position, nor will they be performed in the same way by any two persons as they take the same role. The actual behavior of any individual in taking a role must be sharply distinguished from the role itself, which is stated in terms broad enough to apply to all occupants of any position. Role behaviors are distinguished from other behaviors not by any phenotypic characteristics, but in terms of the degree to which they are a function of shared ways of perceiving whatever roles are involved in the interaction—shared, that is, by the behaving individual and by those with whom he interacts. Role behavior is thus a form of communicative behavior. The operations by which it is identified are not mysterious, though they are not simple.

Every role is thus necessarily defined in relation to one or more other roles. The role of mother is unthinkable apart from that of child. But her role, though functionally defined in terms of the child, also involves relations with other persons—her husband, for example, the child's teacher, or the neighbors. Her role prescription includes sets of behavior referring to them, as well as to her child, but always in ways which involve the child. The meaning of any role is thus to be seen in the entire network of roles, or the role system, of which it is a part.

The significance of interdependent roles is not only that they provide shared frames of reference in terms of which people can communicate *about* one another (as they communicate about sticks and stones); common understandings of roles also make it possible for people to communicate *with* one another. The significant (and probably unique) thing about human interaction is that so much of it has to do with a process by which people share meanings *about* each other *with* each other. And this, if I may venture to repeat myself, is possible because of shared frames of reference in terms of which the communicating individuals perceive themselves, each other, and others about whom they are communicating.

Now let me remind you of another platitude. Frames of reference, as perceptual norms, cannot be divorced from attitudes. Indeed, it seems to me necessary to define an attitude toward something as a persistent state of readiness to perceive, to perform, to think and feel about something in such interdependent ways as to lead to a certain kind of goal. If this is correct, then a pre-disposition to perceive the thing in question in a specified way is simply a part of the individual's attitude toward it. Frames of reference for perceiving people are thus inseparable from attitudes toward people, as Sherif and Cantril have so cogently pointed out. And thus, since people are of such supreme importance to one another, we are led again, along a different path, to the conclusion that the fact of shared frames of reference for perceiving people is of unique significance in human social psychology.

What most psychologists have not adequately understood is that the study of social organization and group structure provides them with far more than a formal map of the territory which their subjects inhabit. Studies of social organization, if properly exploited by the social psychologist, provide him with indispensable information about his own subject matter, namely, communication, and in particular its content and the channels through which it occurs. Group structure and social organization are not only instances of social norms, in themselves; they are also determiners of the processes of communication among group members. What is communicated to whom, and what is the meaning of what is communicated, are determined quite as much by the nature of the group structure as by the private demands of the communicating individuals. If, therefore, we accept as our special province the study of communication, we must make use of all available information concerning group structure as one of the determiners of communication.

The term "group," like the term "role," has achieved no standard meaning among social psychologists. This, on the face of it, is somewhat surprising. Granted that the facts of collective life are enormously complicated, it is a scientific truism that the discovery of genotypic laws and principles presupposes the taxonomic task of differentiating and labelling phenotypic events. Again, if I may run the risk of appearing dogmatic, I should like to outline what seem to me the necessary distinctions between groups, as amenable to social psychological study, and other forms of human collectivities. For social psychological purposes, at least, the distinctive thing about a group is that its members share norms about something. The range covered by the shared norms may be great or small, but at the very least they include whatever it is that is distinctive about the common interests of the group members—whether it be politics or poker. They also include, necessarily, norms concerning the roles of the group members—roles which are interlocking, being defined in reciprocal terms. Thus an American family is composed of members who share norms concerning their everyday living arrangements, and also concerning the manner in which they behave toward one another. These distinctive features of a group—shared norms and interlocking roles—presuppose a more than transitory relationship of interaction and communication. They serve to distinguish, for social psychological purposes at least, a group from a number of persons at a street intersection at a given moment, and also from a mere category, such as all males in the State of Oklahoma between the ages of 21 and 25.

The advantages of this kind of definition of a group are that it takes account of the realities of collective life, as noted by sociologists and cultural anthropologists, and at the same time it is stated in terms which are accessible to the psychologist. It is a definition which is stated in terms of observable behavior (e.g., frequency counts of conforming and deviant behavior, and verbal reports of judgments as to how other people are perceived).

So far I have tried to suggest that the ineluctable facts of group life can be treated in terms accessible to psychologists. Now I should like to indicate that the equally inescapable facts of intra-personal life can and must be treated in terms accessible to sociologists. For purposes of illustrating this point I shall refer briefly to the concept of the self. From one point of view nothing is so private, so strictly intra-individual, as one's own self, by which I mean simply "the individual as known to that individual." And yet the process by which the individual comes to know himself, as well as the content of that "knowledge," is in many ways determined by the social norms—and in particular by the role system—of the society and the sub-groups of which the individual is a member.

We are all familiar with the general outlines of the process by which individuals learn to distinguish themselves from objects and other persons. If I am right in assuming that the more important it is to a person to be able to communicate with others about something, the more certain it is that he will come to share with them the frames of reference within which he perceives that something, then it is practically inevitable that people should come to perceive themselves in terms of shared frames of reference. Inevitably, therefore, self-perceptions come to be figured against the ground provided by group-shared norms for perceiving people—i.e., in terms of positions and roles.

Many students of personality—e.g., Freud, G. W. Allport, Murphy, and Horney—have noted that much of the stability of personality can be understood in terms of the persistence of self-perceptions. Many of them have also pointed out that with successful psychotherapy there is always associated some change in self-perceptions. (Rogers and his associates, in particular, have documented this point.) Not all of them, however, have stressed the fact that the persistence of self-perceptions, in turn, is to be accounted for in large part by their embeddedness in a particular kind of role system. If this is correct, then we should expect to find that changes in the role system in which the individual's self-perceptions are anchored would be accompanied by changes in self-perceptions, too, as well as by changes in observable personality characteristics. This seems to be precisely what we do find, whether the changes in the role system are primarily the result of the individual's own perceptual restructuring (as in psychotherapy), the result of voluntary entry into a new role system (as in class mobility or migration), or the result of enforced introduction into a new role system (as in prison life).

Let me now take one of the ancient and honorable problems in social psychology and indicate, not a solution, but a manner of approach to it. I refer to that process which has been noted by so many, both before and after Gustave LeBon, and which has been variously labelled "group mind," "social facilitation," as well as by other names. What I should like to suggest is that many of the more fruitless aspects of this ancient controversy simply disappear if we view the problem in terms of self-other perceptions and shared norms.

If I may oversimplify the issue, for brevity's sake, LeBon's great contribution was that he viewed the phenomenon which he called "group mind" in terms of shared mental processes. His great shortcoming was that he had nothing to say about the conditions under which such sharing took place. F. H. Allport, on the other hand, saw the necessity of distinguishing among various hypothetical conditions, and of controlling and experimentally manipulating them. His doctrine of social facilitation, however, left only a speculative place (by way of what he called the illusion of universality) for shared norms. The net effect of his doctrine was that in intense group situations the essentially private mental processes of the individual were not modified, but only intensified.

The problem of reciprocal stimulation in group situations, with the often-noted "spiraling" effect, is one which can be handled only in interactional terms. It is a problem which, in my judgment, can be solved only by recognizing that the determinants of overt response are in most respects the same as the determinants of perception of overt response in others. That is to say, the problem is basically one of shared norms, including roles as norms for perceiving behavior.

Social psychologists, by and large, have made more use of the notion of social reinforcement (in one form or another) in trying to account for the extreme forms of crowd behavior than for more commonplace behavior. I should like to indicate, however, that the process of group reinforcement of individual motives and attitudes, if it is understood in the context of social norms, has a very important place in an integrated theory of social behavior. I shall stop briefly to indicate the importance of this process in situations of group conflict and in those of group solidarity.

We have long since learned to look for the *sources* of individual hostility against members of out-groups in the norms of the individual's own groups, as represented in the studies of Horowitz, Murphy and Likert. But we have not always taken adequate account of the part played by social norms in the persistence, the waxing and the waning of hostility toward out-group members. The persistence or change of such hostility, as well as its sources, depend upon norms according to which various degrees or forms of hostile behavior are included in the members' roles.

When hostile attitudes or behaviors on the part of members of one group toward another are on the increase, we must look to interaction among the members of that group as one source (and I think the major one) of the change. Something happens—say an incident which could be interpreted as being warlike or otherwise threatening to one's own group—which reduces the thresholds for hostility on the part of some of the more influential members of that group. They show, by their behavior, their conviction that their own group norms prescribe hostile behavior under these conditions. Because of their influence, other members of the same group perceive the incident as threatening; their thresholds for hostile behavior, in turn, are lowered, and so on. The more extreme the forms of behavior (the classical lynching mob offers the extreme example), then the more extreme the plainly observable limits within which norm-prescribed behavior is permitted. There is nothing especially novel about these remarks, but I do want to stress the point that norms concerning behavior are not merely standards of judgment which have been permanently interiorized by individuals. Rather, they are subject to constant revision in the light of what other people are observed to be doing. Role-taking is not only the result of pre-existing social norms; role-taking also provides their source and continuing support.

The essential feature of the process of social reinforcement is this: the more vivid the behavior perceived in shared ways (i.e., role behavior), the more vividly it is perceived and the more intensely others are stimulated. They are not necessarily stimulated to behave in the same ways (as the doctrine of social reinforcement apparently requires). Rather, they are stimulated to take interlocking roles, which may call for similar or for complementary behavior. In either case, an adequate account of social reinforcement depends, or so it seems to me, upon the fact of group membership, defined in terms of shared norms and interlocking roles.

Social reinforcement does not, of course, tell the whole story of group conflict. It represents communication within a group, and it is equally important to study the process of communication between groups which are in conflict. One important aspect of inter-group communication (as I have elsewhere noted) has to do with the effects upon members of one group of their perception of the behavior of members of another group. With rare exceptions, every individual perceives the behavior of an out-group member in terms of his own group's social norms. To the extent that the members of one group perceive the behavior of out-group members as hostile, the opportunities for communication between the groups tend to be reduced. Suppose, for example, that the norms of middle-class whites in this country prescribe somewhat "condescending" behavior toward American Indians. If so, Indians with whom they interact will tend to become aware that they are undervalued by whites, and to the extent that this happens Indians will feel discouraged about communicating with whites. The more this happens, the more divergent become the white norms and the Indian norms concerning both groups. As Indians are perceived by whites to be uncommunicative, there is added to their other undesirable qualities (according to white norms) those traits assumed to go with uncommunicativeness—like deceitfulness and treachery, perhaps. White people's behavior, as influenced by these revised norms, makes Indians still less inclined to communicate with them, and so on.

I have taken time for this oversimplified analysis of group conflict simply because I think it illustrates how social psychological problems must be attacked in terms of communicative processes. I should be the first to grant that it is not enough to know the conditions and consequences of specified forms of communication within and between groups, but I do maintain that such information is indispensable. Such an approach, moreover, seems to me neither psychological nor sociological, but distinctly social psychological.

Now let me undertake, as a final example, an analysis of interaction within a group characterized by considerable solidarity, or "high morale." The conditions associated with such a group can be studied at either the individual or the group level. We can study them, more specifically, in terms of individual attitudes of belongingness, or in terms of group conditions which are associated with cohesiveness. There are many kinds of satisfactions which it is possible for a person to find in group membership—e.g., doing attractive or necessary things that can be done only with others; or just being with people who are known and liked and with whom one can interact in confident manner; or being recognized by outsiders as belonging to a group which is not accessible to everyone. Without attempting to analyze such sources of satisfaction, we can say that, together, they constitute the attractiveness of group membership for the individual, and his predisposition to find such satisfactions in being a member constitutes his attitude of belongingness.

The attitude of belongingness, as I prefer to think of it, corresponds to a predisposition to take a role as group member. Taking a role is not only a matter of carrying out certain role behaviors; it is also a matter of being perceived, thought and felt about and otherwise responded to by other group members. But a role cannot be taken at all without making use of the shared norms by which roles are defined. Thus the attitude of belongingness includes the more or less confident anticipation of being responded to by others as they take their roles in understood ways. Thus, we may define the individual's attitude of belongingness as a predisposition to find motive satisfaction by taking a member's role in anticipation that his own understanding of the group norms is shared by other members. We know something about the conditions under which such attitudes arise and persist, though I cannot take time to outline them. Whatever they are, we would expect to find that they are also the conditions under which groups are most cohesive.

Various indices of group cohesiveness have been proposed, and again I have no time to indicate what they are. What they have in common is that they are indices which stand for characteristics of a group-as-a-whole. They may or may not be pooled scores referring to single individuals; in any case they are indices which have no meaning as applied to single individuals, but refer to some property of the group as an entity. And we find, not surprisingly, that such indices are highest under the same conditions which most effectively make for individual attitudes of belongingness. There are scattered bits of evidence, at least, which suggest the following conditions: Opportunities for satisfying individual motives related to the group activity; satisfying interpersonal relations; and shared task-involvement.

It is possible, then, to take either individual indices or group indices of group cohesiveness, and to relate them to various independent variables. But these are only rough, empirical approaches to the problem. I see little possibility of a complete or sophisticated theory of social behavior until we have learned to analyze the interaction process itself. The history of the study of perception offers, I think, a good analogy. We are no longer content to observe the covariation of stimulus magnitude and subjective experience. We now see the necessity of studying, à la Postman, the nature of the interdependence between "hypothesis," or expectancy, and the information characteristics of the stimulus. Just so, we cannot be content with observing the covariation of "personal liking," for example, and "morale" on the part of group members. We must go beyond this, studying the exact nature of the interdependence of the behavior of group members.

Our best guess, as of today, concerning the nature of the interaction process in groups characterized by high morale is that suggested by the principle of group reinforcement. The more frequently and the more obviously group members demonstrate by their behavior that a certain kind of role is prescribed by the group's norms, the more vividly they call to one another's attention what the role prescriptions are, and the more they intensify one another's motivation to take their own "proper" roles. This principle, incidentally, is similar to F. H. Allport's *social facilitation* except in one important respect. It depends upon the assumption of shared norms, while that of Allport does not. Group reinforcement is not just a matter of increased motivation to do the same things that others are doing because of increased stimulation in seeing and hearing them do it; rather, it is a process whereby there is, so to speak, cognitive clarification as to what the demands of the situation are, together with increased motivation to take one's own role, whether that role be similar to or complementary to those of others.

Under these conditions we have another example of the interdependence of ego and group membership. As LeBon and many others have noted, individuals sometimes get "caught up" into a group or crowd so that they lose their sense of separate identity. What happens under these circumstances (among other things) is that what the individual wants to do and what he perceives as demanded by his role come to be identical. As he becomes more intensively motivated to take a certain role—say that of torturer in a lynching mob—he also becomes more convinced that it is the one and only possible role demanded of him. For once in his life, others expect him to be exactly what he wants to be. His world of social reality perceives him precisely as he perceives himself. Psychologically speaking, this is probably the same kind of experience as that of the mystic who feels himself "at one with the universe." There is no more complete sense of support for the ego than this experience of being evaluated by the world of social reality (whether in the form of a family, a crowd, or of the powers of the universe) precisely as one evaluates oneself.

So far, I have preferred to outline what seem to me to be the directions in which social psychological theory must move, rather than to present research findings. Some of the propositions which I have proposed are supported by well-controlled research, but most of them, as yet, are not. Nevertheless, I would not have taken your time to outline a program of development for social psychology if I were not convinced that it is susceptible to investigation.

I have stressed, in particular, the necessity of taking into account the field conditions of group life under which psychological processes occur. I have beseeched you to study the interaction process, the conditions and the consequences of its various forms. Now let me indicate some of the requirements of a research program through which—and only through which—it will be possible for social psychology to develop in an integrated and systematic way.

First, there remains a great deal of work to be done at the basic level of taxonomy. We cannot study the conditions or the consequences of interaction unless we know how to distinguish the significant forms which it takes. The most promising work that I know of along these lines is that of Professor Fred Bales, of Harvard, who has shown that it is possible to make reliable observations of different kinds of individual behavior in small groups—behaviors which can be treated not only as dependent variables but also as independent ones affecting the subsequent behaviors of others. By such means he has been able to show that different groups, known to differ in various ways, are characterized by distinctive patterns of interaction—patterns which, of course, are made up of individual behaviors which, in turn, can be studied in terms of all that we know about psychological processes.

As Dr. Volkman suggested yesterday (pp. 273–295), one of the tasks of any science is to make necessary discriminations among its relevant variables. Most social psychologists need to take a less condescending attitude toward the task of making significant distinctions among forms of interaction, and making reliable observations of them. To mention another area in which much work of the same kind needs to be done we have (from cultural anthropologists) only partial taxonomies of role systems that are appropriate to social psychological study. If, as I believe, we cannot understand the psychological processes involved in social behavior apart from the field conditions of social structure in which they occur, then we must learn how to make the necessary distinctions among different kinds of role behaviors, and learn to make reliable observations of them in their different forms.

Secondly, as implied by what I have already said, social psychology suffers from an inadequacy of tools and methods. Here, as elsewhere, theoretical development waits upon methods of obtaining information. During the past quarter-century we have made enormous strides in a few methodological areas—public opinion research perhaps provides the best example. But we are only beginning to develop methods of observing interaction, of analyzing the role structure of a group or a society, of studying the process of communication, of distinguishing among the many variations of social norms. Many of us tend to take a dim view of methodological studies, as we do of taxonomic studies; but I suspect that, as of 1950, these interdependent kinds of investigations represent our greatest need.

Thirdly, of course, is the purpose for which taxonomies and tools exist: the formulation and testing of hypotheses. I shall not stop to give examples of specific hypotheses, but I do want to indicate some of the areas in which whole programs of research are needed. I shall mention seven such areas, devoting a sentence or two to each and trying, in each case, to indicate that it is a problem to be studied in terms of interaction, as a function of both psychological processes and of social organization.

1. We need to know much more about social attitudes (viewed as dependent variables) in relation to personality factors and to group structure (viewed as independent variables). For such purposes, we would want to make use of such intervening variables as perception of self and of the role system—or, as I prefer to say, of self-other perceptions and attitudes.

2. Self-other perceptions and attitudes need to be studied in relation to various forms of interaction. The relation between self-other cognitive processes and social behavior is, of course, a circular one; certain kinds of interaction, under certain conditions, are determined by certain kinds of self-other perceptions and attitudes but these, in turn, are determined by previous history of interaction.

3. We know extremely little about the nature of the communicative process. (Incidentally, our terminology in this area is so undeveloped that we scarcely know how to communicate about communication.) The special part of this problem about which I am particularly concerned has to do with what I might call the perceived overlap between the communicating individuals. That is, what is expressed by each to the others, and what is received by each from the others, is (hypothetically) a function of what is perceived by each to be the area of shared perception. I should place this kind of problem very high on my own list of priorities.

4. Many social psychologists, more or less independently, are now working on problems of "group cohesion." If we consider this group-property as a dependent variable, what are the independent variables with which it is most closely associated? From what kinds of interactions is it most likely to develop and what, in turn, are the situational conditions and the personality conditions which are most likely to facilitate such kinds of interaction?

5. There is no social psychological problem which is more fascinating than that of multiple group membership, as Dr. Hartley's paper indicates (see Ch. 16). One aspect of this problem deals with the conditions under which individuals select among various role behaviors which are potentially available. My own suspicion is that, under most conditions, one set of role behaviors rather than another tends to get the right of way, though of course there are various kinds of compromise formations, too. In any case the problem is one demanding empirical investigation which must, I think, take account of such variables as actual group structure, perceived role demands, and perceived adequacy of the self to meet those demands.

6. Most psychotherapists have given lip service to the significance of the transference phenomenon. Very few of them, however, have studied it in terms of role theory. A particularly important part of such investigations would deal with the process by which a changing role-relationship to the therapist "carries over" to other kinds of role-relationships.

7. Finally, a wide range of investigations is needed in the area of what might be called "symbolic group memberships." As Sherif (borrowing the term from Hyman) has shown, the use of the intervening

variable of "reference group" can throw a flood of light on a great deal of social behavior. This problem is closely related to the distinction which many sociologists have made between formal and informal group memberships. We may consider a reference group to be any group, formal, informal, or symbolic, in which the individual has a psychologically functioning membership. Under what conditions do reference groups most closely and least closely correspond to actual membership groups, and how are these discrepancies, great or small, associated with the variable forms of social behavior?

In summary, the two basic facts with which the social psychologist must deal are those of the organization of group life, and of the organization of individual behavior. Sociology and cultural anthropology have customarily dealt with the one, and individual psychology with the other. It is the unique and supremely difficult task of social psychology to provide an integrated theory of how human life goes on at both levels of organization simultaneously. We shall never arrive at such a theory if psychologists regard social behavior as merely an applied field of their own discipline, in which the environment happens to deal with other people, or in which the emphasis is on "social problems." This, if I may adapt a phrase which has been used here in several other contexts, would be individual imperialism. Group imperialism is an equally unacceptable doctrine. The assumption that social psychological problems represent merely a special branch of sociology, in which the facts of individual differences are duly noted, is equally inimical to the development of an integrated theory of social behavior. As I have tried to indicate, it is only by erecting a theory of behavior which is at the same time a theory of *inter*action that the task can be accomplished.

We have, I believe, the beginnings of such a theory. The sociologists and cultural anthropologists have shown us how groups and societies are organized in terms of positions and roles. The individual psychologists have shown us how individual behavior is organized, particularly by way of cognitive processes. The social psychologist must learn to observe and study human behavior as socially organized because so much of it is cognitively experienced in shared ways—both by the behaving individual himself and by those who observe him. Interaction, particularly in the form of taking and perceiving roles, is a necessary part of process by which individual organization and social organization simultaneously take place. Hence I want to see social psychology develop in ways which are not only psychological but also social. I look forward to a theory which takes account of the nature of psychological processes no more and no less than it takes account of the field conditions of group life in which they occur.

Part Two

Biological Factors and Human Behavior

CHAPTER 3

ᒐᒐᒐᒐᒐᒐᒐᒐᒐᒐᒐᒐᒐᒐᒐᒐᒐᒐᒐᒐᒐ

Genetic Variability
and Human Behavior

PAUL R. DAVID
and
LAURENCE H. SNYDER

University of Oklahoma

Geneticists cannot pretend to have made conspicuous contributions toward the analysis of human behavior patterns, and it is not likely that they will do so in the very near future. No final answer is available to the question of what part genetic variability plays in human individuality, and it is indeed quite certain that there is no single answer to this question (cf. **26**).[1] Nevertheless, recent research, especially in the fields of developmental and population genetics, has made possible the formulation of certain principles regarding the action of genes and the distribution of genes which we believe to have real implications for the social sciences.

Since genetics until rather recently has been almost exclusively a laboratory science, it is not surprising that many attempts have been made to apply its findings to problems of human society without adequate consideration of the very fundamental differences between human materials and laboratory materials, and between human populations and laboratory populations. We shall of necessity lean heavily on laboratory observations in the ensuing discussion, but we shall try carefully

---

[1] The boldface numbers in parentheses apply to the References at the end of the respective chapters.

to evaluate their possible implications for human society in human, and not in zoömorphic, terms.

We have already mentioned *genes,* and we shall have a good deal more to say about them. We should therefore perhaps make it clear at the outset that a description of the classical genes of the genetics laboratory, to which the greater part of standard genetics textbooks is devoted, is only a first step in the analysis of heredity. Limitations in the early concept of genes as individual "determiners" of mendelian characteristics, and of a one-to-one correspondence between gene and characteristic, were exposed by the discovery of genic interactions and of environmentally contingent gene effects. The newer concept of *genic balance* implies that genetic variability is a function of the genotype as a whole and that isolation of individual gene effects involves an artificial disjunction of gene and total genotype. The disjunction is both valid and necessary at certain levels of analysis (cf. the disjunction of time and space in classical mechanics), and it has been eminently successful in helping to clarify certain problems involving patterns of hereditary transmission and some aspects of developmental processes. It should be anticipated, however, that at complex levels of interaction a preoccupation with individual genes as isolates would prove methodologically inadequate (cf. 50), and we shall see later some substantiation of this suspicion. In the meanwhile, a preliminary consideration of properties of the genes of the laboratory may serve two useful purposes: (1) it will give some indication of why the isolation of individual gene effects has held so prominent a place in the history of genetic investigation; and (2) it will call attention to characteristics of genic action, discovered through the classical atomistic approach, which will inevitably be relevant to the behavior of more complexly interacting systems.

It is a commonplace of observation that no two animals, human or otherwise, are identical either in appearance or in physiologic activity. It has been amply demonstrated that individual differences among animals, in so far as they are hereditary, are predominantly contingent upon differences in the chromosomes of the respective individuals' cells and, most frequently, upon differences in their genes. Genes may roughly be defined as narrowly localized peculiarities of the chromosomes. We are commonly inclined to think of genes as discrete particles which are joined together in chain-like fashion. It is rather more accurate to consider them as regional differentiations of the chromosomes.

Thus, the difference between a color-blind man and a man with normal color vision is referable to a difference, most likely of a chemical nature, in a particular region or *locus* of their respective X-chromosomes. The difference between a man with hemophilia and a non-hemophilic individual is attributable to a difference between their respective X-chromosomes at another locus.

The high degree of precision with which the locus of a given gene difference can be defined under favorable circumstances is best seen in that animal which has been most exhaustively studied from a genetic standpoint, the fruit fly, *Drosophila melanogaster*. In this creature, gene differences with phenotypically distinguishable effects have been identified at more than 600 different loci (10). The loci have been proven to lie on the chromosomes in linear sequence. The aggregate length of the four chromosomes is less than 10 micra. Consequently, the average linear extent of the chromosomal material involved in a single gene difference is less than one-fiftieth of a micron, a distance which is well below the resolving power of even a theoretically perfect optical microscope. Nevertheless, it is possible to specify, for any gene difference in *Drosophila,* both the chromosome on which its locus lies and the exact position of that locus relative to all other loci on the same chromosome. For a variety of reasons, the same kind of mapping in human chromosomes presents almost insuperable difficulties. However, a slight beginning has been made. For certain loci on the X-chromosome, it is possible to state which of two general regions of the chromosome they occupy, and something is known even of the relative positions of a few of them (36, 39, 86). A first step may have been made toward accomplishing a similar feat for an autosome, when one of us recently reported evidence that the genes for sicklemia and the M,N blood groups, respectively, have their loci in the same chromosome (87).

We usually speak of color-blindness (as contrasted with normal color vision), or of hemophilia (as contrasted with the non-hemophilic condition) as the effect of a single-gene substitution, or more briefly, as the effect of a single gene, and we shall use these convenient though inexact phrases frequently in the ensuing discussion. You may recall that except for the sex chromosome in the male all chromosomes in the body cells of higher animals are present in physiologically equivalent, or homologous, pairs and that each chromosome of an homologous pair possesses the same series of gene loci. It follows that the gene for albinism, for example, may be present on either one or both of a pair of homologous chromosomes; or more technically, the gene may be in heterozygous (single-dose) or homozygous (double-dose) condition. In general we shall not distinguish between these two situations, and the term single-gene substitution, unless qualified, will be understood to mean a gene substitution at a single *locus* in whichever dosage (heterozygous or homozygous) the gene in question requires to produce a discernible effect.

Any relevance genetic findings may have for social psychology necessarily depends on the role genes play in determining the phenotypic characteristics of individuals, especially such characteristics as may be presumed to affect behavior, and on the *distribution* of different kinds of genes in the population. We propose to discuss these matters, first with reference to their probable significance for individual differences, and second, with reference to their probable significance for group differences. As a preliminary to the discussion, it is necessary to review some of the more important features of gene action which have been discovered in 50 years of laboratory research:

First, there is no structure or organ, and no physiological process of the organism that cannot be altered, and radically altered, by a single-gene substitution at one or another locus.

In *Drosophila,* a single-gene substitution reduces the wings of the fly to mere vestiges; another results in the development of two pairs of wings, instead of the characteristic single pair; others respectively alter the size, shape, or venation of the wings; still others affect the size, shape, or histologic structure of the eyes; a gene substitution at any of several different loci prevents development of the eyes altogether; more than 40 different loci have been identified at which a single-gene substitution alters the pigmentation of the eye, with effects which range from varying degrees of darkening or lightening, to complete elimination of one or both of the pigments that are responsible for the brick-red eye color of the wild-type fly. Antennae, legs, bristles, sclerites, body color, and body size, are a few of the other features of the animal which may be discernibly affected in a variety of ways by various single genes. Finally, gene substitutions at any of a large number of loci interfere so radically with the development of the animal that they have a lethal effect, causing death in the egg, larval, or pupal stage (10).

Many of the genes we have referred to produce more than one read-

ily observed effect. Thus one of the gene substitutions which reduces
wing size also modifies the wing muscles, changes the angle of certain
bristles, and affects the balancers, the shape of the spermatheca, growth
rate, fecundity, and length of life; another single gene simultaneously
affects the structure of legs, wings, antennae, and bristles.

For obvious reasons, the genetics of laboratory mammals has not
been studied with nearly so much thoroughness as the genetics of *Drosophila*. Nevertheless, it is apparent that the variety and extent of
single-gene effects are comparable to those exhibited in the fruit-fly. To
take the house mouse as our single example, the effects of perhaps a
hundred different single-gene substitutions are known (34). The most
familiar are those affecting pelage color, of which there is a considerable variety. Other single-gene substitutions affect the texture or growth
of the hair; any one of at least three genes at different loci produces
nearly complete hairlessness. Further single-gene effects in this animal
include skeletal abnormalities, eye abnormalities, short ears, two or
three types of anemia, harelip and cleft palate, hydrocephalus, pituitary
dwarfism, complete absence of rods in the retina, and absence of the
corpus callosum; any of several genes may produce a nervous disorder
symptomatized by choreic movements. As in *Drosophila*, a single-gene
substitution is frequently seen to affect the animal in more than one
way. Thus the gene which shortens the ears also predisposes the animal
towards spontaneous muscle contractures in the tail; the gene for yellow pelage besides affecting the development of hair pigment, produces
obesity and reduces the likelihood of spontaneous mammary carcino-
mata.

The identification of genetic mechanisms in man is of course very
much more difficult to accomplish than in laboratory animals, because
controlled matings cannot be made as desired. Since the pioneer work
of Weinberg and of Bernstein in the 1920's, however, a number of special statistical approaches have been developed which make critical genetic analysis of human material feasible within certain limits (1, 21,
22, 23, 39, 43, 44, 70, 74, 89, 91).

In the enormous, and mostly *un*critical, literature which contains reports on human heredity there is presumptive evidence that more than
a hundred variations (chiefly pathologic) in the skin and its derivatives
(18), more than a hundred eye abnormalities (95), and a comparable
number of skeletal anomalies (2) may be attributable to single-gene

substitutions. Other organs are somewhat less accessible to observation. Nevertheless, we may include among conditions for which there is some evidence of single gene determination, a dozen or more blood dyscrasias, similar numbers of metabolic and endocrine disturbances, of nervous disorders, of aberrations in the muscular system and of neoplasms in a variety of organs (30, 83).

We must emphasize that the evidence for single-gene determination in the majority of the pathologic conditions included in the preceding enumeration is no more than presumptive. But critical evidence is available for a substantial proportion of the conditions in each of the categories mentioned; and there is little doubt that in the human species the effects of single gene substitutions are at least as numerous, varied, and far-reaching as in the laboratory animals that have been studied.

Variations of non-pathologic nature in man which can safely be attributed to single-gene substitutions have been found for remarkably few characteristics; those whose genetic mechanisms are most soundly established concern serologic characters, which are detectably affected by single-gene differences in a number of loci; these include the A,B,O antigens, the M,N antigens, the Rh-series of antigens, and others (98); high taste thresholds for phenylthiourea appear to depend on a single-gene substitution (82); and quite probably variations in the direction of the vellus or fine hair of the forehead are single-gene effects (48). This modest list represents a substantial portion of our current knowledge of single-gene variations in *normal* human characteristics.

A second important feature of gene action concerns the principle that the phenotype of an organism is not a mere mosaic of independently expressed single-gene effects. The dependence of genic expression on environmental factors will be considered in a moment. Here we wish to stress that an animal's phenotype depends on developmental interactions involving the entire aggregate of genic material as well as the materials of the extragenic protoplasm. Examples of striking interaction effects from the combination of two or more identifiable genes at different loci will be found in any standard genetics text (77, 88, 96). Interactions less conspicuous than those cited in the textbooks are probably far commoner; and it seems fairly safe to say that the effect of a gene substitution at any given locus is influenced by the character of the genic material at virtually every other locus (32).

A third important principle of gene action is that the phenotype of an organism is a function both of its genetic constitution and of the environment in which the organism develops; the statement that a given peculiarity is hereditary does not mean that it is not subject to environmental modification. Different genes vary widely in their responsiveness to environmental conditions. The effects of certain genes appear to be expressed with great uniformity within any range of environmental conditions that permit the organism to survive at all, whereas the effects of many known genes show conspicuous differences in different environments (44). In *Drosophila,* for example, flies possessing a gene called *Giant* (in the third chromosome) are about 75 per cent larger than individuals without this gene; and the size difference is apparent even when the larvae have been reared on a minimal diet (9). On the other hand, there is another *Giant* gene (in a different chromosome) which has the same effect on body size, but only when an abundant food supply is available to the developing larvae; when the larvae are reared on starvation rations, flies carrying this gene are indistinguishable in size from their genetically non-giant messmates (29).

Flies with a gene for *abnormal abdomen* exhibit the abnormality only if they are reared in a moist culture medium (57). An indistinguishable abnormality of the abdomen may also result from the presence of another gene—in this case the effect of the gene is maximally expressed when the flies have been reared in a *dry* culture (8). In the same animal, the effects of a number of other genes are to a large degree dependent on temperature during incubation (38). The manifestation of the gene *Antennaless* is significantly affected by the adequacy of vitamin B_2 in the culture medium (33), and so on. The effect of the Himalayan gene in rabbits is to prevent pigment formation except at the extremities of the animal; but if a newborn rabbit of the Himalayan genotype is subjected briefly to a moderately low temperature (11° C.), the entire pelage develops pigmentation (45).

Intrauterine conditions during pregnancy can also be shown to influence the expression of several genotypes in mammals, inasmuch as consistent differences either in degree or frequency of manifestation of certain genetic characters are found with increasing age of the mother. Conditions which show this effect include white spotting (104) and polydactyly (101) in guinea pigs, and harelip in mice (90). Many congenital malformations in man, it may be recalled, appear to exhibit this phenomenon; in most cases the incidence is highest in children born to older mothers (**62**, **68**); in at least one case (pyloric stenosis) the incidence appears to be highest among first-born children (**19**).

Excellent examples of human genes whose effects are uniformly expressed within any range of environment consistent with survival are those upon which the A and B, or M,N antigens depend. Instances of environmentally conditioned gene manifestation in man are difficult to cite with assurance. This does not imply that they are rare, but merely that the technical difficulties of identifying them are very great. Pattern baldness, however, is possibly an example (**89**). There is evidence that in most cases this is dependent on a single-gene substitution, and that baldness appears in females only if they are homozygous for the gene, whereas it is manifested regularly in males who are heterozygous. It is commonly stated that eunuchs never show baldness. This suggests that the expression of the pattern-baldness gene in heterozygous condition is contingent on the presence of male sex hormones, and therefore that any environmental agency (e.g., castration or injury) which prevents elaboration of these hormones also prevents phenotypic manifestation of the baldness gene in single dose.

A fourth principle relating to gene action which requires mention is that the effect of a gene substitution can be simulated, in the absence of the gene in question, by the effect of appropriate environmental conditions. The environmentally induced modifications have been called *phenocopies* and they are phenotypically indistinguishable from gene-effects (**32**). By subjecting *Drosophila* larvae to nearly lethal high temperatures for different intervals of time and at different stages of development, Goldschmidt has produced phenocopies of almost every known genetic variation in this animal. In mice, phenocopies of several morphologic gene effects (pseudencephaly, flexed tail, hydrocephalus, etc.) have been produced by X-radiation of developing embryos of different ages (**47**).

It should be emphasized that the environmentally induced phenocopies do not reappear in the progeny or descendants of the treated animals unless the decendants are exposed to similar treatment. The phrase "environmentally induced" is an oversimplification, however, because genetically different stocks differ in their response to heat and other treatments, and exhibit different predilections for yielding specific kinds of phenocopies (**15**, **31**, **32**, **71**). The principle illustrated in the production of phenocopies is therefore essentially a special case of the principle stated earlier, that the phenotype of an organism is a function both of its genetic constitution and of the environment in which it develops.

In man, there is reason to believe (based in part on the heterogeneity of familial incidence) that several pathologic conditions occur as single-gene effects in some families, and as sporadic phenocopies in others. These conditions include microcephaly (70), lobster claw (5), deaf-mutism (52), and diabetes insipidus (72). In particular, it appears from data assembled by Murphy that an embryo can on occasion be induced to develop into a microcephalic by X-radiation of the mother during early pregnancy (62). There is likewise evidence that certain infections during early pregnancy (e.g., rubella) may cause the development of malformations which in other families occur as single-gene effects (62).

A final point regarding gene action which must be kept in mind is that multiple effects are highly characteristic. We have given examples of possibly extreme cases in *Drosophila* and mice. Equally striking illustrations could be drawn from a large number of hereditary syndromes in human pathology. What we wish to call special attention to here, however, are the *viability* effects of gene differences. Virtually every gene difference that has been studied in experimental animals has been found to affect viability in one direction or the other, and this is almost certainly a nearly universal phenomenon. The overwhelming majority of the single-gene substitutions whose phenotypic effects we have mentioned affect viability adversely, at least under standard laboratory conditions. A few, however, improve the viability of the animals possessing them, and in some cases the same gene substitution impairs viability under some environmental conditions and improves it under others (24).

We may turn now to a consideration of the question of the degree to which the kind of gene effects we have been discussing are significant as factors in human variability.

The effects of the single-gene substitutions to which we have referred are so striking and their variety so great that one might be pardoned for supposing that, collectively, they must play a major role in the determination of individual differences in human (and other) populations. In recent years, however, it has become more and more widely recognized that single-gene differences which produce readily distinguishable discontinuities in phenotypic variation are completely *non-representative* of the bulk of genetic variability in any species. Gene differences, of course, arise originally as *mutations,* and the rate of appearance of mutations is enormously accelerated by X-rays. Many of the mutated genes produced by X-ray treatment have conspicuous phenotypic effects and are identical with those which have appeared spontaneously in natural populations and in laboratory stocks; a much larger number are lethal; by far the largest number, however, have been shown to have very slight effects on viability, about as often in a favorable as an unfavorable direction (93). The viability of an organism necessarily depends on morphologic or physiologic characteristics, or both. There is, moreover, a general, though not absolute, parallelism between the conspicuousness of the visible effect of a gene and the degree to which it impairs viability. By and large the more striking the phenotypic effect, the more drastically is viability reduced. Consequently the *largest class* of mutated genes produced by X-rays comprises those genes which individually do not have readily discernible phenotypic effects. There is abundant reason to believe that the same is true of genes which appear by spontaneous mutation (59).

Mather and his collaborators have been particularly impressed with the special problems posed by this class of genes, and they designate them as *polygenes,* in distinction from the single genes responsible for conspicuous phenotypic discontinuities, which they call *major genes* (53). The latter, as we have seen, can be individually identified (in laboratory material at least, and to some extent in man) by the discontinuities they produce, and can be assigned to precise loci on one or another chromosome. Polygenes on the other hand, tend to have quantitatively equivalent cumulative effects, and cannot be individually identified and assigned to chromosomal loci. Their reality cannot be doubted, however, because their existence is revealed by the effectiveness of selective breeding for almost any continuously variable quantitative character in a genetically heterogeneous population of laboratory or domestic animals. Mather, moreover, has adduced what appears to be critical evidence that polygenes possess the essential genic characteristics of classical genes, viz., that they exhibit segregation and crossing-over.

If our reasoning was correct about the relative frequencies with which polygene and major gene mutations, respectively, occur, it follows that there must be available in any animal species an enormous store of genetic variability contingent upon very large numbers of polygenes, with individually minute, but cumulatively appreciable, effects.

We should also expect to find that a far greater portion of the phenotypic variability in natural populations depends on polygenic differences than on major-gene effects. This follows from the fact that, in general, the viability impairment produced by genes with discernible individual effects should result in their being kept down by natural selection to very low incidences; and this, in fact, seems to be the usual rule. The only discernible single-gene effects with incidences of 5 to 50 percent in human populations are those few which are approximately neutral as to viability effect. Mostly, these involve differences which are detectable only by special techniques, such as abnormalities in color vision, and the blood-group antigens. Of the hundreds of presumptively single-gene abnormalities in man which we have referred to, only a small minority have a population incidence above one in 10,000, and the vast majority are very much rarer than this.

If we pick two unrelated people at random from any human population, we shall probably find that they differ in respect to one or another of the blood antigens, and we may find that one is a taster and the other a non-taster. Beyond this it is highly probable that few, if any, of the observable phenotypic differences between them will be referable to known major genes. Yet we know that the physical characteristics which distinguish individuals are to an appreciable degree determined by genetic differences because of the almost complete physical identity of individuals who are known to have *identical* genotypes, viz., members of monozygotic twin pairs.

Predominantly, then, such genetic differences as are involved in the non-pathologic range of human variability are likely to be of the polygene rather than the major-gene class. This is very probably true also for genetic differences which may be significant in many of the commoner conditions which are classed as pathologic, including cancer and hypertensive disease, as well as for genetic differences which may be involved in resistance and susceptibility to specific infections.

It is possible, we may add, that the expression of polygenic variability may in general be especially sensitive to environmental conditions, as was noted by Wright more than thirty years ago (**99**, cf. **102**) in the case of polygenic variation in physiologic processes relevant to the productive characters of livestock.

We shall try to indicate in a moment some of the ways in which the polygene concept, the facts regarding the nature of genic action, and modern knowledge of the distribution of genetic variability in populations may affect our views on genetic components in behavioral differences. Right here, however, we should like to point out that recognition of the fact that the overwhelmingly greater part of genetically conditioned variability in man depends on polygenic differences rather than on clearly segregating major genes has vital methodologic implications for research in the field of human genetics itself, because it sets a limit to the amount of information that we may expect to gain through analysis of single-gene differences.

This does not mean that further search for individual gene differences in man should be eschewed. Quite the contrary, we regard it as essential to continue the refinement of statistical methods for detecting major-gene effects, and to continue an assiduous quest for variations contingent upon single-gene differences. The collection of *critical* data, which means systematically assembled data and not those culled from casual observations reported in the literature, has hardly more than begun in the field of human heredity. The various ways in which these data can be useful, even indispensable, in certain areas of medical practice and research, and in anthropology, have been discussed by Snyder and by others on several recent occasions and will not be reviewed here (6, 7, 12, 20, 61, 64, 67, 84, 85).

On the other hand, it appears evident that if human genetics is to progress along fresh pathways, the traditional atomistic approach must be supplemented by methods which will yield information on the significance of genetic variability without recourse to analysis in terms of individual gene substitutions. The beginnings of the new methods are perhaps to be found in the various kinds of twin studies that have been undertaken by workers in several fields. These include, of course, innumerable quantitative comparisons of intra-pair differences in monozygotic and dizygotic twins, studies of separated identical twins, co-twin control and concordance-discordance studies with or without investigation of sibs and other relatives (13, 91). We refer to these studies as beginnings, because it is clear that methods of research involving twins need to be both elaborated and refined a good deal before they can be expected to yield the kind of information we are after. But we feel that twin materials can be and should be exploited more fully and more systematically than in the past.

We return now to the question of the probable significance of hereditary components in the development of behavioral patterns.

In experimental animals, the existence of polygenes and perhaps of major genes which affect temperament and behavioral responses is well established. Hall found it possible, through selective breeding, to establish strains of rats differing in aggressiveness (41); Scott has reported a number of differences in social behavior among different inbred strains of house mice (75); Tryon was successful in breeding high and low maze-running abilities, respectively (94); and Heron, in a similar experiment, found that he had obtained genetically differentiated strains with respect to general activity level and motivation (42).

It is of course possible, indeed to us it seems probable, that there exists in the human species a genetic basis for differentiation in respect to analogous organic drives; but we think it extremely dangerous to press the analogy to the point of equating "boldness" in rat behavior, for example, with "boldness" in human behavior (cf. 63). There very probably are in man innate neuro-endocrine variations comparable to those which presumably distinguish "bold" and "shy" rats. But, as Schneirla has ably stressed, there are striking *qualitative* differences between the significance of organic drives for animals whose interindividual relationships are on a physiological or a biosocial level, and the implications for human, psychosocial, behavior (73). The aggregate effects of the manifold variables significant for human behavior which are consequent upon the unique functional development of the human cerebral cortex must inevitably, we think, overshadow the effects of any but the most extreme organic deviations in neurophysiologic mechanisms.

The existence of major genes in man which produce extreme neurophysiologic aberrations is, of course, well established. Examples are the genes responsible for most or all cases of Huntington's chorea (3, 79), Friedreich's ataxia (80), the infantile (81) and juvenile (78) forms of amaurotic idiocy, phenylketonuric amentia (69), and a number of other severe neurologic conditions. The neuropathologic conditions attributable to single-gene substitutions, however, are individually of extreme rarity (e.g., the incidence of juvenile amaurotic idiocy is in the neighborhood of 1 in 25,000; of phenylketonuria, perhaps 1 in 40,000) and even in the aggregate they are not sufficiently numerous to have appreciable significance for social behavior in general.

On the other hand, even within the non-pathologic range of behavioral variability in man there is little reason to doubt the existence of a considerable diversity of polygenic effects of potential relevance to psychosocial responses. But the word *potential* is extremely important here, and we cannot too strongly emphasize the highly contingent nature of the genetic potentialities we are considering. Thus, it would seem safe to assert that differences in skin pigmentation, in physique, or in facial conformation, dependent on genotypic differences, may indirectly have significant effects upon psychosocial response. The effects would be discernible chiefly in extreme cases, when genetically determined characteristics in these categories might impair (or favor) social acceptability. The degree of social rejection or acceptance which an individual encounters may in turn influence the course of his personality development and ultimately the pattern of his social integration. It seems to us obvious that the *direction* of this latter influence (whether toward submissiveness or aggression, for example), as well as its degree must be contingent upon a multiplicity of still other factors. The character and intensity of the individual's biogenic needs (which are quite conceivably in part conditioned by genotypic constitution) as well as the availability of satisfactions for them (which cannot be genotypically determined) may be involved; almost certainly, his immediate social situation (the status of his family, for example, and his own status within the family) will be significantly implicated.

Thus the genotype of the individual is subjected to a kind of social buffeting throughout his psychosocial development. The course of the development is not a straight line whose direction and ultimate terminus can be neatly analyzed, by a simple parallelogram of forces, into genetic and environmental components. It appears rather that it must be represented by a complex series of meanderings, turning and twisting in response to a variety of social and other influences, all along the way. Each inflection marks an effective interaction of environmental influences, and if at the appropriate point, the strength of one or another of these influences exceeds some threshold value (which itself must be a function of all preceding developmental history) this factor may become critical as a determinant of certain features of the final pattern. According to this concept, genotypic constitution is but one of a large number of factors whose dynamic interactions ultimately establish the pattern of the individual's social relations. Except where genotypic deviations from the norm are extreme (as in the cases of major-gene substitutions with neuropathologic effects which have been mentioned above) we should not expect them to be in any rigid sense deterministic, either in direction or degree, of differences in psychosocial phenotype.

We think there is some measure of support for the kind of concept we have just outlined in the observations of Newman et al. on monozygotic twins separated from infancy, which they interpret, perhaps a little mechanically, as evidence for the existence of several "levels of behavior" (65). Thus in one of Newman's cases (No. XVIII) the members of a twin pair were remarkably similar in personality and temperament, as well as could be judged both by tests and observation; nevertheless, they had adopted very different ways of life, which in this instance were rather clearly related to differences in the respective environments in which they were reared. In other cases (perhaps that described by Muller (58) belongs here) rather marked personality differences appear to have developed between the members of a separated pair, whose adaptations to their social group environments were nevertheless similar both in character and degree. We interpret these observations as indicating that environmental differences which are critical at one level do not necessarily produce divergent responses at another.

Well-known observations on the sexual differentiation of individual and social behavior bring support from another angle. Within the range of non-pathologic variability in the human species, there are probably few genotypically conditioned differences in morphology and physiology more striking than those which distinguish the sexes. As Mead especially has shown, however, the social roles of women may actually be reversed in different social contexts (54), and even within the same society we find a great diversity of individual role (in terms of behavior socially regarded as sex-conditioned) among the members of either genotypic sex. There seems little reason to doubt, in fact, the essential plasticity even of the more immediately biologic (more "basic"?) aspects of sexual behavior. Ethnologic evidences bearing on the social conditioning of homosexual or ambisexual versus heterosexual responses have been adduced by many anthropologists (e.g., 4, 17); evidence of another kind may be found in Lange's single case of presumptively monozygotic twins whose histories of overt sexual behavior would seem to place them almost at opposite ends of the homosexual-heterosexual scale (49); a third line of evidence is to be found in the histories of pseudohermaphrodites, in whom the direction of sexual interests and form of overt sex expression more frequently is consistent with the sex they have been brought up to believe they belong to than with the sex of their gonads (27).

The foregoing and similar considerations lead us to conclude that in spite of the remarkable diversity of genotypic differences within the human species, the plasticity of individual response to the social environment is even more remarkable; and that as determinants of social roles and attitudes, genetic factors are, on the whole, of very limited significance.

We could end here, were it not for the fact that the animal experiments of Hall, Tryon, and others, cited above, have been interpreted by some as lending plausibility to an assumption that human races, nations, or social classes may have become genetically differentiated from one another in temperament or behavioral potentialities as a consequence of selection and other evolutionary processes. Those who espouse this interpretation point also to the fact that human ethnic groups often are significantly differentiated with respect to skin color, stature, and other morphologic characteristics which have a genetic basis; why, they ask, is it not likely that they are similarly differentiated in physiologic or other characteristics which may affect their behavior as groups?

Now, it is clear that there is a vast difference between the population dynamics of laboratory animals mated according to their breeder's choice, and natural populations such as are approximated by racial and other groups in man. Drastic selection, such as was practiced by Tryon and by Hall would be expected to result in the accumulation of a large number of polygenes favoring the characters selected for in the respective strains. Differentiation of the stocks studied by Scott did not result from selection, but was a consequence of close inbreeding, which is the most rapid way of producing genetically homogenous strains differing in their residual (i.e., polygenic) heredity. Close inbreeding is not, and as far as we know, never has been characteristic of the human species.

The basic question here, then, is whether the processes of biologic evolution in human populations have been of such a nature as to permit or encourage racial differentiation of the type suggested.

Current genetic theories regarding the evolution of biologic races (theories which are almost daily receiving fresh substantiation from field and laboratory observations) recognize *selection* and *genetic drift* as two of the processes which may be involved, in varying degrees under varying circumstances, in establishing racial differentiation. Other processes, such as migration, hybridization and, more rarely, mutation pressure are also highly relevant, and may on occasion assume paramount importance; but their consideration here would not affect the main tenor of the argument (24, 28, 35, 46, 76, 103).

Genetic drift comprises the random shifts in gene frequencies which may occur as a cumulative result of the sampling fluctuations inherent in the mendelian mechanism. The implications of the process have been extensively analyzed by Sewall Wright (103; see also 51; an elementary treatment of the principles involved will be found in 88).

In a small population, a gene which is present initially in only a few individuals may, in the course of a large number of generations, increase in frequency through genetic drift until it is found in most or all members of the population; the same process, alternatively, can result in a reduction of the frequency of the gene, or even in its complete elimination from the group in question. In small populations, where genetic drift tends to dominate evolutionary changes in gene frequency, selection, unless quite intense, is virtually without effect. In larger populations, where selection may become a major factor in determining the course of evolution, the effects of genetic drift become negligible. It appears that a good deal of the early racial differentiation of man (and of many other animals) may have occurred in mutually isolated populations of small size (perhaps a few score or a few hundred individuals). Under these circumstances, differentiation in gene frequencies at a large number of loci would be expected to occur. Subsequently, if individual populations underwent considerable expansion (as they apparently did in some cases) the relative gene frequencies existent at the time of the expansion would tend to be preserved *in the case of genes with approximately neutral effects from the standpoint of selection,* i.e., effects which neither impair nor improve viability, fertility, etc. Major genes whose effects involve slight selective disadvantages could also become disseminated through large ethnic groups in similar fashion, provided the entire population, while it was still numerically small, had become completely homozygous for these genes through genetic drift, i.e., more technically, if the genes in question had become *fixed* in the population prior to its expansion. The observed distribution of such genes as those determining the various blood groups, taste-blindness, color-blindness, etc., in different racial groups can in large part be explained on these principles; and it is possible that the distribution of striking physical discontinuities (e.g., stature difference between the pygmies and neighboring groups) may be similarly explicable.

More generally, after expansion of small populations into large ones, genes whose effects confer selective advantage or disadvantage on their possessors would tend to have their frequencies increased or decreased accordingly by natural selection. It is quite possible that the widespread presence of dark pigmentation in most Negroid, and some Caucasoid, races is to be accounted for in this fashion.

Phenotypic differentiation (whether in the morphologic or physiologic sense) in characteristics whose variability is chiefly dependent on polygene differences would seem rather less likely to result from genetic drift than differentiation in characters contingent on major genes, because the effects of individual polygenes appear to be in large part mutually interchangeable (53, p. 17). Thus, while genetic drift might well lead to the accumulation of different constellations of polygenes in different populations, the relative proportions of loci occupied by genes with plus and minus effects, respectively, on any given character more often than not should tend to be about the same from one population to the next. If genetic drift should lead to differentiation in polygenically determined characteristics, the differentiation would not have an appreciable likelihood of persisting after the populations expanded, unless it should then be maintained by selection: evolutionary changes in characteristics whose variability is polygenically determined are essentially more reversible than changes in characteristics which are contingent on major genes, because of the improbability of complete fixation through genetic drift of genes affecting the same character at a very large number of loci.

This leaves us with only the hypothesis that more or less fixed tendencies toward different kinds of behavioral response might have evolved in different racial groups through natural selection. This would require that certain types of behavior had *adaptive value* (selective advantage) in some populations while different types of behavior were favored by selection in others. But change in the genetic composition of a population through natural selection is an excessively slow process, especially in the case of polygenic systems concerned with characteristics whose expression is sensitive to environmental influences (35, 60). Its rate would usually have to be measured in terms of tens or hundreds of thousands of years, rather than in terms of centuries or millenia; *and it seems highly improbable that tendencies toward fixity of response in any type of social behavior have ever had persistent adaptive value in a human population.*

As Dobzhansky and Montagu have pointed out, there are two general ways in which adaption to environment has been achieved through evolution (25; cf. 73, 76). One is through the selection of ever more precise specializations which fit the organism to cope with specific environmental situations; the other is through the development of increasingly plastic responsiveness to any of a variety of environmental situations. Adaptation through the evolution of structural specializations and genetic fixity of behavior is most conspicuously exemplified in the insects. Adaptation involving the preservation of relatively generalized structures such as the human hand, which can be put to a variety of uses, and plasticity of responsiveness, permitting adjustment to a variety of situations, has been strikingly characteristic of the human species.

The forms of human society which mankind has developed in the course of its history as a species have been varied in the extreme, Dobzhansky and Montagu also remind us, and in terms of evolutionary time, they have succeeded one another with considerable rapidity. Even in any one social organization, flexibility of behavioral adjustment to different situations is likely to have had a selective advantage over any tendency toward stereotyped reactions. For it is difficult to conceive of any human social organization in which plasticity of response, as reflected by ability to profit from experience (that is, by intelligence) and by emotional and temperamental resilience, would not be at a premium and therefore favored by natural selection. It therefore seems to us highly improbable that any significant genetic differentiation in respect to particular response patterns, personality types, temperaments, or intellectual capacities among different populations or races has occurred in the history of human evolution (cf. 56).

The conclusion reached above applies equally, of course, to subdivisions of human populations, such as socio-economic levels and the like. The fact that reference is frequently made to "superior stocks" or "superior strains" in human society (with the implication that they may be found in all nations, races, classes) calls for some comment. In the first place, as might be inferred from facts regarding gene action which were presented in the early part of this chapter, the terms "superior" and "inferior" cannot reasonably be applied to genotypes *unless the environment in which they are to develop is specified.* This is clearly evident even on the level of physiological behavior: Guernsey cows pastured on their native island yield 8 or 9 gallons of milk daily; on the same pasturage, scrub cattle imported from Africa yield only about three gallons. If both breeds are reared in the African bush country, however, the yield of the Guernseys drops to zero, while the African cows continue to produce a gallon or two of milk a day. It is clearly impossible to designate either breed as superior in any absolute sense. Other types of interaction between genotype and environment involve similar difficulties for defining "superiority" and "inferiority" (37, 38). A further and equally strong objection to the expressions quoted concerns the lack of precision (coupled with misleading connotations) in the words "stocks" and "strains." To the laboratory geneticist, these terms have rather exact meanings. They are usually qualified by the adjective "isogenic," or some comparable expression, or else the qualification is understood. In laboratory usage, the terms *imply complete or very nearly complete genetic homogeneity.* To the animal breeder, the term stock or strain has a somewhat less exact meaning, but carries similar implications; it usually connotes high degree of uniformity of pattern, etc., among individuals in the stock, and a moderate to high degree of genetic homogeneity. Now genetic homogeneity is something which can be measured, at least in part. Its degree is usually expressed in terms of Wright's coefficient of relationship (100). This coefficient applied to a breed of animals, for example, gives the average probability, for pairs of animals chosen at random, that any given gene will be present in both of them through inheritance from a common ancestor. It can also be interpreted as giving the average fraction of all genes shared in common by the members of pairs chosen at random from the breed, by virtue of common ancestry. For reasons we cannot go into here, the coefficient of relationship is usually an underestimate of genetic homogeneity when applied to livestock. The scale of the coefficient can perhaps be appreciated from the fact that its value is unity for pairs of identical twins, 0.50 for sibs, 0.125 for first cousins, and .031 for second cousins. The average coefficient of relationship for an isogenic strain of *Drosophila,* or for a stock of mice which has been derived from 18 or more generations of brother-sister mating is well over 0.95, i.e., the individual members of such a strain or stock are very nearly identical in genotype. Average coefficients of relationship in livestock breeds range as high as 0.40, but mostly appear to be much lower. Referring to these breeds (or to individual herds, which are likely to have greater genetic homogeneity than the breed as a whole) as stocks or strains is justified as implying at least that there is genetic identity at a number of loci which contain genes determining the breed characters. Reference to current descendants of Jonathan Edwards or of the Wedgewood-Darwin families as a strain or stock is not justified on this basis, and can hardly have any meaning at all unless some estimate is made of the degree of genetic homogeneity among them.

Questions of the evolutionary effects of selection on the one hand, and of the identification of "superior stocks" and "inferior stocks" on the other, have pertinence to the widely publicized allegations that the civilized world (Great Britain and America, at least) is facing a downward evolutionary trend in average test intelligence (11, 14, 92). Whatever may have been the nature of selective processes in the past, according to these allegations, fertility differentials today are such that we must anticipate a decline of from one to four points I.Q. per generation in the average intelligence level of the population. Those who maintain this thesis appear to be fairly convinced, moreover, that the predicted decline will involve genotypic, and not merely phenotypic, deterioration.

The earlier arguments in support of the theory of the declining I.Q. were based on observed socio-economic differentials in average I.Q. level and reproductive rate, respectively. These arguments have largely been abandoned, for the simple reason that the assumptions which they involved were soon seen to be unsubstantiable (cf. 66). Currently, those who maintain the thesis that intelligence is declining base their predictions on what they believe is evidence of a negative association between test intelligence and fertility which appears to them to be at least partly independent of socio-economic stratification. The actual data on which this belief is founded, however, show merely that there is a negative correlation between the test intelligence of children and the number of their sibs. That the relation between intelligence and *fertility* need not parallel this becomes self-evident when we consider the fact that mental defectives of imbecile and idiot grades, whatever may be the average size of the sibships in which they occur, are themselves almost completely infertile. A valid argument that fertility differentials are such as to result in phenotypic selection favoring low test intelligence must, then, show that any negative regression of fertility on I.Q. over one portion of the I.Q. range is not compensated by a regression of opposite sign in another part of the range.

It seems to us quite conceivable that fertility differentials could be such as to produce a rather rapid *phenotypic* change of average test-intelligence level *in either direction* from one generation to the next. But in any case, no prediction of phenotypic change based on reproduction differentials would be valid if it failed to consider general trends in environmental conditions which might tend to raise (or lower) test intelligence throughout all levels of the population. Wheeler's report (97) of a 10-point increase in average I.Q. among samples taken only ten years apart in Tennessee mountain communities suggests that trends of this character may have effects which it would be unsafe to ignore. It is of interest to note that the recently published results of the second (1947) series of tests in the elaborate Scottish survey initiated in 1932 indicate that over the 15-year interval involved the average test-intelligence level in the population studied has possibly shown a slight improvement, and has certainly not declined (55).

To admit the conceivability that phenotypic changes in population I.Q. may occur with some rapidity, however, is not to concede that genotypic changes are likely to occur with comparable speed. The protagonists of the declining intelligence theory appear to be persuaded that phenotypic selection (acting through fertility differentials at different I.Q. levels), if it exists, must have a rather direct effect on the genotypic composition of the population. The belief seems to rest ultimately on the well-established correlation in I.Q. between parent and child; and it appears to involve a rather elementary confusion of correlation with causation. The potential genetic effects of the kind of selection which has been postulated cannot, in fact, be envisaged except on the foundation of some *causal* hypothesis.

We cannot pretend to any detailed knowledge of the conditions which determine human fertility; but it seems to us fairly evident that, in general, the limiting factors are social rather than biologic. There appears also to be evidence that factors in the social environment which encourage fertility are broadly the same as, or intimately related to, those which tend to depress the phenotypic development of high test intelligence in many, if not all, genotypes. If this is the case, it should be obvious that fertility differentials will have minimal effect on the frequencies of genotypes which may conceivably be involved in determining different innate potentialities for intelligence-test performance. Alternatively, we might hypothesize that factors in the social environment which stimulate fertility *do not* appreciably militate against optimal expression of genetic potentialities for intelligence-test performance. On this hypothesis we might expect that the postulated phenotypic selection would favor systematic alterations in genotype frequencies; but we think that the hypothesis is rather improbable.

One might legitimately ask what all of this means for the prospects of future human evolution. Does it imply that the human species has ceased to evolve in the biologic sense, or perhaps even that further evolution, either progressive or retrogressive, is impossible? The answer is largely a matter of time scales. The earliest fossil primates are found in strata that are approximately 70,000,000 years old. The earliest known anthropoid is placed at about 40,000,000 years ago, although in view of the sketchiness of the primate fossil record, the Anthropoidea may be considerably older than this (16).

The fossil record, then, indicates that an interval of some 40,000,000 years elapsed between the time that the first anthropoid appeared and the emergence of *Homo sapiens*. It is estimated that the human species has existed for a quarter of a million to half a million years, and it appears to have undergone little or no alteration, in skeletal parts at least, during that time; one would hardly expect that human evolution in the biologic sense would proceed very rapidly on a merely historic time scale. On the other hand, the whole of human *social* evolution has occupied only a microscopic fraction of the geologic time scale, but it is hardly probable, either on theoretic grounds or on the basis of inferences from human history and archeology, that the biologic basis of human abilities or behavioral potentialities, whatever these terms may mean, has appreciably changed during this period.

Nevertheless, enormous changes have taken place in the last 5000 years, and even in the last 500 years, in human social organization, in man's control over phenomena in the world about him and, to some extent, over his own personal resources. It should be evident from what we have said that we regard Galton's golden dream of man directing the course of his own biologic evolution as an eventuality not likely to be realizable within the very near future. Haldane suggests that it is a possibility, but he is convinced that the knowledge of past evolution, of genetics, and of cytology necessary for accomplishing it would considerably exceed the entire body of scientific knowledge on which our present civilization is based (40). If this seems to some a counsel of pessimism, to us it seems precisely the reverse. We have seen evidence of the enormous constructive potentialities existing in the human species as it is today and as it has been, biologically, for some time. We have ample reason to believe that mankind is not, either individually or collectively, utilizing these potentialities to anywhere near their full extent. We believe, therefore, that even with its present genetic composition, the human species has before it enormous possibilities for further advance. We see no evidences of a decline in the hereditary "quality" of our species; and we are convinced that if mankind goes to the dogs within the next ten or twenty centuries it is far more likely to do so as a result of inexcusable bungling in the management of social relationships than as a consequence of genetic deterioration.

REFERENCES

1. *Annals of Eugenics, 6* (1934) *et seq., passim* (especially papers by D. J. Finney, R. A. Fisher, J. B. S. Haldane, L. S. Penrose).
2. Aschner, B.   1929.   Zur Erbbiologie des Skelettsystems, *Zeitschr. f. Konst.-Lehre, 14,* 129–211.
3. Bell, Julia.   1934.   Huntington's chorea, *Treas. Human Inher., 4,* 1–67.
4. Benedict, Ruth.   1939.   Sex in primitive society, *Amer. J. Orthopsychiat., 9,* 570–574.
5. Birch-Jensen, Arne.   1949.   Congenital deformities of the upper extremities, *Opera ex Domo Biologiae Hereditariae Humanae Univ. Hafn., 19,* 1–285.
6. Boyd, W. C.   1940.   Critique of methods of classifying mankind, *J. Phys. Anthropol., 27,* 333–364.
7. Boyd, W. C.   1947.   The use of genetically determined characters, espe-

cially serological factors such as Rh, in physical anthropology, *Southwest. J. Anthropol., 3,* 32–49.

8. Braun, Werner. 1938. Opposite effect of environmental factors on similar phenotypes, *Amer. Nat., 72,* 189–192.

9. Bridges, C. B., and Morgan, T. H. 1923. The third-chromosome group of mutant characters of *Drosophila melanogaster, Pub. Carneg. Inst.,* No. *327,* 1–251.

10. Bridges, C. B. and Brehme, K. S. 1944. The mutants of *Drosophila melanogaster,* Carneg. Inst. of Washington, Pub. *552,* 1–253.

11. Burt, Cyril. 1946. Intelligence and fertility, *Occasional Papers on Eugenics, 2.* London: Hamilton Hamish Medical Books.

12. Cappell, D. F. 1947. The blood groups of mankind: A new approach to anthropology, *Glasgow Med. J., 28,* 397–413.

13. Carter, H. D. 1940. Ten years of research on twins: Contributions to the nature-nurture problem. *39th Yearbook,* Nat. Soc. Stud. Educ., Part I, 235–255.

14. Cattell, R. B. 1940. Effects of human fertility upon the distribution of intelligence and culture. *39th Yearbook,* Nat. Soc. Stud. Educ., Part I, 221–233.

15. Child, G. P., Blanc, R., and Plough, H. H. 1940. Somatic effects of temperature on development in *Drosophila melanogaster.* I. Phenocopies and reversal of dominance, *Physiol. Zool., 13,* 56–64.

16. Clark, W. E. Le Gros. 1949. *History of the primates.* London: British Museum (Natural History).

17. Cline, W. 1936. Notes on the people of Siwah and El Garah in the Libyan Desert, *Gen. Ser. in Anthropol.,* No. *4,* Menasha, Wisc. (*Cited in* Ford, C. S. 1945. A comparative study of human reproduction, *Yale Univ. Pubs. in Anthropol.,* No. *32*).

18. Cockayne, E. A. 1933. *Inherited abnormalities of the skin and its appendages.* London: Oxford Univ. Press.

19. Cockayne, E. A., and Penrose, L. S. 1943. The genetics of congenital pyloric stenosis, *Ohio J. Sci., 43,* 1–16.

20. Corwin, E. H. L. (Ed.), 1949. *Ecology of health.* New York: The Commonwealth Fund.

21. Cotterman, C. W. 1942. The biometrical approach in human genetics, *Amer. Nat., 76,* 144–155.

22. Cotterman, C. W., and Snyder, L. H. 1937. Studies in human inheritance XVII. The gene-frequency analysis of double recessive inheritance involving one autosomal and one sex-linked gene substitution, *Genetica, 19,* 537–552.

23. Cotterman, C. W., and Snyder, L. H. 1939. Tests of simple mendelian

inheritance in randomly collected data of one and two generations, *J. Amer. Statist. Assn., 34*, 511–523.

24. Dobzhansky, Th. 1941. *Genetics and the origin of species.* 2nd ed., revised. New York: Columbia Univ. Press.

25. Dobzhansky, Th., and Montagu, M. F. Ashley. 1947. Natural selection and the mental capacities of mankind, *Science, 105*, 587–590.

26. Dunn, L. C., and Dobzhansky, Th. 1946. *Heredity, race, and society.* New York: New Amer. Library of World Lit., Inc.

27. Ellis, A. 1945. The sexual psychology of human hermaphrodites, *Psychosom. Med., 7*, 108–125.

28. Fisher, R. A. 1930. *The genetical theory of natural selection.* Oxford: The Clarendon Press.

29. Gabritschevsky, E., and Bridges, C. B. 1928. The giant mutation in *Drosophila melanogaster.* Part II. Physiological aspects of the giant race. The giant "caste." *Zeitschr. induk. Abstamm.-u. Vererb. Lehre, 46*, 248–284.

30. Gates, R. R. 1946. *Human genetics.* 2 vols. New York: The Macmillan Company.

31. Glass, Bentley. 1944. The effect of X-rays upon the action of a specific gene in *Drosophila melanogaster, Genetics, 29*, 436–446.

32. Goldschmidt, R. 1938. Physiological genetics. New York: McGraw-Hill Book Company, Inc.

33. Gordon, C. and Sang, J. H. 1942. The relation between nutrition and exhibition of the gene Antennaless (*Drosophila melanogaster*), *Proc. Roy. Soc., B, 130*, 151–184.

34. Grüneberg, Hans. 1943. *The genetics of the mouse.* Cambridge: The Univ. Press.

35. Haldane, J. B. S. 1932. The causes of evolution. New York: Harper & Brothers.

36. Haldane, J. B. S. 1936. A search for incomplete sex linkage in man, *Ann. Eugen., 7*, 28–57.

37. Haldane, J. B. S. 1938. *Heredity and politics.* New York: W. W. Norton & Co.

38. Haldane, J. B. S. 1946. The interaction of nature and nurture, *Ann. Eugen., 13*, 197–205.

39. Haldane, J. B. S. 1948. The formal genetics of man, *Proc. Roy. Soc., B, 135*, 147–170.

40. Haldane, J. B. S. 1949. Human evolution: Past and future. In Jepsen *et al.* (46), 405–418.

41. Hall, C. S., and Klein, S. J. 1942. Individual differences in aggressiveness in rats, *J. Comp. Psychol., 33*, 371–383.

42. Heron, W. T. 1941. The inheritance of brightness and dullness in maze learning ability in the rat, *J. Genet. Psychol., 59,* 41–49.

43. Hogben, L. T. 1932. *Genetic principles in medicine and social science.* New York: Alfred A. Knopf.

44. Hogben, L. T. 1933. *Nature and nurture.* New York: W. W. Norton & Co.

45. Iljin, N. A. 1926. Studies in the morphogenetics of animal pigmentation. II. Investigations of the temperature influence of the Himalayan rabbits pigmentation, *Trans. Lab. Exp. Biol. Zoopark Moscow, 3,* 12–63. (Russian, with English summary.)

46. Jepsen, G. L., Mayr, Ernst, and Simpson, G. G. (Eds.) 1949. *Genetics, paleontology, and evolution.* Princeton: Princeton Univ. Press.

47. Kaven, A. 1938. Röntgenmodifikationen bei Mäusen, *Zeitschr. f. Konst.-Lehre, 22,* 238–246.

48. Kiil, V. 1948. Inheritance of frontal hair directions in man, *J. Hered., 39,* 206–216.

49. Lange, Johannes. 1929. Verbrechen als Schicksal. Leipzig: Georg Thieme. Translated by Charlotte Haldane 1930: *Crime and destiny.* New York: Charles Boni.

50. Levy, Hyman. 1938. *The universe of science.* rev. ed. London: C. A. Watts & Co.

51. Li, Ching Chun. 1948. *An introduction to population genetics.* Peiping: Nat. Peking Univ. Press.

52. Lindenov, Harald. 1945. The etiology of deaf-mutism with special reference to heredity, *Opera ex Domo Biologiae Hereditariae Humanae Univ. Hafn., 8,* 1–268.

53. Mather, K. 1949. *Biometrical genetics.* New York: Dover Publications, Inc.

54. Mead, Margaret. 1935. *Sex and temperament in three primitive societies.* New York: Wm. Morrow & Co.

55. Mental Survey Committee (Godfrey H. Thomson, Chairman). 1949. *The trend of Scottish intelligence: A comparison of the 1947 and 1932 surveys of the intelligence of eleven-year-old pupils.* London: Univ. of London Press, Ltd.

56. Montagu, M. F. Ashley. 1945. *Man's most dangerous myth: The fallacy of race.* 2nd ed. New York: Columbia Univ. Press.

57. Morgan, T. H. 1915. The role of environment in the realization of a sex-linked Mendelian character in *Drosophila, Amer. Nat., 49,* 385–429.

58. Muller, H. J. 1925. Mental traits and heredity, *J. Hered., 16,* 433–448.

59. Muller, H. J. 1940. Bearings of the 'Drosophila' work on systematics.

In Huxley, J. (Ed.) *The new systematics,* 185–268. Oxford: The Clarendon Press.

60. Muller, H. J. 1949. Redintegration of the symposium on genetics, paleontology, and evolution. In Jepsen, G. L., *et al.* (46), 421–445.

61. Muller, H. J., Little, C. C., and Snyder, L. H. 1947. *Genetics, medicine, and man.* Ithaca: Cornell Univ. Press.

62. Murphy, D. P. 1947. *Congenital malformations.* 2nd ed. Philadelphia: J. B. Lippincott Co.

63. Murphy, Gardner. 1947. Genetic and social significance of differential fertility III. A review of relevant research on the inheritance of mental traits, *Milbank Mem. Fund Quart., 25,* 373–382.

64. Neel, J. V. 1947. The clinical detection of the genetic carriers of inherited disease, *Medicine, 26,* 115–153.

65. Newman, H. H., Freeman, F. N., and Holzinger, K. J. 1937. Twins: A study of heredity and environment. Chicago: Univ. of Chicago Press.

66. Osborn, Frederick. 1940. *Preface to eugenics.* New York: Harper & Brothers.

67. Penrose, L. S. 1942. Future possibilities in human genetics, *Amer. Nat., 76,* 165–170.

68. Penrose, L. S. 1946. Familial data on 144 cases of anencephaly, spina bifida, and congenital hydrocephaly, *Ann. Eugen., 13,* 73–98.

69. Penrose, L. S. 1946. Phenylketonuria. Lancet 1946–1, 949–952.

70. Penrose, L. S. 1949. *The biology of mental defect.* New York: Grune & Stratton.

71. Plough, H. H., and Child, G. P. 1936. Developmental modifications in unhatched pupae induced in genetically different stocks of *Drosophila* by high temperatures, *Amer. Nat., 70,* 60 (abstract).

72. Roberts, J. A. F. 1940. *An introduction to medical genetics.* London: Oxford Univ. Press.

73. Schneirla, T. C. 1946. Problems in the psychobiology of social organization, *J. Abn. & Soc. Psychol., 41,* 385–402.

74. Schulz, Bruno. 1936. *Methodik der medizinischen Erbforschung.* Leipzig: Georg Thieme.

75. Scott, J. P. 1942. Genetic differences in the social behavior of inbred strains of mice, *J. Hered., 33,* 11–15.

76. Simpson, G. G. 1949. *The meaning of evolution.* New Haven: Yale Univ. Press.

77. Sinnott, E. W., Dunn, L. C., and Dobzhansky, Th. 1950. *Principles of genetics.* 4th ed. New York: McGraw-Hill Book Co., Inc.

78. Sjögren, Torsten. 1931. Die juvenile amaurotische Idiotie, *Hereditas, 14,* 197–425.

79. Sjögren, Torsten. 1935. Vererbungsmedizinische Untersuchungen ueber Huntingtons Chorea in einer schwedischen Bauernpopulation, *Zeitschr. f. Konst.-Lehre, 19,* 131–165.

80. Sjögren, Torsten. 1943. Klinische und erbbiologische Untersuchungen ueber die Heredoataxien, *Acta psychiat. et neurol.,* Suppl. XXVII, 1–200.

81. Slome, D. 1933. The genetic basis of amaurotic family idiocy, *J. Genet., 27,* 363–376.

82. Snyder, L. H. 1932. The inheritance of taste deficiency in man, *Ohio J. Sci., 32,* 436–440.

83. Snyder, L. H. 1941. *Medical genetics.* Durham: Duke Univ. Press.

84. Snyder, L. H. 1946. Medical genetics and public health. *Bull. N. Y. Acad. Med.,* 2nd Series, *22,* 566–587.

85. Snyder, L. H. 1947. The principles of gene distribution in human populations, *Yale J. Biol. & Med., 19,* 819–833.

86. Snyder, L. H. 1947. Human heredity. In Muller, H. J. *et al.* (61), 109–127.

87. Snyder, L. H. 1949. Studies in human inheritance XXXV. The linkage relations of sickle cell anemia, *Proc. 8th Int. Cong. Genetics,* 446–450.

88. Snyder, L. H. (in press). *The principles of heredity.* 4th ed. Boston: D. C. Heath and Co.

89. Snyder, L. H., and Yingling, H. C. 1935. The application of the gene frequency method of analysis to sex-influenced factors, with special reference to baldness, *Human Biol., 7,* 608–615.

90. Steiniger, F. 1939. Ueber die experimentelle Beeinflussung der Ausbildung erblicher Hasenscharten bei der Maus, *Zeitschr. f. Konst.-Lehre, 24,* 1–12.

91. Stern, Curt. 1949. *Principles of human genetics.* San Francisco: W. H. Freeman & Co.

92. Thomson, Godfrey. 1947. The trend of national intelligence, *Occasional Papers on Eugenics, 3.* London: Hamilton Hamish Medical Books.

93. Timofeeff-Ressovsky, N. W. 1937. *Experimentelle Mutationsforschung in der Vererbungslehre.* Dresden & Leipzig: Theodor Steinkopf.

94. Tryon, R. C. 1940. Genetic differences in maze-learning ability in rats, *39th Yearbook,* Nat. Soc. Stud. Educ., Part I, 111–119.

95. Waardenburg, P. J. 1932. Das menschliche Auge und seine Erbanlagen, *Bibliogr. Genet., 7,* 1–631.

96. Waddington, C. H. 1939. *An introduction to modern genetics.* New York: The Macmillan Company.

97. Wheeler, L. R. 1942. A comparative study of the intelligence of East Tennessee mountain children. *J. Educ. Psychol., 33,* 321–334.

98. Wiener, A. S. 1943. *Blood groups and blood transfusion.* 3rd ed. Springfield, Ill.: C. C. Thomas.

99. Wright, Sewall. 1920. Principles of livestock breeding. *U. S. Dept. Agric. Bull.* No. *905,* 1–67.

100. Wright, Sewall. 1922. Coefficients of inbreeding and relationship, *Amer. Nat., 56,* 330–338.

101. Wright, Sewall. 1934. An analysis of variability in number of digits in an inbred strain of guinea pigs, *Genetics, 19,* 506–536.

102. Wright, Sewall. 1939. Genetic principles governing the rate of progress of livestock breeding, *32nd Ann. Proc. Amer. Soc. Animal Prod.,* 18–26.

103. Wright, Sewall. 1940. The statistical consequences of mendelian heredity in relation to speciation. In Huxley, J. (Ed.). *The new systematics,* 161–183. Oxford: The Clarendon Press.

104. Wright, Sewall, and Chase, H. B. 1936. On the genetics of the spotted pattern of the guinea pig, *Genetics, 21,* 758–787.

CHAPTER 4

⊓⊔

The "Levels" Concept in the Study of Social Organization in Animals[1]

T. C. SCHNEIRLA
American Museum of Natural History

INTRODUCTION: NATURE OF THE "LEVELS" CONCEPT

Individuals and groups in the animal world may be thought of as being more or less advanced with respect to one or more series of different but related stages. Such a concept, which concerns the theory of "levels," may afford a useful and effective way in which to evaluate both the biological and psychological properties of individuals and the psychological properties of individuals and groups (Needham, 1929; Woodger, 1929; Redfield, 1942).

Organisms of different types exist under similar or widely different conditions. Even the "same" conditions may be met in terms of very different adjustment patterns in different groups. For the student of social phenomena it is important to know what similarities and what differences may underlie the adaptations of both solitary and collective organisms of different types in their respective settings. Widely different scientific opinions are encountered on this question. Some are inclined to believe that the similarities of the "lowest" and "highest" organisms have been underestimated (e.g., Chauvin, 1947), others take

---

[1] The writer's field and laboratory investigations upon certain phases of group behavior in insects and in mammals, contributive to this paper, have been supported to a large extent through a contract with the Office of Naval Research, and through a grant from the Committee on Problems in Sex, National Research Council, to the Department of Animal Behavior, American Museum of Natural History.

the view that vast and inescapably significant differences exist (e.g., Maier and Schneirla, 1935).

Metaphysical Devices in Characterizing Functional Levels

Although the writer has discussed the more philosophical aspects of this problem elsewhere (Schneirla, 1949), one question will bear consideration here. One of the most trammeling habits in traditional studies of individual and society is the tendency to characterize complex phenomena in the simple terms of some metaphorical expression. Thus organized community functions are conceptualized on the insect level by Maeterlink as "spirit of the hive" and on the human level by McDougall as "group mind." A fallacy of metaphor is inherent in such naming. The conceptual term is so reified that functional characteristics of the phenomenon, which represent problems demanding investigation, are viewed as aspects of some vaguely generalized entity and are thereby held as already explained. Procedure in studying the phenomenon thereby becomes descriptive, and analytical, comparative investigation becomes superfluous.

The tendency to analogize individual and society is strong, and opens the way for irresponsible ethnocentric and subjective projections on the part of the individual who chooses the analogies. Thus, once Strecker (1940) has found the "mass mind" paranoic, it follows for him that world society must be saved by small elite groups of superior intellects, presumably participants in a non-paranoic mind. Analogies may be useful, of course, for introductory, pedagogical purposes, to emphasize and stress the characteristics of the phenomena under study. Certainly, for example, a most dramatic point is made when nervous conduction in an individual is analogized with communication in a social group. Events are no less dramatic when someone like Goebbels takes the analogy seriously, and sets himself up as the social neocortex sending out impulses to the spinal sub-groups of society. Concern about the scientific adequacy of theoretical procedures is excluded when analogical devices are relied upon uncritically in studying adaptive processes.

It would seem necessary to develop the central conceptual terms in our study of individual and society in accordance with scientific standards of reliability and validity, recognizing that analogy is only introductory and illustrative and possesses no inherent dependability as a means of understanding the nature of individual and of group. Since the time H. Spencer seriously analogized human society as an organism, wide advances have been made both in biology and psychology which reveal the misleading character of this metaphor (Schneirla, 1946, 1949). Perhaps the most important risk inherent in this analogy is that it distracts attention from the extent to which a social group, composed of individuals, develops properties of its own that are not realizable within an organism considered as unit.

Views such as "supraorganism" (Emerson, 1939, 1942), are reductionistic from their inherent implication that the physiological integration and interaction of the cells, tissues, and organs in an organism are somehow qualitatively equivalent to the interactions of individuals and of sub-groups in a society. In contrast, on the principle of levels, we recognize the necessity for constructing an appropriate new set of concepts when qualitatively distinctive functions are encountered. Thus, the alternative postulation to the supraorganismic interpretation is that the biology of the organism and the biology and psychology of individual and of group represent phenomenal levels which may be similar and even related to some extent but which possess important qualitative differences.

"Levels" as Differentiated Adaptive Systems

The levels concept postulates the existence of intra-organic and organic systems of phenomena which are comparable in their evolution and ontogenetic function but which also exhibit significant qualitative differences and in some important sense may be described as related but distinctive stages. Considered as surviving adaptive systems, the viruses, independent unicellular organisms, colonial organisms, metazoan organisms, and sub-social and social groups of different kinds, may be studied as members of a hierarchy of related functional systems in which basic relationships are present in very different settings of special functional properties and functional patterns (Woodger, 1929; Redfield, 1942; Novikoff, 1945). The expansion and development of each system represents not only a different condition of internal complexity, but, more important, a very different stage of qualitative integrity, marked by a capacity of the higher systems to function adaptively under more inclusive and more heterogeneous and variable surrounding conditions. A group or society, for example, has the advantage over an individual in adaptive resourcefulness in that it more freely plays multiple roles in space and in time. Hence groups and societies on the whole represent qualitatively superior systems in adaptive function.

In abstract terms, perhaps the most important qualitative similarity among surviving functional levels is that they are all more or less adaptive, presumably in basically related ways in some respects, in basically unrelated ways in others. What conditions may make for the survival or extinction of a system is obviously an important consideration for our entire discussion. Their most important differences evidently arise in their degrees of plasticity under conditions of environmental emergency and their properties for admitting opportune and well-integrated changes in the characteristic patterns. In order to evaluate the adaptive adequacy of a whole system, however, it is necessary to proceed from the objective fact of relatively successful environmental adjustment to an examination of the internal make-up or organization which is evidently responsible for the functional characters in question.

CHARACTERISTICS OF LEVELS AND THEIR INTERRELATIONSHIPS

Internal Organization and Resemblances of Levels

Implicit in the concept of levels is the assumption that, in adaptive systems representing qualitatively inferior or superior stages, the part-processes exhibit important differences in their mutual interrelationships and in their various relationships with the inclusive aggregate. First of all, this brings up a fundamental question in the interrelationship of different levels; the question whether, as Collias (1944) states, "integrated systems at one level of organization may themselves be units of a more inclusive grouping. . . ." This might be the simplest basis for a relationship among levels, except that the objective world does not appear to function in the way implied.

Actually, when a part-process of a higher level resembles a "whole" of some lower level, it is likely at the same time to have a qualitative uniqueness by virtue of the setting in which it is incorporated (rather, has *become* incorporated *through elaboration in development and growth*) in the superior system. In other words, to say that evolutionary doctrine implies that higher integrative levels are derivatives of lower levels does not mean that "lower wholes" are repeated as such, as units, in the higher systems.

Two very different examples are: (1) the "cell" that has grown into relationship with an organismic matrix is not the same kind of functioning system as the independent, unicellular (rather, *acellular*) organism which may be *loosely* designated a "cell"; (2) there exists no such entity as "instinctive man" or "emotional man" considered as "animal nature" with a "cortical component" overlaid. A component functioning as a closely meshed unit in an organismic whole, or an individual organism functioning in a group, is qualitatively very different from the same component or individual when alone. The point here is that the concepts "whole" and "unit" as concepts actually are only abstract conveniences to be considered as preliminary devices in the study of adaptive systems. It is unfortunate that they can be very misleading.

Part and Whole as Relative in the Study or Organization

We may think of adaptive systems as physical, biological, biopsychological, psychological, sub-social and social. In a sense, these may be regarded as overlapping and interrelated adaptive stages. In evaluating and comparing their respective conditions of organization, it is often necessary to study parts or part-processes intensively as though they existed separately from the whole. This procedure is methodologically and theoretically sound only if it is combined appropriately with an investigation of the pattern as a whole. It is necessary to bear in mind that the "part" is only an abstraction and that the concept of parts as isolated units is paradoxical and unreal. As Sloane (1945) has suggested, our preoccupation with the part or unit as isolated may be considered a derivative of our folkways and socialized thought-patterns which conceptualize the individual as an independent object making social contacts.

From the failure of "atomistic" theories in biology and social psychology we learn, on the contrary, that the part functions or units may be adequately conceptualized only in view of their relations to and their dependence upon the wholes to which they belong. Actually, an atomistic conception of adaptive systems seems most adequate on the lowest organic levels, in which the "whole" (e.g., a sponge) may be described with a measure of validity as not only a morphological but also a functional sum of its parts. Even here, however, the view becomes false and misleading if carried very far in a functional study of the whole. It is inevitably less and less applicable to the understanding of progressively higher levels.

Preliminary Comparison of Individual, Association, and Social Group

The metazoan ancestral forms which were presumably first differentiated from protozoan organisms are conceivable as hollow masses of flagellated cells among which functional differences appeared, opening the way for specialized properties of the whole in nutrition and in locomotion (Hyman, 1931). In the course of evolution, further versatility of the whole appeared with additional differentiations among component parts, and at the same time with greater dependence and interconnection among the parts. With such changes, the organic unity imposed upon the mass through growth and division was supplemented by an increasingly complex and qualitatively superior functional unity. Living sponges, which are essentially colonies of growth-aggregated individuals having only a limited neuroid-mechanical transmission system, are decidedly more limited in the scope, variety, and orientation of their activities than is a jellyfish, in which diversified parts are unified functionally through a simple nerve-net system. Behavior of the sponge as an aggregate is little more than a summated action of individual parts or chimneys, with a virtual absence of diversified patterns of function, whereas in the insect one observes a variety of behavior patterns smoothly performed in a well-co-ordinated fashion by a well-integrated individual. The advances in whole-function were gained through greater intra-individual specialization coupled with a wider range of interrelationship among individual units, and the correlative reduction of autonomy and of functional independence in the components.

A contrast of colonial organism and metazoan organism is not to be taken *a priori* as a direct parallel of a contrast between social group and individual. The first pair represents different kinds of organic aggregates, all appearing through growth from a basic form, possessing in the metazoan organism a closer physiological interrelationship of the components. Sub-social aggregates (e.g., "associations") did not appear through the internal specialization of an ancestral unit-type, but through the assembling of individuals which in the most generalized associations became incidental parts of one another's environments by virtue of generalized properties. In contrast, in the more specialized social groups, individuals began to be environmental necessities of one another. Even wider and more important differences are found between organism and social group in the relation of the part to the aggregate. Study of individual variations through the animal series is in a sense preparatory for the study of social organization, but not in the sense that intraorganic relationships are directly parallel to those of animal groups.

PREREQUISITES FOR ADVANCED ORGANIZATION IN INDIVIDUAL AND GROUP

Discarding the analogy of individual and group on theoretical grounds does not mean that we turn away from the study of individuals in their group settings. Rather, we gain thereby a healthy skepticism concerning attempts to find common principles which will hold for part-to-whole relations in both individual and group situations. It seems clear that in the scientific study of individual and social group the problem of organization must be approached by different although not entirely independent methods. We may expect to find that advances in integration have different prerequisites in individuals, considered as a series of adaptive types, than in groups.

Individual Properties Underlie Group Functional Pattern

An intriguing picture is presented by studies of progressive organization in individuals through the animal series. The morphological basis may be sketched somewhat as follows: in the lower metazoan invertebrates (e.g., jellyfish), there first appear various patterns of radial symmetry in structure, with interchanging dominance-subordination relationships among the parts in physiological function and behavior. There next appear (e.g., in flatworms) patterns of bilateral symmetry and cephalization (antero-posterior polarity), a condition which admits stable patterns of physiological function and behavior. The radially symmetrical types have generalized nervous centers of limited properties; a "brain" or clearly dominant center first develops with bilateral symmetry, as an efficient transmitter from sensitive anterior regions (e.g., in earthworms). In the arthropods and especially in the insects it has also become a co-ordinator, while the co-ordinating efficiency of the nervous system as a whole is on the increase. With the appearance of cerebral cortex, in the higher vertebrates, the controlling function of the brain reaches its highest point, the co-ordination of parts and the unity of the organism are at their maximum in the animal series. These characteristics roughly set the limits of individual attainment and the pattern and qualitative level of intra-individual organization, hence are correlated with differences in the psychological level of the individual organism (Maier and Schneirla, 1935).

Those properties of individual organisms which set limits for the level of individual behavioral capacity also are among the factors involved in setting the qualifications of individuals, as wholes, for participation in group situations—considered as wholes of qualitatively different types. We are concerned here with what individual properties influence the *kind* of group pattern which emerges. Perhaps the most significant organic factor conditioning the qualitative level of the social pattern is the extent to which the central nervous system has developed. In the lower invertebrate organisms, capable only of temporary behavior changes largely involving peripheral sensory and motor processes (e.g., coelenterates), the persistence of more than the simplest type of group through active individual responses is hardly to be expected. The capacity for conditioning and stereotyped learning evidently contributes to the persistent integrity of groups in insects, but on the other hand, it is subordinate to the stereotyped mechanisms insuring inter-individual responsiveness which predominate in the insects (Schneirla, 1946). It is difficult with our present knowledge to discern precisely what organic and functional characteristics contribute to the presence of social life on different animal levels and what characters influence variations in its form. The fact seems to be that organic maturation makes somewhat similar but also very different contributions on different levels, in both of these respects. Differences in the potential capacity to learn must be involved in very different ways, both setting limits upon the elaboration of organization and upon its relative plasticity in different animals.

In a preliminary way, the speculation may be advanced that a social pattern which is dominated by specific and reflexively stereotyped organic mechanisms must have definite qualitative limitations. Insect social patterns are an example. On the other hand, when individual capacities for perceptual development and learning through experience are greater (e.g., in primates), the social pattern may not only gain in complexity and in stages of organization within a species, but also become more versatile and more variable according to conditions. The relative plasticity of the social pattern in relation to new emergencies presented by the environment would appear to depend particularly upon the extent to which a capacity for conditioning and learning can modify the influence of specific organic factors underlying social behavior. Group comparisons on this basis afford an advantageous approach to the understanding of levels in social patterning.

Individual Properties Limiting the Level of Group Function

It is apparent that the characteristic organic and psychological qualifications of the component individuals must basically condition the nature of the social structure attainable by the species. In the lower animals the individual functional contributions are more or less uniform for the species, hence the species social pattern is highly predictable under the species-typical environmental conditions. Although in such cases individual capacities limit group function more rigidly than in higher forms, for reasons suggested above, group function even then is not to be considered a simple aggregate or sum of individual components. However limited the individuals may be, biologically and psychologically, every group pattern must be regarded as the product of components functioning in a system. To understand the level of organization, it is evident that its dynamic properties must be examined under conditions which are sufficiently varied to reveal representative properties of the pattern.

The *complexity* of group function and its *adaptive adequacy* are not necessarily dependent upon superior individual capacities in the psychological sense. To take what may be a somewhat extreme example, the behavior of certain army-ant species in their mass raids under forest conditions is amazingly complex, and the observer might well be led by the sight of highly adaptive collective maneuvers to an exaggerated estimation of the level of behavioral capacities of individuals functioning in the raid. Analysis of the complex function, however, shows that the workers themselves are capable of only very simple reactions, which within the progressively more complex group situations of daily raids carried out in a heterogeneous forest environment, can result in a seemingly very intelligent social strategy. In a homogeneous action setting, however, with the possibility of progressive developmental stages excluded through smaller numbers of participants, the group either is virtually unorganized or is limited to a simple milling phenomenon (Schneirla, 1944).

SIMILARITIES AND DIFFERENCES AMONG ANIMAL SOCIAL PATTERNS

Outstanding Similarities Between Insect and Mammalian Societies

One of the most common sources of analogies in animal societies is that between insect and mammalian societies. In the hands of Emerson (1938, 1942) this procedure has advanced to a serious and specialized stage at which analogies are offered as a means of scientifically studying the respective social phenomena, and the process is extended to include individual organisms. Some of the outstanding analogies are as follows:

1. *Communication within the whole*. Within the individual organism, nervous impulses from one locality arouse other localities to a simultaneous action, or hormones transmitted through the blood stream co-ordinate the action of separate organs or systems. The insect community is aroused through the propagation of excitement from individual to individual; for example, excited termite soldiers rap their heads repeatedly against wooden gallery walls, transmitting a vibratory effect which arouses other individuals close by or at a distance. An ant excites her nest mates through antennal vibrations; a man sends a message by telegraph, arousing certain distant individuals to action.

2. *Division of labor*. The differentiation of gametes and somatic cells in individual organisms is analogized to the presence of fertile individuals and infertile workers in insect societies; the transmission of food by infertile insect workers may be analogized to the function of cells in an individual's gastrovascular tract. The worker and soldier castes of insect colonies may be compared with the various strata or castes in human society.

3. *Rhythms, life cycles*. The individuals of many animal forms produce their gametes at fairly regular intervals in a recognizable rhythm; social insects characteristically produce their sexual forms seasonally. The life cycle of birth, development, and senescence in an individual organism is paralleled in social insects by colony foundation, expansion, and degeneration.

4. *Phylogeny in organism and superorganism*. Many biologists be-

sides Emerson believe that similarities such as those outlined above afford a valuable basis for studying the nature of organisms and social groups. From their point of view, essentially the same biological processes have been involved in the evolution of individual organism and of social group considered as supraorganism. Natural selection is regarded as having been involved in closely comparable ways in the evolution of individual and of group; that is to say, individuals or groups have been eliminated in an equivalent fashion whenever the internal processes of the system have been maladaptive to a sufficient extent.

To be sure, the assumption that selection has worked comparably in the evolution of individual and of group at different phyletic levels has been utilized as a theoretical tool by numerous biologists (e.g., Fisher, 1930). On the other hand, this preliminary, trial conception of evolutionary processes at different levels is now opposed by evidence indicating that natural selection frequently has different properties for the individual organism than for the social group (Simpson, 1949). The bold deductive leaps of analogy certainly afford a stimulating set of devices for general and preliminary comparisons, but do not call attention to important differences among organism and group levels.

Individual Properties Which Promote Group Formation

The analogical procedure really is teleological in that individuals and social groups are compared in terms of the end results of their functions, without emphasizing underlying processes which may be very different. Hence, analogy has serious shortcomings as a means of understanding the nature of different types of functional systems in the animal world. If we are seriously comparing individual organism and social group, we must attempt to find what characteristics of individual organisms permit them to aggregate on different levels of group function. This is the problem raised, but not really answered in any sense, by traditional concepts such as "symphilic instincts" or "gregarious instinct" (Schneirla, 1949).

Jennings (1942) has described in some detail the groupings which appear in Paramecium, the ciliate protozoan. The appearance of such groups contrasts with the fact that solitary activity is common among Paramecia. Paramecia frequently alter their direction of swimming, and frequently come by chance close to the borders of zones containing weak acids. Thereupon they typically move toward and enter such zones (Jennings, 1906). Since faintly acid products are given off by these ciliates themselves, groups of the Paramecia are likely to form where a few have concentrated. Groups of genetically related Paramecia (clones) form most readily, since the free daughter individuals produced by the division of a single parent are alike organically, and react more similarly to outer conditions than do the progeny of different parents. Because one of the adequate conditions for eliciting the reaction may be brought about through Paramecium activity, groups frequently form among these organisms. Because the reactions are not given to other individuals as such but to specific biochemical conditions which elicit the approach reaction, the grouping thus depends directly upon physiological conditions.

In simple association or in sub-social aggregations, groups commonly form through the approach reactions of different individuals to environmental conditions influencing all of them separately (Allee, 1938). Thus swarms of dance flies form through similar individual responses to local conditions such as light, humidity, and temperature. The example of Paramecium represents a somewhat more advanced case, in which the products of individual metabolism may exert a stimulative effect equivalent to that of an attractive environmental stimulation. Aggregations on the latter basis are common among otherwise solitary Arthropods such as the sowbug, *Oniscus* sp., groups of which may be found under stones and in similar places, where they assemble through common environmental effects but remain together for a time by virtue of added individual stimulative effects commonly available as chemical products of metabolism. In such aggregations the unity of the group is incidental to the presence of the individuals as such, and the role of individuals may be replaced by essentially equivalent environmental influences.

What differentiates a social group of any complexity from the above situation is that in social aggregations the unity rests upon an interdependence of individuals, a condition deriving from the effects exerted by group members as individuals with given qualities. In persistent social groups, the attractive effect of group members for one another has become more fixed and specialized, and typically produces in some characteristic manner a fixation of individuals for the group situation as well. The assemblage is thus held together particularly by the approach-responses of members based upon the individual properties of members. These reactions may be simple and primitively physiological, as when based upon characteristic "colony odor" effects in the case of social insects, or more elaborate and dependent upon a recognition of cues through learning as in higher mammals. Hence important psychological differences must be recognized in the "knowing of kind" in various types of social groups.

Adaptive Adequacy not a Criterion of Levels

The influences of individuals upon one another vary greatly among sub-social groups as well as among the social types. Incidental aggregations under similarly effective environmental conditions, and even accidental collections of individuals, introduce a variety of possible adaptive benefits, as Allee (1938) in particular has pointed out. For example, in swarms of various small flies, the meeting of sexual forms often is thereby assured, an advantage even more specific to stable social groups. Another kind of adaptive outcome, demonstrated in the associations of various lower invertebrates, is the modification of the microclimate or effective local environment through the products of individual metabolism, or, in some instances, even of organic degeneration. Both overcrowding and (frequently) undercrowding may result in results harmful to many or to all of the animals concerned. The involvement of what Allee has called "unconscious mutualism" in incidental assemblages and in environmental-response associations must be considered a potentially important factor in the survival or extinction of population segments or entire species, also in the rise of new factors influencing aggregation-responsiveness. Even under the simplest conditions of grouping, other individuals of the species may function as parts of the effective environment of each component individual, and thereby constitute factors in its potentialities for reproductive function and for survival.

The significance of grouping for individual and species survival is potentially great in representative social types, in which the interdependence of individuals is more specialized and group integrity is more systematic and persistent. In a pattern which is at the same time more stable and persistent and more varied and complex in its characteristics, the aggregation of individuals and its potentialities for mutuality may have a considerably greater adaptive significance than in the case of pre-social groupings. The meeting of the sexual forms is assured through their proximity and also through the rise of facilitative behavioral (epigamic) situations in the social group. Furthermore, in the social setting, increasingly complex and systematic controls may function which introduce characteristic selective processes in the operations of pairing and mating. The behavior patterns of vertebrate groups frequently involve inter-individual relationships describable as dominance hierarchies, involving differential individual adjustments based upon relationships of aggression, ascendancy, or some other form of priority which is demonstrably important for pairing and mating in many species. Thus in the prairie grouse a well-marked dominance hierarchy is present in which the apical male individual or "master cock" carries out most of the mating operations (J. W. Scott, 1941). In clans of howler monkeys, on the other hand, which have low dominance gradients within the group, priority in mating is virtually absent except in the case of "marginal males" excluded from the group proper but loosely affiliated with it (Carpenter, 1934).

There are many and varied additional consequences of the social condition on various levels, which have recognizable survival values for the functional groups, their individual members, and for the species. Defensive functions are promoted, not only through various kinds of individual specialization (as in insect castes) but also through the establishment of a more or less regular territory (as in various vertebrates) which is more defensible by virtue of group behavioral properties. Through the construction of nests or shelters, an increased environmental control is attained which promotes the longevity of individuals and also supports group survival through facilitating propagation and the raising of young. Obtaining a regular food supply is promoted through the rise of routine foraging operations, and on the side of group health, a social stimulative effect upon feeding (very probably accompanied by a facilitation of digestive processes) through the presence of other individuals has been demonstrated (Allee, 1938) in various bird and mammal groups.

It is doubtful whether adaptive adequacy is a criterion of diagnostic value in the evaluation of "levels," since groupings of all types, both pre-social and social, are more or less effectively adaptive in relation to their respectively different settings. There is little point, for example, in comparing insect and mammalian social groups in terms of adaptive success, for very different environmental conditions have been met successfully by each in its characteristic way. The properties influencing behavior on different levels, according to how they restrict the potentialities for group function, open environments which are narrow or broad, and simple or complex, to which the respective aggregations adjust according to their behavioral and biological capacities.

It is not the relative adequacy of environmental adaptation, then, but the potentialities for qualitative elaboration and for plastic modification of group organization under emergencies which may be present in different patterns of animal aggregation, which are most relevant to the question of "levels."

FACTORS UNDERLYING GROUP UNITY
ON DIFFERENT SOCIAL LEVELS

Differential Organic Thresholds—A Process Basic to All Aggregations

Preparatory to a consideration of group organization on different levels, it is desirable to look more closely at the question of group affiliations and group unity. The primary consideration, as already mentioned, is the problem of the gregarious tendency itself. It is probable that in most types of groups, from incidental associations to specialized social patterns, the coming together and remaining together of individuals is based in some essential way upon fundamentally similar biological factors. An important basis for such factors may be found in threshold differences in sensitivity, and in motor function (and probably also neural function), which directly or indirectly promote orientation toward the source of weak stimulation (Schneirla, 1946, 1949). This type of factor also is identifiable in characteristically solitary animal types, varying in nature according to organic condition (e.g., in normal feeding, cf. pairing and mating reactions), and in their case often promoting the temporary survival of incidental aggregations.

Although this condition, which may be termed the factor of "differential organic thresholds," appears to be a basic physiological contribution promoting gregariousness on all levels, there seem to be important differences in its relative organic specialization in different animal types. For example, on the level of associations, the groups are relatively unstable and internally uncomplicated and become formed in response to environmental stimulus effects rather than specifically to stimulation from other individuals. In various sub-social groups such as the ear-wigs, the young of which remain with the mother for some time after their appearance, a specific individual-attractiveness factor enters as a specialization with greater potentialities for group cohesion. The effectiveness of this factor, as concerns biological mechanisms underlying both individual attractiveness and responsiveness to others of the species, is greatest in the animals capable of social organization. As a common biological basis for all types of animal aggregation, we are thus postulating organic (threshold) properties as a basis for individual processes of approach to stimuli of low intensities and individual capacities to contribute attractive effects in the group situation. Theoretically, these two types of mechanisms must have evolved in relation to each other.

Although the fundamental basis of the grouping tendency apparently is broadly similar throughout the animal series, the manner and the relative directness of its expression (i.e., the variables intervening between organic basis and behavioral outcome) are widely different in various social patterns. On the lowest aggregational levels (e.g., *Paramecium*) the "threshold" factor is evidently simplest and most directly expressed in the sense that it is least subject to ontogenetic modification. In the complex social forms of some insects, some ontogenetic modification is identifiable, although stereotypy dominates the patterns; on the higher mammalian levels stereotypy is least and implementation through learning is greatest. The organic process underlying the origin and maintenance of aggregation on different levels evidently lies in the biologically prepotent effect of weak stimulation in eliciting a form of approach reaction peculiar to the given level. Comparisons of food-taking and other approach responses in the animal series show that through this process essentially similar functional results may be achieved in very different ways on different animal levels (Maier and Schneirla, 1935). How different the expression of this "approach" process may be on different levels is revealed in a contrast of insect and mammalian aggregations.

The "Trophallaxis" Factor in Social Insects and Mammals

In both social insects and social vertebrates, hereditary factors centering around the "differential organic-threshold factor" have become elaborated to an extent which permits the maintenance of a more or less involved form of group behavior pattern. In addition to factors of sensory threshold in social insects, Wheeler (1928) outlines in some detail the availability and function of larval exudates and other nutritive and sensory sources of effects insuring approach responses in the social group. Organic mechanisms of this type are identifiable in the various types of social insects in the brood, reproductive individuals, and developed workers, providing a basis for establishing and continuing adult relations to the brood and to other adults. Wheeler's term for the resultant social condition is "trophallaxis," which may be taken to signify a more or less widespread process of mutual stimulation and responsiveness among all members of the colony, underlying both colony unity and colony organization. In the foundation of the insect colony, the social process begins when the queen licks and handles her eggs, responding to attractive fluids upon them, and on a similar basis licks and feeds the larvae as they develop. A comparable process is involved in the attraction of adult workers to the brood, the queen, and to other workers, in various mutual relationships involving licking of body surfaces, stroking with antennae, and feeding with liquid food regurgitated by adequately stimulated individuals.

The nature of the trophallaxis process as a basis for colony function was first described by Wheeler (1928) and has been discussed in relation to colony behavior by Schneirla (1941). It is significant that in the ants, which exhibit social organization universally in all species, some form of trophallactic process is recognizable in all cases. Moreover, corresponding to the relative development of trophallactic properties in the species, the elaboration of the social pattern may be limited or expanded. For example, colony unity and organization are near their peak in the Formica species in which inter-individual stimulation processes are most extensive, and near their low point in certain Ponerine species in which inter-individual stimulation is limited in type and in scope, and feeding by regurgitation is absent.

There is much evidence that the "trophallaxis" factor is also basic to the appearance of social behavior in mammals. In insects, the function of the organic basis (i.e., differential thresholds, glandular attractants) is expressed in a relatively stereotyped way which depends upon learning and ontogeny to a relatively low although evidently essential extent. Here factors pertaining to the germ plasm and arising through organic growth more directly canalize the elaboration of individual behavior in the characteristic environment than in the case in mammals.

On the other hand, in mammals the role of factors promoting plasticity and learning is wide, and the potentialities for modification and elaboration through experience are much greater than in insects. The influence of trophallactic factors begins to be exerted in the earliest relations between mother and newborn infant, which progressively become specialized and elaborated in the social situation according to its make-up. The hereditary basis for trophallaxis in mammals includes not only properties of differential thresholds in exteroceptive sensitivity and in the principal antagonistic muscle systems, but also in the autonomic nervous system and viscera (Schneirla, 1949). On mammalian levels, however, and especially in primates, these factors are not themselves finally determinative of the nature of social pattern, except that through learning they insure the presence of one or another type of socialized adjustment.

Contrasting Social Levels: Insect and Human Societies

Although the organic basis for group formation by animals appears to be broadly similar on all levels, the genetic factors also differ both in complexity and in degree of specialization from the pre-social to the social, and from one social level to another. Even more striking differences are attributable to the involvement of ontogenetic processes centering around learning on different social levels.

Differences of this type may be illustrated in a further comparison of insect and mammalian societies. As Emerson (1942) has pointed out, some of the most prominent similarities between these societies are in the involvement of communication and the presence of division of labor (i.e., functional specialization).

"Communication" in the social insects may be understood as a direct transmission of excitement from individual to individual through tactual encounters (e.g., of antennae) or through substratal vibrations or even air-transmitted vibrations in some species. In ants and other social insects, a finder individual returning to the nest from a food-place is able to arouse her nestmates, which thereby are often enabled to find the food source sooner than by chance. If the secondary individuals are not merely aroused by the finder but also are oriented to some extent, the latter effect is attributable to incidental stimuli which differ in character according to the species. For example, certain ants are able to find a new food source through following chemical traces incidentally deposited on the substratum by the excited finder during her wandering return to the nest. The situation in honeybees is not altogether clear at the present time. Although it has been demonstrated that finder bees may present directive olfactory stimuli to secondary bees in an incidental manner during their stay in the hive after foraging flights, von Frisch (1948) has recently reported that presumably non-olfactory directive effects may be received by secondary bees through the finder's "dance" on the comb. Until the actual nature of the effect transmitted from the finder to secondary bees becomes known, it seems preferable to consider this type of communication qualitatively similar to the types which are already known for insects. Only in its general adaptive function as social transmission does insect "communication" resemble human language.

In the language processes of human society, the following distinctive characteristics are identifiable: (1) the words are typically symbolic, in that they have meaningful and representational identifications with objects and situations, and as abstractions are frequently conventionalized; (2) the items are directive, in that they are used to influence the behavior of other individuals as well as to influence oneself; (3) they are used in social situations in relation to anticipated effects, i.e., intentionally, with the expectation of producing given desired or expected results; (4) the symbolic items or words are patterned and rearranged according to the effective motivation of the user or the nature of the anticipated outcome (Bierens de Haan, 1930). As parts of the process of their individual socialization, children normally master the meanings and composition of language so that the symbols can be expressed in spoken and also in a written form if appropriate education is available. The capacity to learn and to elaborate symbolic cues in anticipatory ways apparently depends upon the relative development of cerebral cortex as a basis for advances in perceptual and conceptual learning. The chimpanzee's inability to use vocal sounds as language cues thus seems attributable to his failure to reach the essential level in organizing meaningful perceptual and conceptual relationships, a level which the human infant normally attains before the end of his first year.

The essential characteristics of language as it appears on the human level are not apparent in social insect communication, which evidently is not conceptualized or abstract but is limited to a generalized excitation effect performed in a stereotyped way without anticipation of given social results. In contrast, Crawford (1937) found mature chimpanzees able to use gestures such as shoulder tapping in social signalling or perhaps even symbolic ways, with evidence of anticipating a given effect in the signalled individual and a readiness to participate in the joint activities (e.g., rope pulling for food).

To a certain extent, insect and human societies are alike in having caste-like patterns, or a division of labor. Morphological types are characteristic in insect societies, correlated with differences in individual function (Wheeler, 1928). Beyond the sexual dichotomy of male and female, many species have structurally differentiated sub-types in one or both sexes. In many ant species there are polymorphic worker types, sometimes in a clearly dimorphic distribution, sometimes in a continuous series from the smallest or minor type of worker to the largest or major type. Correlated with organic differences, the various polymorphic castes exhibit functional differences: the males and fertile females are more or less completely specialized in reproductive function, with workers major predominant in defensive activities, workers minor as brood-tenders within the nest, and intermediate workers most frequently as foragers. The genetic basis of caste differentiations is typified in most ant species by conditions in which males appear from unfertilized eggs and females from fertilized eggs, the queen-type female from overfed larvae and the worker-type female from underfed larvae raised from eggs of equivalent germ plasm make-up. These differences in feeding are effective during the larval stage, and after the worker individual emerges from the pupal condition as a young adult (incapable of further growth) the characteristic functional capacities of its caste appear within a few days, in a predictable correlation with its organic make-up. The caste functions are stereotyped on the basis of the predominant role of germ plasm factors, and lasting changes can appear only through further organic evolution in the species.

Castes on the human level, in contrast to those of insects, exist in the form of social or functional classes differentiated essentially according to processes of learning in a given social context. The psychological plasticity of human society is evidenced by the frequency with which individuals shift across class lines in a democratic situation, as well as by the possibility of recognizing the cultural and traditional fixation of such barriers when they are impermeable (Newcomb and Hartley, 1947). The one social feature in which there is a distant biological basis for the caste differences of many human societies is a sexual dichotomy, with its differentiation of reproductive functions. Few behavioral differences follow in a fixed manner from this dichotomy, as in the case of insects; rather, in many ways organic differences express themselves indirectly in behavior, and psychological differences in attitudes and values in their characteristic nature are products of social heritage and cultural pattern. Human experience, and in particular the widely different practices of distinctive cultural groups, indicate that in man biological differences between the sexes, in themselves, can have a very indirect influence upon social function, or a very different influence according to individual socialization.

The case is different in insect societies, in which biological factors dominantly channelize social function. Drone bees, like the males of most other social insects, lack any organic basis for brood tending, foraging, or feeding other individuals—these are functions peculiar to the genetically and trophically differentiated workers. The human male on the other hand is capable of performing most of the functions popularly termed "female," other than the specific female reproductive functions.

Although social functions are in many cases generalized among the worker individuals of many insect species, they are often highly differentiated to an extent dependent upon polymorphic differences, and reproductive function in most cases is limited to a relatively small number of individuals. In the higher primates and particularly in man, on the other hand, reproductive function for the most part is a general property of adult individuals throughout the population, and no restrictive biological properties are involved. Crowell (1929) has suggested that this generalization of germinal properties throughout the population has tended away from biologically-based functional specializations and has facilitated a generalization of individual function in the family and social sphere. Highly stereotyped human social forms quite often are characterized by one or another type of arbitrary sexual delimitation (e.g., celibate castes); these however are maintained culturally rather than through the germ plasm as in insects.

It is unnecessary to elaborate upon the vast differences between social insects and man in the matter of how social patterns develop and change. Insect social patterns, arising ontogenetically through the predominant role of hereditary factors, require chromosomal and evolu-

tionary processes as a basis for lasting changes. The individual learning capacity of insects, stereotyped and situation-limited as it is
(Schneirla, 1949) plays a subordinate (facilitative) role in individual
socialization and shows its greatest elaboration in the foraging act (i.e.,
outside the nest). The various individuals make reproductive or nutritive contributions to colony welfare, and no individual learning that
occurs can change the standard pattern of the species in lasting ways.
The society is bio-social in the sense that it is a composite resultant of
individual biological characteristics dominating group behavior.

In contrast, human societies may be termed psycho-social in that cultural processes dominate which are the cumulative and non-genetically
transmitted resultants of experience and learning, under the influence
of human needs and desires interacting variably with the procedures of
labor or conflict, reasoning or routine. That is to say, although the
trophallactic basis of human society is similar in a very general way to
that of insects, it is very different in specific ways in its biological basis,
and quite different in the predominant importance of individual learning and group experience for its realization in social intercourse.

ONTOGENETIC FACTORS INFLUENCING
GROUP ORGANIZATION

Factors Introduced Through Individual Socialization

On all social levels, the formation of the group depends in some manner upon the initial reciprocal stimulative relationship between adults
and young. In all cases this association evidently centers around some
type of trophallactic process, which establishes a basis for a bond between the individual and the social group. For the young individual,
the social group is thereby first represented by the attending parent or
parents. The qualitative differences in the nature of this bond may be
readily seen through carrying further our comparison of insect and
mammalian societies.

In the social insects, the period of development during which the
young individual typically is cared for by adults may involve a limited
behavioral socialization through the trophallaxis process. In connection
with feeding, the individual, as a callow and perhaps earlier as a larva,
may be habituated and conditioned to the characteristic colony odor.
After emergence, in many social insects there is a short period of a few
days in which the callow attains to the adult behavior pattern, includ-

ing particularly trophallactic relations, i.e., inter-individual stimulation and a capacity for mutual feeding.

It has been suggested (Maier and Schneirla, 1935; Schneirla, 1941) that this pattern may be elaborated from a basis of early reflex-like responses, and that the early transition of trophallactic processes within the nest may be a factor in the later appearance of individual foraging outside the nest. The involvement of hereditary organic characteristics as factors in the process is indicated in the honey bee, in which the early socialization of the worker passes through three principal stages ending with adult foraging, each of these stages correlated with a demonstrable change in secretory function. It is our suggestion that this process, whereby the individual is incorporated into the colony, involves a simple learning factor which may be essential to the process although not prominent in it. The fact appears significant that in certain Ponerine ants in which no definite initial socialization process can be identified in the worker, trophallaxis is greatly reduced in the colony, and members of the population are very loosely integrated.

The term "bio-social" seems adequate for the insect social level, with its predominance of specific organic factors accounting for a representatively stereotyped pattern with (at best) only a secondary learning factor. However, it is not adequate in any real sense for the mammalian level.

The development of infant primates entails a far longer and more complex process of acquiring reciprocal relationships with the mother, then with the wide social environment, than in any other animal. The process evidently is one of a developing trophallactic integration of mother and young, involving reciprocal cutaneous stimulation, relief of mammary-gland tension in the mother by the young, and conversely, a relief of food-lack in the young and a presentation of optimal cutaneous stimulation by the mother (Schneirla, 1939, 1946). Apparently a process of conditioned learning in the young, involving an increased responsiveness first to the stimuli accompanying the feeding act, then to secondary accompanying stimuli, sets the stage for a process of selective learning. In the latter type of learning, the individual acquires the capacity to change a situation through particular reactions rather than others, according to the degree or kind of organic "satisfaction" received under different stimulative conditions. In the lower mammals the process of weaning typically initiates a considerable change or even a break in this relationship, and the family association of the young often does not continue into a protracted group affiliation. However, the young have acquired a motivated responsiveness to the exteroceptive cues (e.g., visual, auditory) of the species, which may function later in the initiation of pairing and in its sequel events, and in the formation of loose social groups (e.g., rat colonies) or of temporary groups.

In primates, including man, a similar process is based upon and is energized by certain physiological factors and the trophallactic interchanges to which they lead. The infra-human primate mother, like that of many lower mammals, typically consumes the fetal membranes, licks the embryo and her own sexual zones, and consumes the afterbirth. For the infant the major initial effects are optimal cutaneous stimulation and relief of physiological tensions in feeding, for the mother, comparable cutaneous effects and organic relief through a reduction of tensions. However, the resulting process of learned attachment between mother and young is manifestly more complex and highly organized than in lower mammals (Yerkes and Tomilin, 1935). The primate parent-young attachment typically leads beyond the weaning stage and constitutes a basis of great importance for the subsequent wider affiliation of the young animal with the social group.

On the human level the initial organic processes have substantially the same role in principle, and their effect as a basis for some kind of trophallactic reciprocal relationship between mother and young is also the same in principle. Yet it is manifest that the socialization process may be very different in its outcome, depending upon the social context in which the early family relationships develop. Whereas the human mother typically anticipates the infant as such, it is doubtful that the lower primate mother's growing attentiveness to her changing sexual zones during pregnancy has a forward reference of definite perceptual expectancy, even in multiparous females. The chimpanzee mother is much quicker to become attached emotionally and perceptually to the infant as a social object than are the mothers in lower mammals, yet the relative complexity of her perceptual schema and understanding of this object has its limitations far below the psychological level attainable by the human mother.

It is possible that we shall begin to find the solution to the difference in the patterning of social behavior in different mammals in the characteristics of the early socialization situation. In all cases the basic aggregation-responsiveness of the young apparently arises through the initial trophallactic situation of the young. Approaches to the mother afford a basis for approaches to others of her kind, and expand inevitably into the social group. Dependence upon the mother generally shifts after weaning into a dependence upon the social group in primates, but not as closely or as continuously in lower mammals. The lower mammals and particularly the rodents generally have more than one young born at a time, which inevitably introduces a competitive factor into their demands upon the mother. Such experiences, together with other factors such as the abruptness of weaning, may exert important influences upon the later sociability of the young and hence perhaps the entire species social pattern.

It is possible that the character of the early social environment of the young mammal may have a considerable influence upon its capacity for subsequent group behavior. Preliminary evidence suggests that the amount of time spent by young rats with their mother and the opportunity for free trophallactic relationships with her and for associations with litter mates have bearing upon the later "sociability" of the individual. Early deprivation of this sort seems to result in an abnormally great tendency for aggressiveness toward species mates or independence from them. A female lamb which J. P. Scott (1945) raised on the bottle from birth, and kept apart from other sheep until nine days of age, never became an integrated member of the flock. She showed almost no tendency to play with other lambs, and as a rule behaved independently of the other sheep. She did not approach the flock to any extent until her first heat period, and only briefly then. When Jacobsen, Jacobsen, and Yoshioka (1932) raised a young chimpanzee apart from others of its kind from the time of birth, and at nine months of age this animal was placed with another chimpanzee infant, he was at first disturbed and aggressive, and required a few weeks of companionship before relations became acceptant and dependent between them.

Priority Factors and Dominance Hierarchies

As an approach to the study of vertebrate groups, the "dominance hierarchy" concept has occupied a foremost position since the first studies of Schjelderup-Ebbe (1922) with barnyard fowl brought the "peck-right" type of social pattern to contemporary attention. This type of hierarchy is the most readily identified in birds as well as in numerous other vertebrates, and lends itself easily to quantification. Within less than two decades a relatively voluminous literature has developed concerning this type of group structure in all of the principal vertebrate groups from fishes to primates (see summaries by Allee, 1938, 1948, and Collias, 1944).

The "dominance-hierarchy" concept usually implies a series of aggression-subordination relationships in the group, in which one member forces the submission of another by attacking fully or partially, or "threatening" an attack. A dominance hierarchy centering around aggression-submission relationships is an outstanding characteristic of group behavior in many vertebrate animals. As Allee (1948) has pointed out, however, the best known cases of dominance hierarchy are from studies of captive animals. In the forefront of attention are the results of studies with domestic fowl artificially confined in enclosures which hold all animals in the situation. The results of such studies do not necessarily suggest what kind of group pattern if any might arise if the group had been formed on another basis, or if the subjects had been free to group in dependence upon their initial responsiveness to one another.

It would seem that the ecological, psychological, and sociological conditions which lead to clear-cut dominance-subordination relationships must become better known before the real significance of this characteristic in social study may be appraised. In mammalian groups in their natural situation, the appearance of dominance patterns in a species may depend first of all upon the characteristic early parental and family relationships of the young, and its prominence in the group situation may also depend upon the manner of feeding and other typical environmental conditions. It is an interesting fact that whereas dominance relationships are minimal and co-operative relationships outstanding in the organization of the bisexual clans of Central American howler monkeys (Carpenter, 1934), male despotism and relative differences in dominance are prominent in groups of rhesus monkeys (Carpenter, 1942). One important difference in the origin of these patterns may concern the fact that young rhesus males separate from their groups in early adolescence and live in distinct groups with other young males until early adulthood, when they join a bisexual group and compete for social rank. Not only the trophallactic situation in the family and in early group life, but also factors influencing sexual behavior apart from these, must be considered as a basis for understanding typical group patterns in a species.

The problem is of course much more complex on the human level. Investigations with human groups in the United States have shown that the extent to which hostile aggressive behavior is involved in the group relations of children depends for one thing upon the individual's experience of aggression in previous group contacts according to how they involve dominance relations or group integrative patterns (Lewin, Lippitt, and White, 1939), and in experiences of aggression contacts with adults (Anderson, 1939).

It seems desirable to subject the dominance concept to a thoroughgoing appraisal, in order to identify more validly its relationship to other factors and characteristics in group organization. If trophallaxis factors may be postulated as the source of individual behavioral properties leading to aggregation and group unity, it seems necessary also to recognize the intervention of factors which lead to intra-group conflict according to their "strength." The administration of testosterone propionate to vertebrate subjects results in behavior changes through which group status of the injected individuals is likely to rise. Exclusive possession of females by certain males is outstanding in groups of prairie grouse (J. W. Scott, 1941) and rhesus monkeys (Carpenter, 1942) in which the dominance hierarchy is strongly developed, whereas generalized intercourse between the sexes is more prevalent in groups of howler monkeys (Carpenter, 1934) in which dominance differences are low.

If dominance status is a matter of aggressive tendencies for the most part, and has its main basis in factors such as adult sexual drive and individualistic food-taking, it is a process which concerns inter-individual "distance" in social patterns and not group unity. As a distance-governing pattern in the more solitary vertebrates it is involved in the warding off of other males from territory held by a male in breeding season, in more social vertebrates it is a source of pair conflicts which may hold the group to a low degree of cohesion (Collias, 1944; Allee, 1948). In the Scottish roe deer, as Darling (1937) has reported, the group is male-led and is held to a small size by intra-group aggressive relationships. On the other hand, the female-led groups of red deer, with far lower aggression-dominance, become much larger and retain the young animals in the herd for a longer time than do the roe deer.

It is probable that when aggression-dominance as a source of intra-group conflicts exceeds a given intensity and persistence, an effective social group with cohesion and stability may become impossible.

If it is true as Zuckerman (1932) states that "an adequate primate sociology is impossible without reference to the principle of dominance," it is even truer that if this principle is not viewed in its proper relation to other social factors, an adequate animal sociology is still less attainable. A reductionistic motif is not lacking in dominance doctrine, for when inter-group relationships are stated as matters of aggression or withdrawal, social patterns are most readily compared in terms of the relative prominence of dominance-hierarchy characters, and phyletic differences receive less attention. As Anderson (1946) has put the matter for social-adjustment studies on the human level, we are aware of domination but are not sufficiently aware of socially integrative behavior.

As a matter of fact, the dominance concept itself cannot validly be used as though it referred to a qualitatively equivalent process on all vertebrate levels. In the social behavior of lower vertebrate animals the dominance characteristic seems to be outstandingly of the peck-order type, although there are known to be many exceptions. In mammals the status of dominance relationships is much more complex and variable. In primates such as howler monkeys and chimpanzees, an ascendance factor must be recognized independently of a conflict-based dominance. In herds of red deer the leader usually is an experienced female, who does not gain her position through fighting (Darling, 1937). Scott (1945) reported no significant correlation between dominance and leadership order in a flock of sheep, and Stewart and Scott (1947) found a similar absence of any indication of relationship between these characteristics in a flock of goats. The "Spitzentier" animals (Fischel, 1927) which act for short times as pioneers in groups of fishes or birds, although they require facilitation from the group to maintain their role and typically hold it only in a temporary and limited sense, nevertheless represent a function of ascendancy which must be considered as important for group organization. The point holds even in the simpler situation of insect group function, in which some of the workers in a colony are "leaders" in the sense that they exert a greater facilitative effect through their work-rate in the group than do others (Chen, 1937) or as in the mass activities of army ants, the "leadership" is generalized and held briefly by any members of the group in dependence upon their happening to reach the front border of the swarm (Schneirla, 1940).

Although Maslow (1936) has defined a dominant animal as "one whose behavior patterns (sexual, feeding, aggressive, social) are carried out without deference to the behavior patterns of his associates," it is doubtful that this statement would be valid for the whole pattern of any functioning social group, even for those of very sharply defined dominance character. In monkeys and chimpanzees, even the most dominant male changes in behavior and attitude toward his sexual partner when she is sexually receptive (Yerkes, 1939). Grooming, or mutual preening, is one reciprocal activity in which the dominant animal is responsive to and dependent upon the subordinate, or the reverse (Yerkes, 1933). Chapple (1940) concluded from his study of human group relations that, basically, hierarchies as developed in human society tend to rest upon the ability of one individual to evoke responses from others at a given time.

Individual Motivation and Group Pattern

The primary factor underlying social aggregations on all levels appears to be the capacity of the mother or both parents to stay with the young, which opens the way for relations of mutual stimulation, response, and dependence to be set up as the young are reared. On all levels the evolution of organic factors underlying this capacity has involved the appearance of special mechanisms insuring mutual stimulation of parent and young. Larval secretions and adult regurgitation in social insects have a function basically similar in this sense to that of mammary glands in mammals. It is evident that the complexity of superimposed factors is greatest in the mammals, which are far less stereotyped in their social patterns than are most insects. The contrast is greatest with the primates, in which a prolonged association of the young with parents opens the opportunity for an extensive learning in group functions (Yerkes and Yerkes, 1935). Presumably the organic factors which facilitate the lengthy associations of parents and young, and those accounting for a slow and complex maturation process, have evolved in relation to those underlying a superior capacity for behavior modification through learning.

The socialized modification of the insect worker individual is relatively simple and is dominated by stereotyped processes arising through the involvement of the individual in group-feeding situations. That of mammals is infinitely more complex and variable, also very different in complexity and in elaboration on different levels, as new factors become involved. In higher mammals, learning contributes increasingly to individual socialization, which therefore is subject to wider differences in dependence upon group and environmental conditions of development than is the case in lower forms. This also means that maladaptive social behavior may appear more readily than in the stereotyped patterns of lower levels.

We have suggested that the limits of individual psychological capacities, particularly as they affect the socialization process, constitute an important factor imposing boundaries on the kind of group organization possible under given conditions. For example, when the parents are able to participate actively in the selective learning of the young, as some birds evidently can do to an extent and many mammals to a greater extent, the social environment of the young individual is inevitably limited or expanded in dependence upon the social and psychological capacities of the parents. The human ability to develop an abstraction of "one's kind" is a vastly less space-limited and more versatile process for group unity than is the dependence of lower mammals upon direct sensory cues and that of insects upon odor.

The ontogeny of the individual approach to the group underlies his group motivation. The human infant first reaches for his mother incidentally and on a physiologically-forced basis (Schneirla, 1946, 1949), then through a learned act of skill in manipulating his arm in a simple "purposive" manner, later through the use of a learned perceptual symbol, first in language, then in thought. Thus reaching toward social objects is fundamentally a matter of an action-based perception, then may also become symbolic and represent the consequences of an approach far more effectively. Throughout the process, there function social taboos and encouragements which influence learning selectively and serve to control the conditions under which the individual participates in the group. The socialization of young animals in lower primates is far simpler especially because no ability to initiate vocal "reaching" symbolically in the group situation is present.

The socialization process in man may be viewed as a matter of progressive interrelated stages, each arising upon the basis of previous ones, in which through the development of socialized motives and "goals" the individual is assimilated into the culture. In another connection the writer has discussed the relationship between the basic physiological processes and the socialized outcome, on different levels (Schneirla, 1949). In man, the process seems to depend upon the occurrence together of certain interruptive (disturbance) or vegetative (relief) processes in the organism with respectively different environmental situations which arouse them. This type of coincidence provides the basis for simple conditioning processes which open the way for a more complex selective learning of incentives, adjustments, and goals, in which the parents assist. In lower mammals the nature of incentives and goals and the whole pattern of motivation is always rather directly related to the underlying organic conditions ("drives") and the related environmental situations themselves. In man even adjustments to sustenance and security incentives (and of course, to those of sex) become highly modified according to cultural factors concerning prestige, dominance, social approval, and the like. Because the young of lower mammals receive a more standardized and stereotyped preparation for social participation, the result in their case is typical of the species.

SUMMARY CONSIDERATION: ORGANIZATION IN INDIVIDUALS AND IN GROUPS

How well a "whole" is organized depends upon the extent to which its parts function together as a system. The degree to which a system is organized may be evaluated in terms of the complexity and qualitative elaborations in the interaction of its parts and in the formation of interactive sub-systems among them. In an important sense these remarks may be applied both to individual organisms and to aggregations of organisms, so far as these may both be considered as types of whole systems.

The levels of individual organisms and the levels of aggregated organisms presumably are interrelated, if the view is correct that aggregations must have arisen and developed selectively in evolution when the daughter products of fission or of sexual reproduction remained together or associated in some sense other than one of common growth. Despite this consideration, individuals and groups cannot be considered parts of a single continuous series of levels, and the parts of an organism do not necessarily function together in the same way that individuals function together in a social group. Some of the similarities are striking; the differences are also significant and essential to a diagnostic, analytical study.

Our real problem in this paper has been to consider the principal forms of animal aggregation in terms of their comparable characteristics. The first question in understanding group organization concerns the basis on which the component individuals happen to be together, the second their behavior (i.e., group pattern) in remaining together. The *gregarious factor* as it may be called appears to have basic similarities on all levels, although its relation to the eventual group pattern is very different in dependence upon superimposed factors. Incidental associations, insect groups, and the various forms of vertebrate aggregation all possess widely similar reaction tendencies to stimulative effects which may be encountered by individuals. In the simplest forms, the associations, the reactions are to localized environmental effects; in the higher types of aggregations they emanate from the individuals themselves. The attraction of individuals to one another forms and holds the group together, in the simplest cases through similar responses throughout the group, then on the basis of more specialized types of adjustment which become progressively more modifiable in the course of ontogeny on the respective higher levels.

The similar genetic basis underlying the gregarious factor in different organic settings we have characterized as a physiological process accounting for a turning toward weak stimulation. The incidental facilitation described by Allee for the association level typically involves physiological effects of the products of metabolism,—the bio-social cooperation typical in insect groups is qualitatively superior in that through a certain development in ontogeny a "trophallaxis" or specialized stimulus-exchange relationship of individuals can develop. This process is traceable through all higher levels, although it appears in different organic forms and in very different psychological and social contexts. Pattern differences among the levels may be understood in terms of (1) the different psychological capacities of individuals which limit potentialities for individual function and for plastic ontogenetic socialization, and (2) the ecological, environmental, and social conditions under which the early stages of group development have occurred.

The second type of influence (i.e., the "social setting") is more or less standard for lower levels; however, its variability becomes increasingly important in progressively higher levels. Social-aggregation tendencies are initially elaborated in many forms through behavioral relationships arising in the early association of parents and young. In the higher levels, this situation contributes important new formative potentialities for the assimilation of the individual into the social group. In insect groups and higher types, more or less specialized responses are established to group members as distinct from strangers, as an outcome of the trophallactic process and initial individual socialization.

Numerous other processes may be termed *social distance* factors in the sense that they tend to modify, reduce, or to vitiate the influence of the aggregational factor. That is, while the gregarious factor promotes the formation of some type of group which may be close and maximally facilitative or loose and diffuse according to the strength of this factor, the "social distance" factors tend to modify the pattern by complicating the conditions of inter-individual approach and by introducing tendencies for withdrawal from other individuals or from the group situation. Individualistic sexual factors, in the males particularly, frequently serve this function, leading to the formation of group patterns or "dominance hierarchies" the nature of which depends upon intragroup aggressive relationships. The formation of groups of this pattern apparently requires the fixation of social position through individual discriminative learning of differences among others in the group, hence such groups are size-limited in sub-human animals. In some animal forms the establishment of dominance hierarchies apparently depends to a great extent upon access to reproductive relationships within the group, and may thereby play a selective role. Whether the aggression-dominance process accounts for a distinctively organized group, is minimal in the group pattern, or prevents any group formation except sexual pairing, seems to depend in particular upon the nature of the reproductive biology of the species. Dominance patterns are also facilitated through the overpopulation of small areas or through the availability of limited incentives (e.g., food) when the organic needs of associated individuals are high.

By definition, the highest social levels are those in which qualitative elaboration and plasticity in new emergency situations are greatest. The effective environments of primate social organizations are much more complex and variable than are those of social groups in lower organisms. Under different environmental conditions the capacities for modi-

fiability in individuals and group are expressed differently and to varying extents. Under laboratory conditions when problems arise demanding collective effort, chimpanzees become able to co-operate on an
adjustment level which is not apparent in the field (Nissen, 1931), utilizing gestural abstractions as means of influencing the behavior of others
(Crawford, 1937) and hence as an effective group co-ordinating device.
In human social situations, the amount of individual conformity required under given conditions differs from one culture to another, and
within any one culture may vary temporally in dependence upon current social conditions. In the socialization of Hopi Indian infants, there
is a noticeable lack of avoidance training, a characteristic which stems
from an absence of social emphasis upon individual possession of objects (Dennis, 1940). American college students solve syllogistic problems very differently according to whether the problems are presented
in terms of emotionally-loaded political and social symbols or in less
preceptually coercive terms (Lefford, 1946); in the first case their solutions are dominated by the social-conformity (J-curve) factor (F. Allport, 1934), but in the second there are indications that individual
reasoning abilities have been involved much more effectively. The vi-
tiation of reasoning and higher psychological capacities in complex
mammalian societies does not mean that what emerges will be equivalent to the non-reasoned stereotyped patterns of lower levels. The conditions are very different, and the result is very likely to be maladaptive
with respect to group welfare.

On the social levels which are potentially highest in the above sense,
factors may intervene which favor the retention of a stereotyped culture, or in other cases a plastic and progressive culture. The outcome is
especially dependent upon whether a demand for maximal individual
emotion-supported adherence to traditional forms excludes from the
social situation the species potentials in new contributions from individuals and from sub-groups. On lower levels, the characteristic species
social patterns arise through an effective domination of the underlying
biological processes over the inter-individual relationships involved in
socialization and in environmental adjustment. For example, studies of
group function in lower mammals indicate that the characteristic pattern of group leadership depends to a considerable extent upon species
reproductive processes. On the human level, a wide range of processes
may be involved, producing leadership relations which are contracted

or wide in their intellectual, economic, and social representation of sub-processes throughout the group, or on the other hand represent few or none of the sub-processes.

In order to dispense with sharp distinctions between individual and group which are actually paradoxical in studying social patterns, the tendencies expressed in individual socialization must be studied on different levels in terms of the growth and elaboration of group dependence and group relationships. Even in social patterns showing a maximal individual articulation, a socialized individual always lives with reference to a group in some sense in the processes of group integration, and co-ordination. Also according to the nature of social pattern, there exist various transitional stages between individual and group, individual and sub-groups. Group organization needs to be studied in terms of inter-individual dependence and sub-group interrelationship in their bearing upon group patterns on different levels. Further evidence is needed concerning what types of factors dominate individual and sub-group contributions to group organization on the respective levels.

In the last analysis, the utility of postulating different social levels depends upon our discerning the relative roles of biological factors underlying aggregation and those modifying or opposing it. Particularly important is the relationship of these processes in various animal types to psychological capacities which can facilitate or oppose aggregation and well-integrated group organization according to the special conditions of culture and social situation. It seems clear that any progressive modification of social patterns on the lowest levels is rigidly dependent upon the slow processes of natural selection and biological evolution. This long-time process occurs, as we have seen, in a variety of ways as concerns the entrance of qualitative specialization and behavioral versatility in group function. The importance of discernible differences in this process in different animals makes analogizing by similarity from level to level a procedure of doubtful validity, unless the analogies lead to thoroughgoing comparison.

Man, due to his potentially great freedom from the restrictions of biological processes, or to the opportune utilization of socially beneficial biological factors in the evolution of social patterns, can attain a far higher standard than in lower levels, depending upon how his psychological capacities are permitted to influence social progress. As Simpson

(1949) puts the matter, "Under our ethics, the possibility of man's influencing the direction of his own evolution also involves his responsibility for doing so and for making that direction the best one." The problem of what is "best" for man's social welfare is properly a preeminent concern of the scientist in his investigation and theory.

REFERENCES

1. Allee, W. C. 1938. *The Social Life of Animals.* New York: Norton.
2. Allee, W. C. 1948. Animal sociology, *Encyclop. Brit.,* 1948 ed.
3. Allport, F. W. 1934. The J-curve hypothesis of conforming behavior, *Jour. Soc. Psychol., 5,* 141–183.
4. Anderson, H. H. 1946. Domination and social integration in the behavior of kindergarten children and teachers, *Genet. Psychol. Monogr., 21,* 287–385.
5. Bierens de Haan, J. A. 1930. Animal language in its relation to that of man, *Biol. Rev., 4,* 249–268.
6. Carpenter, C. R. 1934. A field study of the behavior and social relations of howling monkeys (*Alouatta palliata*), *Comp. Psychol. Monogr., 10.*
7. Carpenter, C. R. 1942. Societies of monkeys and apes, *Biol. Sympos., 8,* 177–204 (Redfield, R., Ed.).
8. Chapple, E. D. 1940. Measuring human relations: an introduction to the study of the interaction of individuals, *Genet. Psychol. Monogr., 22,* 1–147.
9. Chauvin, R. 1947. Le progrès de la psychologie animale moderne et leur intérêt en psychologie, *Rev. Quest. Sci., 20,* 188–204.
10. Chen, S. 1937. The leaders and followers among the ants in nest-building, *Physiol. Zool., 10,* 437–455.
11. Collias, N. E. 1944. Aggressive behavior among vertebrate animals, *Physiol. Zool., 17,* 83–123.
12. Crawford, M. P. 1937. The cooperative solving of problems by young chimpanzees, *Comp. Psychol. Monogr., 14,* 1–88.
13. Crowell, M. F. 1929. A discussion of human and insect societies, *Psyche, 36,* 182–189.
14. Darling, F. F. 1937. *A Herd of Red Deer.* London: Oxford University Press.
15. Dennis, W. 1947. Does culture appreciably affect patterns of infant behavior? Ch. 6, Sect. I, "Readings in Social Psychology," Newcomb, T., & E. L. Hartley (Eds.).
16. Emerson, A. E. 1939. Social coordination and the superorganism, *Amer. Midl. Nat., 21,* 182–209.

17. Emerson, A. E. 1942. Basic comparisons of human and insect societies, *Biol. Sympos., 8,* 163–176 (Redfield, R., Ed.).

18. Fishel, W. 1927. Beiträge zur Sociologie des Haushuhns, *Biol. Zent., 47,* 678–695.

19. Fisher, R. A. 1930. *The Genetic Theory of Natural Selection.* Oxford: Oxford University Press.

20. Frisch, K. von. *Aus dem Leben der Bienen.* 4th ed., Wien: Springer.

21. Galt, W. 1940. The principle of cooperation in behavior, *Quart. Rev. Biol., 15,* 401–410.

22. Hyman, Libbie H. The transition from the unicellular to the multi-cellular individual, *Biol. Sympos., 8,* 27–42.

23. Jacobsen, C. F. and M. M., and J. G. Yoshioka. 1932. Development of an infant chimpanzee during her first year, *Comp. Psychol. Monogr., 9,* 1–94.

24. Jennings, H. S. 1906. *Behavior of the Lower Organisms.* New York: Columbia University Press.

25. Jennings, H. S. 1942. The transition from the individual to the social level, *Biol. Sympos., 8,* 105–119.

26. Lefford, A. 1946. The influence of emotional subject matter on logical reasoning, *Jour. Gen. Psych., 34,* 127–151.

27. Lewin, K., R. Lippitt and R. K. White. 1939. Patterns of aggressive behavior in experimentally graded 'social climates,' *Jour. Soc. Psych., 10,* 271–299.

28. Maier, N. R. F. and T. C. Schneirla. 1935. *Principles of Animal Psychology.* New York: McGraw-Hill.

29. Maslow, A. H. 1936. Dominance-quality and social behavior in infra-human primates, *Jour. Soc. Psych., 11,* 313–324.

30. Needham, J. 1929. *The Skeptical Biologist.* London: Chatto.

31. Newcomb, T., and E. L. Hartley (Eds.), 1947. *Readings in Social Psychology.* New York: Holt.

32. Nissen, H. W. 1931. A field study of the chimpanzee, *Comp. Psych. Monogr., 8,* 1–105.

33. Novikoff, A. 1945. The concept of integrative levels in biology, *Science, 101,* 209–215.

34. Redfield, R. (Ed.). 1942. *Levels of Integration in Biological and Social Systems, Biol. Sympos., 8.* Lancaster: J. Cattell, Pr.

35. Révész, G. 1944. The language of animals, *Jour. Gen. Psych., 30,* 117–147.

36. Schjelderup-Ebbe, T. 1922. Beiträge zur Sozialpsychologie des Haus-huhns, *Ztschr. Psych., 88,* 225–252.

37. Schneirla, T. C. 1939. A theoretical consideration of the basis for approach-withdrawal adjustments in behavior, *Psychol. Bull., 37,* 501–502.

38. Schneirla, T. C. 1940. Further studies on the army-ant behavior pattern.—Mass organization in the swarm-raiders, *Jour. Comp. Psychol., 29,* 401–460.

39. Schneirla, T. C. 1941. Social organization in insects, as related to individual function, *Psych. Rev., 48,* 465–486.

40. Schneirla, T. C. 1944. A unique case of circular milling in ants, *Amer. Mus. Nov.,* No. 1253, 1–26.

41. Schneirla, T. C. 1946. Problems in the biopsychology of social organization, *Jour. Abnorm. Soc. Psych., 41,* 385–402.

42. Schneirla, T. C. 1949. Levels in the psychological capacities of animals. Chap. in *Philosophy for the Future,* pp. 243–286 (Roy W. Sellars, et al., Eds.). New York: Macmillan.

43. Scott, J. P. 1945. Social behavior, organization, and leadership in a small flock of domestic sheep, *Comp. Psychol. Monogr., 18,* 1–29.

44. Scott, J. W. 1941. Behavior of the sage grouse during mating cycle, *Bul. Ecol. Soc. Amer., 22,* 38.

45. Shaffer, L. F. 1936. *The Psychology of Adjustment.* Boston: Houghton Mifflin.

46. Simpson, G. G. 1949. *The Meaning of Evolution.* Yale University Press.

47. Sloane, E. H. 1945. Reductionism, *Psych. Rev., 52,* 214–223.

48. Stewart, Jeannie C., and J. P. Scott. 1947. Lack of correlation between leadership and dominance relationships in a herd of goats, *Jour. Comp. Physiol. Psychol., 40,* 255–264.

49. Strecker, A. E. 1940. *Beyond the Clinical Frontiers.*

50. Wheeler, W. M. 1928. *The Social Insects.* New York: Harcourt, Brace.

51. Woodger, J. H. 1929. Biological Principles—a Critical Study. New York: Harcourt, Brace.

52. Yerkes, R. M. 1933. Genetic aspects of grooming, a socially important primate behavior pattern, *Jour. Soc. Psych., 4,* 3–25.

53. Yerkes, R. M. 1939. Social dominance and sexual status in the chimpanzee, *Quart. Rev. Biol., 14,* 115–136.

54. Yerkes, R. M. and M. I. Tomilin. 1935. Mother-infant relations in chimpanzee, *Jour. Comp. Psychol., 20,* 321–458.

55. Yerkes, R. M. and Ada W. Yerkes. 1929. *The Great Apes.* New Haven: Yale University Press.

56. Zuckerman, S. 1932. *The Social Life of Monkeys and Apes.* London: Kegan Paul.

CHAPTER 5

⊓⊔⊓⊔⊓⊔⊓⊔⊓⊔⊓⊔⊓⊔⊓⊔⊓⊔⊓⊔⊓⊔⊓⊔⊓⊔⊓⊔⊓⊔⊓

Levels of Integration Along the Phylogenetic Scale

Learning Aspect

HARRY F. HARLOW
University of Wisconsin

In the discussion of the general topic of levels of integration along the phylogenetic scale with special emphasis on learning, I shall emphasize a single great biological order—the order of primates. This emphasis is justified not only because it is the order to which man belongs, but also because it is the order in which social learning has attained a peak. Further observation and experimentation with subhuman primates should give us additional insight into human social learning.

The primate order comprises lemurs, tarsiers, monkeys, apes, and man. Man himself must have evolved from some simple form that branched off the primate tree before the differentiation of any of the presently existing anthropoid apes, including the gibbons. Some proto-gibbonoid type devoid of anything approaching human culture may have provided the stem from which evolved multiple millions of years ago a rather atypical primate, the human being, unusual for his degree of terrestrial adaptation, his carnivorous tendencies, and his slightly exaggerated cerebral development. Unfortunately, the history of the development of enculturation in this species, the only primate species to attain a highly organized culture, is unknown and probably will be forever lost. This enculturation includes the development of a system of communication designed to express more than emotional states and physiological needs, the development of social groups that carry out specialized functions within a larger social milieu, and the development and control of the basic tools and implements—fire, the knife, the axe, the bow, the fabrication of stones and metals—that made it possible for neural structure to gain ascendancy over bone and muscle.

Although man is not descended directly from any existing primate, and although man's cultural evolution is forever lost, study of the behavioral characteristics of present primate forms and the nature of their social organizations may give limited information as to the kinds of problems which the human species must have faced during its cultural development and may even provide insight into the reasons for basic problems which the present-day still only semicivilized *homo,* somewhat *sapiens,* faces.

PRIMATE SOCIAL BEHAVIOR

Many millions of years ago, probably before the emergence of the proto-human being, the primate stock was split into two separate divisions or sections: the New World or Catarrhine monkeys and the Old World or Platyrrhine monkeys. The New World monkeys never produced a higher form—gibbonoid, anthropoid, or humanoid, whereas multiple higher forms were produced by the Old World primates. From a social psychology point of view this may have been a vast evolutionary error, for the scanty evidence that we have suggests that the New World forms were inherently more social in their behavior than the Old World primates. There is some reason to believe that these South American monkeys are by native disposition less cruel and less savage, more kindly and more social in relationships with other members of their group than are Old World monkeys. They come far closer to being born into the ten commandments than their Eurasian relatives. The studies conducted by Maslow (27) at the Wisconsin Laboratory indicate that dominance is less strong, less generalized, less brutal, and less cruel in the New World monkeys than it is in the Old World forms. Unfortunately, Maslow's studies represent only preliminary investigations; the subjects were few and species sampling was incomplete. But it is striking to note that Maslow's experimental data correlate with behavioral observations of New and Old World monkeys in their natural, state-in-the-wild kind of social organization. It is always possible, of course, that all or part of the apparent difference between the two divisions in social amity derives from differential experiences from early infancy rather than differential inheritance.

The species of Platyrrhine monkeys whose social organization has been most intensely studied is that of the howling monkeys. *Alouatta palliata,* according to Carpenter (6), form social groups averaging about 17 animals and including as many as 35 members. These bands frequently contain several mature males and several mature females, providing a sufficient number of adult animals for serious internecine strife. Yet the howling monkeys live in a state of social bliss probably unmatched by any other primitive primate "culture," not even excluding the highly co-operative Zuni, Dakota, or Bathonga cultures (29). Adult howler males do not fight adult males, adult females do not fight adult females, and there exists not even a battle between the sexes. The infant animals struggle and tussle as they romp and play, but when they reach an age and state in which such play could result in pain and injury, they abstain from these activities and live a proper howling life of peace at any price. It is an interesting observation that these are the only primates that are not polyandrous, polygynous, or monogamous. Instead, they are completely promiscuous—the only primate group to be so described. Whether this is to be regarded as a compensatory penalty for an otherwise idyllic existence or a reward for social virtue lies beyond the province of a psychologist to decide.

Each howling monkey band has its own territory, even though the geographic outlines are neither precisely marked nor mapped. Because of this imperfect mapping, border disagreements occasionally arise between two howling monkey groups, but there is never physical violence or bloodshed. Instead, the battle is one of words, or more precisely, vocalizations—greater in amplitude, shorter in duration, and infinitely more effective than anything that has come from the Chamber of the Security Council of the United Nations. There are, of course, no Russian howling monkeys. The group vocalization contests have a faint homologue in the Ammassalik Eskimos' individualistic drum-matches in which the competitors try to best each other in the volume of sound they produce by their drum beating and singing. But these Eskimos do not reach the howling monkey ideal of battle by pure vocalization, since Mirsky reports (32, p. 69) that "the singer mocks the other in a number of ways, by snorting and breathing right in his face, by butting him with his forehead so that he tumbles over."

From one point of view a tragedy and from another a parodox, the section of primates probably by nature the more anti-social, was destined to produce the species that were to form the largest and most complex social groups culminating in those organized by man. In Maslow's studies of dominance it was the Old World monkeys that were brutal, savage, and quick to behave in a manner mirroring man's inhumanity to man. Perhaps the largest primate social organizations, aside from human, are formed by baboons whose social groups may include some dozens or hundreds of members. Such communal living is a triumph for an animal that gives every indication of being anti-social from an early age. Baboons are completely rugged individualists. Large male baboons steal food from middle-sized male baboons, who in turn steal from small male baboons, all of whom steal food from female baboons, who will snatch food from their children's mouths. All baboons are born free and equal, but the large baboons catch on very quickly.

Zuckerman (37) has described the behavior of Hamadryas baboons in the fabricated rocky caves of Monkey Hill in the London Zoo, an environment still more limiting and offering less chance for escape from other baboons than the natural habitat. The most striking observation in this situation was the shrinking population as the baboons gradually decimated their ranks in a series of gladiatorial combats surpassed in their sadistic fury only by the Roman emperors who, according to historians, were human beings. Baboons fought for females, they fought for food, and they fought apparently because there were available baboons and nothing else to fight. If any baboon uttered what Zuckerman calls the fear-threatening cry, other baboons quickly assembled dressed to the teeth with their most intense emergency reactions. In the wild, no doubt, they destroyed a common enemy, but in the absence of a common enemy in the captive state, they sublimated by destroying each other. Zuckerman recounts the case of a large male baboon who, for some unaccountable reason, was just sitting quietly. A small baboon gave the fear-threatening cry in his presence and rushed away. The unfortunate animal was quickly surrounded by other male baboons who, after a hasty Senate investigation, probably decided he suffered from guilt by association and promptly tore him limb from limb. Baboons killed in the wild typically give evidence of having been lacerated by toothy animals and the commonest tooth marks are baboon tooth marks.

But the baboons have no monopoly on brutal dominance. Maslow's experimental studies indicate that brutal dominance is the rule and not the exception among Old World or Catarrhine monkeys. Maslow and Flanzbaum (28) tested ten pairs of three different species of macaques for dominance. The tests were made in a cage approximately three feet square and five feet high. Daily twenty-minute tests were made until the behavior of the pair of animals was judged to have stabilized or until 30 observation periods had been completed. Twenty small pieces of apple were automatically introduced into the test cage during each test period. Results indicate consistency in the dominance responses of the individual animals, and in the behavioral repertoire characterizing dominance. Bullying, pre-empting the limited available food, initiating of fighting, and assumption of the masculine position in copulatory behavior regardless of sex were prominent ascendant traits. The only indication of positive social responses lay in grooming behavior, which was usually initiated by the dominant animal.

The extremely strong and brutal dominance responses of the monkey under relatively natural living conditions have been described by Carpenter (9) for the Santiago Island Rhesus Colony. The strength of this dominance is indicated by the fact that a group of seven males observed for a month showed a straight-line dominance order. The supremely dominant male was judged to be more than fifty times as dominant as the least dominant male on the basis of the frequency of observed behavioral patterns indicating precedence or aggression. Brutal dominance was also described by Harlow and Yudin (18) who observed cage-mates in the Vilas Park Zoo. Two young mandrills were so attached that, when separated, they cried and wailed for hours until reunited, but when they were put together and offered food, the female quickly returned to her most frequent cage avocation of beating the smaller male. When food was offered to a green monkey in another group, all other monkeys in the cage fled, but even so, he did not touch the food until he had first brutally assaulted the other monkeys. Rhesus monkeys, even adult rhesus monkeys, will usually live amicably paired in cages if they survive the original pairing procedure. But the initial pairing of adult animals is frequently a breath-taking experience. We originally built our monkey cages in a manner that enabled the animals to reach into neighboring cages, but it became necessary to remodel the quarters because we were losing so many rhesus fingers there was threat of disruption of our entire test program.

Little is known about the social organization of the anthropoid apes. The orangutans (8) and gibbons (7) probably live in family groups and the chimpanzees (33) and gorillas (5) may form small multiple-family organizations. It is possible that the anthropoids show less brutal dominance than the lower Old World forms. Perhaps their social organization is so simple that there is little cause for frequent elicitation of anti-social behaviors. It may be that the individual members of anthropoid social groups learn more readily to adjust to their respective roles and, by appropriate techniques, minimize violent forms of behavior. But even in the small chimpanzee social groups that Nissen sought to observe in Africa, there were frequent sounds of fighting and cries of pain from the locations in which the groups had established their temporary quarters for the night and morning.

The picture we have given of the Old World primates, including man, is that of an anti-social animal that, nevertheless, may live in fairly large social groups. In all likelihood this picture is correct. It is probable that all Old World primates are highly self-sufficient, self-reliant animals whose primary concerns are strongly self-centered. It is highly probable that they are inherently efficient fighting units whose aggressive responses are easily released and are supported by intense emergency-type internal responses. Certainly the primates are not truly social animals like many of the insects. The social role of any individual in a primate society is continually subject to change, whereas by original nature different members of certain social insect species throughout their life span automatically subserve diverse specialized, socially-useful functions.

ROLE OF LEARNING IN PRIMATE SOCIAL BEHAVIOR AND PERSONALITY

It is possible, of course, that men, baboons, and rhesus monkeys are inherently as social as the howling monkeys and that the conception of the Old World animal as a societal-living but anti-social creature by nature is fallacious. We mentioned earlier Maslow's studies on the differential strength of the dominance drive in New and Old World monkeys, but we should frankly recognize that neither these studies nor the observations of monkeys in the wild give any definitive answer to our questions. Almost all of Maslow's animals were approaching maturity. Much of their life history was unknown, but undoubtedly included the influences of maternal controls and other within-species social behaviors. Actually we know all too little about the nature and strength of the dominance response or any other kind of social response in monkeys of different ages, or in monkeys of different species with factors of age and experience controlled.

We have already stated that no animal other than man has a true culture in the sense of an organized body of knowledge passed down from generation to generation. In a limited sense, however, any animal living in a group and capable of facile learning must develop a semblance of a culture, since it must have learned to be influenced in its behavior by the ways of its fellows. It is possible that dominance responses in howling monkeys and baboons would not differ if the members of the two species were reared in isolation or in an environment devoid of representatives of their own species, or if the young of both species were reared in social environments equally benign or equally savage.

Maslow's pioneering studies show that efficient and reliable measures of primate social behavior can be obtained. It would be a comparatively simple matter to test the effect of various environments upon such basic social patterns as dominance and grooming in rhesus monkeys, in New World monkeys, and, if sufficient funds were available, in anthropoid apes. Since rhesus monkeys breed readily in captivity and are imported in quantity, it would be relatively easy and inexpensive to obtain newborn animals (or 6-week-old animals if one wished to dispense with bottle feeding), rear them under a variety of social environments, and test the effect of these diverse environments on personal-social traits. This would be particularly easy in any school sufficiently far south that the animals could be housed and maintained in unheated outdoor living and test cages. Even the infant rhesus monkey is a hardy animal and could easily maintain himself after weaning in unheated outdoor living quarters if the temperatures did not fall below freezing for any long period of time. Groups of four animals would no doubt be sufficient to give representative data on the effects of any experimental social environment one wished to study.

The first obvious situation to investigate would be isolation, except for specified social test periods made perhaps at six-month or one-year intervals. One can only conjecture what the results might be on such responses as grooming and dominance. It is entirely possible, of course, that the animals might show as much disregard for members of their own species as members of different species have been reported to show for each other in the wild. Carpenter, for example, has reported that howling monkeys and spider monkeys may cross paths in their natural habitat without aggressive social interchange. It may well be that animals in isolation would show strong positive social responses such as co-operative playing and grooming and either fail to show the violent dominance responses involving assault or threatened assault which characterize the adolescent and adult rhesus monkey, or show them in much milder form. It is possible, of course, that the essentially antisocial and egocentric brutal dominance responses are maturationally determined and would appear as early and in as violent a form in animals reared in isolation as in animals reared in a rhesus monkey or baboon environment. Stone's observations (35) of the effects of interchanging the litters of wild rats and albino rats soon after birth demonstrate the feasibility and importance of techniques such as we suggest.

Carpenter (10, pp. 256–257) has already conjectured concerning the results of an experiment similar in type but somewhat more pretentious in scope than ours. He writes as follows:

Raise in isolation animals of the species, but of the right sex and age to compose a group which meets the requirements of the formula for the average group characteristic of a species. These individuals will then be released together. What will happen? Some may so fear others that they flee. Some will be antagonistic and fight. Others will form into groups and remain together. In general, the synthetic group experiment will not fall together, as had been hoped or predicted, into a single organization. Why? Even though the social drives are operative and social incentives are present, the monkeys have not been conditioned to each other. They have not been socialized—i.e., they have not learned to make fitting responses to each other as complexes of stimuli. What is lacking is what I have called *integration*.

Social integration is conceived to begin with birth and to involve definable processes of social learning and adjustment. These processes are organic and involve the expressions and satisfactions of physiological drives. From one viewpoint, effective social integration of an individual conditions it in a manner to make it responsive to the communicative acts, motor expressions including gestures, and vocalizations. These communicative acts, involving specific stimuli patterns and fitting responses, constitute the core of group coordination. Let it be remembered that the stimulus aspects of communicative acts cannot be operative except on a background of social integration—i.e., animals which are conditioned to each other.

A second kind of environment that would provide interesting data would be the environment of abundance in which the satisfying agents of the animals' needs would be ever available. Multiple shelters and multiple play and exercise devices would always be present. All desirable foods would be obtainable in numerous, separate places. In short, competition would never be required to supply any of the animals' basic wants. If it were feared that this kind of plenty would introduce an uncontrolled variable of obesity, one could accustom the animals from the time of weaning to eat at appropriate times in individual feeding compartments. Initially and individually the animals would be trained to obtain food in a particular locality and to avoid the feeding places of the other animals. In preliminary ventures it might be well if all of the monkeys trained to expect the more abundant life were of the same sex. It is not inconceivable that an environment such as this might lead to an augmentation of the positive social responses and to reduction or even elimination of aggressive behavior.

An obvious third social environment would be one stimulating strong competition for the satisfaction of essential needs throughout the life span of the animals. Individual living cages of varying degrees of desirability would be arranged in the living pen. A single exercise or play device would be available. At the primary feeding interval, food would be offered from a single dispensing unit, thus putting a premium on aggression by delaying the feeding of some animals in the group. Two hours after the basic ration had been dispensed—a time which should allow all four animals to obtain a maintenance diet—a limited quantity of tidbit foods such as grapes, oranges, and bananas could be presented in a single container and thus provide a situation to induce overt aggression in some and timidity and avoidance in other animals. It is possible that animals reared under these conditions would make few or no positive social responses. Howler monkeys so trained might show the cruel dominance patterns characteristic of rhesus monkeys and baboons.

The effects of our different social environments could be measured not only by observation of the animals in their living quarters, but also by periodic tests under experimental conditions utilizing basic techniques that have already been rather well explored—experimental techniques such as those reported by Maslow for measuring dominance, by Harlow for social facilitation of feeding, and even perhaps those by Crawford for co-operative behavior measures in the chimpanzee.

There can be no question that such experiments would give striking and significant data. All authorities recognize that the nature of primate social organizations is greatly influenced by learning. The experiments would supply data concerning the extent and permanence of learning.

Once social groups are formed by monkeys, they show considerable degree of solidarity and cohesiveness, and even though there is quarreling among the members of the "in-group," the reactions to any "out-group" members are far more violent. Thus Carpenter reports (10, p. 251): "Only a short time may pass after a 'foreign' female has entered the sphere of a well organized group until she would be recognized and usually attacked and driven from the group or killed." Particularly he recounts the case of one female who, when sexually receptive, was accepted by a foreign group but upon termination of estrus was driven from the group. And, with regard for her own well-being, she apparently departed with less fury than that commonly ascribed to the female scorned.

The speaker has observed groups of monkeys in adjacent cages both in the Madison Zoo and in the Wisconsin Primate Laboratory. No matter how much quarreling there is within cages, all members of a cage group put up a common front when threatened by the foreigners in the next cage. When the common enemy threatens, a "cage consciousness" quickly develops and a temporary strong national feeling is engendered that would do credit to any Balkan country. This "cage consciousness" is an obviously learned process, and its study under experimental conditions should provide information concerning the forces operating in the formation and maintenance of basic primate social groups.

The effect of varied and extreme environments upon the behavior of animals has, of course, frequently been studied. There are many studies, such as those by Louttit (25), Stone (36), and Beach (2), of the effect of isolation on the sex behavior of guinea pigs and rats. At the present time there is a considerable number of studies completed or in progress relating to the influence of some special condition introduced early in life on the behavior of the animal later in life. These have been primarily inspired by Hunt's pioneer investigation (21) of the effect of food deprivation in infancy on subsequent hoarding behavior in rats. As far as I know, however, there are no studies of the effects of extreme environments maintained for prolonged periods on the total personality of any animal. The rhesus monkey would be an ideal animal for such study. The young rhesus is small, sturdy, and easily and cheaply maintained. At the same time he exhibits a wealth of behavior that can be tested effectively. The prime requirement for conducting such a study is space in a relatively mild climate. Since Wisconsin does not afford such an environment, we have not been able to conduct these researches ourselves, but we might be able to provide newborn or infant animals to an interested experimenter who has the requisite facilities.

Our knowledge of cultural groups, both human and subhuman, has been primarily derived from the study of continuous cultures in which each generation is subjected to the pre-established patterns of the previous generation or generations. Our knowledge of the effect of cultural impacts should be extended by the technique of discontinuous cultures —the study of the development of animals, and as complex and humanlike animals as possible, brought up uninfluenced by their parents or other uncontrolled members of their group. A semblance of this has been applied by Dennis (13) to a pair of human twins in early infancy, but the environmental restrictions were necessarily limited and experimental controls were lacking.

Desirable as such human studies might be, it is obviously impractical to continue them through any considerable portion of an individual's life. There can hardly be any question that a systematic study of prolonged exposure of a subhuman primate such as the rhesus monkey to an extreme environment would vastly influence later behavior. Riesen (34) has shown that an environment of extreme visual deprivation profoundly influences chimpanzees' and monkeys' visual responses and ability to learn such responses. There are three cases of chimpanzees studied in an extreme environment, a human environment: the original study of Gua by Kellogg (22), the longer study of Fin by Finch (15), and the current research by Hayes (17) on Viki. The human environment seems to have influenced markedly the social behavior and personality of all three subjects, a finding that lends credence to the hypothesis that the imposition of even more extreme environments might produce still more drastic deviations from the typical behavior of the various primate species.

The anthropologists, on the basis of studies of comparative culture, have recently emphasized the role of the effect on basic personality structure of early training and regulation of the basic physiological drives of hunger and elimination. Permissive versus restrictive cultures have been studied and interpretations have been made, usually in terms of psychoanalytic concepts. Unfortunately, it is not possible to carry out controlled studies, since cultures do not vary in single characteristics but always show multiple differences based on a host of uncontrollable factors. There is an obvious need to supplement these observational anthropological studies with rigorous experimental studies on subhuman animals subjected to various permissive and restrictive training procedures during infancy and even the subsequent years. Levy's pioneer researches (23) on the sucking behavior of puppies give some indication that this type of training can affect a behavioral trait. Puppies fed through free-flowing nipples showed extra-feeding sucking to a far greater degree than puppies obtaining milk through small-holed nipples.

At the Wisconsin Laboratory we have reared two rhesus monkeys isolated soon after birth from mothers unable to nurse them adequately. Both of these monkeys were fed by medicine droppers and both became persistent and prolonged thumbsuckers. Indeed, one of these animals developed an elongated and deformed thumb. A third infant was separated from his mother at six weeks of age and sent to the University of Chicago where he, too, developed habitual thumbsucking. We have never observed thumbsucking in any other of the dozen infants born and reared by their mothers at the laboratory, nor have we ever observed thumbsucking in any other monkey. Such incidental observation of a persistent behavioral difference associated with an atypical, though uncontrolled, training procedure, suggests that striking results might be obtained if rigorously controlled studies were conducted of the response variations resulting from varying degrees of adequacy of satiation of the physiological drives.

It is probably not feasible on the basis of comparative studies of cultures to assay the exact effect of infantile training procedures independent of the effect of procedures carried out in post-infancy. Cultures and also individuals that are either restrictive or permissive in inculcating routine habits in early childhood show a strong tendency to continue such procedures in other training throughout childhood and, indeed, until the period of independence or partial independence of the progeny. Thus, if we wish to study not only the effect of a special type of training on personal-social development, but particularly the influence of such training during a limited period of an individual's life, we are of necessity forced to go beyond the data afforded by comparative culture techniques. Information bearing on such matters might be obtainable from subhuman animals and we should, of course, recommend the use of subjects as closely akin to man as possible. Certainly with monkeys it would be possible to measure the influence on personal-social traits of either permissive or restrictive training techniques carried out consistently throughout infancy, to measure the effect of early permissive techniques followed by restrictive techniques at any given period, and to measure the effect of restrictive techniques followed by permissive techniques at any desired age. The possibilities latent in such experiments, or the limitations intrinsic to such an approach, cannot even be guessed since the background researches for such studies are either incomplete or nonexistent.

Failure to carry out studies of this type partially arises from their long-term, longitudinal nature. They are, unfortunately, not the kind of investigations which can be farmed out conveniently to our graduate students. At the same time we must face the fact that the future progress of psychology, and especially social psychology, depends in large part upon our willingness, if not eagerness, to conduct such studies.

STRESS, LANGUAGE, MOTIVATION, AND LEARNING

Research on subhuman animals, particularly learning studies, may provide social-psychological theory with valuable data of a more general type than those represented in the previously reviewed studies or hypothetical studies. Basic and theoretical information about neuroses, anxiety states, fundamental personality mechanisms, motivation, and even the nature of learning, can be obtained using subhuman animals. Comparative psychology has already built up a very considerable literature on the role of learning in the development of neuroses. These studies stem from the classical researches of Pavlov and his pupils and include a long series of studies by Liddell and co-workers (24) who investigated experimental neuroses in dogs, sheep, and goats. Subsequently, studies by Cook (11) at Minnesota and Bijou (3, 4) at Iowa have shown that such behavioral states can be developed in the rat. The essential conditions for the experimental neuroses appear to be an extremely strong drive, either hunger or shock, from which the animal has no escape except by correct responses to a problem which is deliberately designed to be beyond the limits of his ability and thus to provide no more than partial reinforcement.

Conditions analogous to human neuroses have been set up in these animals and in many cases the abnormal behavior has generalized beyond the experimental training situation. These studies have perhaps elucidated basic conditions for neurosis, and have shown that states similar to the neurotic state in man can be produced in lower animals. It must be admitted frankly, however, that the studies have provided little or no new information concerning the nature of human neuroses, and some authorities have even questioned the comparability of experimental neuroses in animals with the various neurotic conditions in man. It may be of interest here to note that human neurotic conditions are typically based on the failure of social adjustments—the inability of the individual to adjust to his social group. As far as the speaker knows, no comparative psychologist has attempted to induce experimental neurosis in subhuman animals by use of an inescapable motive of a social nature which drives the animal to attempt solution by an adjustment to members of his species, even though constantly rebuffed. Increasing information about social motivation in animals and knowledge of their affectional needs might enable us in the near future to conduct far more efficient studies of experimental neuroses than have yet been reported. A goal, of course, in the production of experimental neuroses in animals is to produce a subject better adapted than the mentally ill patient for the study of basic re-educational techniques and procedures.

A number of investigators have developed in subhuman animals response patterns that either are analogous or homologous to various basic Freudian personality mechanisms. Illustrative of these experimentally induced response patterns is that of displacement, reported by Miller (31) in a study of rats.

Six pairs of rats were placed, one pair at a time, on a charged electric grid and trained to strike vigorously at each other to effect cessation of shock. The animals were subsequently tested in a balanced temporal order under two conditions: in pairs with a doll and singly with a doll. Paired, the animals struck at each other more frequently than at the doll, and the difference was significant. Placed alone with the doll and shocked, all of these rats knocked down the doll, half by striking and half in irrelevant ways. Only one of an untrained control group struck at the doll before knocking it down in irrelevant ways. The difference approaches statistical significance.

In spite of the fact that there is almost no literature on the problem, it would appear that language, especially vocalized language in animals, merits investigation. Carpenter's field studies of the howling monkey and the gibbon have suggested that perhaps vocal language is a more efficient tool in guiding the social behavior of these animals than may have been supposed. Carpenter believes that howler monkeys may possess fifteen to twenty different vocal signals, even though he could clearly describe and analyze only nine. The same number of different types of vocalization have been identified for gibbons. It is not at all unlikely that this extremely careful and cautious investigator, working under the unfavorable observational conditions of the wild, underestimated rather than overestimated the total range of meaningful vocalizations.

Casual observations in our own laboratory have indicated a very considerable ability of cage-mates to communicate with each other. Thus, calls of one member of a pair restrained in the living quarters will cause an animal in a test-room to cease work even though these sounds are only faintly audible to the human tester. Yet the same animal will test undisturbed and indifferent when similar and far more vigorous calls are being made by animals other than the cage-mate. Indeed, the faint call of a cage-mate may cause cessation of all work, whereas even the sounds of fighting by other monkeys may go largely ignored. Equally striking results have been observed in the response to vocalizations of separated mothers and infants. It is more than possible that primates make far more use of vocalizations in the wild than is commonly recognized, and it is possible that this range of calls and cries might be extended by appropriate training procedures. Certainly most laboratory housing conditions are designed to extinguish experimentally acquired language communications between animals.

The language limitation of the great apes has always remained a mystery, since these animals apparently possess effectors capable of differential articulation and since their intelligence, as indicated by their ready adaptation to most laboratory tests, appears to be far more than adequate to effect verbal responses. Many years ago the naturalist Furness (16) reported that he had trained a young orangutan to speak two words in a meaningful manner. Since Furness, unlike most naturalists, reported failures as well as successes in his training techniques, special credence might be placed in his observations. At the present time Hayes (17) at the Yerkes Laboratory of Primate Psychology, is carrying out a long study designed, among various other goals, to teach a young chimpanzee to speak. At last reports, Viki had attained an English vocabulary of three spoken words, although the meanings associated with these words apparently lack precision. Hayes believes that at least part of his success results from deliberate training of the animal to acquire an imitative "set"—a learned set to mimic the behavior of his human associates. It is possible that by learning the social psychology of the chimpanzee, information will be gained on fundamental mechanisms essential to acquired meaningful articulation, or conversely, it may turn out that study of the spoken language in the chimpanzee may indirectly lead to further knowledge of basic types of social motivation. Frankly, we are by no means hopeful that the study of language in animals will prove to be an unusually productive field, even though this problem has been and will continue to be particularly intriguing and beguiling.

It is our belief that the study of the subhuman mammals, particularly the more advanced subhuman mammals, offers a rich field of research for the student of basic motivational theory. Present theory places too much emphasis on the physiological drives of hunger, thirst, elimination, and sex. It explains social drives as learned derivations of the physiological drives. Many authorities even suppose the social drives remain dependent on physiological drive reinforcement after their derivation.

During the last two years Meyer (30) has carried out extensive studies at the Wisconsin Primate Laboratory on the effect of hunger drive, measured by periods of food deprivation up to 47 hours, on a variety of performances by monkeys. Somewhat to our surprise it has been found that the food deprivation period is a variable of *no importance* in determining the learning performance of the monkey. Learning by the monkeys is equally efficient 1 hour, 23 hours, and 47 hours after eating. Likewise, the latency of their responses, their orientation to the test situation, and activity in the test cage do not vary significantly with time since eating. It is possible, of course, that monkeys are not familiar with modern motivational theory. It is also possible that the monkey is so closely related to man that he must be regarded as an "atypical" animal.

It seemed only reasonable to us that hungry monkeys should be less discriminating in their choice of food than satiated monkeys and should show some tendency to choose on the basis of quantity rather than quality. Initially, norms were obtained on a group of eight monkeys for frequency of choices of small pieces of a preferred food against larger pieces of a semi-preferred food. Then we tested the same animals following 1, 23, and 47 hours of food deprivation. No significant differences were uncovered among the deprivation groups, although it is interesting to note that the 23-hour hungry animals were, in fact, more responsive to quality than to quantity and to a greater degree than the 1 and 47-hour groups (14). Again, our monkeys displayed a distressing faith in psychological hedonism rather than in the importance of drive condition. It is possible, of course, that the critics who so ably refuted hedonistic doctrine thirty years ago may have made one small mistake —they may have been wrong.

We have found that monkeys can learn to solve mechanical problems which have never been associated with extrinsic incentive, and we have formally described their behavior as motivated by a manipulation drive (20). Some monkeys, at least, apparently solve problems as efficiently under this condition as the most skillful monkeys solve these puzzles for a food reward. There are, of course, many observations of chimpanzees' and children's solving mechanical puzzles where the only obvious motivation has been curiosity or manipulation.

Common sense tells us that our basic theories of motivation are erroneous or at least incomplete. It is our obligation to devise experiments of sufficient ingenuity and precision to reduce the obvious to quantification. We once observed, at the Vilas Park Zoo in Madison, an adult orangutan playing with two blocks of wood, one containing a cylindrical hole and the other a square hole, and two plungers, one with a circular and the other with a square face. He tried repeatedly to fit the square plug into the round hole. It is not the intellectual error which is of interest, however, but the fact that he would frequently work for many minutes on a task which was not reinforced by thirst, hunger, elimination, or sex—unless one is willing to adopt an extreme psychoanalytic interpretation.

We do not believe that monkeys, apes, and men are the only deviant mammals with respect to current motivational theory. We are convinced that cats can learn on the basis of a manipulatory drive which is not derived from primary physiological needs; we strongly suspect that an affectional drive can be demonstrated in dogs under conditions which would preclude secondary conditioning to hunger; our faith is so boundless, we are even experimenting on rats.

We are convinced that social motivation is, in large if not predominant part, learned, but we remain unconvinced that the nature of all important fundamental mechanisms is now understood and we are skeptical if present learning theory is adequate to explain this important phase of the process. The subhuman animals, particularly those species capable of rapid and efficient learning, should and eventually will provide us with basic information for a comprehensive learning theory applicable to a wide variety of social situations.

During the last five years we have studied the inter-problem or between-problems learning in a long series of problems of a particular kind and have found that there is progressive improvement from problem to problem in each series. Problems of a kind, originally solved only after many errors, are eventually solved immediately and without errors. We have investigated this phenomenon in monkeys and children in a wide variety of behavior situations. We have found no exceptions to our "learning set" theory and believe that it has broad applicability.

After we had published a formulation of our theory we found that it had in principle already been proposed by the anthropologist Bateson (2), who had described the phenomenon as "deutero-learning" and had italicized the words which we believed most descriptive of the theory, the animal *learns to learn*. Our contribution has been to provide extensive, rigidly controlled experimental data in support of such a theoretical formulation. Bateson wrote (2, p. 122): "We need some systematic framework or classification which shall show how each of these habits is related to the others, and such a classification might provide us with something approaching the chart we lack."

Our own researches, we believe, provide or have begun to provide this "systematic framework." Bateson in his paper discusses the anthropological implications of such a theory. We have indicated its possible role in personality formation in a theoretical paper (19). Magaret (26) has suggested its operation in the clinical field in a later paper. Our researches illustrate the kind of contribution that comparative psychology can make to theoretical social psychology and the psychology of personality.

In summary, we believe that the study of the lower animals with particular reference to learning can be of service in aiding our understanding of problems of social psychology in two ways. We may study in these animals the forces operating in the formation, maintenance, and dissolution of their social groups, and we may study by appropriate experimental procedures the social forces operating to influence the formation of basic social and personality traits. But the study of the behavior of subhuman animals will make a less direct but equally important contribution to social psychology in its service of analyzing, under rigidly controlled experimental conditions, the fundamental nature of neuroses, personality mechanisms, motivation, and learning.

REFERENCES

1. Bateson, G. Social planning and the concept of "deutero-learning." In T. H. Newcomb and E. L. Hartley (Eds.), *Readings in Social Psychology.* New York: Henry Holt and Co., 1947. Pp. 121–128.

2. Beach, F. A. Comparison of copulatory behavior of male rats raised in isolation, cohabitation, and segregation, *J. genet. Psychol.,* 1942, *60,* 121–136.

3. Bijou, S. W. The development of a conditioning methodology for studying experimental neurosis in the rat, *J. comp. Psychol.,* 1942, *34,* 91–106.

4. Bijou, S. W. A study of "experimental neurosis" in the rat by the conditioned response technique, *J. comp. Psychol.,* 1943, *36,* 1–20.

5. Bingham, H. C. Gorillas in a native habitat, Carnegie Instn. Publ. No. 426, August, 1932.

6. Carpenter, C. R. A field study of the behavior and social relations of howling monkeys, *Comp. Psychol. Monogr.,* 1934, *10,* 1–168.

7. Carpenter, C. R. A field study in Siam of the behavior and social relations of the gibbon (Hylobates lar), *Comp. Psychol. Monogr.,* 1940, *16,* 1–212.

8. Carpenter, C. R.　A survey of wild life conditions in Atjeh, North Sumatra, with special reference to the Orang-utan.　Comm. No. 12 of the Netherlands Committee for International Nature Protection, 1938, Amsterdam.

9. Carpenter, C. R.　Sexual behavior of free ranging Rhesus monkeys (Macaca mulatta), *J. comp. Psychol.*, 1942, *33*, 113–162.

10. Carpenter, C. R.　Characteristics of social behavior in non-human primates, *Trans. New York Acad. Sci.*, 1942, *4*, Ser. II, 248–258.

11. Cook, S. W.　The production of "experimental neurosis" in the white rat, *Psychosom. Med.*, 1939, *1*, 293–308.

12. Crawford, M. P.　The co-operative solving of problems by young chimpanzees, *Comp. Psychol. Monogr.*, *14*, 1937, 1–88.

13. Dennis, W.　Infant development under conditions of restricted practice and of minimal social stimulation, *Genet. Psychol. Monogr.*, 1941, *23*, 143–189.

14. Fay, J. C., J. D. Miller and H. F. Harlow.　Food preferences under varying conditions of deprivation.　Unpublished manuscript.

15. Finch, G.　Personal communication.

16. Furness, W. H.　Observations on the mentality of chimpanzees and orang-utans, *Proc. Amer. phil. Soc.*, 1916, *55*, 281–290.

17. Hayes, K. J. and C. Hayes.　Vocalization and speech in chimpanzees. Paper, 1950, M.P.A.　22nd meetings.

18. Harlow, H. F. and H. C. Yudin.　Social behavior of primates: I. Social facilitation of feeding in the monkey and its relation to attitudes of ascendance and submission, *J. comp. Psychol.*, 1933, *16*, 171–185.

19. Harlow, H. F.　The formation of learning sets, *Psychol. Rev.*, 1949, *56*, 51–65.

20. Harlow, H. F., M. K. Harlow and D. R. Meyer.　Learning motivated by a manipulation drive, *J. exp. Psychol.*, 1950, in press.

21. Hunt, J. McV.　The effects of infant feeding-frustration upon adult hoarding in the albino rat, *J. abnorm. soc. Psychol.*, 1941, *36*, 338–360.

22. Kellogg, W. N. and L. A. Kellogg.　*The ape and the child.*　New York: McGraw-Hill, 1933.

23. Levy, D.　Experiments on the sucking reflex and social behavior in dogs, *Amer. J. Orthopsychiat.*, 1934, *4*, 203–224.

24. Liddell, H. S.　Conditioned reflex method and experimental neurosis. Chap. VI in J. McV. Hunt (Ed.) *Personality and the behavior disorders,* Vol. I.　New York: Ronald Press, 1944.

25. Louttit, C. M.　Reproductive behavior of the guinea pig: II. Ontogenesis of the reproductive pattern, *J. comp. Psychol.*, 1929, *9*, 293–315.

26. Magaret, Ann.　Generalization in successful psychotherapy, *J. consult. Psychol.*, 1950, *1*, 64–70.

27. Maslow, A. H. Dominance-quality and social behavior in infra-human primates, *J. soc. Psychol.*, 1940, *11*, 313–324.

28. Maslow, A. H. and S. Flanzbaum. The role of dominance in the social and sexual behavior of infra-human primates: II. An experimental determination of the behavior syndrome of dominance, *J. genet. Psychol.*, 1936, *48*, 278–309.

29. Mead, Margaret. *Cooperation and competition among primitive peoples.* New York: McGraw-Hill, 1937.

30. Meyer, D. Food deprivation and discrimination reversal learning by monkeys. In press, *J. exp. Psychol.*, 1951.

31. Miller, N. E. Theory and experiment relating psychoanalytic displacement to stimulus-response generalization, *J. abnorm. soc. Psychol.*, 1948, *43*, 155–178.

32. Mirsky, J. The Eskimo of Greenland. In Margaret Mead (Ed.) *Cooperation and competition among primitive people.* New York: McGraw-Hill, 1937, pp. 51–86.

33. Nissen, H. A. Field study of the chimpanzee, *Comp. Psychol. Monogr.*, 1931, *8*, 1–122.

34. Riesen, A. H. Innate and experimental factors in visual perception, *Sci. Amer.*, 1950, in press.

35. Stone, C. P. Wildness and savageness in rats of different strains. In K. S. Lashley (Ed.), *Studies in the dynamics of behavior.* Chicago: University of Chicago Press, 1932, pp. 3–55.

36. Stone, C. P. Counteracting the retarding effects of inanition on the awakening of copulatory ability in male rats by testosterone proponate, *J. comp. Psychol.*, 1942, *33*, 97–105.

37. Zuckerman, S. *The social life of monkeys and apes.* New York: Harcourt, Brace and Co., 1932.

Part Three

Interaction in the Cultural Setting

CHAPTER 6

ЛЛЛЛЛЛЛЛЛЛЛЛЛЛЛЛЛЛЛЛЛЛЛЛЛЛЛЛЛ

On Cultural and Psychological Reality

MELVILLE J. HERSKOVITS
Northwestern University

If, as has been stated, the concept of "society" dominated the emergent social science of the nineteenth century, it may equally well be said that the exploration of the concept of "culture" has been one of the outstanding heuristic and operational concerns of the social sciences during the first half of the twentieth. This has been especially true of the latter portion of this period when, the groundwork of preliminary analysis having been laid, the fruitfulness of the idea of culture in clarifying the understanding of all aspects of human behavior began to diffuse into new fields.

At this turn of the half-century, then, it is particularly appropriate to explore some of the epistemological and methodological implications of this concept which we use with such increasing frequency when we study the life of man. Twenty-five years ago, the University lecturer who employed the term found it necessary to devote an hour's discussion, or even more, to distinguish "culture" in the scientific sense from the conception of "culture" as something which marks the behavior of a specialized segment of our society. Today a word of caution suffices, and one may then safely pass on to developing the theme of the nature and function of the phenomenon as a subject for scientific analysis.

Nor are definitions of culture any longer the subject of appreciable controversy. There are few social scientists who today would refuse to accept, in principle at least, the classical statement of Tylor that culture is "that complex whole which includes knowledge, belief, art, morals, law, custom and any other capabilities and habits acquired by man as a member of society" (1). Even short delimitations, such as "Culture is the learned behavior of a people," or "Culture is the man-made part of the environment," bring on no more than critiques of detail as concerns implication or scope. In this category of discussion may be placed the current controversy, largely turning on points of method, whether language is to be studied as a part of culture, or as a phenomenon to be analyzed in terms of an autonomy of its own (2).

What are some of the points on which all students of culture share common ground? It is essential that this solid conceptual base be made explicit as we move toward the far more debatable questions that constitute the terms of reference for this discussion. All students of culture agree, in the first place, that though man's physical structure and inherent mental endowment afford the starting-point for culture in the sense that culture is a peculiarly *human* phenomenon, there is no genetic explanation, such as racial endowments, for the many particular characteristics of the many different cultures that comprise the ways of life of different human groups. They are, further, agreed that culture is the instrument whereby men meet the demands of their natural setting —their habitat, or environment, in the strict use of the term—molding it to their purposes within the limitations placed by technological and other aspects of their ways of living. All agree that every culture constantly changes; the search for an understanding of the dynamics of culture has always prominently marked the work of students of culture. It is likewise accepted that culture, as a phenomenon susceptible of scientific study, exhibits regularities of structure and process. These, it is recognized, permit the drawing of generalizations that will ultimately allow us to achieve prediction in terms of those probabilities that must always be taken into account in scientific analysis, and, in these terms, similarly to achieve some measure of scientific control.

Of all agreements, however, the most basic is the proposition, derived from the first two points just indicated, that culture is *learned*. Whether it be held that a culture subsumes the behavior of a group of individuals, or that it is something which, existing by and of itself, holds individuals in its grasp as puppets dancing on the strings of custom, none denies that the adaptation of the individual to the way of life of his group derives from his capacity to learn that way and to cope with its demands. The phenomenon of learning, in the broadest meaning of the term, thus affords us an all-important lead in our attempt to analyze the problem of cultural and psychological reality, and points the path which we must now explore.

Learning is essentially a process which marks the maturation of the individual, and, in the final analysis, is employed best to designate the non-biological or modified biological responses he comes to control in effectively mastering the demands of his total setting. In the process of growing up, that is, the individual must, if he is to survive, adapt himself to his natural setting, and to the other individuals with whom he is to come into contact. But this is not all; he must also come to control those resources of the ways of life of the particular group into which he is born that are essential to his survival as an individual. He must acquire its language, he must have a measure of awareness of its traditionally sanctioned conceptions of the universe, he will come to know its accepted modes of self-expression in musical and artistic and literary forms, he must order his life in terms of its value-systems and recognized goals. He must, in short, make a triple adaptation—to his natural setting, to the fellow-members of his society, and to the patterns of his culture.

Holding the natural environment as a constant, something given in the experience of all members of a particular society, we thus have these three dimensions of human experience—behavior, society, and culture. These terms will at once be recognized as the key concepts of the three disciplines of Psychology, Sociology, and Anthropology. They are phenomena that, in decreasing numbers, mark off organisms as we move up the phylogenetic scale in the biological series. All animals, that is, have characteristic modes of behavior, but by no means all are social animals, while none but man has culture. From another point of view, and as concerns man, the order of magnitude is reversed; behavior always reduces itself to the behavior of an individual in a given situation; social institutions reflect modes of behavior in inter-personal relations; cultural behavior comprises the totality of the sanctioned responses of a people.

Now these facets of human existence, or of the life of lower orders where any of them is germane, are acquired as the result of processes which can be differentiated in a manner similar to that in which the phenomena themselves are to be distinguished. Adult behavior of any creature, it scarcely needs be pointed out here, is in the main the result of those conditionings or of those imitative or volitional reactions that we have termed *learning*. Those particular learned elements in behavior that have to do with the adjustment of one member of a social group, animal or human, to his society, is termed *socialization*. The third process, under which culture is learned, less well known than the two that have been given, is to be termed *enculturation*. The necessity for this last term arises from the fact that, since by general agreement, only man has that body of learned behavior we call culture, cumulatively handed on from generation to generation by the symbolisms of language, while man shares with many other forms the designation "social," the concepts of society and culture are thus to be differentiated and the processes whereby the organism adapts himself to the two must likewise be distinguished.

It would be fallacious to conceive these three processes as mechanisms operating independently of one another. In man, that is, much of behavior is the result of the particular conditioning the individual receives as a member of his society, in terms of the accepted patterns of its culture. Phrased somewhat differently, it may be said that learning is channelled, especially during the early years of life, by the experience of socialization, while his relations with other members of his society, in terms of his creative efforts no less than of his conformity, will be effected through the process of enculturation. Essentially, it depends on the focus of interest as to which term—learning, socialization, enculturation—will be most relevant in approaching a given topic in the study of human behavior. The results of learning, as far as the individual is concerned, are manifest in a social setting and in terms of his culture; cultural patterns are the consensuses of individual behavior patterns; and both are maintained in orderly form by the social structures and web of inter-personal relations that knit every human group into the functioning unit we find it to be.

Let us, then, turn to that aspect of the learning process whereby the individual is prepared to function in terms of the totality of sanctioned ways of behavior of his group we call their culture. The entire procedure—education in the broadest sense of the word—is lifelong, but understandably bears down with most force in the earlier years of life, when as a relatively passive figure in the family constellation, the human being is molded to conformity with the basic elements of his culture. There are those who hold that at this period the enculturative experience shapes his entire personality, so that, in a sense, he lives his life in terms of predetermined configurations, in a frame from which he cannot emerge. This, however, has by no means moved out of the realm of hypothesis, and need not be examined here, since it is not critical for the point under consideration. From whatever point of view we regard the enculturative process—whether in terms of conditioned responses, gestalt, or the psychiatric-psychoanalytic approach—we cannot but conclude that the basic lines along which a vast proportion of later behavior will be manifest are laid down in the first years of life.

What is impressive in considering the enculturative experience is the relative ease and the thoroughness with which it achieves its end. While evidence is not lacking to show that the disciplining of the child to bring him into line with accepted canons of behavior is not accomplished without a certain degree of stress, we undoubtedly tend to overlook the painlessness of much of the process. One of the reasons for this tendency arises from the fact that so much of our attention has been fixed on the socializing aspects of enculturation, where formal discipline does enter to a larger degree than in other phases of the process. There is punishment, for example, for a repeated breach of discipline whereby an improper term of address is used to an elder, to say nothing of those cases where graver breaches entailing excretory or sexual functions are involved. But we need also consider those numerous elements in culture where the child failed to follow accepted standards as he learns how to sing the songs of his people, to manipulate words and ideas, to dance, to model, to paint, to carve—to name but obvious instances where learning is exploratory, eager, and immediately rewarding—and where the child is not only not punished, but may be encouraged in his experimentation.

How much of culture is acquired by simple, voluntary imitation, especially as regards these aspects where the creative drives are called into play, cannot be said, for the matter has not been studied. One may, for instance, ascribe the deep-seated pattern of rhythmic expression in music that marks African culture to the fact that the infant is carried everywhere in a cloth astride its mother's back, and is not removed when she dances, or pounds her mortar, or walks to market. Even as a young ambulant child, it will be present at all manner of rites where singing and drumming reinforces the conditioning of the earlier experience. But it is one thing to note the concomitant occurrence of two phenomena in a single setting, and quite another to adduce scientific proof that the two stand in a causal relationship to each other.

Yet the importance of the creative aspects of human life, not only for an understanding of what might be termed the positive as against the inhibiting forms of enculturation, but also for the analysis of broad questions of cultural dynamics, becomes apparent as soon as the point is made. It is not easy, however, to find controlled studies of such a problem as the role of fantasy in the creative process—in technology and the realm of ideas no less than in the arts, and in later no less than in early life—and thus arrive at an understanding of its function in adjusting men to their total setting. One cannot, when contemplating the slight attention given such an important phenomenon in human life, refrain from speculating whether the very semantics of the term "social," which logically focusses the attention of social psychologists almost exclusively on the "socialization" process, has not stood in the way of those concerned with the problem of the psychology of man in society from taking the total scene into account. The point may well be raised whether the sub-discipline of social psychology itself does not need to be supplemented by a complementary sub-discipline of cultural psychology.

There is another reason why a stress, so strong as at times almost to seem compulsive, is laid on the study of the inhibitory, "socializing" devices of a society to the well-nigh exclusion of those mechanisms which encourage self-expression, fulfilment, and adjustment. If we approach this question with the objectivity for which we strive in assessing any problem in the analysis of cultural developments, we find it not too difficult to comprehend. After all, it was the psychiatrists and psychoanalysts who discovered the role played by the experiences of early childhood in shaping the reactions of the adult. Their concepts and techniques have thus understandably been paramount in influencing the whole field of child-study and child development. But the subjects of these students, it must be recalled, by no means represented even the total range of variation in the personality configurations of the particular societies of Western Europe and America in which they worked. Their subjects were the repressed, the maladjusted, the overtly aggressive—the non-functioning or malfunctioning individuals. Those who have applied their methods and concepts to the larger cross-cultural problems of the relation between personality and culture, despite the many data accumulated and the stimulating hypotheses that have been advanced, are still hampered by the bonds laid down by a discipline derived from the study of the pathological, rather than the total gamut of personality forms.

Because of this, the idea of enculturation affords a conceptual tool for the assessment of the relation between psychology and culture that transcends the limitations of approaches that stress, where they do not lay exclusive emphasis on, those elements in culture that produce mal-adjustments, and that obscure study of the total range of reaction to all the stimuli provided by a culture. The concept of enculturation, that is, opens the way toward a psychology rather than a psychopathology of culture, and in this manner gives us a further tool in our analysis of the reality of culture and the psychological basis of this reality.

Why is the question raised at all concerning the objective reality of the phenomenon we call culture? The answer, in terms of encultura-tion, is strikingly similar to that we find when we seek to understand the hold that instinct theory, or the various theories of human nature, or the hypothesis of the group mind, have had on students of human behavior at one time or another. For all of these derive their force from the fact that the enculturative process is so subtle and pervasive, that the human being lives most of his life demonstrating, albeit un-wittingly, by the automatic character of a vast proportion of his re-sponses, how well he has learned the lesson of living in accordance with the ways of his group.

In the case of the first two psychological theories that have been mentioned, the fallacies that eventually emerged were in large measure discovered and understood by an increasing use of cross-cultural data. This approach, in essence the comparison of ways of life of peoples whose cultures appertain to quite different historical streams, has given us a fresh perspective on the psychological plasticity of man, and repre-sents one of the primary contributions of anthropological science. This result was accomplished by the technique of comparing the responses to all manner of situations met with in our own society by presumed "instinctive" reactions, or because of the assumed existence of overall reactions caused by "human nature," to responses to similar stimuli in societies that lie outside our own particular historical stream. Even such responses as the reaction to pain have been shown to be so varied in different groups that they must be regarded as culturally conditioned, while types of motor behavior, so closely related to the biological organism and restricted by its demands, are today recognized as the result of a process of cultural conditioning that, selected from an admittedly somewhat narrow range of possibility, holds behavior to a yet more restricted range of variation. What appeared to be instinctive, the result of the functioning of human nature, we now know to be automatic, learned, enculturated. We can see, through the analysis of how an identical end of life-subsistence, procreation, aesthetic satisfactions —is achieved by different people in different ways, that throughout his life man is exposed to a continuous bombardment of stimuli which, volitionally or unwittingly, cause him to observe the limits set by his culture for accepted modes of thought and action.

What is important to understand is that, in any given society, the behavior of individuals will be more alike than the behavior of any one of them is like that of members of another society. The enculturative experience, that is, plays on every individual of a given group, etching his conduct in patterns that closely resemble, even though they may not be identical with, those of his fellows in his society. And, though changes always occur, the total body of custom seems to move as a unit, even in changing, while its stability over the years is such as to make persuasive the proposition that it has a life of its own, over which individuals can exert but little influence.

Here we come to the crux of the argument. For to what degree is a man a creature of his culture, to what extent can he be said to be the instrument that shapes it? If we consider culture as something that exists by and of itself, then he is, perforce, its creature. If we regard culture as a reflection of the psychological conditionings plus those accruals that result from the operation of man's inventive ability, then the reality of culture is psychological, and man its master. Both points of view must be assessed in our present analysis.

The argument for the independent existence of culture cannot be lightly brushed aside. There is, first of all, the fact of the continuity of every culture, that far transcends the life of any member of a society that lives in accordance with its patterns. To use the well-known, and best, illustration of this, we may point out that while many cultures concerning which we have adequate historical documentation are recognizable today as developments out of, and in many respects as having identical patterns with, their forerunners several centuries removed, none of the individuals who lived in the earlier times, behaving in accordance with the common body of custom, remains alive today. That is, to put it concisely, cultures continue in recognizable form, while personnel constantly changes. To point the conclusion that culture is the reality which, existing of its own right, provides the path that men follow from birth to death, and that the path is something distinct from the men who traverse it, seems but an exercise in logic that gives the analogy the force of conviction. It is a theorem which, in terms of this logic, needs but to be stated to bring the finality, *quod erat demonstrandum*.

Or we can approach the matter from the point of view of the individual, and develop another theorem leading to an identical conclusion. In this we take into account the conditionings of the enculturative process. The individual is born into a society whose customs, that will frame his conduct, are present before his birth and will continue after his death. His culture, like his society, is a going concern. He has had no hand in its formation, and whatever the degree of creativeness with which he may be endowed, no matter how strongly he may rebel against any of its dictates, his efforts will result, at best, in no more than changes of detail. In the main, though, he will not rebel against his culture at all. Most persons do not question. Those who do rarely realize how slender a proportion of their total culture is comprised by the elements of it they do question. The political revolutionary does not refuse to cast his revolutionary songs in the modal structure and scale progressions of the culture he is in process of changing; his formations, if his organized forces are strong enough, will operate in terms of accepted patterns of military procedure. The one who rebels against the religious and moral system of his time will couch his appeals in the linguistic patterns of his people, use established affect symbols, and employ accepted aesthetic standards in heightening the responses of his followers.

In these terms, culture may be thought of as a kind of psychological iceberg of whose totality but a small portion appears above the level of consciousness. This is why the student of a culture not his own often discerns much of interrelationships, of sanctions, of organization which is quite unapparent to those who order their lives by it. Every student of unwritten languages can testify to the astonishment with which native informants come to realize the existence of the structural patterns of the language they have spoken all their lives, quite unconscious of how regularized their speech was. The same is true of other elements in culture, especially those that comprise implicit sanctions as against the overt manifestations of a way of life. Can it not be argued, then, that a phenomenon which orders the life of a man, despite the fact that he is not conscious of the influence exerted on him by so large a part of it, must be regarded as having an existence of its own?

Still another argument for the autonomy of culture is cast in terms of the independent discovery or invention, in our own culture, within a short space of time, of identical principles, mechanisms, formulae, machines, and other items by two or more persons, working quite without knowledge of each other's efforts. It is on the basis of these facts, and of a study of the manner in which changes in women's fashions occur through the accumulation of small variations from the standard of a given year which, with time, produce a regular cycle of changes, that the concept of culture as a superorganic phenomenon has been advanced by Kroeber. Data of this kind are too well known to need more than mention here; but the relation between the point of view concerning the existence of culture as an independent phenomenon they have been used to document, and the concept of cycles and revolutions of civilization associated with the names of Flinders-Petrie, Spengler, Toynbee, and, most recently, Kroeber himself, is not as well understood. For in the thinking of these writers, man is impotent in the face of culture which, in ordering his existence, carries him as its creature as it grows, flowers, and decays.

The ontological implications of this position, especially in terms of the age-old controversy between the proponents of philosophies of free-will and determinism, are self-evident. The shifts of emphasis in the writings of these later cultural determinists are, however, not so immediately discernible. A moment's reflection makes it apparent that the determining force assumed to exist has changed, in terms of the scientific orientation of our times, from the supernatural to the cultural—though this holds only partially in the instance of Toynbee. But what has also occurred has been a shift from emphasis on the individual to emphasis on culture. In the earlier discussions of the problem, the debate centered on the question of the freedom of man—of *a* man—in the face of Destiny. For the neo-determinists, while the problem of the ability of man as an individual to influence the course of his existence is present by implication, the argument and its documentation is couched in terms of how cultures change, the ways in which change is effected, the degrees of change to be expected and the regularities to be perceived. The individual, that is, has been quite lost sight of despite the formal recognition of his existence given by those who take this point of view.

The response to propositions of the kind we have just sketched is contained in the question, "What is the *locus* of the phenomenon, culture, which under the deterministic hypothesis is something that exists by and of itself?" Psychologists will at once recognize the identity of this question with that raised concerning the group mind. For in that case, it was also asked, "If there is a group mind, where is it to be found?" And it is not without significance for the problem of our present concern to point out that the answer was that the group mind was no more than a reification of the similar reactions of individuals who found themselves responding in a similar manner to a particular stimulus or series of stimuli.

It would seem impossible to frame any other answer to such questions that did not call on belief as a substitute for objective proof. The concept of culture as a phenomenon with an existence, a reality of its own, cannot but be a mystical concept, no matter how skillfully the language of science is called on to phrase the argument in technical terms—terms, which, in practice, call on analogy rather than experimentation to bring conviction. Try as one may to envisage culture as something apart from those who live by it, to think of it as something "carried" by man, the inexorable question, "Where is it? How can one isolate it?" must eventually be faced.

As a matter of fact, the thesis of cultural determinism has never been carried to its logical conclusion. Those who have advanced it, even in most vigorous terms, have always included an escape clause in their contractual obligations concerning it. Too often these reservations have gone unnoticed, or the portrayal of an uncompromising determinism has resulted from the high-lighting of this outstanding feature of their position as a didactic device in the discussion of various points of view when studying theories of culture. There is, for example, no more uncompromising determinist than White, yet we find ample evidence in his writings that he, like others who hold with him, anchors culture firmly in the human organism. "Cultures can no more exist without men than vehicles can move without friction," he says. "But one may regard culture *as if* it were independent of men just as the physicist may consider vehicles as if they were independent of friction . . ." (3). In another place he writes, "The culturologist is well aware that culture does not and cannot exist without human beings. . . . But . . . culture may be treated *as if* it had a life of its own, quite apart from human organisms, just as the physicist may treat a falling body *as if* there were no atmospheric friction" (4).

Kroeber, too, has been at some pains to make quite clear that, as he phrases it, "The *as if* attitude gives us a perfectly adequate way to proceed" in studying cultural phenomena. "I take this opportunity," he wrote in 1948, "of formally and publicly recanting any extravagances and overstatement of which I may have been guilty through overardor of conviction, in my 'Superorganic' and since. As of 1948, it seems to me both unnecessary and productive of new difficulties if, in order to account for the phenomena of culture, one assumes any entity, substance, kind of being or set of separate, autonomous, and wholly self-sufficient forces . . . I would now say that culture was *primarily* intelligible in terms of itself, not *only* in terms of itself" (5).

The *locus* of culture, then, cannot be regarded as anything other than the individuals who, responding to the enculturative process, live in accordance with the traditions of their group. Because the overall conditionings of each member of a group resemble those of every other member, there is given to the totality of the ways of life of the group as a whole, at any given moment and over the years, a degree of solidity and stability that justifies us in treating this totality *as if* it existed in its own right. This is a recognized and essential technique in the procedures of science. Because friction presents a subject for study does not mean it operates as an independent entity in the physical world, instead of as a function of the movement of certain types of bodies. In the study of culture, by taking a comparable position, we remove the question from the realm of subjects for philosophical debate and treat it as a problem for scientific analysis.

We see how important is the enculturative approach to the problem when we consider culture not as an entity which controls man, but rather as a series of definable reactions which mark the behavior of all members of definable reactions which mark the behavior of all members of a given society to the multifarious situations of life with which all must cope. These reactions vary from those which make up the gross, immediately discernible blocks of culture we term aspects, and the institutions that implement the ends of adjusting men to their setting that must be achieved by each of these aspects, to subtleties of motor behavior, of thought, of attitude, and of affect that only become apparent under the skilled utilization of the most sophisticated techniques of field research.

As so often in current discussions of the nature and function of culture, especially in probing the psychological springs from which it flows, we profit from the insights into this problem from the pen of Edward Sapir. "Culture is not, as a matter of sober fact," he said in one paper, "a 'given' at all. It is only so by a polite convention of speech. As soon as we set ourselves at the vantage-point of the culture-acquiring child, the personality definitions and potentials that must never for a moment be lost sight of, and which are destined from the very beginning to interpret, evaluate, and modify every culture pattern, sub-pattern, or assemblage of patterns that it will ever be influenced by, everything changes. Culture is then not something given but something to be gradually and gropingly discovered. We then see at once that elements of culture that come well within the horizon of awareness of one individual are entirely absent in another individual's landscape" (6). The new member of a society, that is, learns while exposed to the situations of his culture, and by the accepted methods of training, but as an individual reacts to this continuum of experience in terms of his particular bio-psychic composition, and the particular concatenations of circumstances which, both as an infant and in later life, he may encounter.

This makes of culture a most complex phenomenon, introducing the important concepts of variation and consensuses which, whether explicitly named or employed without designation, have been responsible for most of the advances in recent research. For a culture, in these terms, is first of all seen as a series of limits to behavior, ordered in terms of those institutionalized forms we call cultural patterns. From this, we arrive at a recognition of the factor of individual variations in behavior which, when pressing against these limits, afford a rationale for the dynamics of cultural change, just as the failure of these limits to give under the pressure of creative individuals explains the stability of culture. Here again, though, we recognize that this is in a manner of speaking, for in psychological terms the problem is recast as acceptance or rejection of innovations by the persons who comprise a group. There are no cultural walls as such.

It is from the point of view of this approach, however, that the significance of the concept of enculturation is seen to stand out in bold relief. There is implied here no denial of the importance of those aspects of the total conditioning process subsumed under the heading of socialization, by which the developing child learns the proper modes of implementing his relationships with his fellows. From this point of view, it is these processes which, as has been pointed out, bring the individual into line with accepted canons of social behavior, that operate most strongly to give stability to the culture of his group. But the enculturation of the individual spreads farther over the totality of his culture, and endures throughout his lifetime. In the early years, a person is enculturated to those elements in his culture where the creative forces can play most freely, as well as to those that exact conformity. Moreover, the process continues throughout his life, whenever he comes upon facets of his culture that are new to him—a circumstance that occurs to adults of even the least complex societies far more frequently than is generally recognized.

One needs but to think back on current usage to recognize that the term socialization can be used in the case of adults only in a negative sense. The "difficult" deviant, whose conduct is not in accord with accepted modes of behavior, is said to be "badly socialized," or one may speak, in such a case, of the need for an individual of this kind to become socialized—that is, of the need for the person in question to learn to conform. Yet, again, if we turn to the individual who is not aberrant but who, in our own society, let us say, comes on a style of poetry or art with which he is unfamiliar, it is immediately relevant, in terms of cultural analysis, to say that, to the degree he accepts it, he is being enculturated to a newly discovered element in his own culture. And if he develops a new form of verse and enough of those to whom he recites it, or who read it, find it acceptable, and thus develop a new tradition in poetry, each additional person who discovers it thereby furthers the process of his own enculturation.

It has been pointed out that the enculturative experience is extraordinarily subtle, extraordinarily effective, producing men and women so many of whose reactions are automatic that it is not surprising that human beings have come to be regarded by some students as automatons. One of the enculturative mechanisms whose role in bringing about this result has received little attention is the well-known mechanism of cue-reduction. To say that the process of enculturation is extraordinarily subtle is but to say that the cues which initiate responses are extraordinarily fine. It is presumably because of the operation of a mechanism of this sort, where the reduction of stimuli to the level of subliminal perception occurs over a vast proportion of the total range of every individual's behavior, that we gain so strong an impression that man is to such a degree the creature of his culture.

How effective this is can be seen if we reflect on how confusing it is to move into a culture other than one's own—even into another subculture, where broad, overall cultural elements such as language and basic social configurations are shared in common. Even in the most obvious aspects of behavior, it takes time to learn how to behave. A young man will move out of a group where not a word has been spoken and return with a desired object; the cue has been so remote from one's experience that it is impossible to imagine how communication has been established. A cross-cultural study of what we term, with scientific disdain, intuition, might be pursued with considerable profit. To what degree is the fact that certain peoples react surely to other personalities, even on the basis of slight contact, the result of a pattern whereby subliminal cues are, as a matter of course, taken into account rather than, as with ourselves, distrusted?

The problem of cultural and psychological reality is thus one of defining in the most precise terms the reaction of the individual to his total setting, and the manner in which this setting conditions the individual. It is here that the studies in the relationship between personality and culture have made their primary contribution. When extended by concern for the positive as well as the negative aspects of personality structure, and by a more considered utilization of the concept both of individual and intra-cultural variation, it is to be expected that the fallaciousness of the dichotomy too often drawn between the individual and culture will be replaced by a concept of interaction between custom and people that, both in cultural and psychological terms, is the scientific reality.

Our discussion has thus far dealt primarily and properly with the methodological aspects of our subject. It would, however, fail to set the question in adequate perspective were its epistemological implications left entirely unexplored. This is a vast field, but certain considerations of this order can be mentioned in terminating our analysis.

In essence, the matter here before us is best indicated by the phrase "cultural relativism." Granting that man's approach to reality is through his bio-psychic endowments as shaped by his personal experience, and that that experience is bounded by the limits of the culture of his group, does it not follow that there are as many realities as there are cultures? Here the problem of ultimate values enters intimately, but the matter by no means rests there. For one may raise the question as well concerning the reality of what is termed the objective world, the world perceived by the senses, in such of its aspects as mass and volume, time and space. It involves, ultimately, the question of the validity of the findings of science, a point that has not been ignored by the philosophers who have taken the problem into account.

Thus Suzanne Langer, in her consideration of the role of symbolism in shaping thought, commenting on the psychological interaction between percept and understanding says, "The eye and ear make their own abstractions, and consequently dictate their own peculiar forms of conception. But these forms are derived from exactly the same world that furnished the totally different forms known to physics. There is, in fact, no such thing as *the* form of the 'real' world; physics is one pattern which may be found in it, and 'appearance' or the pattern of *things* with their qualities and characters, is another. . . . The world of physics is essentially the real world construed by mathematical abstractions, and the world of sense is the real world construed by the abstractions which the sense-organs immediately furnish" (7). This, of course, in terms of cultural analysis refers essentially to differences in perception as influenced by sub-cultures, essentially of our own cultural orientation. How much the more impressive is the position when carried into the cross-cultural field where, one is tempted to say, there are as many variations in logical presuppositions as there are cultures. It was this that prompted another philosopher, Grace deLaguna, to write, "If the scientific mode of thought can sustain itself only through continuous growth and self-regeneration, it can survive only in a social order permeated by its own philosophic faith and itself capable of cultural transcendence. Physical science deprived of these conditions must eventually wither like a plant cut off at the roots" (8).

Science, itself, is continuously presented with difficulties arising from the need to cope with relativistic symbols. Consider, for example, translation of time into distance. In the study of slaving operations in Africa, for years it seemed self-evident that slaves had been transported from great distances inland to the slave markets of the coast because of the long time required for the journey. It was only after repeated analyses of the available documents that it became apparent that no attempt had been made to ascertain how far the daily trek might have been, or how often the coffle might have stopped on the way, and for how long. Or, cross-culturally, one has only to discover that for some peoples day-after-tomorrow is three, and not two, days, or a week of what to us would be seven days is eight. All that is needed is a convention whereby both ends of the time sequence in question are counted in reaching the total. And as regards perception of color, the data are so rich that one needs only mention the confusion of designation and the arbitrariness with which lines of distinction are drawn to make the point—how, for many peoples, dark blue and black are held to be the same color, or orange and brown are classified together.

Certain very important aspects of the problem of objective reality are raised when such matters as the cultural definition of pathological states are taken into account. This is particularly true of psychopathological categories. Again, it is a commonplace to say that the saint of yesterday might well, in terms of present patterns, today have been regarded as manifesting a degree of withdrawal from reality that would have resulted in his being confined. In discussing the problem recently with a group of practicing psychiatrists, it was interesting to note that one very practical problem raised was whether a Negro from the South Side of Chicago, brought in for treatment because he talked with the Holy Ghost and purported to be able to heal the sick because of a gift of tongues, should be confined as a psychotic. Is a man or woman, enculturated to patterns of belief wherein the nearness of the beings who control the universe is accepted as a basic tenet, beyond dispute, to be diagnosed properly in terms of the system of thought that arises out of a mechanistic world-view? Far from being an academic question; it is something that rises to the level of national policy in dealings between peoples whose epistemologies derive from differing premises.

It is in the field of values that relativism is most discussed. It should be made clear in this context that a cultural relativistic point of view does not entail moral anarchy in the area of values, since it is essentially a cross-cultural and not an intra-cultural matter. The question of relativism within cultures need not be raised here, for the degree of similarity in the enculturative experience of all the members of a given society is sufficient to ensure that all will be inculcated with the tenets of a single body of standards. As a result, a low degree of variation in the values held by these persons will restrict the range of common attitude and characteristic reaction. From the cross-cultural point of view, it is a matter of sifting out those *universals* in the ordering of conduct that comprise the least common denominators in the code of all human groups, from the *absolutes* that the people of a given society may devise, and then insist on as universally valid in their dealings with groups of differing orientations. The psychology of *ethnocentrism* is a subject—an all-important subject—to which far too little attention has been paid by social psychologists. For this attack holds the solution to the baffling question: Where is even the most objective among men to find the cultural boot-straps with which to elevate himself above his own conditioning, and above his own deeply enculturated reactions to customs that are in conflict with the values of his own system?

The ambivalence manifest in reactions to the relativistic position itself documents the point. On the one hand, all the findings from the study of many cultures point to its validity. In each, the system of values, techniques, sanctions calls forth intense devotion from the members of the society who live in accordance with it. On the other hand, the absolutist tradition, manifested in many centuries of evangelical religion, and the basic assumption as to the superiority of the society in which we live, has enculturated us with a militant ethnocentrism that dies hard. Relativism is thus at once acceptable and not acceptable. One anthropologist, commenting on a discussion of it, held it to be a denial of the importance of the study of values—which, obviously, is not the case. A philosopher, declaring that it was the only possible conclusion to be drawn from the study of cross-cultural data, followed with a statement that its acceptance would render moral judgments impossible—which might be true cross-culturally, but scarcely so within a society.

This is not the place, however, for an extended discussion of the questions raised by the relativistic position. For our purpose, it is enough that its significance for the problem of cultural and, to no less extent, of psychological reality be recognized; and that the psychological no less than the anthropological study of culture take into full account the role of the enculturative experience in giving men that view of the world which, for them, frames the ultimate reality of their existence.

REFERENCES

1. Tylor, E. B. *Primitive Culture* (New York, 1874), p. 1.
2. Voegelin, C. F. and Z. S. Harris. "Linguistics in Ethnology," *Southwestern Jour. of Anth.,* vol. i (1945), pp. 455–465; C. F. Voegelin, *Word* (1949), pp. 33 ff.; C. F. Hockett, "Language 'and' Culture: a Protest," *Amer. Anthropologist,* vol. lii (1950), p. 113.
3. White, L. A. *The Science of Culture,* (New York, 1949), p. 408. Italics added.
4. *Ibid.,* p. 144. Italics as in the original.
5. Kroeber, A. L. "White's View of Culture," *American Anthropologist,* vol. L (1948), p. 410, pp. 407–408.
6. Mandlebaum, D. (Ed.). *Selected Writings of Edward Sapir in Language, Culture and Personality* (Berkeley, 1949), p. 596.
7. Langer, S. K. *Philosophy in a New Key* (New York, New American Library—Mentor Books), pp. 73–74.
8. deLaguna, G. A. "Cultural Relativism and Science," *Philosophical Review,* vol. li, p. 166.

CHAPTER 7

⊓⊔⊓⊔⊓⊔⊓⊔⊓⊔⊓⊔⊓⊔⊓⊔⊓⊔⊓⊔⊓⊔⊓⊔⊓⊔⊓⊔⊓⊔⊓⊔⊓

Cultural Factors in the Structuralization of Perception

A. I. HALLOWELL
University of Pennsylvania

INTRODUCTION

In recent years some psychologists, psychiatrists, psychoanalysts, and anthropologists have discovered a common field of interest in the exploration of the relations between cultural variability and personality structure. This is not the only area, however, in which significant problems of an interdisciplinary nature are to be found. In 1947, two psychologists, Goodenough and Anderson, published an article entitled "Psychology and Anthropology: Some Problems of Joint Import for the Two Fields" (1). They selected a few problems for brief discussion which, they said, "constitute only a small sample of the endless number that are of joint concern to anthropologists and psychologists." "The major problem of interest to the psychologist and perhaps also to the anthropologist," they wrote, "is the problem of the organization of perceptions and the manner in which *sense data* are integrated and tied in with the *practical experience* of the individual to produce effective adaptations in a particular environment." (Italics ours.) As a concrete example they point out that reputed superiority in distance vision in one group as compared with another "may arise not so much from greater acuity as from experience and training in interpreting cues that are available to both."

This illustration defines a problem by indication that perceiving, when measured in terms of a scale of efficiency, may not be a simple function of an individual's organic make-up alone but be related to his group membership and thus involve differential cultural factors. However, the actual variables in perceptual experience are much more complex than this simple example would suggest since much more than "sense data" are involved and areas of behavior far beyond "practical experience" require analysis. What the authors failed to point out in this article was the radical shift in emphasis which, in the past two decades, has been occurring among psychologists themselves in approaching the study of perception.

It has been this shift in emphasis that now makes possible, it seems to me, a closer rapprochement between anthropologists and psychologists. And it is worth noting that this revitalization of the investigation of perception seems to have been due to the interest which social psychologists have taken in the problem. As early as 1935, for example, Sherif pointed out that "Social psychology has studied individual differences in *response* to a social environment, but it has never recognized that each one of us *perceives* this environment in terms of his own personal habits of perceiving; and that cultural groups may differ from one another in behavior, because of fundamental differences in their ways of perceiving social situations" (2). At any rate, in the present state of our knowledge, we have departed a long way from the notion often held by the proverbial man in the street and, to some extent, by nineteenth-century psychophysics, that we literally see with our eyes and hear with our ears; the logical inference from this being that the world is mirrored in the perceiver. The myth of the passivity of the perceiver already has been disposed of.

A more inclusive formulation of the relevant variables involved has led, first, to an increasing interest in "behavioral" or "functional" factors of perceptual organization, i.e., "those which derive primarily from the needs, moods, past experience, and memory of the individual" in contrast with "autochthonous" or "structural" factors "derived solely from the nature of the physical stimuli and the neural effects they evoke in the nervous system" (3); secondly, to a fuller appreciation of the extent to which non-sensory or directive factors such as purpose, need, value, stress, tension, etc., are functionally significant in perceiving (4); and, thirdly, to a consideration of the relation between personality organization and perception (5).

Thus the door has been thrown open to the investigation of a wide gamut of problems in the functional area which, on the one hand, include the question of the cultural constituents of perception and, on the other, idiosyncratic determinants rooted in the personality structure of the individual. What now seems more clearly indicated than hitherto, perhaps, is the need for the formulation of a theoretical framework which will resolve any initial separation of structural and functional factors (6). Some such framework of theory would be valuable for anthropology, too, since in actual life situations what we observe is an integral picture of perception in all its functional complexities. What I have tried to do in some of the concrete illustrations that follow is to discriminate analytically different classes of significant variables in perception. Among these are culturally derived variables which, to my mind, fall nicely into place in the more inclusive frame of reference which is now becoming established in psychology. But before going into a more detailed discussion of these I should like to state briefly in my own words why it seems to me that cultural variables are inevitably constituents of human perception.

Dynamically conceived, perception is one of the basic integral functions of an on-going adjustment process on the part of any organism viewed as a whole. While its cognitive aspects are necessarily of importance, the traditional interest in these led to an overemphasis upon them with a concomitant underemphasis upon the relation of perceptual processes to the molar aspects of behavior. For once viewed in its total behavioral context perception cannot be isolated from action (7), that is, from motivated and goal-directed behavior (8). Consequently, the perceptual field of the organism must be structuralized in a manner that bears a direct relation to its activities, no matter what these may be. One of the basic questions, therefore, is how a particular type of organism becomes prepared for action.

In the case of an organism with man's zoological status we know that at birth the human individual is never prepared for the full round of activities that will be eventually demanded of him. Thus we can make a postulate that holds for human behavior everywhere. Whatever capacities members of our species may possess because of their phylogenetic background, nevertheless, past experience, acquired behavior patterns, an organized personality structure, comprise a set of variables that are *always* relevant to the question of how the human organism becomes prepared for action. This generic postulate, a commonplace in anthropology, accords with Bruner and Postman's basic axiom in the study of perception, viz., "that perceiving is a process which results from the stimulation of a prepared or *eingestellt* organism" (9).

But there is also a corollary empirical fact that must be taken into account so far as human behavior is concerned. If we keep mankind as a whole in view we must say that different segments of the human species, or *groups* of human individuals, are prepared for quite different patterns of activity through different modes of training and experience, through orientation to different systems of value, motivations toward different goals and through the creation of different needs. In our species, therefore, what is learned and the content of acquired experience in one society as compared with another constitute important variables with reference to the full understanding, explanation, or prediction of the behavior of individuals who have received a *common* preparation for action. That is to say, the overt behavior and the meaningful content of the experience of the human being is demonstrably related to the traditional cultural attributes of a group, to the socially transmitted culture patterns that distinguish one human society from another. What becomes perceptually significant to the *eingestellt* human organism cannot be considered apart from a continuum that views the human individual as an adjusting organism, motivated, goal-directed, and psychologically structured as a functioning unit in a socio-cultural system. Culture patterns considered as traditional instrumentalities of human existence function as selective agencies in the emergence of the kind of behavioral environment in which a group of human beings carry on their activities. Consequently the psychological field in which human behavior takes place is always culturally constituted, in part, and man's responses are never reducible in their entirety to stimuli derived from an "objective" or surrounding world, in the physical or geographic sense. Inevitably then, personal adjustment in a behavioral environment with culturally constituted properties produces variability in the phenomena of set and expectancy so that in any given perceptual situation such factors take on a differential directive importance.

In this connection, I should like also to point out that if we conceptually integrate perception to adjustment as an on-going process and recognize that cultural variables in man imply different modes of adjustment in different behavioral environments, then the three generic processes in perception that Bruner and Postman (10) have stressed—

selection, accentuation and fixation—fit into the conceptual picture from a cross-cultural point of view. The fact that the human organism becomes selectively sensitized to certain arrays of stimuli rather than others is most certainly a function of the individual's membership in one cultural group, rather than another, whatever other factors may be involved. Likewise the fact that certain stimuli "are accentuated and vivified at the expense of others" may be examined with reference to the differential experience of groups of individuals, as well as with reference to idiosyncratic determinants. Bruner and Postman seem to have recognized this possibility themselves since in another article (11) in which they refer to the fact that "there is experimental evidence that objects which are important or personally relevant are remembered as larger than neutral objects." A footnote is appended in which they say: "We may inquire if it is a universal thing to find the good and important associated with largeness, or whether this is a characteristic of our culture. Certainly our language is full of size-value linkages. A successful man 'grows in stature,' an important problem 'looms large,' etc. We even have moral dicta warning us against the linkage, 'good things come in small packages'—a maxim not readily taught the young child." The question raised is directly related to the general question of cultural variables. The same is true of the process of fixation. For the statement that "what is 'habitually seen' in any given perceptual situation is a function of the fixation of past perceptual responses in similar situations" might well be taken as an hypothesis demonstrable in terms of the emphasis given to perceptual experiences of a certain class that occur in a particular socio-cultural system. Since the human being makes his personal adjustments with reference to the attributes of a particular socio-cultural system, his basic perceptual processes will, in part, be influenced by the "cultural set" imposed by his group membership.

From the standpoint of human adjustment, then, culture has an instrumental function that is co-ordinate with the function of perception. If, as Postman and Bruner assert, "The goal of perception in its broadest sense, is the construction of a meaningful behavioral environment—an environment congruent with 'reality' on the one hand and the needs and dispositions of the organism on the other," in the concrete instance perception in man only fulfills this generic function by means of cultural instrumentalities. Perception in man is not simply a process by which he adjusts to the world at large. And, while it is true that, as compared with other animals, man always builds up a meaningful world with reference to the accumulated and socially transmitted experience of past generations of his kind, this is not the main point. What is of prime psychological significance is that man does this in terms of an organized *schema* for living in which, to some degree, a *provincial* world of articulated objects become defined, characteristic values and goals are represented and institutionalized means of reaching them are emphasized. The human being in every society is motivated from the start to make full and constant use of the provincial and traditional cultural instrumentalities at his disposal. Perception functions integrally with these in the construction of a meaningful behavioral environment defined by culturally constituted attributes.

Finally, I should like to point out that the fundamental reason why cultural constituents in human perception cannot be ignored lies in one of the most characteristic and basic features of man's psychological level of adjustment. This is the ubiquitous role which symbolic mediation plays in building up a meaningful world in our species. This is what has made possible the differential cultural systems that have been investigated and described by the ethnographer (13). At the human level of psychological adjustment, that is to say, we are faced with the empirical fact that the *representation* of various classes of objects, events, relations, and qualities become functionally integrated with the aspects of the world that we meet in direct perceptual experience. In this respect man is set off from other species of animals in which perception is not complicated by the symbolic transformation and representation of experience and among whom the autochthonous factors in perception undoubtedly play a more determinative role, even though modified to some extent by individual needs and experience. Human social life at its very root is functionally dependent upon the role which the symbolic representation of objects, events, and relationships play in establishing a novel kind of behavioral environment which transcends the more simply perceived world of the lower animals. Through the creation, development, and transmission of highly elaborate systems of extrinsic symbolization—hundreds of different languages, a great variety of forms of the plastic and graphic arts, oral and written narratives, etc.—human beings have not only been able to give articulate form to quite differently structuralized cultural worlds; their perceptual responses to the world in which they live and act become mediated, in part, through the kind of concrete symbolic means provided by the cultural tradition of their society. Consequently, it seems to me, it is of some importance to determine what aspects of culture are relevant to perception, how they become involved in the perceptual experience of individuals, the role they play in the total structuralization of the perceptual field and the consequences of this fact for the actual conduct of the individual.

LANGUAGE AND PERCEPTION

It has long been recognized that speech must be considered as a constituent factor in the structuralization and functioning of human perception. But it is somewhat paradoxical that among those who have been the pioneers in stressing this basic fact, we discover philosophers like Ernst Cassirer and Grace deLaguna and, among anthropologists, Edward Sapir, rather than psychologists (14).

One of the major points made by Cassirer, for example, is that "Language does not enter a world of completed objective perceptions only to add to individually given and clearly delimited objects, one in relation to the other, 'names' which will be purely external and arbitrary signs; rather, it is itself a mediator in the formation of objects. It is, in a sense, the mediator par excellence, the most important and most precise instrument for the conquest and the construction of a true world of objects" (15). It is this "objectifying" function of language which permits man to perceive so much of his surrounding world in terms of the discriminations, the concepts, etc., that he not only learns to make but can represent and express. The role of language in self-objectification is not only well recognized but a unique attribute of man. The human world, therefore, takes on qualities and attributes that are completely out of the psychological realm of any other animal, however this difference may be phrased. deLaguna in her book on *Speech,* published in 1927, points out that, "The ability to speak . . . to attach names to things and to make statements about them, does not leave unaltered the world which we see and hear. Perception remains primarily a preparation for direct primary response toward things, but there is superadded the capacity for a more detached and disinterested sort of scrutiny, in which the response that is 'constituted' (to use Dewey's term) is not a bodily act, but the utterance of a descriptive word or phrase. We look at things to see in a new sense 'what' they are. Even when the descriptive epithet, the verbal tag, is not spoken, its utterance is prepared in tentative movements, so that all our attentive scrutiny of things is informed by speech. Human perception is, then, conceptualized to an indefinite degree. Compared to those of men, the percepts of animals are 'blind' (to use Kant's expression) being without concepts" (16). A few years later we find Sapir writing: "Human beings do not live in the objective world alone, nor alone in the world of social activity as ordinarily understood, but are very much at the mercy of the particular language which has become the medium of expression for their society. It is quite an illusion to imagine that one adjusts to reality essentially without the use of language and that language is merely an incidental means of solving specific problems of communication or reflection. The fact of the matter is that the 'real world' is to a large extent unconsciously built up on the language habits of the group. No two languages are ever sufficiently similar to be considered as representing the same social reality. The worlds in which different societies live are distinct worlds, not merely the same world with different labels attached. Even comparatively simple acts of perception are very much more at the mercy of the social patterns called words than we might suppose. . . . We see and hear and otherwise experience very largely as we do because the language habits of our community predispose certain choices of interpretation"(17).

More recently psychologists have shown how, under experimental conditions, "the reproduction of forms may be determined by the nature of words presented orally to subjects at the time they are first perceiving specific visual forms" (18). What is of general significance in these experiments is the fact that the words employed were the bearers of meaningful *concepts*. What the subject did was to modify *objectively neutral* figures in a meaningful manner which corresponded to the concepts of the objects connoted by the stimulus words.

Many years ago when I was trying to demonstrate the relation between language and perceiving to a class I used the stellar constellation we call "the dipper" as an example. I pointed out that this constellation was given a different name in other cultures as, e.g., "the plough" or "the bear" and that although the constellation itself remained constant in form, the actual perception of it was a function of language and associated concepts as well as of our organs of vision. The members of the class seemed to have grasped the point so I was about to pass on to something else when one young lady raised her hand and said, "But it *does* look like a dipper!" And of course it *does*—to us.

Since, by its very nature, the representative function of speech permits a wide variation in the selection of the kinds of objects, events, qualities, and relations that are abstracted and conceptualized, it is fairly clear why the cognitive aspects of man's perceptual experience in a given socio-cultural system cannot be completely isolated from the articulated world of objects and events which is also his behavioral world. We must also remind ourselves that without a cross-cultural linguistic perspective, man's world is likewise a provincial world and that the categories of a language are not objectively apparent to the speakers of it. Furthermore, even aside from the formalized aspect of language, speech may become the bearer of ideas and concepts that reflect one kind of world rather than another and thus be relevant to perception. Köhler has pointed out, for example, that the transition in western culture from a period in which a scientific world view was first articulated in "theoretically formulated sentences" to a later period when this world view became an integral part of the outlook of the man in the street, was mediated through the symbolic representation of it in the functioning of everyday speech. "Long ago," he says, "the most basic convictions of scientific culture lost the character of theoretically formulated sentences. Gradually they have become aspects of the world as we *perceive* it; the world *looks* today what our forefathers learned to say about it; we act and we speak accordingly. In this form the consequences of a few centuries of science are present in the remotest corners of the civilized world" (**19**).

While I do not have time here to elaborate the manifold relations between language and perception, I should like to emphasize the fact that these relations involve much more than the cognitive function of perception. Two rather simple illustrations will, I hope, be sufficient to exhibit the role of language as an integrative factor with respect to the functioning of perceptual discrimination, conceptualization, evaluation, and motivation.

In the vocabulary of the Northern Ojibwa Indians, with whom I have spent considerable time, there is a word—*kinebikominin*—which means "snake berries." Unlike other terms of its class, which usually apply to a single plant species, *kinebikominin* is applied to a number of species. The common feature that is shared by these plants is that their berries are considered inedible by the Indians. Thus the word referred to not only discriminates a special category of berries and provides a verbal symbol that represents them in discourse; at the same time it is a *value* symbol. *Kinebikominin,* as compared with other berries, are no good to eat. I may also say that this evaluation is by no means a simple "adaptive" function to the intrinsic properties of the berries. None of them are poisonous and some other people might place them in the edible category. Thus we can see at once how language provides the Ojibwa with a means of conceptually discriminating one class of berries from another at the cognitive level and at the same time furnishes him with an evaluation of the edible properties of different species of berries. This evaluation, in turn, is integrated with *motivation* in that such berries, once perceptual recognition takes place, are shunned as food. I have seen more than one mother smack the hands of a child who was about to put berries of the tabued category in his mouth or snatch them away, saying at the same moment— *kinebikominin!* Consequently, the child is not permitted to secure firsthand knowledge of the actual properties of these berries but learns instead to discriminate, evaluate, and avoid objects of this class through the symbolic mediation that language provides. "Snake berries" are not simply objects perceived in the surrounding geographical environment. They are selectively discriminated objects of a special category in a behavioral world conceptualized through language. *Kinebikominin* becomes a word that is emotionally toned for the child. It connotes something forbidden, something to be avoided, something one may be punished for eating; a class of objects with a negative valence. So it is quite easy to see how *both* perceptual discrimination and avoidance of such objects are motivated through the integrating function of language.

It is also worth noting that in this society *snakes* are disliked, too, even though there are no poisonous ones about. They are not only avoided, but, if caught, sometimes killed and burnt on a pyre. I was traveling with some Indians once when this happened, the victim being not more than a foot long and entirely harmless. At any rate, the negative evaluation of *kinebikominin* as food is at the same time, through language, tied in with an equivalent attitude toward a class of *animals* that are disliked, avoided, and not eaten. The Ojibwa child soon learns to recognize a class of "snake berries," to discriminate them from edible species and to act toward them in accordance with their culturally evaluated and linguistically symbolized properties, rather than their actual ones. In no other animal, of course, do we have perceptual discrimination, categorization of objects, their evaluation and conduct towards them all integrated through a convential means of symbolic representation. This is one of the novel functions of language in man which any thoroughgoing account of perception considered in the context of adjustment must take account of.

Kinship terms offer another illustration of a type of linguistic phenomena that may be viewed as exercising an integral function in the perceptual discrimination, conceptual classification and motivation of individuals in social interaction. Among other things they may assume directive importance in lowering the threshold of perception with reference to the sexual qualities or attractiveness of women who are culturally sanctioned as sexual objects, or raising in it the case of women of a tabued class.

The Northern Ojibwa furnish one example. Here all women of the forbidden class in a man's own generation are "sisters" in the classificatory sense. They belong to this category because a man *calls* them "sister," not because they are siblings of the same parents and thus genetically related. A man may not even know just how he is related to a "distant" sister or whether there is any blood connection at all. What language does is to override completely the genetic facts in the interest of a discrimination, classification, and sexual evaluation that is socially significant. So *all* women of this category are perceived as "sisters," not just as women in a purely biological sense or as differentiated individuals. Women of this category take on the culturally constituted qualities of their class, i.e., women who are tabu as sexual objects, women who should not even be thought about as such, women who must not be looked at too closely or even talked of too freely. They should be avoided as much as possible in everyday life, so an Ojibwa man would find himself embarrassed to find himself alone with a "sister" and even today if they both happened to be attending the same church service, he would never accompany her there.

The other category of women in a man's own kinship generation are all called by the term *niñ∝m*. This word is roughly equivalent in meaning to the English "sweetheart." Women of this linguistically defined class *always* are "seen" as potential sexual objects. It is practically compulsory to joke with them in the most bawdy fashion on every possible occasion. And they may be pursued and won as actual sexual objects. These are the women whose eyes are continually noticed, whose hair is seen as glossy black and among whom a fat pudenda will not only be noticed but commented upon with admiration.

Language in this illustration, as well as the previous one, is not only integrally related to perceptual experience, it cannot be separated from a total adjustment process in which the individual functions as a unit in a socio-cultural system. In this last illustration the perceptual discrimination that language assists in promoting is a factor in the organization of attitudes and motivational patterns toward sexually approved and sexually disapproved women which is basic to the pattern of social organization in this group. Language plays an important role in building up the necessary attitudes, in maintaining them and in channeling the motivational patterns which, in their turn, reinforce the discrimination of sexual objects by playing their role as directive factors in the perceptual experience of the individual.

ART FORMS AND PERCEPTION

The fact that the graphic arts and literary narratives also may be the source of constituent factors in perception has been noted by those who were neither psychologists nor social scientists. These complex symbolic forms may act as determining influences through a set created in the individual which, in turn, may operate selectively in the perception of objects, qualities, and the values in actual life situations.

In 1889, for example, Oscar Wilde published a famous essay entitled *The Decay of Lying* (20), which took the form of a conversation between two sophisticated young men. Although it teems with some of Wilde's most notorious paradoxes, his fundamental point must be taken quite seriously. It is observed by one of the participants in this literary conversation that one of the popular cries of the time is "Let us return to Life and Nature" (p. 20) but he comments that if "we regard Nature as the collection of phenomena external to man, people only discover in her what they bring to her. . . . (Wordsworth) found in stones the sermons he had hidden there" (p. 21). "Life," it is maintained, "imitates art far more than art imitates life (p. 32). . . . The 19th century, as we know it, is largely an invention of Balzac. . . . We are merely carrying out, with footnotes and unnecessary additions, the whim or fancy or creative vision of a great novelist" (p. 35). We can, indeed, go farther. "Nature follows the landscape painter . . . and takes her effects from him . . . (p. 40). Things are because we see them, and what we see, and how we see it, depends on the arts that have influenced us (p. 41). Where she (Nature) used to give us Corots and Daubignys, she gives us now exquisite Monets and entrancing Pisaros. . . . Nobody of any real culture, for instance, ever talks now-a-days about the beauty of a sunset. Sunsets are quite old fashioned. They belong to the time when Turner was the last note in art" (p. 42).

Andre Gide in his lectures (1922) on Dostoievsky (21) comments on Wilde's paradox as follows: "His meaning is undoubtedly that, accustomed to looking at Nature in a manner that has become conventional, we recognize only what art has educated us to discern. When a painter essays to transmute and express in his work a personal vision, Nature's new aspect seems at first blush paradoxical, insincere, freakish even. However, we speedily grow used to contemplating her with the bias given by this new method, and recognize only what the artist pointed out to us. Hence, to eyes unprejudiced, Nature would really seem to imitate art." Gide then goes on to apply the same principle to Dostoievsky who, he points out, made his readers percipient to traits of human character never noticed before—"I do not necessarily mean rare ones," he says, "but simply phenomena to which we had been so far blind." "We exist on given premises," observes Gide, "and readily acquire the habit of seeing the world, not so much as it actually is; but as we have been told and persuaded it is." An equivalent statement may now be found in any up-to-date textbook in social psychology.

With reference to the problem of cultural factors in perception the observations of Wilde and Gide might be phrased in the form of the general question: To what extent are the symbolic representations of life and nature found in the art of a people of determinative importance as constituent factors in the perceptual organization and experience of individuals (22)?

Recently John Gillin (23), on the basis of the drawings of Northwest coast children studied by Anastasi and Foley, concludes that "children of some of the Northwest coast tribes have apparently so internalized the bizarre and dismembered designs of animals current in their own group that they have great difficulty in seeing, to say nothing of draw-ing familiar animals naturalistically. Both perception and performance tend to remain within the cultural form." In this case the mere fact that children represent animals graphically in the traditional art style does not in itself, it seems to me, indicate that the actual animals of their environment are seen as they are drawn. But Gillin's interpreta-tion sharpens the problem because of the extremely bizarre characteris-tics of the art style itself as viewed by outside observers like ourselves.

To my mind, there is a large area open to empirical investigation once we begin to give serious thought to the relation between the na-ture of objects, qualities, relations, values, etc., as symbolically repre-sented in the art forms of a culture and the the perceptual experience of individuals. With respect to the non-literate peoples the question has a negative as well as a positive import. What perceptual differences, if any, result from the total absence of certain arts, like painting, or the absence of certain features we now take for granted, like three dimen-sional perspective which in Western culture is only about five centuries old? (24) In other words, did the rise of the representation of scientific perspective in Western painting as a convention lead to any changes in the manner in which subsequent generations of Europeans have come to perceive the spatial aspects of their world?

The fundamental complexity of human perception, then, when viewed in an inclusive frame of reference, arises from the fact that while the perceptual world of the human being is dependent upon the nature of immediate objects and events, it is not dependent upon them alone. It is also dependent upon objects and events not immediately given at the moment but mediated through representative processes. As G. Murphy puts it: "We do not really see with our eyes or hear with our ears. If we all saw with our eyes, we should see pretty much alike; we should differ only so far as retinal structure, eyeball structure, etc. differ. We differ much more widely than this because we see not only with our eyes but with our midbrain, our visual and associative centers, and with our systems of incipient behavior, to which almost all visual perceiving directly leads" (25). In consequence the symbolic represen-tation of meaningful forms, entities, and values in art and, in language, the discriminations of significant classes of objects and events and their conceptualization become important constituents operating through memory, imagination, fantasy, attitudes, or beliefs in the total structuralization of perceptual experience (26). But once we take account of such functional factors in perception we can go a step beyond this.

BELIEF AND PERCEPTION

I shall attempt to demonstrate, by reference to the Northern Ojibwa, how entities that have *no* tangible or material existence may become perceptual objects in the actual experience of individuals. That is to say, the reality of what to outsiders are only symbolically mediated and concretely elaborated images may receive perceptual support through the experiences of individuals for whom such entities are reified in an established system of traditional beliefs. Under these conditions it is even predictable, I think, that some persons will not only report perceptual experiences involving such entities, but will *act* as if they belonged in the category of tangible or material objects.

From a descriptive point of view the belief system of the Northern Ojibwa includes several different classes of non-human "spiritual" entities, i.e., orders of sentient beings that are not classed as *Anicinabek* (men-Indians). It will be unnecessary to describe these in detail here since the major point I wish to make is that the Ojibwa themselves distinguish between these orders of being with respect to the manner in which they become manifest to *Anicinabek*. Their most characteristic manifestation is in dreams and the generic term *pawaganak* may be translated as "dream visitors." Furthermore, *pawaganak* become closely associated with an individual in so far as they function as his guardian spirits. He obtains these guardian spirits in the dreams of his puberty fast and he does not expect these particular *pawaganak* to manifest themselves to him in any other way. In short, the Ojibwa does not *expect* to perceive them under the same circumstances as the objects and events of daily life. By cultural definition *pawaganak* are "perceivable" only in the "inner world" of dreams. But if a man is a conjurer, he may call some of his guardian spirits to his conjuring tent where they become audible to other persons. Consequently, it is particularly interesting to note that there is one reified being, the High God, who never becomes the guardian spirit of an individual, nor appears as a "dream visitor," nor becomes an object of perception even in the conjuring tent. The existence of this being is a matter of faith. By cultural definition the High God is not a perceptible object in any context. If any

Indian reported that he had seen or heard *kadabendjiget,* his veracity would be challenged, or he might be thought "crazy."

Now in addition to these types of spiritual beings, there is another category of special interest. The Ojibwa believe in the existence of certain animals of exceptionally large size, despite the fact that animals of this type are seldom seen. Among others, there are Big Turtles, Big Snakes, Big Frogs, and Thunder Birds. Although these large animals are classed by the Ojibwa with the other fauna of their habitat, in only one or two cases are there actual species of animals of the same family that differ markedly in size. One example would be the Turtles. In this case, there exists one species of large turtle—along with smaller ones that are called the "younger brothers" of *mikinak.* Considered as a class, therefore, the "big" animals are "mythical" animals from our point of view. What is of special interest, even if confusing to us, is that there is a "mythical" *mikinak,* too. I call attention to this because it is likewise paradoxical that the faunal counterpart of this "mythical" turtle is very rare and seldom *seen* whereas the reified *mikinak* has been *heard* by everyone. For along with other *pawaganak* he speaks, and even sings, in the conjuring tent (27). In this conjuring rite a small structure is built which conceals the conjurer. He has the power to invoke the *pawaganak* who happens to be among his guardian spirits. They manifest themselves audibly to the Indians who sit on the ground, outside the tent. These *pawaganak* talk and sing like human beings and the dogma is that it is not the conjurer's voice that you hear. From the standpoint of perceptual experience, therefore, the conjuring rite is a device whereby spiritual entities become reified through sound as the sensory medium. Since *mikinak* always has something to say in a conjuring performance, he becomes a familiar figure to everyone. On the other hand, his actual faunal counterpart is scarcely ever seen.

As I have already pointed out, Thunder Birds, Great Snakes, and Great Frogs have no faunal counterparts. But since they are classified with the fauna of the region in the conceptual scheme of the Ojibwa, it follows, logically enough, that these animals *may* be heard, seen, or some other evidence of their "actual" existence be perceived by any one, even though rarely. Rarity of observation is irrelevant to the conviction that animals of this category actually exist.

Among the large animals, Thunder Birds are familiar to everyone because thunder is their cry. They are put in the avian category, moreover, for a very good reason. Their cries are only heard from late spring until early fall, so it is said that they belong in the same class with the Summer Birds who migrate north at this time and leave the country before winter sets in. As a matter of fact, I once compared the meteorological facts on record regarding the occurrence of thunder with the facts on bird migration to this region and there is an almost perfect correlation (28). So the reification of Thunder Birds like the Great Turtle of the conjuring tent is actually supported by auditory experience, but in a different context. On the other hand, although Thunder Birds may appear to an individual in dreams, they are *rarely* seen. Some years ago there was a man who claimed to have seen *pinesi* (a Thunder Bird) "with his own eyes" when he was about twelve years old. During a severe thunderstorm, he ran out of his tent and there on the rocks lay a strange bird. He ran back to get his parents but when they arrived, the bird had disappeared. He was sure it was *pinesi* but his elders were skeptical because it is almost unheard of to *see* a Thunder Bird. Sometime later the veracity of the boy's experience was clinched when a man who had dreamed of *pinesi* verified the boy's description.

In the case of Big Snakes, Big Frogs, and certain other animals of the same category who are believed to be terrestrial in habitat, it is thought that there are relatively few of them about. And since they are never sought out, like other animals, it is not expected that they will be frequently observed. But there is always the possibility that these animals, or their tracks, may be seen in the most literal sense.

Thus Maman, the best hunter of the Little Grand Rapids Band, a man of high intelligence, and vivid imagination as judged both from common sense observation and his Rorschach record (29), told me he saw one of the Great Snakes when he was hunting moose up a small creek that runs into Family Lake. He was so surprised, he said, that he did not shoot. The creature was moving into the water. He saw the head, which looked something like that of a deer, but without horns. The snake was white around the chin. I asked him about the diameter of the body. "It was as big around as that" he said, pointing to a stove pipe. He said he saw as much of the snake as the diagonal distance across the cabin in which we were sitting at the time, which was about 15–16 feet. The Great Snake moved in a straight path, not this way and that, as the smaller snakes do. I also have another eye-witness account of a Great Snake seen by my informant Chief Berens and his two sons when they were on a hunting trip. Both these accounts document the fact that culturally reified images may, under given conditions, become directive factors in the perceptions of the individual. But these cultural constituents of perception may have much deeper implications than these relatively simple instances demonstrate. For in any given situation they may also evoke deep-seated attitudes and emotions that precipitate action. Congitive and motivational factors become inextricably linked. Great Frogs, for instance, are greatly feared, so that no one wishes to meet one. On one occasion when four Indians were crossing Lake Winnipeg in a canoe and landed on an island where they expected to spend the night, one of them discovered what he interpreted as tracks of a Great Frog. His companions examined the tracks and agreed. All of these men became stricken with fear so although night was approaching and they had a considerable distance to paddle, nevertheless, they felt compelled to leave the island at once.

What I should like to stress in this example is the fact that all of these men were excellent hunters and were accustomed to differentiate the tracks of the various animals that inhabit this region. Yet *all* of them agreed that the marks they saw indicated traces of a Great Frog. Hence the significant thing to be noted is the depth of the affect associated with the conceptualization of Great Frogs. Once this was touched off, it was impossible for any of them to examine the tracks on the beach in the *unemotional* way the tracks of the ordinary fur-bearing animal or a moose or deer would be inspected. And then fear, in turn, made it inevitable that they should leave the island with the greatest haste, since the whole perceptual situation became meaningfully structured in terms of flight. The psychological field in which these Indians were behaving, although culturally constituted, was much more complex than the accounts I have cited in the case of the Great Snakes. Furthermore, the conduct of these men would be completely *unintelligible,* if viewed or analyzed in terms of the "objective" situation alone. Their belief in and attitude toward Great Frogs alone give it meaning and explain their overt conduct (30). It is a concrete exemplification of the general assertion of MacLeod that: "Purely fictitious objects, events and relationships can be just as truly determinates of our behavior as are those which are anchored in physical reality" (31).

As a final example, I wish to discuss another case in which I happen to have a more detailed personal account of the experience of an Indian who "met" and took flight from a cannibal giant—a *Windigo*. A belief in such monsters is an integral part of Northern Ojibwa culture. There are two categories of *Windigowak*. The first comprises actual persons who have turned into cannibals. In this discussion, I am not concerned with *Windigowak* of this class. The second category consists of mythical cannibal giants who may be found roaming the country, especially in the spring, avid for human flesh. They are conceptualized as horrible in appearance, they have hearts of ice and every time they call out they get taller so that to hear the shouts of a *windigo* is enough to make one shudder with fear. Only a few such shouts and he is taller than the towering spruce which are so characteristic a feature of the landscape.

Both categories of *windigowak* are the focus of a considerable number of anecdotes. For just as it was considered necessary to kill actual persons who had turned into cannibals, there are parallel anecdotes which relate the heroic battles between human beings and monster mythical cannibals. Besides anecdotes of this sort there are those told in the first person by individuals who have heard the blood-curdling shouts of a *windigo* in the bush, or by those who have seen the tracks of such a creature. The following anecdote of this class is of particular interest with reference to the total structuralization and functioning of perception since Adam Big Mouth became convinced that a *windigo* was close by, although he never saw him, and only toward the end of the anecdote is there any reference to a shout. The circumstances under which an objectively innocuous situation became perceived as an extremely dangerous one can best be conveyed in Adam's own words:

Once in the Spring of the year, I was hunting muskrats. The lake was still frozen, only the river was open, but there was lots of ice along the shore. When it began to get dark I put ashore and made a fire close to the water edge to cook my supper. While I was sitting there I *heard* someone passing across the river. I could *hear* the branches cracking. I went to my canoe and jumped in. I paddled as hard as I could to get away from the *noise*. Where the river got a little wider I came to a point that has lots of poplars growing on it. I was paddling quite a distance from the shore when I came opposite to this point. Just then I *heard a sound* as if something was passing through the air. A big stick had been thrown out at me but it did not strike me. I kept on going and paddled towards the other side again. But he went back and headed me off in that direction. This was in the spring of the year when the nights are not so long. He kept after me all night. I was scared to go ashore. Towards morning I reached a place where there is a high rock. I camped there and when it was light I went to set a bear trap. Later that day I came back to the river again. I started out again in my canoe. Late in the evening, after the sun had set, there was a place where I had to portage my canoe over to a lake. I left my canoe and went to see whether the lake was open. There were some open places so I went back to get my canoe. Then I *heard* him again. I carried my canoe over to the lake—it was a big one—and paddled off as fast as I could. When I got to the other end of the lake it was almost daylight. I did not *hear* him while I was traveling. I went ashore and made a fire. After this I *heard* something again. I was scared. "How am I going to get away from him," I thought. I decided to make for the other side of an island in the lake. I was sitting by my canoe and I *heard* him coming closer. I was mad now. He had chased me long enough. I said to myself, "The number of my days has been given me already!" So I picked up my axe and my gun and went in the direction of the *sounds I had heard*. As soon as I got closer to him he made a break for it. I could *hear* him crashing through the trees. Between the shore and the island there was a place where the water was not frozen. He was headed in this direction. I kept after him. I could *hear* him on the weak ice. Then he fell in and I *heard* a terrific yell. I turned back then and I can't say whether he managed to get out or not. I killed some ducks and went back to my canoe. I was getting pretty weak by this time so I made for a camp I thought was close by. But the people had left. I found out later that they had *heard* him and were so scared that they moved away.

In the foregoing anecdote there are thirteen references to *hearing* the *windigo*. Auditory stimuli alone appear to have been the chief *physical* source of the subject's interpretation of the initial presence of a *windigo* and all his *subsequent* overt behavior. In principle, therefore, there is some analogy to a linguistic situation although, in speech sounds, there is a very high order of patterning. But in principle a succession of sounds is heard which, although they are physical stimuli, become significant to the perceiver because they also convey a conventional *meaning*. This meaning is only understood because the perceiver has undergone a learning process which makes the meaning intelligible. And intelligibility in linguistically conveyed meanings always involves concepts. Analogously, the sounds heard by Adam "meant" *windigo* to him. But this was only possible because cannibal monsters were among the traditionally reified concepts and imagery of his culture. Furthermore, just as a word or a sentence may induce an affective response, or immediately define a situation as dangerous and thus call forth appropriate conduct, such was the case here. Once the situation became perceptually structuralized in this way, subsequent sounds likewise became meaningful in terms of the same pattern. I should also like to stress the fact that, at the time, a premise for action became established in terms of which Adam's behavior becomes thoroughly intelligible. It is important to recognize this because we see exemplified in this case, too, the integral relation between perception and action that is characteristic of all organisms. In actual life situations, perceptual responses never occur in a behavioral vacuum. Considered in cross-cultural perspective I think we may say that, in addition to enabling man to adapt himself to a world of physical objects and events, like other animals, perception in our species enables human beings to adjust to a realm of culturally constituted objects as psychologically "real" as other orders of phenomena. Consequently, motivation and appropriate conduct must be judged with reference to a culturally constituted order of reality. Adam's behavior, therefore, was highly appropriate in his own frame of reference.

But there is another side to this coin which may, at first, seem paradoxical. Perception in man may be said to have acquired an overlaid *social* function. For is it not true, that in the light of the foregoing material, perception serves such a function to the extent that it is one of the chief psychological means whereby belief in reified images and concepts as integral parts of a cultural order of reality, are *substantiated* in the experience of individuals? It is through the activity of the same sensory modalities that always have been considered sufficiently reliable in bringing us into contact with the "reality" of the outer world that the "reality" of objects that have their roots in man's inner world are reinforced.

PERSONALITY FACTORS AND PERCEPTION

Part of the psychological interest of Adam Big Mouth's experience with a *windigo* lies in the fact that he himself was responsible for the perceptual structuralization of *this particular situation*. Another Indian in the same objective situation and belonging to the same cultural group may, or may not, have perceived a *windigo*. Consequently, it is inaccurate and misleading, I believe, to speak of cultural *determinism* in such a case. It is for this reason that I have deliberately referred to culturally constituted factors in perception, when speaking of individuals. This leads to a more general question. While given a belief in giant cannibals, it may be predicted that *some* Ojibwa Indians will report perceptual experiences which offer tangible evidence for the actual existence of *windigowak,* are there not selective factors that determine which particular individuals have these experiences under given conditions? I am sure that everyone agrees that there are such factors even though it may be difficult to identify them and to demonstrate their relevance in a given instance. Let us call them idiosyncratic or personal determinants.

Is there any evidence for the operation of such determinants in the case of Adam Big Mouth? I think that there is some evidence, although I do not have sufficient details to push it too far. (1) Adam's father was a very powerful medicine man. (2) He was also one of those who was reported to have *killed* mythical cannibals. (3) Adam was the man who told me more anecdotes about cannibals than anyone else. (4) When he was a small boy Adam had also seen a *windigo* a short distance from where his family was camping. He reported this to his father. (5) Adam's Rorschach record is characterized by the fact that out of a total of thirteen responses he gave a whole answer to each card. This was always his first answer and he responded with considerable rapidity. Furthermore, in this immediate interpretation of each successive blot as a whole Adam was almost unique in my series. And when I add that his wholes were not particularly good ones, I believe that the relevance of his Rorschach performance to his responses in the situation narrated is even more fully evident. His rapid but not too accurate structuralization of an ambiguous situation gave free play to the influence of traditional belief as well as personal determinants.

Although Adam was a conjurer and medicine man too, he did not enjoy the reputation of his father. One might guess that all this indicates that Adam wished to be like his father and to have his power but he had never succeeded in his inner striving for identification. I also suspect that the anecdote I have narrated might be psychologically interpreted to mean that although Adam unconsciously wished to be able to face a *windigo* and kill it as his father had done, he was not quite up to it. He did not have the courage of his father. Nevertheless, he managed to escape from the *windigo* alive. At first he was terrified; ultimately he regained his courage for he says; "I was mad now. He had chased me long enough." So at that point he starts off in the direction of the *windigo* and the *windigo* becomes pursued and falls through the ice! In the end, Adam became a kind of hero to himself, which satisfied an inner need. From the personal angle, therefore, it matters little whether his account is strictly accurate. It is quite possible that he may have elaborated it as time went on. But taken at its face value, his experience not only illustrates cultural factors in the structuralization of perception but, at the same time, personal needs as directive factors in perception.

Another case that illustrates the integral functioning of cultural and idiosyncratic variables has quite a different setting than the one just described. It will serve to demonstrate the importance of directive factors in perception in the area of interpersonal relations among a non-literate people. On the face of it the facts look very simple. An old man named Kiwetin (North Wind) told me that a married woman who was his neighbor was using sorcery against him. He had been sick and Catherine, he said, was back of it.

From a cultural point of view, therefore, we have a belief in sorcery to consider and the general attitudes it engenders among a people who are convinced of its reality. On the personal side we have to ask: Why did Kiwetin think that Catherine was responsible? Was it simply because she had the reputation of being a witch or were there selective factors of a more idiosyncratic nature rooted in the psychodynamics of his personality? Since I do not have all the necessary facts in this case, including any personal impressions of Catherine, whom I never met, my main purpose in discussing it at all is to use it as a sort of paradigm. I want to call attention to some of the possibilities that the investigation of the role of perception in interpersonal relations affords in a primitive society.

A belief in sorcery, of course, is based on the assumption that human individuals may possess, and exercise at will, malevolent powers against other individuals. Such a belief is found in many human societies. Among the Ojibwa there are certain provincial features that must also be understood. (1) Typically, men rather than women are thought to possess powers of sorcery. If women have magic power they use it principally to protect themselves and their children. (2) Power that can be used malevolently comes from the same sources of power that can be used benevolently, such as curing people who are ill. These sources are the *pawaganak,* already referred to. They are a man's guardian spirits. They confer certain powers upon him and stand ready to do his bidding. (3) Since such powers are acquired in a lonely vigil at puberty, no one can tell how much power another individual has, or whether it enables him to do evil or not. (4) Sorcery, by cultural definition is always practiced covertly. No one ever admits he possesses evil power, or that he has acted malevolently, except under circumstances I need not go into here. The only really tangible evidence of the practice of sorcery is that in some cases of illness, believed to be due to malevolent action of this kind, a special kind of doctor removes an object from the body of the patient—a piece of hair, a quill, a sharp piece of bone.

Among the Ojibwa there are certain obvious psychological consequences of a belief in sorcery. Men in particular are wary of one another; they cannot fully trust each other. For sorcery is always a potential threat to the central value of these people—*pimadaziwin*—Life, in the sense of longevity and freedom from illness and misfortune. Interpersonal relations are affectively toned by suspicions that may arise from the manner, tone, facial expression, gestures, attitudes, and conduct of persons with whom an individual is associated in daily life. There is always a latent anxiety that can be easily aroused because sorcery is believed to exist and may threaten *pimadaziwin*. If I fall ill my anxiety increases, because someone may have bewitched me. In consequence I am highly motivated to reflect upon the whole matter, my purpose being to discover *who* it might be. To arrive at a satisfactory answer I have to have some evidence on the basis of which I can make a judgment. So I appeal to the "evidence of my senses." Where else, indeed, could I turn?

The chief point I want to emphasize is the important psychological fact that the Ojibwa have to pick out sorcerers for themselves. With reference to our central topic we may ask: What kind of perceptual evidence becomes important in the identification of a particular sorcerer? And what kind of directive factors influence perception. The situation would be quite different, of course, in a society where there was a cultural definition of the traits of sorcerers or even where ordeals of a public nature were customary so that an accused individual could be put to some test. Where ordeals exist, everyone can see for himself whether an accused sorcerer passes the test or fails. But among the Ojibwa sorcery itself is not only covert. If I am sick I may privately make up my mind who is responsible and take whatever measures I see fit. If I have any power myself, I may sorcerize my enemy covertly in turn. This is the essence of the situation. So it is easy to see how in this sort of socio-psychological field it is inevitable that projective mechanisms will operate with the utmost freedom. There are culturally constituted barriers to any kind of reality testing.

Returning now to the particular case I mentioned, there are several facts to be noted which seem to me to have special importance. In the first place, Catherine, although I never saw her was, from all accounts, an unusual woman. She was even notorious. She was large in size, terrifically dynamic for an Indian woman, and she had had many husbands. Besides this, many Indians were convinced that she had a knowledge of sorcery which, in itself, made her unusual. Kiwetin at the time of which I speak was a widower, living by himself. I had gone to see him because he had once been active in the *Midewiwin* whose major function was curative. He was a medicine man reputed to have considerable power. How did Kiwetin arrive at the conclusion that *Catherine* was using sorcery against him? In the first place he had been sick. Since he did not respond at once to the medicine used, his suspicions became aroused. Someone must be using malevolent power against him. But why Catherine? What struck me so forcibly when Kiwetin told me his story was the kind of evidence he regarded as decisive. It was the woman's *outward display of amiability and kindness toward him* that made him think she had malevolent intentions. She smiled pleasantly at him. But he knew this was put on. "It was only on her face, not in her mind," he said. She also had invited him into her house to have something to eat. But he always refused. She might put something in his food. The selection of outward amiability as evidence of covert malevolence in this instance is not unique. I have heard the same thing in one or two other cases. On one occasion when I heard a rumor that one old man was a very wicked sorcerer, I naïvely said, "But he is such a nice old man." "That's just it," my informant said, "That's why you have to watch him." I do not wish to create the impression that outward amiability among the Ojibwa is *institutionalized* as indicative of malevolent intentions. This is far from being the case. What is interesting is the fact that what might be supposed to be a universal expression of positive attitudes in interpersonal relations may be perceived as having a completely negative meaning. How far it would be possible to institutionalize a negative appraisal of *all* expressions of kindness and amiability in any culture is a nice question. In the case of Catherine, I may add, I think there is good reason to believe that, in reality, there was no actual malevolence involved.

This leads us to a consideration of directive factors of a purely idiosyncratic nature that may have been responsible for Kiwetin's "choice" of a witch. What finally clinched the whole matter for Kiwetin was the fact that, in a dream, one of his *pawagan* informed him that Catherine was responsible for his illness. This suggests that unconscious as well as conscious forces were operating in the same direction. This fact is of importance because, as I pointed out in the beginning, men, rather than women, are the chief manipulators of malevolent power. So why choose a woman? My hypothesis would be that Kiwetin's choice of Catherine was involved with his basic psychosexual adjustment. His interpretation of the whole situation was a projection on his part which served as an effective personal defense against Catherine, whom he could not help seeing and being aware of constantly since she was his neighbor. At the conscious level, therefore, he made use of a belief well-entrenched in his culture, backed up, of course, by the "evidence of his senses," to build up a rationalization that enabled him to avoid her and condemn her. Unconsciously, I have no doubt, he was fearful of women and Catherine in particular, while at the same time he was attracted to her.

In this case, therefore, we find perception linked to complex personal needs which influence it selectively. At the same time we see another instance in which perception served a social function in so far as it helped to corroborate the belief that witches, even if unusual, existed. Faced with the same personal problem, in some other culture, Kiwetin would have had to make use of some other means of rationalization. Defense mechanisms and perception are universal processes in human adjustment. Culturally available means are local and variable. But in the whole adjustment process the central role which perception plays is evident. Perception is made the basis of judgment, decision, action. Abstractly stated, this is an old axiom in psychology. A case such as the foregoing suggests that the kind of judgments made, the nature of the decisions arrived at, and the consequences in terms of motivation and conduct are related to both cultural and idiosyncratic variables. Consequently, the dynamics of perception are not entirely clear if we do not approach the whole problem in a fashion that enables us to take account of non-sensory as well as sensory determinants.

An inclusive approach such as is now being more systematically pursued than formerly, and which stresses functional factors, is directly relevant to a deeper understanding of the role of cultural factors in the structuralization of perception and even necessary for the explanation of concrete behavior in cross-cultural perspective.

REFERENCES

1. Florence L. Goodenough and John L. Anderson in the *Southwestern Journal of Anthropology,* Vol. 3, 1947, pp. 5–14.
2. Muzafer Sherif, "A Study of Some Social Factors in Perception," *Arch. Psychol.,* 1935, no. 187. Cf. *The Psychology of Social Norms* (New York, 1936) and *An Outline of Social Psychology* (New York, 1948). With reference to the subject of this paper I think it is worth noting that, in England, F. C. Bartlett, who has long been interested in anthropology and has had personal associations with anthropologists, wrote in 1932 (*Remembering: A Study in Experimental and Social Psychology,* Cambridge University Press, p. 31): ". . . to perceive anything is one of the simplest and most immediate, as it is one of the most fundamental, of all human cognitive reactions. Yet obviously, in a psychological sense, it is exceedingly complex, and this is widely recognized. Inextricably mingled with it are imaging, valuing and those beginnings of judging which are involved in the response to plan, order of arrangement and construction of presented material. It is directed by interest and feeling, and may be dominated by certain crucial factors of the objects and scenes dealt with." A few years later in "Psychological Methods and Anthropological Problems," *Africa,* Vol. 10, 1937, p. 407, he again touched upon perception and among other things said: "Everybody now realizes that perceptual meanings, which have an enormous influence upon social life, vary from social setting to social setting, and the field anthropologist has a golden opportunity to study the limits of such variation and its importance."
3. The more inclusive formulation referred to is well represented by the recent text of D. Krech and R. S. Crutchfield, *Theory and Problems of Social Psychology* (New York, 1948), who devote two systematic chapters to perception. The quotations are from pp. 81–82. Their contrasting terms are "structural" and "functional" and they point out that the use of the latter term as applied to such factors was first suggested by D. Muenzinger (*Psychology: The Science of Behavior,* 1942). "Autochthonous" and "Be-

havioral" are the contrasting terms of J. S. Bruner and C. C. Goodman in "Value and Need as organizing factors in perception," *J. Abnormal and Social Psychology*, Vol. 62 (1947) pp. 33–44 (Reprinted in T. M. Newcomb and E. L. Hartley, *Readings in Social Psychology*, New York, 1947).

4. Hadley Cantril, *Understanding Man's Social Behavior, Preliminary Notes* (Princeton, 1947) observes that "the nature and function of perception are understandable only with reference to purpose and causality. Our approach to the psychology of perception may appear extremely radical. This is because our approach is 100% functional as contrasted to classificatory and structural analysis for the study of personality as a series of relationships as seen in some recent work in the field." Major references to the experimental work designed to throw light on the validity of the proposition that perceiving may be functionally guided by non-sensory or directive factors may be found in the article of Bruner and Goodman, op. cit., and in the articles and bibliographies in the *Symposium* on "Interrelationships between Perception and Personality" in the *Journal of Personality*, Vol. 18, Nos. 1 and 2, 1949. Recognition that the complexities of human perception present special difficulties for the experimental psychologist, who has traditionally approached the problem from the standpoint of autochthonous factors, is explicitly stated by J. J. Gibson in his contribution to Andrews (Ed.) *Methods of Psychology* (New York, 1948). In the chapter "Studying Perceptual Phenomena," p. 185, he says: "The problem of meaning and the nature of symbolic perception presents a variety of problems for psychology. Most if not all meanings are also perceptual experiences and in this respect they are difficult to study by experimental methods. The meanings of situations, objects, pictures and words are difficult or impossible to arrange in accordance with their modes of variation as colors can be arranged, because of their seeming uniqueness and almost infinite variety."

5. In addition to the sources noted in the previous footnote see Gardner Murphy, *Personality: A Biosocial Approach to Origins and Structure* (New York, 1947). Representative statements are those of L. L. Thurstone, *A Factorial Study of Perception* (Chicago, 1944), that "In these days when we insist so frequently on the interdependence of all aspects of personality, it would be difficult to maintain that any of these functions, such as perception, is isolated from the rest of the dynamical system that constitutes the person" and Jerome S. Bruner "Perceptual Theory and the Rorschach Test," *J. of Personality*, Vol. 17, 1948, p. 160, who writes, "Perception is an activity of the total organism and, like all other activities, is an aspect of the economy of personality." Perhaps it is also worth noting that in a popular book entitled *The Evidence of Our Senses*, by A. W. P. Wol-

ters (London, 1933), an organismic approach to perception, although phrased in general terms, was clearly emphasized.

6. See Heinz Werner, e.g., in his "Introductory Remarks" to the Symposium mentioned (*J. of Personality*, Vol. 18, 1949, p. 2). An even broader framework of theory is thought to be a necessity by others. See D. Krech and Jane Torrey in the same source.

7. Wolters, op. cit., p. 7, was writing in 1933, "He (the percipient) perceives in order to act, and reciprocally his will to act governs his perception. He develops a rich system of particular purposes which must be guided by knowledge of the environment, and here again his purpose affects what he perceives . . . cognition implies conation. . . ." More recently, Cantril, op. cit., p. 19, quotes the statement of Adelbert Ames, Jr. "In a concrete situation, a perception is a potential prognostic directive for furthering of purpose by action." It is of more than passing interest to note further that Lewis E. Hahn, a philosopher, in his monograph, *A Contextualistic Theory of Perception* (University of California Publications in Philosophy, Vol. 22, 1942), stresses the basic relation of perception to action. Hahn, in turn, has been influenced by the word of E. C. Tolman. This emphasis is quite different from what H. Proshansky and Gardner Murphy, "The effects of reward and punishment on perception," *J. Psychol*. Vol. 13, 1942, pp. 295–305, refer to as the traditional *dualism* of perception *versus* action, "the separation of cognitive activity from behavior." It is their thesis that "perception develops by virtue of its capacity to mediate adjustments, to serve needs and that it may reasonably be expected to show the basic learning phenomena including trial and error and the consolidation of the successful phases of response." They also remark that "Perception has other functions besides mediating *correct* reports," an observation directly relevant to the section of the paper dealing with "Belief and Perception."

8. As Leo Postman and J. S. Bruner phrase it in one of their articles "Perceiving is goal-directed behavior." "Perception Under Stress," *Psy. Rev.* Vol. 55, 1948, p. 314.

9. Jerome S. Bruner and Leo Postman, "On the Perception of Incongruity: a paradigm," *J. of Personality*, Vol. 18, 1949, p. 207.

10. Jerome S. Bruner and Leo Postman, "Tension and Tension Release as Organizing Factors in Perception," *J. of Personality*, Vol. 15, 1946–47, p. 300.

11. Jerome S. Bruner and Leo Postman, "Perception, Cognition, and Behavior," *J. of Personality*, Vol. 18, 1949, p. 22.

12. Leo Postman and Jerome S. Bruner, "Perception Under Stress," *Psy. Rev.* Vol. 55, 1948, p. 314.

13. See A. I. Hallowell, "Personality Structure and the Evolution of Man," *American Anthropologist*, Vol. 52, 1950.

14. If we wish to go even farther afield we find that poets have sensed the same relationship as, e.g., Wallace Stevens "Variations on a Summer Day," *Kenyon Review*, Vol. 11, No. 1, p. 25.

> Words add to the senses. The words for the dazzle
> Of mica, the dithering of grass,
> The Arachne integument of dead trees,
> Are the eye grown larger, more intense.

15. Ernest Cassirer, "Le langage et la construction du monde des objets," *J. de Psychologie Normale et Pathologique*, Vol. 30 (1932) pp. 18–44 (quotation from p. 23). Reprinted in *Psychologie du langage*, H. Delacroix et al (Paris, 1933). Cf. *Language and Myth* (New York, 1946), pp. 28–29 (this is a translation of a book originally published in 1925); "The Concept of Group and the Theory of Perception," *Philosophy and Phenomenological Research*, Vol. 5 (1944) pp. 1–35; "The Influence of Language upon the Development of Scientific Thought," *J. of Philosophy*, Vol. 39 (1942) pp. 309–327.

16. Grace Andrus De Laguna, *Speech, Its Function and Development* (New Haven, 1927, p. 290. See also, "Perception and Language," *Proceedings of the 9th International Congress of Psy.*, 1930, pp. 278–279, and an article under the same title in Human Biology, Vol. 1 (1929) pp. 555–558, which recently has been reprinted in Irving J. Lee (Ed.) *The Language of Wisdom and Folly. Background Readings in Semantics* (New York, 1949).

17. Edward Sapir, "The Status of Linguistics as a Science," *Language*, Vol. 5 (1929) pp. 209–210. Reprinted in *Selected Writings of Edward Sapir in Language, Culture, and Personality*, ed. by David G. Mandelbaum (University of California Press, Berkeley and Los Angeles, 1949).

18. L. L. Carmichael, H. P. Hogan and A. A. Walter, "An Experimental Study of the Effect of Language on the Reproduction of Visually Perceived Form," *J. of Experimental Psy.* Vol. 15 (1932), pp. 74–82. Reprinted in *"The Language of Wisdom and Folly*, op. cit., and also included in L. W. Crafts, T. C. Schneirla, E. E. Robinson, and R. W. Gilbert, *Recent Experiments in Psychology* (New York, 1938). See also the previous experiment of J. J. Gibson, "The Reproduction of Visually Perceived Form," *J. of Experimental Psychol.* Vol. 12 (1929).

19. Wolfgang Köhler, "Psychological Remarks on Some Questions of Anthropology," *Amer. J. Psychol.*, Vol. 50, 1937, p. 274.

20. Oscar Wilde, *Intentions* (New York, 1912), pp. 1–55; "The Decay of Lying" was first published in *The Nineteenth Century* (1889).

21. Andre Gide, *Dostoievsky* (New York, 1926), p. 119. These lectures were delivered in Paris in 1922.

22. L. J. Russell in his Presidential Address to the Aristotelian Society, 1932, (See *Proceedings of Aristotelian Society* (London), Vol. 33, 1933) remarks "that the illustrations in the modern books and newspapers tend to modify the vision of man today, so as to produce a common pattern of organization of the visual field very different from that of the man living in Medieval England or of the Ancient Egyptians," and E. Bevan (*Symbolism and Belief*, 1938), p. 277, writes: "All our admiration of nature is now mixed up with reminiscences of innumerable paintings and drawings we bring to the contemplation of landscapes and figures. We use the term picturesque, and truly. It is in this way that when a new school of art begins to represent things in nature which had not been represented before, men come to see those things in a new way, they instinctively [sic] imagine natural scenes as pictures of that particular kind. I remember once at Oxford, at the Ashmolean, looking through, not very carefully, a series of watercolours by Turner of Oxford, and when I went out again from the Museum into the Oxford streets, it all looked different, there were new lights on trees and houses; it all looked like a painted picture by Turner." Heinz Werner in his "Introductory Remarks" to the *Symposium* (*J. of Personality*, 1949, op. cit.) refers to the fact that "after Goethe visited the Dresden Gallery with its marvelous collection of Dutch landscape painting, he remarked how for days the visible world had transformed itself for him, how he saw things and sceneries in the mood and—metaphorically speaking—with the eyes of the Dutch artists."

23. See John Gillin, "Personality Formation from the Comparative Cultural Point of View," in C. Kluckhohn and H. A. Murray, (ed.) *Personality in Nature, Society and Culture* (New York, 1948), p. 167.

24. Cf. Cantril's remarks, op. cit., p. 25.

25. Gardner Murphy, op. cit., p. 333.

26. Krech and Crutchfield, op. cit., p. 77, write: "How we perceive the world is a product of memory, imagination, hearsay, and fantasy as well as what we actually are 'perceiving' through our senses. If we are to understand social behavior, we must know how all perceptions, memories, fantasies are combined or integrated or organized into present *cognitive structures.*"

27. For further information see A. I. Hallowell, *The Role of Conjuring in Saulteaux Society, Publications, Phila. Anthropological Society*, Vol. 2 (University of Pennsylvania Press, 1942).

28. Cf. A. I. Hallowell, "Some Empirical Aspects of Northern Saulteaux Religion," *Amer. Anth.*, Vol. 36, 1934, pp. 389–404.

29. He had an extraordinary number of M's; not only more than any other subject, but excellent in quality.

30. Donald W. MacKinnon in his chapter on "Motivation" (E. G. Boring, H. S. Langfeld and H. D. Weld, *Introduction to Psyc.*, New York, 1939), p. 159, stresses the need for distinguishing the physical situation, i.e., the environment "considered as having independent real existence" from the psychological field, viz., "the situation as it exists psychologically for the individual." "The psychological field," he goes on to say, "is not to be equated merely to what is consciously perceived or known but rather to everything that at the moment determines the behavior of an individual." In the case described there was no "fearful object" in the situation, objectively viewed; the source of the fear was in the *psychological field*.

31. Robert B. MacLeod, The Phenomenological Approach to Social Psychology, *Psychol. Rev.*, Vol. 54 (1947) p. 205.

CHAPTER 8

ᒣᒧᒣᒧᒣᒧᒣᒧᒣᒧᒣᒧᒣᒧᒣᒧᒣᒧᒣᒧᒣᒧᒣᒧᒣᒧ

The Psychological Habitat of Raymond Birch[1]

ROGER C. BARKER
and
HERBERT F. WRIGHT

University of Kansas

Problems of social psychology have two sides. On one side there is the problem of discovering the laws of social behavior. This is the systematic side; it presents theoretical and experimental problems. On the other side there is the problem of measuring the parameters of these laws for different cultures and different conditions of life. This is the ecological side; it involves descriptive and field-study problems.

Psychology has been concerned largely with the systematic problem. Much time has been spent on the basic question of how to conceptualize social interaction and personality. A great amount of effort has been directed at determining the roles of learning, perception, imitation, identification, gratification, frustration, and other psychological processes in socialization, acculturation, and personality development. Psychology has been little concerned meanwhile with the ecological problem. Little has been done toward the development of psychological field methods. We do not know with precision for different cultures and different conditions of life the degree of occurrence of the factors thought to be of importance for social behavior and psychological development. Before we can understand why Germans behave as Ger-

---

[1] The research upon which this paper is based has been supported by a grant from the National Institute of Mental Health, U. S. Public Health Service.

mans, why Kansas children become Kansans, why city children differ from country children, and why the behavior of lower-class children differs from that of upper-class children, we must know more than the laws of social behavior. We must know also how the variables of social behavior are distributed in society.

At the University of Kansas, we have recently directed our efforts toward one aspect of the ecological problem, namely, the development of methods for describing the psychological environment of children under non-experimental, field conditions. Others have made important contributions to this problem. We cannot review their work here, but we would recall to your minds the important accomplishments of Baldwin in measuring some situational factors within the family, of Anderson in studying domination in the schoolroom, and of Lippitt, White, and Lewin in diagnosing democratic and authoritarian atmospheres in children's groups. Recognizing that psychological ecology is in a pioneering stage where a variety of approaches has value, we shall proceed immediately to the description of our own methods and to the presentation of some results obtained by them.

Here is a specific example of our general problem: We wish to describe as completely as possible the psychological world of Raymond Birch, a seven-year-old who lives in the small Kansas town of Midwest. With current theories in view, we want to know the extent to which Raymond's behavior is influenced by conditions such as those of frustration, failure, rejection, gratification, success, freedom, punishment, and reward. We want to know the kind of world that Raymond, his family and community, in interaction, provide for him. We want this information in a form that will allow us to compare Raymond's world with the worlds of other children in Midwest and with those of children in other cultures and circumstances of life.

THE SPECIMEN RECORD

Raymond's psychological environment has to be inferred from his behavior and from the physical and social situations in which his behavior occurs. To get a sample of Raymond's behavior and situation, we have used a kind of record that was popular in the early days of psychology, but which, in recent times, has been almost completely abandoned as a scientific instrument, namely, the anecdotal record. We have secured detailed records of this kind, and in so doing we have tried to avoid the well-known deficiencies of the early use of this method. Here is a sample of our record of Raymond's behavior and situation on April 26, 1949. It begins at 7:00 A.M. when his mother awakened him:

7:00. Mrs. Birch said with pleasant casualness, "Raymond, wake up." With a little more urgency in her voice she spoke again: "Son, are you going to school today?"

Raymond didn't respond immediately.

He screwed up his face and whimpered a little.

He lay still.

His mother repeated, "Raymond, wake up." This was said pleasantly; the mother was apparently in good spirits and was willing to put up with her son's reluctance.

Raymond whimpered again, and kicked his feet rapidly in protest.

He squirmed around and rolled over crossways on the bed.

His mother removed the covers.

> Raymond wore a T-shirt and pajama pants.

He again kicked his feet in protest.

He sat up and rubbed his eyes.

He glanced at me and smiled.

I smiled in return as I continued making notes.

> Mrs. Birch took some clothes from the bureau and laid them on the bed next to Raymond. There were a clean pair of socks, a clean pair of shorts, a white T-shirt and a striped T-shirt. Raymond's blue-jean pants were on a chair near the bed, where Mrs. Birch continued to stand.

Raymond picked up a sock and began tugging and pulling it on his left foot.

As his mother watched him she said kiddingly, "Can't you get your peepers open?"

Raymond stopped putting on his sock long enough to rub his eyes again. He appeared to be very sleepy.

He said plaintively, "Momie," and continued mumbling in an unintelligible way something about his undershirt.

7:02. His mother asked, "Do you want to put this undershirt on or do you want to wear the one you have on?"

Raymond sleepily muttered something in reply.

His mother left the room and went into the kitchen.

Raymond struggled out of the T-shirt which he had on.

He put on the clean striped T-shirt more efficiently.

7:03. He pulled on his right sock.

He picked up his left tennis shoe and put it on.

He laced his left shoe with slow deliberation, looking intently at the shoe as he worked steadily until he had it all laced.

7:04. He put on his right shoe.

He laced up his right shoe. Again he worked intently, looking at the shoe as he laced it.

His mother called, "Raymond, do you want an egg for breakfast?" in a pleasant inquiring tone.

Raymond responded very sleepily, "No." His voice showed no irritation or resentment; he just answered in a matter-of-fact, sleepy way, "No."

7:05. As he finished lacing his shoe, he called out in a rather plaintive voice, "Momie, come here."

Mrs. Birch didn't respond verbally, but her footsteps signaled her approach.

When his mother came into the room, Raymond still had on his pajama pants; his shorts were lying on the bed next to him.

Mrs. Birch came over to the bed and bent down close to Raymond.

He whispered something to her.

Mrs. Birch chuckled with slight embarrassment and said, laughingly,

"Well, take them off and put them on," meaning that he was to take off his pajama pants and put on his underwear pants.

She stood next to him as he made the change.

Out of deference to Raymond's embarrassment, I turned away as he changed his pants. The mother returned to the kitchen. She re-

entered Raymond's room and said to me, "Won't you have break-
fast with us?" I declined, explaining that I found it difficult to
write and eat at the same time, and that I had just had breakfast
before I left home.

As his mother and I talked, Raymond put on his blue jeans.

7:06.   He stood up next to the bed and buckled the belt for his pants.

The pet dog, Honey, ambled into the room. Honey was a fox ter-
rier, quite old, fat, and broad.

While buckling his belt Raymond said, with a little sleep in his voice,
but friendly and pleasantly, "Hi, Honey."

Honey put her front paws on Raymond's knees.

He finished buckling his belt and, at the same time, patted Honey and
scratched her back in a friendly way.

7:07.   Raymond turned to the dresser and rummaged among some things.

He came out with a piece of candy.

He held up the candy and said to the dog, in a pleasant, yet ordering
tone, "Sit up, Honey, sit up."

Honey promptly sat up and Raymond shoved the candy into her
mouth.

Just as he finished doing this, Mrs. Birch walked by the door and said,
"Are you dressed, son?" Seeing that he was, she added pleasantly, "Then
go and wash up."

Raymond immediately went to the bathroom, leaving the door open.

He washed briefly at the sink.

7:08.   He came out of the bathroom carrying a bottle of vaseline hair oil.

He went into his bedroom.

He shook a few drops of oil into the palm of one hand, and set the
bottle on the dresser.

Then he put the oil on his hair and began massaging his scalp with
his hands and fingers.

As he was doing this, his father, who had been in the front room
reading the morning paper, came by in the hallway on his way to
the kitchen for breakfast.

He turned into Raymond's room and greeted him in a friendly, jocular way: "Well, Clam, are you ready to eat?"

Raymond promptly and easily replied, "Sure."

7:09.   Mr. Birch patted Raymond on the back, then turned and started toward the kitchen.

On his way to the kitchen Mr. Birch called out teasingly, "Well, let's get on the stick, Bub," and repeated, "Let's get on the stick, Bub."

Raymond said nothing, just went on combing his hair.

Raymond finished with his hair rapidly, stroking it a few times with the comb.

7:10.   Raymond went quickly, almost eagerly, into the kitchen.

He went directly to the table.

I took the chair near the table at Raymond's left.

Raymond sat down before a glass of milk, a piece of buttered toast, and a dish of piping hot oatmeal with milk on it, ready to eat.

Raymond picked up his piece of toast.

He began stirring the cereal.

The record continues minute by minute without any breaks until Raymond went to sleep 13½ hours later. We call this a specimen record because it has some of the characteristics of other scientific specimens. It provides an unanalyzed sample of the behavior-situation continuum which can be used for many purposes. This specimen of Raymond's behavior is by no means complete or fully valid. But neither is a dried plant, an Egyptian mummy, or a photograph of the sun's corona a complete and valid specimen of a living plant, an Egyptian pharaoh, or the sun's corona. Yet these specimens are invaluable for many purposes. There is reason to believe that a specimen record of behavior can be similarly valuable despite its imperfections. Its chief advantage appears to be in preserving undisturbed some of the simultaneous and successive complexities of behavior. Let us see how this specimen of a day in the life of Raymond Birch can be used to study the world in which Raymond lived on April 26, 1949.

THE NON-PSYCHOLOGICAL MILIEU

As a matter of fact, an observer sees Raymond living in three worlds. The first world is the non-psychological milieu; it is made up of the geography, the temperature, the sociology, the economy, the ideology of Midwest. The non-psychological milieu does not affect Raymond's behavior directly, but it does provide the physical and social raw materials of his psychological situation.

Our record of the behavior of Raymond Birch tells us something about the alien physical and social facts with any of which Raymond might have interacted to form his own psychological world. We learn that Raymond was an only child, that the school was two blocks from his home, that both his father and mother worked outside the home. We do not know from the record if Raymond's home was of brick or of wood, if the barometer was falling or rising, if the economic conditions were good or bad, if the political climate of Midwest was conservative or liberal. The specimen record provides much indirect evidence regarding the non-psychological milieu, but it does not provide a systematic survey of it. For this, the data of the geographer, the meteorologist, the economist, the agriculturalist, the sociologist, the pollster are required. Such data, however, even if very complete, would not tell us much about the psychological habitat of Raymond Birch, or of any other Midwest child. However, those limited aspects of the non-psychological world described in the specimen record do provide important evidence upon which to base inferences regarding Raymond's psychological situation.

THE BEHAVIOR SETTINGS AND BEHAVIOR OBJECTS

The second of Raymond's worlds on April 26, 1949, was the world of *behavior settings* and *behavior objects*. Midwest provided Raymond with a stage already set with properties appropriate for certain scenes. It provided him with streets for walking and running, for playing ball, for riding a bicycle and for riding in an automobile. It provided him with a time, a place, and behavior supports for getting up and getting dressed, for eating breakfast, for going to school. It presented him with a friendly dog to pet and feed, with a jacket to wear against the cool, threatening weather, and with a courthouse lawn on which to play games.

We have called the larger of these *behavior settings* and the smaller *behavior objects*. Behavior settings and objects are the parts of the infinite number of discriminable physical and social aspects of Midwest that are generally seen by the people of the town as appropriate for particular kinds of behavior. A behavior setting has two characteristics:

It is a discriminable part of the non-psychological milieu, and it is generally perceived as being necessary or appropriate for the transaction of some particular behavior. In Midwest, grocery stores are easily recognized parts of the physical-social milieu that are usually perceived as appropriate places for buying and selling food and for conversing with acquaintances. They are perceived as inappropriate places for dancing, singing, or playing hopscotch. Some behavior settings are imposed by the more or less direct effects of physical-social conditions upon the human organism. The stage that is Midwest is cold in winter and warm in summer and the people behave accordingly; they see winter as a time to wear warm clothes and summer as a time for cool clothes. Other settings are selected from the infinite number of physical-social differentia that exist and are seen as appropriate for particular behaviors. This is true of the behavior setting "getting-up-time"; for example, 6:30 to 7:30 A.M. is generally seen in Midwest as the appropriate time for children to wake up and get dressed. On the other hand, 10:30 to 11:30 A.M., while equally discriminable, is not a behavior setting. Yet other settings, rather than just being selected, are created by the people of Midwest. The bandstand is a covered platform where the band presents concerts, on which small boys play and on which park benches are stored. It was erected by the citizens of Midwest.

In what behavior settings and with what behavior objects did Raymond transact behavior on April 26, 1949? With what parts of the discriminable physical-social milieu of Midwest did Raymond have commerce? The specimen record provides this information. In the excerpt given above, Raymond entered the behavior settings "getting-up-time," and "breakfast time." Behavior was transacted in these settings with the following behavior objects:

mother	candy
own eyes	wash basin
observer	water
socks	hair oil
undershirt	own hair
T-shirt	father
shoe	comb
underwear	breakfast table
pants	chair
belt	toast
pet dog	cereal

There were many other physical and social parts of Raymond's situation with which he might have interacted but did not:

> pillow
> mother's dress
> own nose
> wall paper
> rug
> handkerchief, etc.

Analyzing the entire specimen record, we find that Raymond entered 27 different behavior settings. The numbers in parentheses indicate the frequency with which each setting was entered and the total amount of time he spent in each.

Home: getting up time	(1, 10 min.)
Home: breakfast time	(1, 10 min.)
Home: free time indoors	(9, 56 min.)
Home: free time outdoors	(8, 72 min.)
Home: lunch time	(1, 19 min.)
Home: supper time	(1, 19 min.)
Home: music practice time	(1, 7 min.)
Home: bed time	(1, 8 min.)
Streets and sidewalks	(7, 38 min.)
Courthouse	(3, 37 min.)
Courthouse lawn	(5, 111 min.)
School: free time on playground	(4, 57 min.)
School: halls and cloakroom	(4, 4 min.)
School: classroom before school	(3, 7 min.)
School: class period before assignment	(3, 14 min.)
School: reading, writing and arithmetic seat work	(5, 89 min.)
School: reading, writing and arithmetic recitation	(2, 32 min.)
School: art period	(1, 28 min.)
School: music period	(1, 18 min.)
School: oral reports	(2, 29 min.)
School: after class period and before dismissal	(3, 6 min.)
School: test	(1, 15 min.)
School: boys' basement	(3, 5 min.)

School: story period	(1,	13 min.)
School: preparation for dismissal	(1,	6 min.)
Vacant lot	(2,	74 min.)
Neighbor's yard	(1,	6 min.)

A sampling count indicates that Raymond engaged in overt behavior transactions with over 500 different behavior objects. This includes only those objects that Raymond listened to, looked at, spoke to, or manipulated overtly enough to be seen by an observer. It does not include objects which he undoubtedly perceived, but which were not used overtly in the course of his behavior. The list is too long to be reproduced here. Some behavior objects were used frequently. Within the first hour and a half, Raymond interacted with his mother 20 times, with his father 10 times, with his jacket 6 times, with his father's fishing pole 3 times. From the partly ambiguous, partly structured ink blot we call Midwest, Raymond chose to use or was required to use some but not other parts as behavior settings and objects. Or, to change the analogy, from the almost limitless number of things to use as stage properties, Raymond chose to use or was required to use some and not others in playing his part on April 26, 1949.

These lists of behavior settings and behavior objects give no indication of their meaning to Raymond. They describe Raymond's world in terms of the general culture of Midwest, not in terms of their unique, personal significance to him. The words used to designate behavior settings and objects, e.g., mother, sock, flagpole, courthouse, are used in their generally accepted dictionary meaning. These definitions have two parts. One part of the definition denotes a portion of the nonpsychological milieu and describes its physical and/or social properties. The other part of the definition indicates the behavior that is generally perceived as being appropriately transacted with the object or setting. Webster has this to say about a flagpole: it is "a long, comparatively slender, usually cylindrical piece of wood . . . or metal [i.e., a discriminable physical object, with the described characteristics] to raise a flag on [i.e., something seen as appropriate for the behavior designated]." This definition is in accordance with Midwest mores.

Usually Raymond perceives the behavior settings and objects of Midwest as being appropriate for the same behavior that other Midwest residents do. Sometimes, however, he perceives them quite differently.

He apparently sees his sock as a "knitted object to be worn on the foot"; both Webster and the residents of Midwest see it in this way too. But on one occasion Raymond saw the flagpole quite differently from these others. He saw it as *an upright, slender tone-producing piece of metal to run around and bang upon.*

It will be seen that behavior settings and behavior objects make up a zone of influence between the non-psychological milieu and the psychological situation of a particular individual. A particular individual's psychological situation may differ from the behavior settings of his community in two ways:

First, it may contain parts that are not usually perceived by others of the community. A New Englander in Midwest may differ from the native resident by discriminating between sugar maple trees (seen as suitable for one set of behavior transactions) and soft maple trees (seen as suitable for other behavior transactions).

Second, a particular individual may perceive the same physical-social part as being appropriate for quite different behavior from the generality of citizens. Thus, Raymond perceived candy Easter eggs as being appropriate for the behavior, *feeding to dog.* This is hardly in accord with the usual perception of Easter eggs. The behavior transacted with a behavior object in any culture falls along a gradient ranging from behavior that is generally seen as fully right, through behavior that is generally seen as unusual but not inappropriate, to that which is usually seen as clearly wrong. The "fully right" behavior is modal and the "clearly wrong" behavior least frequent. The behavior object "flagpole" would be seen by most Midwest citizens as fully appropriate for Raymond to watch during the flag raising. It would be considered unusual, but not inappropriate, for him to run around the pole banging it with a stick. But it would be seen as entirely inappropriate "flagpole behavior" for Raymond to climb the pole to its top.

Behavior settings and behavior objects coerce behavior. Children behave differently in a drug store from the way they do in school or at a ball game. How behavior settings and objects come to possess coercive forces is a matter for students of learning, perception, social induction, etc., to say. At the ecological level, the fact of their coerciveness can be accepted as a clearly manifest property of the setting or object. A hammer is immediately seen by most people of Midwest as an object to be used for pounding, not one to be used for a table decoration, a coat hook, a doorstop, or a paperweight. The source of this perception is not an ecological problem.

The description of behavior settings is a primary concern of sociologists and cultural anthropologists. The behavior settings of a community define the culture; as with knowledge of the non-psychological milieu, knowledge of the behavior settings of a community does not allow us to reconstruct the psychological worlds of any particular child. However, behavior settings and objects do come much closer to the psychological world and are important symptoms upon which to base a diagnosis of the individual environment.

PSYCHOLOGICAL HABITAT

This brings us to the *third,* and for psychology, the most important of Raymond's worlds, namely, his psychological habitat. A person's psychological habitat is his naturally occurring life space, the relevant psychological context of his behavior. It includes factors in both the person and his environment. So far as its directly observed, phenotypic content is concerned, the environmental part of Raymond's habitat is rather well indicated by the behavior settings and behavior objects mentioned above. There is evidence that for Raymond the dictionary meanings or, at least, the common meanings in Midwest, of the words naming these settings and objects describe fairly well what he saw in the world. The most important aspects of the habitat, however, are its structure and psychological dynamics. Let us examine a small segment of the specimen record to see what it reveals about the structure and dynamics of Raymond's psychological habitat. Here is a behavior-situation episode from the part of the specimen record reported above. At 7:06 A.M. Raymond was standing beside the bed buckling his belt.

> The pet dog, Honey, ambled into the room. Honey is a fox terrier, quite old, fat, and broad.
>
> While buckling his belt Raymond said, with a little sleep in his voice, but friendly and pleasantly, "Hi, Honey."
>
> Honey put her front paws on Raymond's knees.
>
> Raymond finished buckling his belt and, at the same time, patted Honey and scratched her back in a friendly way.

What can we say about Raymond's psychological habitat while he was petting Honey? Categories that we have developed for analyzing such an episode enable us to say a number of things about it, some of which are as follows:

General nature of situation to Raymond:	social; not physical, intellectual or autistic
Behavior object:	pet dog
Meaning of dog's behavior to Raymond:	friendliness, liking, affiliation; not abasement, aggression, rejection, etc.
Behavior appropriate to object:	affiliation, nurturance
Centrality of Raymond's need:	could not judge
Strength of need:	could not judge
Sign of ruling valence:	positive; not negative
Strength of ruling valence:	medium
Geniality of total situation:	beneficent; not gratifying, neutral, inhospitable, or hostile
Motivational structure:	consummatory; no task, path, rewards, or punishments present
Strength of frustration:	zero
Degree of conflict:	zero
Degree of freedom:	large; no barriers, resistance to action, or coercion
Clarity of cognitive field:	clear
Size of cognitive field:	medium
Time perspective:	present only; no past or future reference
Aspiration level:	none; no definite task or problem with respect to which a level of aspiration could be set
Degree of overlap	situation overlaps with one other, namely, "getting dressed"
Compatibility of overlapping situation:	"getting dressed" impedes, but does not seriously interfere with, "petting dog"
Reality-phantasy level:	Reality completely

We can summarize these facts about Raymond's psychological habitat for this episode in a paragraph as follows: It was a social situation involving an interaction between Raymond and his friendly, accepting pet dog. The dog was attractive to Raymond, and was seen by Raymond as deserving friendly, supportive behavior from him. The whole situation was easy and beneficent. It was immediately and directly satisfying to Raymond; there was no goal to be set, no task to be performed, no reward to be achieved, no punishment to be avoided. There was no conflict or frustration. No barriers were present; there were no resistances to be overcome; there were no coercive forces. The cognitive aspects of the situation were clear; it had no problem element. It did not include a wide scope of objects and relations; neither was it limited to a single, simple stimulus. The situation was completely in the present; it included no past or future reference. It was entirely on the reality level. The situation, "petting dog," was not isolated; it overlapped with and was somewhat impeded by the situation "getting dressed"; there was no serious interference, however, between the two episodes.

On April 26, 1949, Raymond engaged in this and 711 other behavior-situation episodes. All of these have been analyzed and Raymond's composite psychological habitat for this day has been determined. The following are sample findings from the complete description.

Habitat Characteristics	Frequency of Occurrence (Per cent of 712 episodes)
General Nature of Habitat	
Predominantly social	50
Predominantly physical	33
Predominantly intellectual	2
Predominantly autistic	1
Mixed	14
Associates (social behavior objects)	
Associates present	85
Parents	15
Teachers	15
Other adults	18
Children	38
Associates not present, solitary situation	15
Most Frequent Meaning of Associates' Behavior to Raymond	
Domination	14
Appreciation	5
Affiliation	4
Exposition	2
Exhibition	2

Habitat Characteristics	Frequency of Occurrence (Per cent of 712 episodes)
Curiosity	1
Rejection	1
Miscellaneous, could not judge, no associate	71
Behavior Seen as Appropriate to Behavior Objects	
Curiosity	10
Exhibition	10
Expansion	5
Affiliation	3
Blamavoidance	3
Deference	3
Appreciation	2
Passivity	2
Exposition	2
Miscellaneous, could not judge, no associate	60
Centrality of Need	
Peripheral	48
Intermediate	41
Central	11
Strength of Need	
Below Medium	15
Medium	55
Above Medium	30
Interpersonal Relations	
Competition	4
Co-operation	13
Conflict	3
Parallel and conjunctive activities	59
Could not judge, no associate	21
Ruling Valence of Habitat	
Positive	93
Negative	7
Geniality of Total Situation	
Uncertain	4
Hostile	1
Inhospitable	9
Neutral	16

Habitat Characteristics	*Frequency of Occurrence* (Per cent of 712 episodes)
Beneficent	68
Gratifying	2
Motivational Structure	
Reward	0
Punishment	1
Social pressure	12
Means-end activity	40
Direct interest	34
Direct consummatory	13
Frustrating situation	20
Minimum strength	13
Medium strength	6
Maximum strength	1
Non-frustrating situation	80
Conflict	4
No conflict	76
Time Perspective	
Present dominant	44
Future dominant	4
Past dominant	1
Mixed	51
Aspiration level	
Raymond confronted with no clear task	55
Raymond confronted with a clear task	45
Aspiration above abilities	3
Aspiration below abilities	1
Aspiration at ability level	41
Overlapping Situations	
Isolated	45
Overlapping	55
Success and Failure	
Clear success situation	1
Clear failure situation	1
Gain or attainment	92
Loss or non-attainment	6

Habitat Characteristics	*Frequency of Occurrence* (Per cent of 712 episodes)
Evaluations of Raymond by Associates	
Definite approval of actions	6
Definite disapproval of actions	9
No overt evaluation of actions by associates	85
Expectations of Raymond's Associates	
Expression of definite expectation that	
Raymond should engage in "good" or	
"successful" behavior	8
No expectation expressed, no associates	92
Coercion by Associates	
Attempts by associates to change Raymond's	
behavior	40
By attacking him	3
By helping him	4
By resisting him	3
By social pressure	12
Other	18
No Coercion, no associates	60

From such data as these it appears possible to begin to describe the naturally occurring life situations of boys like Raymond not only in Midwest but, also, in New York City, England, Samoa, in orphanages, on farms and in apartments, and thus make a beginning toward a comparative psychological ecology. Specimen records provide data on the behavior of the subject as well as on his habitat. These data have not been reported in this paper. It will be obvious, however, that the possibility of relating behavior to psychological situation, on the one hand, and psychological situation to behavior setting and non-psychological milieu, on the other, opens up many promising lines of investigation. Such investigations should be pertinent not only to ecological problems but to systematic problems of psychology as well. It is encouraging to remember the important theoretical achievements of such non-experimental sciences as geology, meteorology, and astronomy.

Part Four
Basic Psychological Functions

CHAPTER 9

ЛЛЛЛЛЛЛЛЛЛЛЛЛЛЛЛЛЛЛЛЛЛЛЛЛЛЛ

The Place of Phenomenological Analysis in Social Psychological Theory

R. B. MACLEOD
Cornell University

Psychology may be loosely characterized as the attempt to be scientific about human experience and behavior. Social psychology is, accordingly, the attempt to be scientific about those aspects of behavior and experience which can be called "social." To be scientific is to be curious in a disciplined way, i.e., to try to understand (not merely to predict or control) with the aid of the best available methods of observation, deduction, and verification. The term "social" must mean at least "having to do with relations among individuals of the same kind." Clearly, if we are to use our terms as broadly as this, we shall be robbing social psychology of any distinctiveness whatsoever. If we admit of any relationship between one person and another as social, then obviously there is no psychology apart from social psychology; for there is virtually nothing that we do or feel or think that has not been in some way or another, immediately or remotely, affected by another person. There are those who contend for this reason that we have no right to talk of social psychology at all. There is only psychology. I think that I could without too many qualms of conscience defend this view. It seems to me that in speaking of social psychology as a separate discipline we may be doing violence to the facts, and we may even be impeding the progress of psychological theory. Social psychology did, in fact, develop as a separate discipline. One of our tasks today is to break down the barriers

which segregate it from the rest of psychology, and to develop a unifying point of view from which all experience and behavior can be understood as regulated by the same set of fundamental laws. This attempt to achieve unity, is, I think, one of the prominent characteristics
of psychology at mid-century. The particular approach to the problem
which I shall adopt is only one of several useful, and not necessarily
inconsistent, approaches. The phenomenological approach is certainly
not new; it is not a theory, and it is irreconcilable, as I see it, only with
the more extreme forms of positivism. It provides one way, but not the
only way, of bringing together certain diverging streams of psychological theory, but it does not necessarily dictate any particular final theory
of experience and behavior.

I

As we glance back over a half-century of attempts to be scientific
about social behavior and experience, we can discern a number of different theoretical settings within which social psychologies have been
written. This is not the occasion for an historical review, and in singling
out four such theoretical settings I know that I shall be doing violence
to history and tucking some strange bedfellows under a common blan-
ket. Nevertheless, there are, it seems to me, four recognizably different ways in which social psychological theory has been presented.

1. In the first place, we have social psychology presented as the study
of the psychological processes of social groups. The closing years of the
nineteenth century saw an enthusiastic extension of the scientific
method to the study of societies. The scientist had conquered the physical world—or so he thought; he was beginning to see how the more
complex forms of living matter could be envisaged within the context
of natural law. Why should not the complex interrelations among people be amenable to scientific study? The influence of Auguste Comte
was felt in Germany and England as well as in France, and sociology
as a science became, if not respectable, at least recognized. The facts of
social organization were facts, just as truly as were the facts of molec-
ular organization, and these facts had to be recorded, analyzed, and explained.

Much has been written about the "Group Mind fallacy," and many a
hefty epithet has been hurled against it. I often wonder how strenu-
ously the opponents of the group mind have tried to understand the

thinking of the nineteenth century, and how seriously they take the proverbial injunction about motes and beams. The doctrine of the Group Mind holds essentially that groups have mental characteristics analogous to the mental characteristics of the individual. Now, if we assume that the individual mind is a separate existent, independent of the body, and that groups have analogous non-corporeal appendages, then the doctrine can be attacked in the orthodox way. If, on the other hand, we consider mind as form of organization, or as function—and this is the most orthodox Aristotelianism—the question becomes: Are there characteristics of groups, of a psychological order, which can be studied as such without any necessary reference to the characteristics of any particular member of the group? This, I submit, is a reasonable question for research, and I do not think that the answer is obviously in the negative. In our twentieth-century sophistication we tend to reject the word "mind," because it smacks so much of something that rats do not have and which is therefore not scientific. But we do like the word "attitude"; we feel quite at home with words like "characteristics," "tendencies," "traditions," and "customs," and we grow positively smug when we can work in an expression like "pattern of culture" or "social norm." All these terms can be as readily applied to groups as to individuals, often much more readily. A tradition, for instance, although transmitted by means of processes which we describe in individual terms, is never fully actualized in any single individual. Similarly a language contains more than any individual speaker is capable of expressing. Even such terms as "national character" are beginning to lose their stigma (11). We have, then, identifiable processes and relationships which are properly regarded as group characteristics and which without too much strain on our part can be regarded as mental or psychological. Thus, if we reject the substantival view of mind, and think rather in terms of functions or modes of organization, we may quite properly talk of group mentality or group mind.

From this point of view there can be a legitimate study, and consequently a legitimate science, of the psychological characteristics of groups. In my opinion this kind of social psychology is properly a part of the science of sociology. It has in fact been developed primarily within the sociological tradition (9), although in recent years the anthropologists have been making a progressively richer contribution, and especially in the rapidly developing field of group dynamics, the psychologists have been contributing vigorously and creatively. While it poses important problems for the psychologist, it should be recognized as merely one part of the field of psychological inquiry.

2. The second theoretical setting for social psychology is that of the individual psychology of motivation. The belief that the key to the understanding of social behavior is to be found in the interplay of individual motives is not merely a revolt against the doctrine of the Group Mind—for McDougall, the most influential exponent of this doctrine, made the study of group mentality the central problem of social psychology (22). The casual student of McDougall frequently overlooks the fact that the analysis of instinct and sentiment is presented explicitly as an *introduction,* not as the real subject-matter of social psychology (21). Nevertheless, it is in the interplay of the sentiments, which in turn are rooted in the instincts, that McDougall finds his explanatory principles. The psychological bases of man's social nature are to be found in the springs of human conduct, in the innate psychophysical predispositions which select the objects to which he will respond, determine the ways in which they will arouse him, and steer his behavior with reference to them.

This is not the occasion for an evaluation of McDougall's system. His theory caught the fancy of the public for a decade or two, and then as rapidly lost favor as a new fad began to sweep the country. Not all of McDougall's critics seem to have done him the courtesy of reading his books, and it is my private opinion that when social psychologists eventually take time out to do some reading they will find in McDougall's writings a rich store of keen observation and penetrating thought that will make many of our current discoveries appear somewhat less original. The point to be stressed here, however, is McDougall's insistence that we search within the individual for the principles which will eventually render man's social behavior intelligible. The human organism is a biological organism, the human mind a product of the evolutionary process. If we are to understand why people behave like human beings, i.e., like social beings, we must first understand why they behave like animals; for man brings to the problem of surviving in human society the residues of ages of struggle for survival in less complex but more brutal environments. What is unique about man is the developing capacity for objectification. With the increasing modifiability of the instinctive patterns man's behavior becomes increasingly regulated by objects, ideas and ideals that are no longer simply and directly dictated by the instincts. The sentiments, then, the most powerful of which is centered about the idea of self, become the real regulators of social behavior. The sentiments derive their energy from the instincts, and they must provide an outlet for the instincts, but they can deviate so far from the original instinctive pattern that their origin is virtually unrecognizable. To phenotypic analysis they are functionally autonomous. Nevertheless, when conflict arises, when the structure of the sentiments is shattered, the primitive instincts take command and "natural" man is revealed in all his primitive savagery and nobility.

Individual motivation and the organization of the individual personality are likewise the supporting pillars of the vast disordered structure of Freudian doctrine. If, to maintain the architectural metaphor, we disregard the frightening gargoyles and the subterranean passages, we find a simple and intelligible design. Man's behavior is initiated, directed, and regulated by instinct. Man's social behavior becomes intelligible only when we see it as the expression, in direct or disguised form, of motives which in their essence are non-social. "Sociology," says Freud, "which deals with the behavior of man in society, can be nothing other than applied psychology" (6).

Attempts such as these to find the basis of social behavior in individual motivation are undoubtedly appealing, as one can see from an examination of the textbooks of the past forty years. Until recently it has been conventional to lay the groundwork for social analysis by examining the original nature of man. Even those who rejected McDougall's instincts tended for the most part to maintain McDougall's motivational emphasis. Prepotent reflexes, fundamental human wishes, desires, dependable motives, drives, physiological needs, and even the recently invented pushes, may in some cases represent a challenge to McDougall's emphasis on heredity, but they all imply that for an understanding of social behavior we must seek the origins in primitive motivation.

3. While they stressed primary motivation, both Freud and McDougall recognized the almost limitless modifiability of human behavior, at least on the phenotypic level. In other words, they were fully aware of the importance of learning, although this always remained a secondary principle of explanation. It is natural, particularly within the context of American functionalism, that many students of behavior

should have become more impressed by the fact of individual variation than by the evidence of invariance in the social life of man, and should consequently have accepted the laws of learning as the primary explanatory principles. This is the third theoretical setting for social psychology.

Like the motive-oriented theories, the learning-oriented theories are inevitably biological or quasi-biological in structure. The key concept is the biological process of adaptation or its psychological counterpart "adjustment." The primary fact is the sensitive and responding organism, and the language is usually an elaboration of the S-R formula. The organism, originally neutral or almost neutral, becomes exposed to new and progressively more complicated constellations of stimuli. Simple responses, adequate for adjustment on the level of immediate stimulation, become reinforced, eliminated, or elaborated, and the organism gradually builds up a more complicated system of responses to progressively more complicated stimulus constellations. It is interesting to note in the successive editions of standard elementary textbooks the modification of the original S-R formula, first to S-A-R, then to S-O-R, and finally to W-O-W (35), a change which parallels the increasing preoccupation of psychologists with social behavior. The world to which we respond is in part a social world; the stimuli which represent that world are social stimuli, or situations; and the responses we make are not fully characterized until we describe them in terms of the changes they make in the world in which we live.

From the psychological point of view, however, the symbol in the formula which looms ever larger is the central O, the organism, or organization, which assumes the directive and regulative function in behavior. Whether or not we presuppose certain unlearned initiators of behavior—and most of the "learning" psychologists do—it is the central learned dispositions which maintain control and which are responsible for those types of behavior that are peculiarly social. John Dewey made this point very forcibly in 1922 when he took issue with the instinctivists (incidentally, without even mentioning McDougall). "At some place on the globe, at some time," says Dewey, "every kind of practice seems to have been tolerated or even praised. How is the tremendous diversity of institutions (including moral codes) to be accounted for? The native stock of instincts is practically the same everywhere. Exaggerate as we like the native differences of Patagonians and Greeks,

Sioux Indians and Hindoos, Bushmen and Chinese, their original differences will bear no comparison to the amount of difference found in custom and culture. Since such a diversity cannot be attributed to an original identity, the development of native impulse must be stated in terms of acquired habits, not the growth of customs in terms of instincts" (4, p. 91).

The term "habit" has, of course, yielded place to the more imposing language of conditioning, and those who find the Pavlovian harness too restrictive are now inclined to cluster the acquired determinants of social behavior under the general label of "attitudes." The terminology is not important. What concerns us at present is the way in which the problem of social psychology is being defined. Within this theoretical setting, the primary data of social psychology are conceived as dispositions of the organism, built up through experience. These dispositions select those constellations of stimuli to which the organism will respond and determine the way in which the response will be made. This is quasi-biological language. It leaves room for the eventual restatement of the central determinants in terms of cell assemblies, reverberating circuits, or whatever constructs the neurophysiology of the future may give us. The important fact is that these determinants are lodged within the organism, and even if they are deduced from the analysis of behavior and experience they are conceived as parts or properties of the organism. An attitude is thus treated as a biological fact, as an entity co-ordinate with the other entities of "objective" science, capable of being observed, measured, and eventually controlled.

The central problem for this type of social psychology becomes of necessity that of social learning. Beginning with the fact of cultural diversity, the psychologist must explain how the patterns or themes or norms of a culture become "interiorized" in the individual. This calls on the one hand for an analysis of the culture itself, for which the psychologist must depend on the sociologist and the anthropologist, and, on the other hand, for descriptive and experimental studies of the ways in which the effects of social stimulation become salted away in the form of enduring dispositions, and of the ways in which these dispositions affect behavior. It is in no sense a disparagement of the bio-social approach to point out that in this area of investigation the psychologist is still lagging sadly behind the sociologist and the anthropologist. We have still no theory of social learning capable of dealing competently with the wealth of problems set for us by the comparative study of cultures. Perhaps the difficulty is intrinsic in the concept of "learning" as such; perhaps we have been merely too reluctant to relinquish the language of traditional "learning" psychology. It may be that a pattern of learning theory appropriate to rats in mazes, dogs in Pavlovian harness, and sophomores memorizing nonsense syllables is simply not applicable to the process of acquiring an attitude. Rather than stretch the old laws to encompass the new facts, it might be wiser to concentrate on the new facts with the thought that possibly there may be some different laws.

4. The fourth theoretical setting does not yet represent a well-established tradition in social psychology, although the rest of my discussion will in a sense be a further development of this point of view. This is the attempt to find in the psychology of perception the basis for an understanding of social behavior and experience. The current term is "cognitive structure," which obviously includes more than what have been traditionally considered as perceptual phenomena, and the current epithet is "perceptual imperialism" (16). The main thesis is that if we are to understand the social behavior of man we must understand the structure of the social world to which he is responding—not merely the social world as independently defined by the omniscient sociologist, but the social world as it is actually apprehended by the behaving individual. The problem, then, is essentially a cognitive problem, and the basis of cognition is perception.

Although, as Brunswik (3) has ruefully pointed out, there are at least six kinds of perceptual psychology, it will suffice for present purposes to reduce this number to three. First, we have the approach of traditional psychophysics, with its search for simple correlations between stimulus and sensation and its relegation of the phenomena of organization and meaning to the limbo of the central intellective processes. Although we call it psychophysics it was also a psychophysiology, for it included the attempt to trace the neural connection between the stimulus and the aroused sensation. Classical psychophysics had nothing to say about social perception. In recent years, however, the basis of psychophysical analysis has been broadened, and we now have some promising applications of psychophysical method to the analysis of social judgments (31).

Secondly, we have the revolt against the atomism of the classical school, the rejection of the basic distinction between sensation and perception, and the insistence that meaning and organization are immediately given in perception. Although this emphasis has been popularly identified with the Gestalt psychology, it was by no means peculiar to the Berlin group. In Göttingen, Leipzig, Hamburg, and Vienna the same revolt was taking place, and even William James may be interpreted as having anticipated it. The movement has been marked by a greater reliance on phenomenological observation and, in the Gestalt tradition at least, by a shift of emphasis from psychophysics to psychophysiology. The Gestalt theory of perception is, of course, still a psychophysical theory, in that it attempts to co-ordinate perceptual experience to the variables in the physical world. In the doctrine of isomorphism, however, it is asserted that the all-important parallel to perceptual organization is to be found not in the patterning of stimulus processes but rather in the immediately underlying organization of brain activities. Köhler's field theory of perception is thus becoming more and more explicitly a field theory of cortical functioning (14).

This kind of physiological field theory allows for the study of social perception. As long as it is assumed that for every variable in experience there must be a cortical isomorph, it must also be assumed that even the least tangible of perceptual experiences, like the percept of self, the impression of another's personality, or the dimension of irreality, will eventually be pinned down to a counterpart in somatic process. This point has been made explicitly by Köhler (13, p. 70), and has been elaborated by Koffka (12). The phenomena of social perception have thus been given, as it were, a physiological sanction in advance. The psychologist may study them with a clear conscience, even though he cannot yet specify their physiological isomorphs. Nevertheless, it is the phenomenological rather than the physiological emphasis of Gestalt theory which has led to the broadening of the Gestalt approach to perception. Kurt Lewin never denied the possibility of an ultimate unification of psychological and physiological field principles (17). His position was, rather, that a purely psychological analysis can and must proceed without physiological support. The valence of a phenomenal object is just as truly a property of the object as is its color or shape, and the tension between a self and another self is a fact of psychological field organization, which may rest on but which does not require any theory about a corresponding cortical tension. Thus both the orthodox

Gestalt psychologists and the Lewinian deviants have given the psychology of perception a steer in the direction of the social. The best expression of this is to be found in the recent textbook by Krech and Crutchfield (15).

Finally, we have the perceptual functionalists. Functionalism, as Woodworth (36) has concluded, has settled down to the "middle of the road" American psychology. It is organism-centered, it prefers a verbal form like perceiving to a nominal form like perception, and it conceives of the various psychological processes as specialized ways in which the organism adjusts itself to a real world. We have already noted that the prevailing emphasis on learning in social psychology is a natural expression of the functionalist point of view. But for the functionalist perceiving is also a function, one of the organism's ways of adjusting itself, and in recent years we have had a revival of interest in the social aspects of perceiving. For the groundwork of theory we are indebted particularly to Egon Brunswik (2), who perhaps for the first time has given us a functional theory of perception that does full justice to the rich store of available perceptual research, notably on the perceptual constancies. In the rapidly growing experimental movement spearheaded by Bruner, Postman, and their colleagues we have a fresh appreciation of the significance of perceiving in social behavior. What they are giving us is more than the commonplace demonstration that what we perceive is in part determined by our pre-existing attitudes or sets; it is an indication of the value of perceptual analysis as a major tool of social psychology.

Whether we adopt a functional, a configurational, or some other point of view, there is clearly a growing belief that if we are to understand social behavior we must have an understanding of the processes of perception. Perception, as Werner puts it, is becoming "a meeting ground of general experimental and clinical-social psychology" (34, p. 3). A perceptionist like myself is both encouraged and at the same time a little appalled at this sudden upsurge of enthusiasm for what used to be a modest and eminently respectable branch of psychology.

II

These four theoretical settings for social psychology with their respective emphases on group processes, on motivation, on learning, and on perception, may have been too simply and arbitrarily defined. A more elaborate scheme might have been closer to the facts. Nevertheless, whatever our classification, we are still faced with the same problem, namely, that of finding a way of unifying the different approaches. What I shall now try to do is to indicate some possible contributions of a psychological phenomenology toward this end.

First, then, as to the meaning of the term "phenomenological." One of the social scientist's chief embarrassments is always his terminology. A word will be introduced as a legitimate aid to precise thinking, and suddenly we find that it has become nothing but a social facilitator. One such word is "operational." It makes us feel comfortably scientific to talk about operational definitions, although most of the time we are referring merely to "good definitions." Another such word is "phenomenological." To be able to use it without stuttering is to create an impression of profundity and scholarliness. Having used it several times in print (18, 19, 20), I am beginning to suffer a guilt reaction, and there are moments when I wish we could bury the word. It seems to be too late, however. Snygg and Combs (29) have now presented phenomenology as a new frame of reference for psychology, and the students are already rolling the word on their tongues. Our only alternative is consequently to be as clear as possible in our use of it.

Phenomenology is *not* a new frame of reference for psychology. One dislikes to take exception to a book, the general tone of which is so thoroughly invigorating and the consequences of which may be so good, but the facts must be straightened out. Phenomenology has an impressive history, which no one has yet adequately written. It is primarily a German development, although a variation of it has recently flared up in France as Existentialism, and it is represented in the United States by an active group who publish the journal *Philosophy and Phenomenological Research*. It developed as a branch of philosophical inquiry, but it has both influenced and been influenced by the research of many experimental psychologists. Although it has been labeled as a philosophical school, the basic approach has been accepted by many scholars and scientists who would not identify themselves with the school. Snygg and Combs, in adopting the term "phenomenology," have given us a system which bears only a broad resemblance to the phenomenology we have known for the past fifty years.[1]

There are three points in connection with phenomenology which de-

---

[1] A more appropriate connection would be with the *verstehende Psychologie* of Dilthey, Spranger, and Jaspers. Snygg and Combs make no mention, however, either of these or of any of the phenomenologists.

serve discussion here: (1) the philosophical setting of the approach, (2) its actual application to the problems of experimental psychology, and (3) its possible extension to some of the less tangible problems of social psychology. The first of these we must pass over briefly. In 1900 Edmund Husserl began the publication of his "Logische Untersuchungen," in which he attempted to find in the analysis of experience the basis for logic and epistemology. On the one hand this involved a descriptive psychology of the cognitive processes, in which all assumptions about the nature of the "real" world or about ultimate "truth" are, as it were, placed in brackets, and the phenomena themselves are simply observed, described, and ordered according to their own intrinsic characteristics. On the other hand, and partly on the basis of the descriptive psychology, it involved an examination and ordering of the essences which are revealed in experience but are in no sense created by experience. The basic method he called pure phenomenology. It leads, as one readily sees, in two directions, on the one hand toward a refinement of the methods of descriptive psychological analysis and on the other toward a system of epistemology and, eventually, of metaphysics. The philosophical phenomenology of the later Husserl, and of his pupil Heidegger, need not concern us. It bears no necessary reference to psychological methodology. The psychological phenomenology of the earlier Husserl did, however, have an appreciable influence.[2]

The essential thing about psychological phenomenology is that it is not a school or a system but an approach. A phenomenon is by definition an appearance. Psychological phenomenology is the attempt to suspend biases and to observe and describe faithfully that which appears. Now it is clearly ridiculous to assume that there can ever be such a thing as utterly unbiased observation. The bias of the perceiver, even if it takes the form of a mild expectation, is inevitably a part of the process of perception. One might argue accordingly that any phenomenology is a mere fiction and that we might as well forget about it. Nevertheless, if we stress the word "attempt," we find that our proposition is both meaningful and extremely important. It is possible for us to become aware of many of the implicit assumptions which govern our observation and, through discipline, to suspend them. It would be equally ridiculous to expect even the most accomplished phenomenolo-

---

[2] For a full and competent discussion of the contribution of phenomenology to psychology the reader is referred to the recent book by Merleau-Ponty (24).

gist to be able to suspend all biases simultaneously and observe the totality of experience in one flash of brilliant intuition. It is of the very essence of observation that the whole can never be grasped in a single act of observing.

Is not phenomenology, then, merely a name for what any good scientist does anyway? Does not the scientist always attempt to suspend his biases? The answer is emphatically: No. The scientist is always trying to solve a problem, to test an hypothesis, to refine a measurement. He tries to exclude anything that may jeopardize the accuracy of his observation; but in doing so he is implicitly affirming the existence of a fact or a truth of which his observation is only an incomplete indicator. His observation is directed not toward the experience as such but toward that which is revealed through the experience. A phenomenologist turned loose in a physics laboratory would make a horrible mess of things. In fact, if he remained a phenomenologist for very long, he could not survive; for he would be so busy observing himself growing hungry that he would forget to eat.

It should be clear, then, that there really is no such person as a phenomenologist; there are only people who from time to time adopt the phenomenological attitude. And, indeed, there is probably no such thing as a purely phenomenological psychology; there are merely psychologies which attempt to take as their starting point the unbiased observation of phenomena. The fruitfulness of this approach in the psychology of perception is no longer a matter for dispute. During the Titchenerian days at Cornell the art of introspection was developed to a point probably never attained before or since. Yet when Wertheimer reported the phenomenon, the best the Cornell laboratory could do was dispose of it as a grey flash (5). This is a case in which the phenomenon was slighted because it did not conform to the traditional theory of perception. Similarly the Cornell introspectionism had no place for the modes of appearance of color, so brilliantly described by David Katz (10). Rubin's figure-ground relationships (26) and a host of other phenomena could never have found a central place in the psychology of perception had psychologists had not been willing to look at the phenomena without prejudging them in terms of a reductive-atomistic bias. Yet it is phenomena such as these that are most characteristic of the world of things as we perceive them. The phenomenological approach does not merely permit the inclusion of meaning as a fact of perception;

it reveals meaning as the very stuff of experience, and it invites the psychologist to turn his attention to the meaningful aspects of the world.

Phenomenology is, however, not psychology. Phenomenology is sheer description. Psychology is a science, which attempts to explain; and to explain it must have constructs. There is nothing in the descriptive analysis of experience that can decide whether the explanatory constructs are to be quasi-psychological, quasi-sociological, quasi-biological, or quasi-mathematical. All the phenomenologist can do is insist that the system of constructs be flexible enough to deal with experience in all its richness and variety. No set of constructs thus far proposed has been able to do this. In fact, the history of psychology is studded with cases in which it has been the psychologist, with his more intimate familiarity with phenomena, who had laid down the requirements for physiological theory. This is not to argue that the psychologist should dispense with physiological, or even mathematical, theorizing. It has disciplinary value, and once in a while our theories might even be right. What is of the utmost importance, however, is that the psychologist be not restricted in his observation to those phenomena that can be readily dealt with in terms of the constructs of a neighboring science. As one more illustration one might cite Michotte's brilliant study of the perception of causality (25). For most of us, causality as phenomenon is subtly excluded from investigation by an epistemological bias. Causality is literally before our eyes wherever we turn; yet it required a Michotte to make it a problem for experimental psychology.

So far, we have considered phenomenology as concerned with what I can see with my eyes and you with yours. Is the phenomenological approach restricted to so-called "private" worlds, or can we meaningfully talk about the phenomenal world of the other person? This is, of course, a question that goes beyond psychology, but some kind of answer is necessary if phenomenology is to be of any use to social psychology. Two answers are immediately available. One is the solipsism of George Berkeley, which every freshman student of philosophy finds so delightful and so irresistible, and from which he can be rescued only by an act of God. It is easy to demonstrate that the qualities of objects are merely ideas in my mind, that the objects themselves are nothing more than their qualities and are therefore ideas too, and that people who scowl and make noises, are just scowls and noises, also ideas in my mind; in fact, that my resistance to the consequences of my own logic is nothing but an idea. Communication, from this point of view, presents no problem because there is nobody to communicate with. The behaviorist answer, which also appeals to freshmen, is equally devastating. It assumes, naïvely, that there are other organisms, but that my knowledge of them is limited to the stimuli from them which affect my receptors. (One should really not use mentalistic words like "I" and "mine," but the alternative language is too cumbersome.) My responses may constitute stimuli for the other organism, whose responses may in turn stimulate me, until eventually there is some co-ordination between the responses of the two organisms. But I may not talk of the phenomenal world, or the percepts, or the ideas, or the other organisms. That would be rank anthropomorphism; and anthropomorphism is bad. Indeed it is slightly sinful—or at least undemocratic—for me to talk of my own phenomenal world, since the other organism could never share in it. These are two extreme points of view, which I am sure no one has ever really taken seriously; yet, within the context of their presuppositions, they are relatively impregnable. Each constitutes for different reasons a denial of the possibility of a social psychology based on phenomenological analysis. Rather than attack them directly, may I suggest that we examine from a phenomenological point of view two of the standard constructs of social psychology, namely, the social object and the social agent. In other words, what can phenomenology say about social perception and the ego?

III

The term "social perception" seems to be used in two senses, and the two meanings are not always kept distinct from each other. On the one hand, we have the problem of the social determination of perception, on the other hand the problem of the perception of the social. Neither problem is immediately clear. Let us consider first the social determination of perception.

The problem might be restated as follows: in everyday life we do not always perceive things as they really are. Within wide limits we perceive them as we want them to be, as we expect them to be, or in terms of an unconscious bias. Now our wants, expectations, and biases are in large measure socially determined; therefore our perceptions are to a corresponding degree socially determined. What is the extent of this social determination, and what are the causal processes involved?

When one looks for illustrations one naturally thinks of the hallucina-
tion, the case of mistaken recognition, the Rorschach and TAT observations, and the wealth of examples provided by the anthropologists. In
each case a central disposition or attitude, which has presumably been
built up through experience, constitutes one of the determinants of
what is perceived. This is not a new problem in psychology. It is simply
a modern version of the nativist-empirist controversy of the nineteenth
century, what is modern being merely the word "social." The question
in its classic form is: How much of the determination is central and
how much is peripheral? Stated in this way, the question is as unanswer-
able as the parallel question: How much of behavior is determined by
environment and how much by heredity? Heredity and environment
are simply not co-ordinate and independently definable factors. Both
are involved in all behavior and, except in a most superficial sense, the
relationship between the two is not quantifiable.

The central-peripheral dichotomy is equally illicit. If we talk quasi-
physiological language for a moment, we must assume that an attitude
or an expectation is somehow or other lodged in the cortex. We might
be tempted to say, then, in line with some of the older theories, that the
color of an object is determined in the retina and its meaning in the
cortex. But the color processes, whatever they may be, cannot produce
the experience of color until the excitation has been transmitted to the
cortex. We are forced to conclude, then, that the so-called peripheral
determinant is also cortical. The problem must accordingly be restated
in terms of the orginization of processes in the cortex. Are there certain
neatly segregated cortical processes which, if untampered with, will give
us pure, meaningless sensation? Our ignorance of the cortex is pro-
found, but there is not one particle of evidence, physiological or psychological, to support an affirmative answer. What little we know about
cortical functioning, and certainly all that we know about experience,
would suggest that any process which leads to perception affects and is
affected by other processes in its field. One fact of observation, which
for me is conclusive, is too seldom mentioned, namely, the fact of consciousness. Perception is a conscious process. As such it involves a relationship between a self and that which is not self. If we maintain the
physiological analogy we must assume that there is something in the
cortex corresponding to the self. There must accordingly be some sort of

communication between the self-process and the not-self process. The self is thus the irreducible minimum of context for a percept.

If a percept is always a percept-in-context, our next question becomes that of the degree of stability or independence of the various perceptual processes. This is a problem for concrete research rather than for the either/or kind of argument. The early emphasis in Gestalt psychology was on the importance of autochthonous organization. It was part of the battle against empiricism, and the argument was presented so vigorously as to lead some critics to the conclusion that the Gestalt psychologists were denying any possible influence of past experience on perception. This was obviously a misinterpretation. The problem has recently been restated in clear and sober fashion by Wallach (32) in terms of the conditions under which process and trace can interact. That such interaction takes place cannot be questioned, but how they interact, what kind of trace can affect what kind of process and in what way, can be found out only through patient investigation. I see a circle; it continues to look circular even when it is tipped, and no amount of willing on my part will make it look less circular; but the addition of a few oblique lines will destroy the circularity at once. I see a beautiful, luscious apple, but the mere suggestion of a worm in it will make it look less appetizing. Both circularity and appetizingness are perceptual properties. To say that one is peripherally and the other centrally determined is clearly a gross oversimplification. Every percept is a function of field conditions. In the past we have tended in our perceptual studies to concentrate on the more easily controlled field conditions, namely, those which respond fairly directly to changes in stimulation. What we need now is obviously more and more emphasis on the less easily controlled field conditions, on what Bruner and Postman have called the "psychological mechanisms which mediate between the directive states of the organism and changes in perceptual response" (1, p. 29).

The problem of the social determination of perception is thus not a special problem, but a logical and inevitable development of sound perceptual theory. Using the language of field theory, we are now trying to study more and more complex percepts in more and more complex fields. In this connection there is a lesson we can learn from the history of psychology, namely, that each great advance in perceptual theory has depended in large part on a more careful scrutiny of perceptual phenomena. I have mentioned Wertheimer's phi phenomenon as an example. An even better example is to be found in Katz's pioneer work on color constancy. The crude fact of constancy had been noted before. Katz observed that, when illumination is reduced, although a surface may maintain its essential color (*eigentliche Farbe*) it loses correspondingly in the dimension of *Ausgeprägtheit* (pronouncedness). This is a purely phenomenological distinction; yet it led, as we all know, to extremely important theoretical consequences. Further examples could be added indefinitely, but they are hardly necessary. The point of the argument is simply this, that as we approach the more difficult problems of perception the importance of a sound phenomenology becomes correspondingly greater. Writing in a different context, Brunswik has said: "It must be stressed . . . that act psychology and phenomenology are important, and perhaps indispensable, preliminaries to molar research of the objective kind" (3, p. 59). This from any other functionalist might be considered a concession, but Brunswik's own work makes it amply clear that he takes this proposition seriously.

The conclusion to which one comes, then, is that we shall not get very far in our attempt to explain social determination until we have a thorough phenomenology of the social content of perception, i.e., a study of the perception of the social. May I once more suggest that the content we are interested in cannot be limited by the word "social," and that we may find it necessary to use a more comprehensive term than "perception." We are interested, of course, in the angriness of a face—presumably a social percept, since the face belongs to another person—but we are also interested in the angriness of a cloud, which has nothing to do with another person, unless we impose on our description a projection theory of perception, which would be a denial of our phenomenological approach. Similarly, the person in front of us who threatens us might be considered a percept, but the absent person whose threatening image is vividly present is not ordinarily considered to be a percept. Our conventional psychology speaks of the remembered or imagined person. The distinction is not always easy to draw, and it may not be of primary importance. In the phenomenal world we have things and events, varying in their properties and related to one another in various ways. Some of the variations we observe fit fairly neatly into the conventional categories. Memories, for instance, are usually less clear than percepts, and images are usually less stable; but we have variations in clarity and stability within the category of percepts. As a matter of fact, our customary categories of perception, memory and imagination are imposed on our psychology by a simple, and rather crude, epistemology. We cannot quarrel with this, because it is the naïve realism of everyday life; but we must recognize it as one of the biases that constrict our observation.

The phenomenology of the past has tended to focus on the more objective components of experience, objective, that is, in the sense of being apprehended as essentially independent of the self. We know a great deal about the world of color and the world of touch, about the phenomenology of sounds, and about the organizations of these in space and time. For the most part it is possible to describe these phenomena without bringing in the self except as a relatively neutral reference point. When we approach such phenomena as attractiveness and repulsiveness, however, or reality character, or even the simple sensory qualities of warm, cold, and pain, we find it is not always possible to exclude the self from our analysis. Many of these phenomena are just as truly properties of objects as are redness and roughness; but others are more correctly described as subjective, i.e., as states or properties of the self. Within the phenomenal world objectivity and subjectivity are not independent categories, but constitute rather a direction of variation. A film color is in this sense less objective than a surface color, the pain of a pinprick less subjective than the pain of a headache. The distinction has nothing to do with the degree of dependence on the organism, for all experiences are equally dependent on the organism. It does, however, involve the experience of selfhood. A piece of chocolate possesses, in Lewin's language, positive valence. It looks good and it tastes good, especially when I am hungry. But it may look and taste good even when I am not hungry. The goodness of the chocolate is phenomenally inherent in the chocolate. Yet there may be a subtle difference between the goodness it has when I am hungry and the goodness it has when I am not hungry. I cannot characterize the difference precisely, but it is meaningfully related to a state of me. The hungriness of me does not create the goodness of the chocolate, but there is clearly an intimate relationship. One could pick innumerable, and probably better examples. The cheeriness of a melody, the grandeur of a mountain, the loveliness of a lady in the moonlight, or, to crib from William James, the never-to-be-too-much-sat-on-ableness of a nestfull of eggs. These are all objective phenomena, but their meaning is imbedded in a self-object relationship. The phenomenology of the object will thus be incomplete until we have a phenomenology of the self.

For the purpose of this discussion I prefer the word "self" to the word "ego." The self is a phenomenal datum, or a category of phenomenal data. The ego, in my thinking, is not a datum but a construct. The self can be observed and described; the ego is deduced or postulated. The ego may be conceived in quasi-psychological terms, as in the Freudian system, or in quasi-physiological terms as a sub-system of the organism. All I should argue at the moment is that before we can have a sound theory of the ego we must have a careful phenomenology of the self.[3] The self must also be distinguished from the personality. At the risk of appearing pedantic, might I suggest that the word personality be reserved, in phenomenological analysis at least, for what has sometimes been called the "other self" or the "other person." To tie things together, we might borrow from William Stern (30) the non-phenomenological concept of "person." The person, then, is the neutral entity, the whole individual. The ego is a sub-system of the person. Self and personality are respectively the "inside" and the "outside" views of the person, not necessarily parallel. There can thus be a phenomenology of the self and a phenomenology of the personality (or other self); and both are necessary.

It would not be possible here, even if I were capable of doing so, to give even an outline of a phenomenology of the self. All I can hope to do is to make a few observations that seem to be relevant to the problems of social psychology and to stress the need for systematic research. One of our main difficulties is that we have never really accepted the self as a topic for research. The problems have been brilliantly discussed by William James, James Ward, and others, and more recently G. H. Mead (23) and Kurt Koffka (12) have given it a place of prominence in systematic doctrine; but the admirably thorough review of the literature by Sherif and Cantril (28) reveals disappointingly little that could pass as respectable research. The self is the most important component of the psychological field, yet for every study of the self as percept, or of the development of selfhood, there are hundreds devoted to the perception of squares and circles and the learning of nonsense sylla-

---

[3] The disagreement with Professor Hilgard (7) is perhaps not as fundamental as this statement might suggest.

bles. It is true that the German literature contains more. Careful phenomenological analyses are to be found, for instance, in Scheler's study
of sympathy (27) and in the various volumes of Husserl's *Jahrbuch für
Philosophie und Phänomenologische Forschung*. These are not research
in the sense in which we use the term, although they constitute an indispensable preliminary to research. What we need now is less talk
about the self and more empirical studies.

To study the self empirically we must begin with the phenomenon.
This means that we must temporarily suspend any hypotheses we may
have about the transcendental self, the pure ego, the cognitive agent,
just as in studying objective percepts we bracket our questions about
the "reality" of the physical world. As phenomenologists, we are, of
course, interested in those phenomenal properties of the self which
invite the belief in a pure ego, just as we are interested in the
Dinghaftigkeit of the perceived table or chair; but these, I suggest,
would not be the easiest phenomena to begin with. The inescapable
phenomenon of selfhood is the body, not the organism, but the body
as it is present in the phenomenal world. The self that we begin with
is thus a segregated, bounded entity. It is extended and located in
space; it endures in time; it possesses color, weight, and various other
properties found in other entities of the phenomenal world. As such
it can be studied experimentally, just as we study the perceptual objects around us. We have, tucked away in the literature of somaesthesis,
a great deal of information about the phenomenal body, although
much of it will require reinterpretation.

To this extent the self is in principle just like any other object. Properly speaking, however, it should not be called an object, for it has the
unique characteristic of being the indispensable condition of all ob-
ject-perception. It is an ever-present anchorage point, about which the
frameworks of space and time are organized. It is in a completely literal
and empirical sense the subject of all experience. This, too, is a matter
for experimental investigation.

It is when we approach the more dynamic properties of the self that
we begin to encounter difficulties. The phenomenal world is not static.
It contains purposes, wishes, and anxieties, and at first glance these
seem to be uniquely characteristic of the self. It is intelligible that
many psychologists have been led to the conclusion that the dynamic
properties which seem to inhere in the objective world have all been

projected into it. The projection theory has not recently been defended in systematic fashion, but it comes up implicitly in the interpretation of the studies based on the so-called "projective" techniques. What the individual sees in the Rorschach ink-blot is what he puts into it. I cannot take time to discuss the projection theory in detail, but there are, it seems to me, two points to be made. In the first place, the dynamic properties of the phenomenal world are not limited to the self. We perceive fear or anger in the other person, we perceive direction of movement, we perceive objective causation. In the second place, the self may be a completely passive component of the field, responding and adjusting to the forces around it, rather than generating those forces. There is nothing in phenomenological analysis which requires us to believe that the self is the only, or even the main, point of origin of vectors. Indeed, what used to be called the "pathetic" fallacy may be closer to psychological truth than the theories that have attempted to correct it. This is not to argue that we can learn nothing from the projective methods, merely that the term "projective" is misleading. We do not project the meaning into an object any more than we project the redness or the squareness into it. What looks like projection is just as much a function of the objective as it is of the subjective structure. The less rigid of the two structures will tend to conform in a meaningful way to the more rigid.

To say that the individual organizes his world is thus not strictly in accord with the phenomena. The self and the world organize each other or, better stated, become organized together. There is another way, however, in which such a statement can be misleading. It suggests that there is one world which belongs to one individual and another world which belongs to another individual. For some practical purposes this is not a bad way of speaking. When I try to understand an unhappy child I try to see things as he sees them and to feel myself as he must feel himself. This is in essence the "phenomenological" approach of Snygg and Combs, which they oppose to what they call the "objective" approach, and it is one with which I have great sympathy. We run the danger of confusion, however, if we speak of the phenomenal world as though it were a "private" world. If we had only private worlds we could have no communication.

Let us look again at the phenomena. The meaning of "private" hinges on the meaning of such words as "I" and "mine." We have already discussed the meaning of "I." That is the self. It may not have the same meaning at all times, including sometimes more and sometimes less; and this is even truer of the word "we." The word "my" necessarily bears reference to the self, but it has a still broader range of meanings. "My" may refer, among other things, to a part of me like my head, to a possession of me like my hat, to a property of me like my weight, to a characterization of me like my reputation, and so forth; but it always implies an alternative category of that which is not mine, possibly "yours" or "his" or "its." In other words, "my" properly characterizes only some of the components of the phenomenal world. The bulk of the phenomena are not mine at all, any more than they are yours. You and I observe and describe the same object. We don't describe it respectively in terms of your red and my red, your square and my square, nor would it be meaningful to talk of it as our red square. In fact, as Titchener's pupils always found, it requires great effort to look at an object and treat it as though it were not an object but an experience. This basic fact of phenomenal objectivity is the fact which renders possible the understanding of one person by another. We do not ordinarily live in private worlds. For each of us there are some phenomena of a private or subjective nature but together we live in a public world, a world which contains people as well as things.

IV

What we have covered so far is merely a sample of the problems we encounter when we embark on phenomenological analysis. It has not been possible to discuss them with any degree of thoroughness, nor to pay proper tribute to the many writers who have dealt with them more adequately. May I conclude by repeating three general points which I have tried to make and then returning briefly to the four types of social psychology outlined at the beginning?

First, phenomenology in its psychological context is not a theory but an approach. Its one assumption is that there are things to look at and listen to and think and feel about—in other words, there are phenomena—and that one can gradually learn to observe and describe these without necessary reference to their hypothetical origin, destiny, or status in the universe.

Secondly, phenomenology is not psychology. It is merely a first step in the direction of a scientific psychology. It helps to set the problem, and it serves as a constant check on the adequacy of our methods and the correctness of our thinking. It does not, as such, dictate the constructs in terms of which psychological phenomena are eventually to be explained.

Thirdly, phenomenology is a field for research. True, it is easy and delightful to sit in an armchair and phenomenologize, and beyond phenomenology there is always the lure of epistemology and metaphysics. Nevertheless, one can and must be disciplined about it. The usefulness of the phenomenological approach has been demonstrated beyond question in the experimental psychology of perception and in the psychology of thinking. There are many more phenomena in these fields to be investigated, but we need now to apply the same method of careful descriptive analysis to other fields, notably to motivation and the affective life.

To what extent can a phenomenological approach help to clarify the problems and methods of social psychology, and relate these to the problems and methods of general psychology? The answer, it seems to me, is that there is a challenge and a promise but that most of the work is still to be done. Insofar as our psychology is rooted in the observation of experience and behavior, i.e., in the study of phenomena—and this includes all psychologies except those that deny the existence of phenomena—the unbiased scrutiny of phenomena is a necessary prerequisite to all further work. This is true of all four types of social psychology. In theory, the study of group characteristics can proceed without the aid of phenomenology. In other words I concede the possibility of a sociology that is independent of psychology. In actual practice, however, such a sociology is likely to be formal and barren. A more fruitful study of national, racial, or other group characteristics is likely to include as some of its important facts the ways in which nations, races, and other groups are actually apprehended by people. This is equally true for the study of the dynamics of groups. Before we can understand social roles, for instance, and the ways in which they interact, we must know what in phenomenal terms a role is.

For a motive-oriented social psychology the key problem is obviously that of the nature of motivation. If I had time I should like to argue that the source of most of our confusion in motivational theory lies in our lack of an adequate phenomenology of motive. Our concepts of need and goal have too frequently failed to distinguish between psychological content and logical implication, and we have tended to jump from biological constructs to ego-constructs without pausing to examine the phenomenal characteristics of the self. We cannot have a genuine dynamics of behavior until we have scrutinized the dynamic phenomena themselves.

Insofar as our learning-oriented theories are couched in a quasi-mathematical language without phenomenal content, they are, I am afraid, beyond hope. If, however, their primary concern is to discover how it is that the individual incorporates within his own behavioral system the characteristics of a culture, then there is clearly a role for phenomenology. How are the variables of a culture, its values, its customs, its prohibitions, represented in the psychological field? What is the phenomenal counterpart of an attitude, of a social role? What is the meaning for the individual of reward and punishment? And, above all, through what changes do the structures and relationships of the phenomenal world pass as the individual becomes a social being? These are all phenomenological questions of first importance.

To speak of a cognitively oriented social psychology is in my opinion merely another way of referring to a social psychology that begins with phenomenological analysis, which is clearly the approach I am favoring. If this be perceptual imperialism, I plead guilty to the charge. I think, however, that the epithet is slightly misleading. If one were a functionalist and favored the function of perception over other functions, one would be open to the charge, and one might retaliate by hurling back other epithets, like "motive imperialism" or "learning imperialism" or even "organism imperialism." As I see it, however, phenomenological analysis is prior to the adoption of any systematic theory. Phenomenology ought to be a neutral court where evidence for or against any system may be dispassionately assessed. It just happens that our best examples of phenomenological analysis are to be found in what we have traditionally called the psychology of perception.

One final word of caution, and this, too, is merely repetition. It is easy to list the problems which demand further phenomenological analysis, the physiognomic properties of objects, the self as percept and as agent, the impressions of personality, the dynamic properties of changing psychological fields, the phenomenology of linguistic meaning, and so forth. It is easy to say that we must understand the world as other people see it. But there is a great distance between the recognition of the problem and its solution. We still have to learn how to do it.

REFERENCES

1. Bruner, J. S., and L. Postman. Perception, Cognition and Behavior, *J. Personality*, 1949, *18*, 14–31.
2. Brunswik, E. *Systematic and Representative Design of Psychological Experiments.* Univ. Calif. Press, 1947.
3. Brunswik, E. Remarks on Functionalism in Perception, *J. Personality*, 1949, *18*, 56–65.
4. Dewey, J. *Human Nature and Conduct.* 1922.
5. Dimmick, F. L. An experimental study of visual movement and the phi phenomenon, *Amer. J. Psychol.*, 1920, *31*, 317–322.
6. Freud, S. *New Introductory Lectures on Psychoanalysis.* 1933.
7. Hilgard, E. R. Human Motives and the Concept of the Self, *Amer. Psychol.* 1949, *4*, 374–382.
8. von Hornbostel, E. M. Die Einheit der Sinne, *Melos*, 1925, *4*, 290–298.
9. Karpf, F. B. *American Social Psychology.* 1932.
10. Katz, D. *Die Erscheinungsweisen der Farben.* 1911.
11. Klineberg, O. A science of national character, *J. soc. Psychol.*, 1944, *19*, 147–162.
12. Koffka, K. *Principles of Gestalt Psychology.* 1935.
13. Köhler, W. *The Place of Value in a World of Facts.* 1938.
14. Köhler, W. *Dynamics in Psychology.* 1940.
15. Krech, D. and R. S. Crutchfield. *Theory and Problems of Social Psychology.* 1948.
16. Krech, D. Notes toward a psychological theory, *J. Personality*, 1949, *18*, 66–87.
17. Lewin, K. *Der Begriff der Genese in Physik, Biologie und Entwicklungsgeschichte.* 1922.
18. MacLeod, R. B. The phenomenological approach to social psychology, *Psychol. Rev.*, 1947, *54*, 193–210.
19. MacLeod, R. B. Perceptual constancy and the problem of motivation, *Can. J. Psychol.*, 1949, *3*, 57–66.
20. MacLeod, R. B. The new psychologies of yesterday and today, *Can. J. Psychol.*, 1949, *3*, 199–212.
21. McDougall, W. *An Introduction to Social Psychology.* 1908.
22. McDougall, W. *The Group Mind.* 1920.
23. Mead, G. H. *Mind, Self and Society.* 1934.

24. Merleau-Ponty, M. *Phénoménologie de la Perception*. 1945.

25. Michotte, A. *La Perception de la Causalité*. 1946.

26. Rubin, E. *Visuell wahrgenommene Figuren*. 1921.

27. Scheler, M. *Wesen und Formen der Sympathie*. 2nd ed., 1923.

28. Sherif, M. and H. Cantril. *The Psychology of Ego-Involvements*. 1947.

29. Snygg, D. and A. W. Combs. *Individual Behavior*. 1949.

30. Stern, W. *General Psychology from the Personalistic Standpoint*. 1938.

31. Volkman, J. J. Scales of judgment and their implication for social psychology, chapter 11, this volume, pp. 273–295.

32. Wallach, H. Some considerations concerning the relation between perception and cognition, *J. Personality*, 1949.

33. Werner, H. *Grundfragen der Sprachphysiognomik*. 1932.

34. Werner, H. Introductory remarks, *J. Personality*, 1949, *18*, 2–5

35. Woodworth, R. S. and D. G. Marquis. *Psychology*. 5th ed., 1947.

36. Woodworth, R. S. *Contemporary Schools of Psychology*. rev. ed., 1948.

CHAPTER 10

⊓⊔⊓⊔⊓⊔⊓⊔⊓⊔⊓⊔⊓⊔⊓⊔⊓⊔⊓⊔⊓⊔⊓⊔⊓⊔⊓⊔⊓⊔⊓⊔⊓⊔⊓⊔⊓⊔

Toward a General Theory of Cognition

LEO POSTMAN
Harvard University

The cognitive processes—perceiving, remembering, and thinking—
have occupied a strategic position in the development of psychology.
Cognition has been a focus of interest for many different theories and
schools of psychology—structuralism and Gestalt, learning theory and
psychoanalysis. Common interest, however, has not given rise to unity.
Rather, it is disagreement in the interpretation of cognitive processes
which has been one of the major centrifugal forces in psychological theory. It is, indeed, not surprising that cognition should be an area of
ferment and argument, for it is the complexity and subtlety of these
processes which is above all the hallmark of human behavior.

MAJOR TRENDS IN COGNITIVE THEORY

It is always dangerous to summarize complex historical trends under
a few pat headings, but it is probably fair to say that there have been
two major types of emphasis in the analysis and interpretation of the
cognitive processes: the *formal* and the *instrumental*. The formalists
have tended to study the various cognitive functions as more or less
self-sufficient processes, with little regard to the context of behavior in
which they take place. In the field of perception, their emphasis has
been on the relationship between the dimensions of physical stimulation and the dimensions of experience—the organization of color, form,
and space. Such formal emphasis is equally strong in the classical psychophysical tradition and in Gestalt psychology. For while Gestalt psychology substituted the laws of field processes for the associationism
and mental chemistry of structuralism, it still tended to view percep-

tion as a more or less self-sufficient process. As Brunswik put it, "the dynamic interaction in a closed brain field amounts to a kind of self-sufficient encapsulation of the perceptual system" (**11**, p. 56).

And so in memory. The classical tradition, laid down by Ebbinghaus, focused on the determination of retention by such formal variables as frequency, amount of material, and structure of the series learned. Indeed, to eliminate meaning and personal significance, the nonsense syllable was invented. Again, for the atomism of the associationist doctrine Gestalt psychology substituted the dynamic evolution of the memory trace. The laws governing the fate of the trace, however, were the very same laws of organization and self-distribution—closure and Prägnanz—which determine the autochthonous perceptual process. It is through insistence on the universality of these laws that Gestalt psychology pioneered in the unification of cognitive theory.

The instrumentalists have been mainly concerned with the ways in which cognitive behavior serves the adjustment of the organism to a changing environment. The instrumentalists wanted to know not only what it is an organism perceives and remembers under given conditions and along what general dimensions percepts and memories develop and change; they were interested above all in the relation between cognition and motivated, goal-directed behavior, in the role which cognitive processes play in adjustment and survival. It is primarily the instrumentalist view of the cognitive processes which has articulated with theories of personality and social psychology. For those concerned with personality dynamics and with social processes have always been impressed with the highly selective and idiosyncratic interpretations of the environment rooted in deep-seated motivations and in strongly reinforced social and cultural norms.

These two approaches to cognition are, of course, in no sense contradictory. They represent differences in the range of questions asked, predilections in the variables sampled and intervening processes postulated. Formalist and instrumentalist approaches have also tended to look to different neighboring disciplines—the formalists primarily to physiology for the neural bases of cognitive behavior, the instrumentalists to social psychology, to personality theory, and to anthropology for wider sampling of motives and situations in which cognition serves the needs of the organism. A general theory of cognition cannot emerge unless and until formalism and instrumentalism are fused. They will so fuse when one approach ceases to hold constant or to ascribe to residual error those variables which are of paramount importance to the other. Set, motivation, past experiences, and social context are ever-present parameters in perceptual organization and memory change. By the same token, those who view the cognitive processes as mediating personal adjustment and social interaction must not disregard or hold constant at some arbitrary or unspecified level those variables which define the limits of the organism's response to stimulation. As we have said elsewhere (7), the goal is a "full information" theory of cognitive behavior. All cognitive behavior must be viewed as *jointly determined* by what Krech and Crutchfield have called "structural" and "functional" factors (26), or, as we have described them, "stimulus" factors and "directive" factors. Structural or stimulus factors represent the capacities of the nervous system to respond to stimulation; they determine the range over which response to a pattern of stimuli can vary. The functional or directive factors are those needs, goals, and past experiences of the organism to which the cognitive processes are instrumental; it is these factors which determine systematic differences in cognitive function from individual to individual, from situation to situation, from group to group, and from culture to culture. Cognitive behavior, then, is viewed as jointly determined by both sets of factors. I should like to stress the phrase, *jointly determined*. We must not think of directive factors as sources of distortion away from some true value, rather we must view them as processes contributing to cognitive organization on a par with structural or stimulus factors. Directive factors can and indeed do sometimes lead to greater rather than lesser accuracy and precision of function. The important point is that they do make systematic and predictable differences in cognitive behavior.

Our language at this juncture is dualistic, but only for reasons of experimental expediency, not because we wish to assume a discontinuity among the causes of cognitive behavior. For purposes of experimental manipulation, we think in terms of two distinct sets of variables, often differing widely in the type of operation which they require. Eventually both types of variables may be translated into a common system of statements which would free us of the necessity of switching from one universe of discourse to another.

As the paths of formalism and instrumentalism converge, cognitive theory will become an integral and, I venture to say, a central part of social psychology. For it is a truism that social behavior, like all other behavior, is critically determined by the ways in which the individual perceives, remembers, and thinks about his environment. It is not a one-way street, however, that connects cognitive theory and social psychology. Social psychology has been describing and classifying a wide range of behaviors whose cognitive characteristics a truly general theory of cognition must encompass and has achieved important insights into the motivations and goals of individuals which may well turn out to be important determinants of cognitive functioning. In this sense, social psychology has made, and will continue to make, important contributions to the development of cognitive theory. With cognitive theory a central part of social psychology, and with the facts and problems of social psychology integrated into cognitive theory, we would be well on the road to a general theory of behavior in which the facts of social action and interaction would become special instances of universal laws of behavior.

THE CHARACTERISTICS OF A GENERAL COGNITIVE THEORY

What are the characteristics of a general cognitive theory that can integrate in a unitary scheme the problems of formalism and instrumentalism or at least cause them to converge? It seems that three different roads may lead to this end, and today we find investigators traveling along each of these roads.

Reduction of Instrumental Variables to Formal Variables

In a recent article protesting against the perception-motivation dichotomy which allegedly characterizes much contemporary research dealing with the "effect of motivation on perception," Hochberg and Gleitman write: "Motivational processes can be subsumed under perceptual ones—in the sense that they can be described and predicted by perceptual laws . . . certainly the laws of perceptual organization are more precise, well defined, and on more solid empirical foundations than whatever laws of needs exist at present" (**22**, p. 183). The authors then go on to suggest that motivational processes can be translated into processes of disequilibrium in the isomorphic brain field which continually strains toward the restoration of its own equilibrium. Thus, the law of Prägnanz, embodying the Gestalt-drang toward equilibration, would become a fundamental law of motivation as well as of perception. This type of approach has well been characterized by Krech as "perceptual imperialism" (25, p. 77).

A broader kind of monistic solution has been advocated by Krech (25). For the traditional classification of psychological data and concepts into such categories as "perception," "learning," and "motivation," Krech would substitute hypothetical constructs which he calls "dynamic systems." These dynamic systems, which are the basic units of psychological analysis, are "the resultants of every neural event which is reflected in any kind of brain event (25, p. 75). It is the properties of these dynamic systems and their laws of operation which will provide the models for the description, analysis, and prediction of all the organism's responses to stimulation. The type of model which Krech suggests for the dynamic systems is drawn largely along Gestalt and field-theoretical lines. In this model, there is no room for perception, learning, and motivations as separate and semi-autonomous systems of psychological functions. Rather, dynamic systems vary along certain basic dimensions. The three basic dimensions of the dynamic system suggested by Krech are: isolation—referring to the degree of interaction with other dynamic systems; differentiation—the extent to which dynamic systems have articulated substructures; and tension—the amount of disequilibrium within the system. It is with variations along these dimensions that the phenomena which are described as motives, percepts, and learnings are associated. For example, "needs" are co-ordinated with variations in tension, perceptual organizations with varying differentiations, etc. However, these dimensions are characteristics of *every* dynamic system, and the laws of dynamic systems involve all these parameters. It is, therefore, impossible to vary need while holding perception constant. Varying any of the conditions of stimulation changes all these attributes simultaneously. Hence, the units of behavior are not perceptions, needs, feelings, etc., but "perception-need-feeling-belief-emotion-etc." In such a system, then, the distinction between formal and instrumental variables disappears and they are all translated into variations along the parameters of dynamic systems. This is one road along which a general theory of cognition can travel. Such an approach is as yet highly programmatic, but it is already clear that it must be on the alert against one danger: that it restrict itself unduly to the choice of variables and situations that lend themselves easily to translation in terms of isolation, differentiation, and tension. In terms of actual experimental manipulations, moreover, the distinctions between perceptual, motivational, and learning variables will die hard.

Descriptive Functionalism (Instrumentalism)

The second approach to a general theory of cognition emphasizes not the mechanisms which mediate cognitive behavior but rather the *achievements* of cognition over the total range of conditions that obtain in the habitat of man. Brunswik's theoretical position, which he aptly describes as "probabilistic functionalism" (10) exemplifies this approach in pure form. Experimenters and theorists who grew out of the formalist tradition have in their preoccupation with mediating mechanisms failed to deal with representative samples of behavior. In their experiments, they have studied under conditions of strict artificial control only a few carefully chosen values of stimulus variables, unrepresentative of the vast range of stimulus values which the organism encounters in its natural habitat under a multiplicity of conditions. From an ecological point of view, behavior has not been sampled in anything approaching representativeness. The model builder's need for the control and restriction of variables, moreover, precludes the covariation of variables in their natural, ecologically characteristic manner. The remedy, Brunswik avers, lies in the representative sampling of stimulus situations and objects. Just as we would hesitate to generalize about a population of people unless we were reasonably sure of a representative sample, so we should not generalize about the organism's response to a variable unless we have a representative sample of the values of the variable that the organism encounters and of the conditions under which he responds to it. The results of such sampling can be expressed in terms of correlations between features of the environment and the characteristics of the subject's cognitive responses, and through analysis of the correlations the basic situational dimensions of cognition can be isolated, just as factor analysis through correlation of test performances isolates the basic dimensions of individual capacities. The correlation between the independent measurements of the environment and the subject's cognitive responses defines the *validity* of the responses. Thus, validity refers to the *achievement* of the response for the organism, the extent to which the response attains what the organism intended. For example, correlation between physical size and perceived size defines

the validity of the perceptual response. The greater the validity of the
cognitive response, the more successful is the organism's adjustment to
the environment. The task of cognitive psychology is to sample the
conditions on which the degree of validity of the organism's response
depends. In Brunswik's own words, "psychology is conceived of as a
fundamentally statistical discipline throughout its entire domain, with
'functional validity' taking its place alongside traditional test validity"
(**10**, p. 56).

Just as the first approach eliminates the separation between formal
and instrumental by translating instrumental variables into formal
processes, so this approach mitigates the dichotomy by focusing inquiry
almost entirely upon the description of instrumental achievements.
The role of the stimulus is that of a cue which makes it more or less
probable that the organism will achieve the object which it intends.
Stimulation is not studied as a condition initiating a particular type of
mediating process in the organism. Probabilistic functionalism does not
build models but evaluates the effectiveness of cues in adjustment. Such
an approach can go a long way toward a general cognitive theory which
will encompass the facts of social behavior, for many of the objects
sampled would, indeed, be cultural objects and social traits, and the
range of situations sampled could well include a wide range of social
situations. However, probabilistic functionalism is centered upon the
analysis of *objective achievement*. Failure of achievement is related to
the unreliability of cues in a changing environment. The social psychologist and the personality psychologist are often concerned not only
with the conditions of achievement but also, and sometimes primarily,
with the nature and determinants of errors and distortions. They wish
to relate these errors and distortions to the motives and past experiences
of the individual. To borrow a phrase which Egon Brunswik has used
facetiously, probabilistic functionalism is "cold" and the functionalism
or instrumentalism of those who have been working on a "full-informa-
tion theory" of cognition often is "hot."

Convergence upon Common Constructs

There is still another way. Essentially it consists in building a model
whose properties are defined in terms of *both* formal and instrumental
variables and in which the relation between the two sets of variables
is part and parcel of the theoretical scheme. Formalistic and instru-

mental variables converge upon constructs which are defined in terms of both and do not require the reduction of one to the other. In the next section of this paper I should like to present an attempt at such a theoretical formulation toward which my collaborator, Dr. Jerome S. Bruner, and I have been tending recently as a result of our experimental work.

AN HYPOTHESIS-INFORMATION THEORY OF COGNITION

In developing this view, we have borrowed heavily from several contemporary theorists, notably Tolman, Brunswik, Krech, Bartlett, and Woodworth. Perhaps we have not done much more than to extrapolate from some of their concepts, adapting them to the needs of our own research.

The Concepts of Hypothesis and Information

Central to our analysis is the concept of *hypothesis*.[1] By hypotheses we mean, in the most general sense, expectancies or predispositions of the organism which serve to select, organize, and transform the stimulus information that comes from the environment. A given sensory input has not only energy characteristics which trip off a series of organized reactions in the nervous system, but it has cue or clue characteristics as well—it carries *information* about the environment. It is with respect to these information characteristics of stimuli that hypotheses operate. Thus, a hazy bluish color has not only certain spectral and intensity values, it is also a cue or clue to distance and *qua* clue it is related to the organism's hypotheses about distance.

Hypothesis, then, is an intervening construct defined on the one hand by the patterns of stimulus information to which the organism is exposed and on the other hand by the organism's responses—discriminations, verbal reactions, and motor acts which occur in response to the stimulus information.

We speak of stimulus *information* because we wish to relate hypotheses to the cue or clue characteristics of stimuli. How, then, do we define the information characteristics of stimuli appropriate to a given hypothesis? Suppose the organism has (or we wish to show that it has) an hy-

---

[1] In our thinking about the concept of hypothesis we are especially indebted to Tolman and Brunswik (47).

pothesis A, for example, that a given type of object will appear in the environment. Or the organism has an hypothesis about a linkage of events in the environment, "if A then B." We can now show in independent defining experiments what stimulus variations and patterns of stimulus organization are related to the discrimination of A and/or B. For example, if the hypothesis concerns the size of objects, the various, so-called secondary, cues to distance would be examples of appropriate stimulus information. Similarly, if the hypothesis concerns the color of objects, such stimulus characteristics as the brightness of the object, mixture of wave lengths reflected, and nature of the surround would be sources of appropriate information. In general, then, stimulus characteristics which can be independently shown to be related to the discrimination of that which is expected or hypothesized are sources of "appropriate information." Of course, the more specifically we state the hypothesis, the more precisely can we delimit appropriate stimulus information. We have already mentioned what kinds and patterns of stimuli would be appropriate information for size and color hypotheses. If the hypothesis were as broad as "something will occur," virtually any discriminable stimulus characteristic would constitute appropriate information.

To summarize, then, *hypothesis* is an intervening construct used to account for observed empirical relationships in cognitive behavior. They are conceived as predispositions or expectancies of the organism which organize and transform selectively incoming stimulus information (perception) and continue to transform it after removal of the stimulus (memory). Hypotheses are anchored operationally in discriminable stimulus information on the one hand and various classes of responses (e.g., verbal reactions and motor acts) on the other.

The ultimate tasks of the theory are these: (1) to specify the hypotheses which operate in the transformation and organization of information; (2) to describe the conditions which govern the acquisition of hypotheses; (3) to analyze the information on which the hypotheses operate; and (4) to build a model representing the mode of operation of hypotheses.

Let me now spell out a few first steps toward this objective as they apply to perception and memory. It is hoped that this model will apply equally to perception and memory, and perhaps to other cognitive processes as well. Let us turn to perception first.

PERCEPTUAL HYPOTHESES

The Hypothesis-Information Cycle

We can conceive of the perceptual process as a cycle of hypothesis-information-trial and check of hypothesis-confirmation or non-confirmation. In any given situation, the organism is not indifferently ready for the occurrence of any or all types of objects, or sequences of objects. Rather, the organism expects, is *eingestellt,* for a limited range of events. Into the organism which is thus "tuned" information is put by sensory stimulation. This information serves either to (1) broaden or narrow the range of hypotheses or (2) confirm or deny specific hypotheses. If the information confirms the hypothesis, a stable perceptual organization is achieved. If the information fails to confirm the hypothesis, the hypothesis shifts until it is confirmed and a stable perceptual organization is achieved. Thus, the relation between hypothesis and information is cyclical in nature, with a continuous process of trial and check, trial and check—to use Woodworth's term—until confirmation has taken place (50). The degree of confirmation or the subjective certainty sufficient to terminate the process of trial and check will vary with the subject's task, with the strength of the hypothesis, and with the opportunities for trial and check in the situation.

Those of a phenomenological frame of mind will probably object at this point that this account of perception does violence to the evidence of experience in which percepts are given immediately and compellingly. Perhaps an hypothesis-information analysis is no more than a restatement of Helmholtz' theory of unconscious inference in currently fashionable terms. However that may be, the justification of a theoretical model of perception need not be sought in its introspective validity. Rather the model must stand or fall with its ability to order a large body of data and to produce testable experimental deductions. We now turn to a set of specific propositions generated by the theory which may allow us to gauge its promise.

Determinants of Hypothesis Strength

Let us now consider a series of specific propositions concerning the determinants of hypothesis strength. We shall provisionally define the *strength of an hypothesis* in terms of the amount of appropriate information necessary to confirm it or infirm it. The stronger the hypothesis, the less of appropriate stimulus information is required to confirm it or infirm it. This is tantamount to saying that a very strong hypothesis will tend to be confirmed even when most of the available information is inappropriate or that a weak hypothesis will not be confirmed even when a considerable amount of appropriate information is available. It might be interesting to note here that what is generally described as an "ambiguous" situation would in our terms be a situation in which there is little appropriate information for the trial and check of hypotheses. Now to the specific propositions and the evidence supporting them.

1. *Frequency of past confirmation.* The strength of an hypothesis depends on the frequency with which it has been confirmed in the past. Defining strength in terms of the amount of appropriate stimulus information required for confirming, we mean that the greater the frequency with which an hypothesis has been confirmed in the past, the less of appropriate stimulus information is required to confirm it on subsequent occasions. This proposition finds considerable, although not unequivocal, support from the series of experiments which have dealt with the problem of perceptual learning. In the wake of Gottschaldt's challenging experiments pitting Gestalt factors of organization against frequency of past experience (17), there has been a succession of experiments (4, 14, 20, 28) which in spite of differences in procedure would probably agree on the following generalization: under conditions of reduced stimulation, such as tachistoscopic presentation or peripheral vision, the more frequently a stimulus constellation has been experienced in the past, the more readily is it recognized. We would conceptualize the results of these experiments as follows. Suppose the experiment deals with the recognition of geometric forms. This fact, of course, greatly narrows the range of the subject's hypotheses. Under conditions of highly reduced stimulation (e.g., very rapid tachistoscopic exposure) a small amount of appropriate stimulus information is fed into the organism. Other things being equal, that specific hypothesis is aroused which has been confirmed most frequently in the past in the presence of this type of stimulus information. Further input of appropriate stimulus information then serves to confirm the hypothesis.

It now becomes clear why so-called ambiguous stimuli have been predominantly used in demonstrations of perceptual learning and, for that matter, in the study of many directive factors in perception. Only under conditions of partial information are there degrees of freedom in the arousal of alternative hypotheses. As one approaches full appropriate information, the nature of the hypothesis is uniquely determined.

We have used the evasive qualifier "other things being equal" in predicting that the hypothesis which has been most frequently confirmed in the past will be aroused and more easily reconfirmed in the presence of appropriate information. Other determinants of hypothesis strength may readily override the effect of frequency. A well-known experimental finding of Henle's (20) may serve as an illustration. To demonstrate the effect of past experience under conditions of reduced stimulation, she compared the efficiency of recognition for normal printwise letters and reversed letters presented tachistoscopically or in peripheral vision. She found that printwise letters which, of course, had been experienced so much more frequently than reversed letters were recognized much more often. However, if she set her subjects to expect reversed as well as printwise letters, the difference disappeared. Giving the subjects a multiple hypothesis—"letters in this situation will be either printwise or reversed"—offset the effect of frequency. Our next proposition concerns this very factor of multiplicity of set.

2. *Number of alternative hypotheses.* The larger the number of alternative hypotheses that operate in a given situation, the more of appropriate stimulus information is required to confirm any one of these hypotheses. In any given situation, hypotheses may vary from complete monopoly-expectancy of one event and one event only—to a high degree of multiplicity—expectancy of a large number of alternative events. As the number of alternative hypotheses increases, any given unit of appropriate information may serve partially to confirm several of the alternative hypotheses. Only in the presence of a critical amount of appropriate information can discrimination among competing hypotheses take place. The situation here is closely akin to the phenomena of interference in learning where competition among alternative and incompatible responses leads to a decrease in efficiency of performance —negative transfer, proactive and retroactive inhibition. In terms of our model, the larger the number of alternative hypotheses, the less probable is it that any given unit of appropriate stimulus information will serve to confirm one of the competing hypotheses.

Now for some experimental confirmation of this proposition. First of all, much classical work can be cited in support. The slowness of disjunctive reaction time as compared with simple reaction time may well be attributed at least in part to the difference in number of alternative hypotheses about incoming stimuli and the consequent difference in amount of appropriate information required to confirm one of them. Indeed, as Merkel (36) showed many years ago, the larger the number of alternatives, the slower the disjunctive reaction time. Perhaps even more relevant is Henmon's demonstration (21) that the more similar the alternatives, the longer is the disjunctive reaction time, for the more similar the hypotheses, the more of appropriate information is required to discriminate among them. More direct demonstrations of the relation between number of alternative hypotheses and perceptual efficiency are contained in the classical work of Külpe and Bryan (27) and its extension by Chapman (12) and Yokoyama (52). If a subject does not know before exposure of a complex stimulus which of several attributes of the stimulus he will be required to report on, his discrimination of any single attribute is poor—the range of hypotheses to which the stimulus information is relevant is wide: i.e., there are a large number of competing hypotheses. If, under the very same conditions of exposure, the subject has a single set for a specific attribute, the efficiency of his discrimination is greatly improved—the range of hypotheses to which the incoming information is relevant is greatly reduced. In a recent experiment on the perception of words we obtained parallel results (39). When the subject is set to expect one, and only one, class of words to appear in the tachistoscope, his perceptual performance is much more efficient than under conditions where he expects one of two alternative, and equally probable, classes of words. Under single-hypothesis instructions, moreover, meaningful interpretations are attempted earlier and failures of perception are less frequent. In short, stimulus information is used more efficiently because it is appropriate to fewer competing hypotheses.

When the social psychologist speaks about stereotypes, he is dealing with strong monopolistic hypotheses about classes of objects and people which operate without much competition from alternative hypotheses. As monopolistic hypotheses, they are confirmed by a small or indeed minimal amount of appropriate information. If I have such a monopolistic hypothesis about Negroes, for example, that all Negroes are dirty, this hypothesis is confirmed almost as soon as I have recognized a man as a Negro. For the linkage between Negro and dirty is so strong that information identifying a person as a Negro serves to confirm the fact that he is dirty as well. If, on the other hand, I have alternative hypotheses about Negroes—a Negro may be either clean or dirty like any other man—I must in any given case have more appropriate information about the individual before one or the other hypothesis is confirmed. Such examples may be homely and obvious, but besides emphasizing the continuity between laboratory experiment and social application, they may have implications which are not self-evident. Several investigations have been devoted to the effect of contact with minority groups on prejudiced attitudes toward these groups (37, p. 995). The results have been contradictory: sometimes contact does, and sometimes it does not, seem to reduce this bias. In terms of the argument presented here, we would say that sheer exposure to members of the minority group cannot be expected to have any kind of uniform effect. The crucial question is whether or not the biased individual acquires alternative hypotheses which can be differentially reinforced by contact with the minority group. As long as he continues to operate under a strong monopolistic hypothesis, little appropriate information is sufficient to confirm it, and exposure to the minority group may easily strengthen rather than weaken his prejudice. The teaching of alternative hypotheses is a first indispensable step in the modification of attitudes.

Whether or not a given hypothesis can be modified or lose, as it were, its monopoly will depend on its motivational support. Having dealt with some of the formal determinants of hypothesis strength—frequency and multiplicity—we now turn to motivational determinants.

3. *Motivational support*. The stronger the motivational support for a given hypothesis, the less of appropriate stimulus information is required to confirm it. The usefulness of this proposition will depend on our ability to give substance to the concept of motivational support. As a first approximation, let us think of motivational support in terms of the consequences which confirmation or non-confirmation of the hypothesis has for the organism. Thus, hypotheses whose confirmation signifies rewards and punishment have stronger motivational support than those which are unrelated to either positive or negative reinforcement. These reinforcements may be externally administered or carried

by symbolic surrogates. Our statement does not imply that wish-fulfill-
ing hypotheses will necessarily be dominant in perceptual organization,
but rather that hypotheses gain strength by virtue of their instrumental
significance. By way of an analogy to learning theory, our statement
is much closer to Tolman's law of emphasis than to the law of effect.

Instrumental hypotheses, then, are stronger than non-instrumental
ones and will be confirmed by less of appropriate stimulus information.
Much of the evidence in support of this proposition comes from experiments which investigated the relation between intensity of need and
perceptual organization. The typical procedure in such experiments
has been to induce a need in the subject (for example, the hunger need),
then to present him with ambiguous stimuli and to observe whether
increase in need leads to increased perception of need-related objects
(e.g., food). A rising frequency of need-satisfying responses is, indeed,
often observed as a function of increasing need (30, 44) but the rise
does not continue indefinitely, and the proportion of need-satisfying
hypotheses may actually decline under very strong motivation (30). The
importance of going beyond a simple wish-fulfillment theory of perceptual selection is emphasized by the fact that the hypotheses which
become dominant with increasing need may concern instrumental
rather than goal objects, e.g., objects useful in the attainment of food
rather than food itself (30). Experiments relating personal values and
emotional attitudes to perceptual selectivity have produced evidence
for the strength of both positive, value-congruent hypotheses (5, 34, 40)
and of hypotheses representing dangerous and threatening objects (5,
34). Parallel results emerge from studies of the effects of rewards and
punishments on perceptual selectivity: in situations in which alternative perceptual organizations are possible, percepts associated with rewards are favored over those associated with punishments (43, 45) but
there is greater sensitivity to stimuli which lead to negative reinforcement than to neutral ones (32). It is interesting to note that parallel
results have been obtained in studies of attributive judgment. Both
positively valued and negatively valued objects are accentuated as compared with neutral ones (6).

What, then, about perceptual defense? Is it not true, as several experiments have seemed to suggest, that some subjects will ward off
as long as possible the perception of the inimical or threatening? On
the basis of our analysis we would suggest that what appears to be

perceptual defense results from the dominance of strong alternative hypotheses rather than from active repression of the inimical or dangerous. In the presence of partial information, strong hypotheses incompatible with the threatening stimulus may be evoked. Let us, for example, assume that we present a very conventional, inhibited subject with a taboo word in the tachistocope (5, 35). In the presence of partial information, a series of strong non-taboo hypotheses is aroused which must be infirmed before the weaker taboo hypothesis is aroused and confirmed. If this is the case, the subject will appear to be defending himself against perception of the taboo word.

If, however, hypotheses related to the negative stimuli are strong, the opposite of defense will appear to operate. Now suppose this same subject is very much afraid of, and preoccupied with, illness, and we present him with the name of an illness in the tachistoscope. His illness-related hypotheses are strong and readily aroused, and he perceives the stimulus word very rapidly. Certainly he does not "wish" for illness. Rather, his hypotheses about illness have a high probability of being aroused.

The tendency for groups of subjects to divided into "defenders" and "non-defenders" in the face of threatening stimuli bears out this point. It would seem that those who show perceptual defense against negative stimuli have strong dominant positive hypotheses which require a large amount of appropriate information before they are rejected and before a shift to negative hypotheses is made. On the other hand, those who do not show resistance to the perception of negative stimuli may have stronger negative hypotheses. If this interpretation should be correct, one of the most urgent research problems facing us is the discovery of the conditions which lead to the dominance of positive and negative hypotheses. The recent studies of Frenkel-Brunswik and her associates (16) suggest that the dominance of positive or negative hypotheses and the ability to shift hypotheses—what she calls tolerance of ambiguity— may be deeply rooted in personality characteristics. Frenkel-Brunswik also found that intolerance of ambiguity was much more characteristic of the ethnocentric than of the unprejudiced individual. Clearly, the conditions of hypothesis dominance and hypothesis shift are central in the study of social attitudes.

Confirmation or non-confirmation of hypotheses not only has consequences for immediate goal-striving activities but also affects larger cognitive organizations of which a given hypothesis is part. We must view a given hypothesis not only as a goal-directed instrumental activity but also as part of a larger cognitive structure or matrix (to use Tolman's term). The degree to which a given hypothesis is embedded in such a matrix or forms a stable part of a larger cognitive organization is an important determinant of its strength in any given situation. These considerations lead to our next proposition concerning hypothesis strength.

4. *Cognitive support.* The more firmly an hypothesis is embedded in a larger cognitive organization, the less of appropriate stimulus information will be required to confirm it. A corollary of this proposition would be: the more firmly a hypothesis is embedded in a larger cognitive organization, the more resistant will it be to change. A "larger cognitive organization" is a system of hypotheses which are associated with each other and are governed by common rules or principles. A given specific hypothesis gains strength by virtue of its embeddedness in such a larger cognitive organization, for past confirmations of specific hypotheses have generalized to all parts of the matrix.

Experimental support for this proposition comes from a series of experiments on "incongruity," in which we studied the effect of violating well-established expectancies, more or less strongly embedded in larger cognitive organizations.

The first experiment (41) was designed to show the support given to an hypothesis by broader cognitive context, even when environmental events are contrary to the hypothesis. Like Henle (20), we worked with the well-established and often-confirmed hypothesis about the properties of letters—that they appear printwise rather than reversed. Under the first condition of the experiment, subjects were presented a series of seven unrelated consonants for tachistoscopic recognition. One of the consonants—either at the beginning, in the middle, or at the end of the list—was reversed. Under the second condition, a reversed letter was introduced in the same positions in a meaningful word (the word *plaster*). Under both conditions recognition was slowed down as compared with the performance of the control groups for whom all letters were printwise. More important for our immediate purposes was the following finding: even though recognition of the series of consonants was *in general* slower than recognition of the meaningful word, it took relatively more time to recognize the reversed letter as reversed when it was embedded in the meaningful word than when it was part of a series of unrelated consonants. The context supported the hypothesis that all letters shown were printwise more strongly in the case of a meaningful word than in the case of disjointed letters.

Our finding is closely related to the Gestalt principle that the properties of a substructure depend to a considerable extent on the properties of the larger whole or structure of which it is a part. Our treatment in terms of hypotheses and systems of hypotheses is in no sense a contradiction of this principle. The organization of hypotheses into larger cognitive structures may well be described in terms of configurational principles as well as in terms of associative linkages. Some hypotheses are more readily formed and more resistant to change than others by virtue of their membership in well-organized cognitive structures. We would hold, however, that the concept of hypothesis is more generic in the analysis of cognitive behavior and that laws of cognitive structure and organization may be viewed as determinants of hypothesis strength.

Cognitive support for a specific hypothesis is often carried by a general rule or principle, i.e., a superordinate hypothesis, of which the specific hypothesis is a special instance. Specific hypotheses supported by a general rule or superordinate hypothesis need only little appropriate information for confirmation, and they will be rejected only in the presence of a considerable amount of contradictory information. A further experiment on incongruity illustrates this point (8). Playing cards are presented to subjects for tachistoscopic recognition, some of them normal cards, others with color and suit reversed, e.g., red spades and black hearts. Incongruous cards are recognized much more slowly. Throughout the trials preceding recognition, the hypotheses defined by the general rule ("if a given suit, then a given color") show dominance and sometimes persist for more than 50 trials in spite of contradictory stimulus information. The shift away from the established hypothesis is often gradual. Prior to recognition of the incongruous event, compromise perceptions (cf. Brunswik, 11) frequently occur— red spades seen as purple spades, black hearts as brown hearts, etc. In the presence of objects, then, which contradict general cognitive rules the process of trial and check proceeds slowly, and there may be a sequence of reorganizations by which the dominant hypothesis is gradually discarded.

Our distinction between motivational support and cognitive support is, of course, a highly analytic one. One can readily agree with Krech that motivational factors or attributes are involved in all behavior and that "a dynamic system which is co-ordinate with our experience when we look at a 'lop-sided' figure on the screen will be *under the very same kind of tension* as a dynamic system which is co-ordinated with our experience when we look at a steak after several hours of food deprivation" (25, p. 79). Nevertheless, we believe the distinction between motivational and cognitive support to be analytically useful because it leads to wider sampling of determinants and allows us to make immediate contact with bodies of information which have to some extent developed independently of each other. The distinction between motivational and cognitive support of hypotheses may, however, be only temporary.

CONDITIONS OF HYPOTHESIS CONFIRMATION

We have borrowed Woodworth's phrase, "trial and check" (50), to describe the process of hypothesis confirmation. We assume, then, that in the presence of partial stimulus information an hypothesis is aroused —the strongest hypothesis which fits the information—and is checked against the appropriate stimulus information until hypothesis and stimulus information match sufficiently to give rise to a stable perceptual organization. The basic condition of hypothesis confirmation, then, is the presence of appropriate stimulus information. Appropriate information, it will be remembered, is stimulation relevant to the discrimination of that which is expected or hypothesized. Even in the absence of appropriate information, however, confirmation of hypotheses will take place. Our next two propositions are concerned with the process of hypothesis confirmation in the absence of fully appropriate stimulus information.

5. *Dominance of hypotheses in the absence of appropriate information.* The less of appropriate stimulus information is available, the more the perceptual organization is determined by the dominant hypothesis. Let me spell out this proposition in terms of an experiment in which we worked with well-established hypotheses and systematically varied the amount of stimulus information available (9). The hypotheses concerned the normal colors of objects. Our stimuli were objects whose normal colors varied from red through orange to yellow. There

were two series of objects: (1) a tomato, a tangerine, a lemon, and a control stimulus closely resembling them in shape; (2) a boiled lobster claw, a carrot, a banana, and control patch of comparable shape.

Under the first condition, all these objects were cut out of gray paper and presented against a blue background under a sheet of glass. Through color contrast, the test patches appeared to be of a rather unstable orange color. The subject's task was to adjust a variable color mixer with red and yellow sectors until it appeared equal in color to the test patch. Two series of matches were made with the object present, and one series from memory. Under this first condition, appropriate information for achieving a good match and verifying the hypothesis about the color of an object was rather poor. The color of the test objects was unstable and different in texture and saturation from the colored paper on the wheel. Nor was any attempt made to control the surrounds of color wheel and test patch. Under these conditions, the subject's matches clearly conform to his expectancy about the normal color of the objects. Significantly, more red is used to match normally red objects than to match yellow objects, with the matches for orange objects falling in between. When matches are made from memory, with the amount of appropriate information further reduced, the differences are exaggerated.

Under the second condition of the experiment, the same procedure was used, except that between the first and second matching series, the nature of the stimulus situation was fully explained to the subjects. This was done to ascertain to what extent the effect of the hypothesis could be reduced through knowledge about the situation while the appropriate *stimulus* information for trial and check remained unchanged. Knowledge of the situation produced no appreciable effect, and the naïve group and the informed group were at no point significantly different from each other. Appropriate stimulus information for the trial and check remained unchanged. Knowledge of the situation produced no appreciable effect, and the naïve group and the informed group were at no point significantly different from each other. Appropriate stimulus information for the trial and check of a dominant hypothesis is necessary to produce a shift to a new hypothesis. This conclusion is borne out by the fact that the subjects reported, often spontaneously, that the objects were all of the same color! For all its docility, perception is also, as Brunswik puts it, "stupid," and appropriate stimulus information must be present for an hypothesis to be broken and a new hypothesis to emerge.

Under the third and fourth conditions, we attempted to provide stimulus conditions more appropriate to trial and check by first substituting stable colored orange paper for the unstable induction color, and finally switching from successive to simultaneous comparison with the stimuli exposed side by side against a uniform gray background. With this increase in appropriate stimulus information, the systematic effects of the dominant hypothesis became more and more reduced. In the third condition, it was still present but to a smaller degree than before. In the fourth and final condition, no systematic effects can be detected, and the differences in matches may be assigned to variable rather than constant error.

In some ways we can take this experiment as a model for thinking about the operation of enduring hypotheses about the environment in the presence of varying amounts of stimulus information. The operation of enduring hypotheses or expectancies is continually subject to trial and check in terms of incoming stimulus information, and only in the absence of appropriate stimulus information do such expectancies continue to determine perceptual organization without correction.

Appropriate information is, of course, not an all-or-none affair but may vary in amount from zero to redundancy, where there is more than the minimum amount of information necessary to check an hypothesis.

When there is little or no information appropriate to the checking of hypotheses, we have the type of situation upon which projective techniques are based. The dominant hypotheses of the subject, which have paramount motivational support, prevail in the presence of inadequate conditions for trial and check. When there is a modicum of information which limits the operation of dominant hypotheses but is not adequate for full trial and check, conditions are ripe for the operation of "suggestion." When cognitive situations are ordered along a continuum defined by amount of appropriate stimulus information available, phenomena, like suggestion, which had been treated as separate classes of behavior, are seen as special cases of hypothesis behavior.

Appropriate stimulus information is the basic means of hypothesis validation. In a social environment, however, an individual may, in the absence of appropriate stimulus information, draw on the experiences and judgments of others to confirm or infirm an hypothesis.

6. *Consensual validation.* In the absence of appropriate stimulus information, consensus among the members of a group will serve to validate an hypothesis. Sherif's experiments on the autokinetic movement (46) can be interpreted as supporting this hypothesis. In this situation, the individual's hypotheses about the extent of movement cannot be checked against appropriate stimulus information. The hypotheses do shift, however, under the influence of the judgments of others until they converge on a common norm and become stabilized. It is this convergence and stabilization at a common norm which indicates hypothesis confirmation by consensus.

Social consensus not only serves to confirm hypotheses in the absence of appropriate stimulus information; it is also an important source of hypotheses. The range of hypotheses which an individual carries around with him and which form, to use Tolman's term again, his cognitive matrix, far exceeds his own range of past experiences. Many hypotheses come, as it were, ready-made and can be activated and checked when the environmental situation demands it. One might, indeed, go as far as to say that the process of socialization consists of building into the child a system of hypotheses which will prepare him to perceive and know his environment in the ways which his culture favors.

HYPOTHESES IN REMEMBERING

Hypotheses and systems of hypotheses (schemata) constitute more or less lasting predispositions to selective cognitive responses. It is these hypotheses and schemata which give continuity and consistency to cognitive behavior. As we have seen, well-established, strong hypotheses are most effective as determinants of cognitive organization when the amount of appropriate information for the trial and check of hypotheses is reduced. *Remembering* is a clear case of cognitive organization which must take place without opportunity for trial and check against appropriate stimulus information. We would expect, then, that it is in memory, perhaps even more clearly than in perception, that the directive effect of hypotheses and schemata can be demonstrated.

Much of the classical work on rote learning, which provided us with basic information regarding such variables as frequency and effect, was by its very nature designed to minimize the influence of hypotheses and schemata. There are, however, two major theoretical and experimental approaches which have stressed the organized, constructive nature of the memory process and which are immediately related to hypothesis theory: Gestalt theory of traces (23, 24) and Bartlett's schema theory (3).

The key axiom in Gestalt theory of memory is that the laws of perceptual organization, such as the laws of closure and prägnanz, are general laws applying to all cognitive processes, and that these laws govern the evolution of traces in time just as they determine perceptual organization in the presence of a physical stimulus configuration. This view leads to the prediction that changes in the trace field will not be haphazard but rather should be progressively in accordance with the laws of perceptual organization, producing more and more prägnant organizations as time goes on. There is some experimental support for this prediction (1, 38, 51) although it has been seriously challenged by the result of some recent investigations (18, 19). For the Gestalt theorist, then, schemata are generated by stresses in the trace field resulting in better, simpler, more prägnant organizations. This theory, naturally enough, has had relatively little concern with learned schemata whose strength is rooted in motivational and social factors.

Unlike the Gestalt psychologists, Bartlett was not concerned with demonstrating self-sufficient principles of organization governing the memory processes. Rather, he saw the course of memory determined to a considerable extent by the attitudes and expectations of the subject, attitudes and expectations which are largely determined by previous experiences, habits, and cultural conventions among which the subject lives. The schema into which new experiences are fitted and to which they become assimilated in memory is described by Bartlett as "an active organization of past reactions and past experiences which is constantly changing." It is with the aid of such schemata that remembering—an active process of reconstruction—unfolds itself. The most important schemata are those related to interests and attitudes rather than schemata which follow the lines of sense differences. As the interests change and develop, so do the schemata. Thus, the assimilation of memories to both enduring and temporary interests and attitudes is for Bartlett the crux of the remembering process. Investigators who have related memory loss and change to the subject's political and social attitudes (13, 15, 29, 42, 49) are closely akin to Bartlett in their approach to memory.

Extending the general theoretical position developed earlier to the phenomena of memory, I shall try to make these statements continuous with the propositions on perceptual organization. Let us consider the remembering situation as one in which the subject is faced with the task of reconstructing a past event, and again let us analyze his behavior in terms of hypotheses and appropriate information. His hypotheses derive from his initial perception of the situation. The appropriate stimulus information in terms of which the initial perceptual hypotheses were checked is, however, no longer present but is, we assume, represented by a system of traces. Paralleling the hypothesis-information-confirmation cycle in perception, we now posit an hypothesis-trace-confirmation cycle in remembering. In an oversimplified way we conceive of the process somewhat as follows:

An ongoing perceptual process activates some part of the trace system representing a past perceptual process. For the moment we shall not be concerned with the determinants of trace-process communication and assume it as given. In general, analysis of trace-process communication has been in terms of similarity between process and trace. As Wallach recently wrote, "any recall which is occasioned by a perceptual experience involves a process which brings into function a memory trace of a similar experience of the past" (48, p. 6). This part of the trace system which has been activated is analogous to the partial stimulus information in a perceptual situation and serves to arouse an hypothesis. Trial and check of this hypothesis is now against appropriate *trace information* rather than against appropriate stimulus information. Again, paralleling our perceptual propositions, we would say that the stronger the hypothesis, the less appropriate trace information is required to arouse it and to confirm it. The total body of propositions regarding the strength and operation of perceptual hypotheses is immediately relevant to the strength and operation of hypotheses in memory. We would say, then, that amount of appropriate trace information required to arouse and confirm an hypothesis in remembering varies inversely with frequency of past confirmation, number of alternative hypotheses, degree of motivational and cognitive support.

Building a System of Hypotheses

The proof for these propositions can be obtained in one of two ways. We can observe remembering performance for a variety of materials and in a variety of situations and then try to infer the nature of the hypotheses that have been operating and to generalize concerning their mode of operation. It is on the basis of such procedures that the dimensions of leveling, sharpening, and assimilation in memory change have been formulated (2, 3). An alternative is to establish the hypotheses experimentally, to *build them into the subject* and to predict the memory changes that must occur if the hypotheses are, indeed, operative. If we can thus gain experimental control over the establishment of an hypothesis, the predictive power of the concept is enhanced and the description of its properties can be made more systematic.

I have begun a series of experiments in which the subjects *learn* a system of hypotheses or a schema in terms of which sequences of unfamiliar materials can be organized and retained. The systematic effects of this learned schema on the retention of specific materials can then be demonstrated and predictions made from our theory can be tested.

In these experiments we teach our subjects sets of geometric figures and certain rules governing their sequence. The symbols have no standard meaning and the rules of sequence, though consistent, are arbitrary in principle. The procedure is in some ways analogous to the learning of an artificial language since there is a set of symbols forming a definite group and there is a partial "syntax," i.e., a set of formal rules which governs the sequence of symbols.

Specifically, these rules determine the nature of pair formations, i.e., they determine the relationship which one member of a pair of symbols must bear to the other. As Figure 1 shows, there is a set of basic pairs called *codes* and for each code a set of *breakdowns* into pairs of symbols. Derivation of the breakdowns from the code is by removal of one line from a code figure, and addition of this very same line to the other code figure, in such a fashion that the added line is not obscured by overlap with any other line in the figure to which it has been added. The principle of code derivation, then, is the addition and subtraction of lines. We teach the subjects a series of hypotheses about these figures: pairs of figures always add up to the basic code.

The first series of experiments was designed to demonstrate the ways in which these learned hypotheses influence efficiency of retention and, more important, the systematic nature of the errors which are introduced by operation of the hypotheses. Let me briefly summarize the results of the first series of experiments. First of all, subjects who have learned the principle governing the derivation of breakdowns from codes differ strikingly in their memory for series of symbols from con-

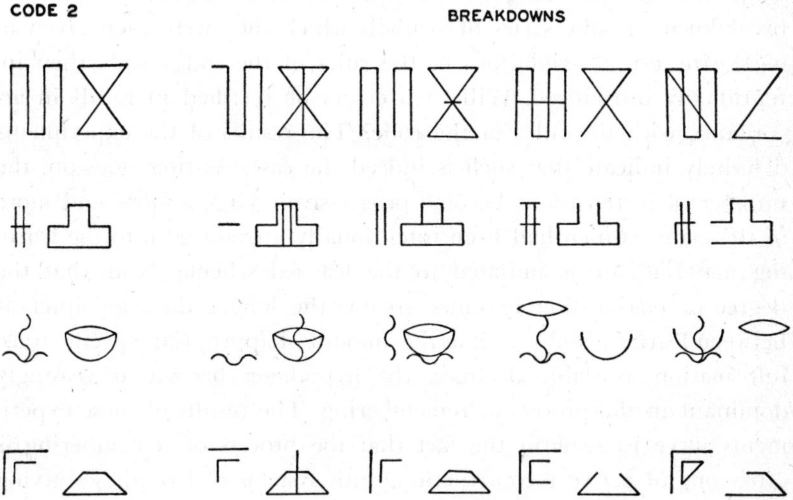

FIGURE 1. Examples of materials used in experiments on the operation of schemata in memory. The code figures appear on the left-hand side and the breakdowns on the right. Derivation of the breakdowns from the code is by removal of a line from one code figure and addition of this line to the other code figure.

trol subjects who have the same amount of familiarity with the symbols but who have not learned a principle of organization. They differ not so much in the number of items correctly recalled, although the code groups show some superiority in sheer amount retained. The major difference between those into whom hypotheses have been built and those who are left on their own to develop a schema is in the nature of the errors made in recall. A large proportion of the errors made by the code learners are errors which *preserve the principle of the code.* Even though the specific details of the individual symbols are incorrectly recalled, the errors are systematic so as to conform to the principle of the code. The codes (hypotheses) are used to reconstruct the series by whatever trace information has remained available.

A second series of experiments was designed to show that learned principles of organization or hypotheses produce effects comparable to the progressive changes of the trace in accordance with Gestalt laws of organization (or comparable to the type of progressive assimilation to a schema which Bartlett had described). In these experiments, subjects were again taught the codes and the rules for deriviation of breakdowns. In the series of symbols which they were then given to memorize, errors—violations of the rules of the code—were then intentionally introduced. Will such errors be rectified in recall in accordance with the rules of the code? The results of the experiments definitely indicate that such is indeed the case. As time goes on, the number of rectifications become progressively larger: more and more of the errors, which had been intentionally introduced into the learning material, are assimilated to the learned schema. Note that the degree of rectification becomes greater the longer the time interval between learning and recall: as the amount of appropriate specific trace information available declines, the hypotheses become increasingly dominant in the process of remembering. The results of these experiments serve to reaffirm the fact that the process of remembering is often one of active reconstruction, with systems of hypotheses giving direction to this process of reconstruction.

CONCLUSION

Many of the experiments which we have used to illustrate our theoretical development are a far cry from the concrete problems of social psychology. Nevertheless, I would reaffirm my conviction that a general cognitive theory is at the very core of a systematic social psychology. The more firmly our model is grounded in experimental fact, the more readily will it generate testable propositions in the field of social behavior. Let me briefly indicate a few of the directions in which hypothesis theory would have to move to maximize its utility for social psychology.

The first task will be to specify the types of hypotheses which are of importance in the description and prediction of social behavior. In arguing for a phenomenological approach to social psychology, MacLeod (31) has suggested three important problem areas on which phenomenological analysis should focus, and it is in these areas that the specification of hypotheses and systems of hypotheses would be most urgent: (1) the self as phenomenal datum, (2) the other person as phenomenal datum, and (3) society as phenomenal datum. As MacLeod says, "the psychologist must first seek to determine without regard to conventional attitudinal categories, exactly what is there for the person, what structures with what properties and related in what ways" (31, p. 202). The results of such phenomenological analysis could be ordered as a set of hypothesis and their conditions of confirmation and infirmation could be determined by the same type of experimental procedures which have proved useful in our exploratory laboratory studies.

Our theory would require us to specify not only the nature and substance of hypotheses about self, others, and society, but also what information is appropriate to the confirmation of such hypotheses. Drawing on the large body of psychophysical knowledge, it was not too difficult for investigators to determine what stimulus information is appropriate to hypotheses concerning size, color, pitch, loudness, etc. The type of hypotheses, however, which may be of paramount importance to the social psychologist will be about such attributes as warmth and coldness of people, security and threateningness and stability and instability of situations. What type of stimulus information is appropriate to the verification of such hypotheses? It is unlikely that the appropriate stimulus information can be specified in energy terms but we should be able to specify it in terms of relevant cues. Brunswik's technique of representative sampling of objects and situations (10) may prove invaluable to this end. Correlating judgments of socially relevant traits with a multiplicity of stimulus situations might enable us to isolate those cues and patterns of cues which are most relevant to the perception of such traits. Brunswik's own work on the perception of such traits as intelligence and leadership has already pointed the way. We must not forget, moreover, that we can often measure the strength of hypotheses about social values indirectly in terms of the amount of stimulus information required for perception and retention of symbols representing these values.

We would hope, then, that such central concepts of social psychology as attitudes and cultural norms can be translated into cognitive hypotheses varying in substantive content and in strength. The advantages of such translation would be many: it would serve to render the determinants of social behavior more amenable to direct experimental manipulation and would bring to bear on the problems of social psychology the growing body of knowledge in cognitive theory. On the other hand, cognitive theory would be rescued once and for all from the isolation that threatened it when it devoted itself to the study of the generalized adult mind. If we travel along this road, the prospects seem bright for a general science of behavior in which the divisions between traditional fields will have lost their significance.

REFERENCES

1. Allport, G. W.   Change and decay in the visual memory image, *Brit. J. Psychol.*, 1930, *21*, 133–148.
2. Allport, G. W., and L. Postman.   *The psychology of rumor*.   New York: Holt, 1947.
3. Bartlett, F. C.   *Remembering*.   Cambridge: Cambridge University Press, 1932.
4. Braly, K. W.   The influence of past experience in visual perception, *J. exp. Psychol.*, 1933, *16*, 613–643.
5. Bruner, J. S., and L. Postman.   Emotional selectivity in perception and reaction, *J. Personal.*, 1947, *16*, 69–77.
6. Bruner, J. S., and L. Postman.   Symbolic value as an organizing factor in perception, *J. soc. Psychol.*, 1948, *27*, 203–208.
7. Bruner, J. S., and L. Postman.   Perception, cognition, and behavior, *J. Personal.*, 1949, *18*, 14–31.
8. Bruner, J. S., and L. Postman.   On the perception of incongruity: a paradigm, *J. Personal.*, 1949, *18*, 206–223.
9. Bruner, J. S., L. Postman and J. S. Rodrigues.   Stimulus appropriateness and ambiguity as factors in judgment.   Paper read at Eastern Psychological Association, 1950.
10. Brunswik, E.   *Systematic and representative design of psychological experiments*.   Berkeley: University of California Press, 1947.
11. Brunswik, E.   Remarks on functionalism in perception, *J. Personal.*, 1949, *18*, 56–65.
12. Chapman, D. W.   Relative effects of determinate and indeterminate Aufgaben, *Amer. J. Psychol.*, 1932, *44*, 163–174.
13. Clark, K. B.   Some factors influencing the remembering of prose material, *Arch. Psychol.*, July, 1940.
14. Djang, S.   The role of past experience in the visual apprehension of masked forms, *J. exp. Psychol.*, 1937, *20*, 29–59.

15. Edwards, A. L.   Political frames of reference as a factor influencing recognition, *J. abn. soc. Psychol.*, 1941, *36*, 34–50.

16. Frenkel-Brunswik, E.   Intolerance of ambiguity as an emotional and perceptual personality variable, *J. Personal.*, 1949, *18*, 108–143.

17. Gottschaldt, K.   Über den einfluss der erfahrung auf die Wahrnehmung von Figuren, *Psychol. Forsch.*, 1926, *8*, 261–317; and 1929, *12*, 1–87.

18. Hanawalt, N. G.   Memory trace for figures in recall and recognition, *Arch. Psychol.*, 1937.

19. Hebb, D. O., and E. N. Foord.   Errors of visual recognition and the nature of the trace, *J. exp. Psychol.*, 1945, *35*, 335–348.

20. Henle, M.   An experimental investigation of past experience as a determinant of visual form perception, *J. exp. Psychol.*, 1942, *20*, 1–21.

21. Henmon, V. A. C.   The time of perception as a measure of differences in sensations, *Arch. Phil., Psychol., and Sci. Meth.*, 1906, #8.

22. Hochberg, J. E., and H. Gleitman.   Towards a reformulation of the perception-motivation dichotomy, *J. Personal.*, 1949, *18*, 180–191.

23. Köhler, W.   *Dynamics in psychology*.   New York: Liveright, 1940.

24. Koffka, K.   *Principles of gestalt psychology*.   New York: Harcourt, Brace, 1935.

25. Krech, D.   Notes toward a psychological theory, *J. Personal.*, 1949, *18*, 66–87.

26. Krech, D., and R. S. Crutchfield.   *Theory and problems of social psychology*.   New York: McGraw-Hill, 1948.

27. Külpe, O., and W. L. Bryan.   Versuche über Abstraktion, *Ber. I Kongr., exp. Psychol.*, 1904, 58–68.

28. Leeper, R.   A study of a neglected portion of the field of learning—the development of sensory organization, *J. genet. Psychol.*, 1935, *46*, 41–75.

29. Levine, J., and G. Murphy.   The learning and forgetting of controversial material, *J. abn. soc. Psychol.*, 1943, *37*, 507–517.

30. Levine, R., I. Chein and G. Murphy.   The relation of the intensity of a need to the amount of perceptual distortion, a preliminary report, *J. Psychol.*, 1942, *13*, 283–293.

31. MacLeod, R. B.   The phenomenological approach to social psychology, *Psychol. Rev.*, 1947, *54*, 193–210.

32. McCleary, R. A., and R. S. Lazarus.   Autonomic discrimination without awareness: an interim report, *J. Personal.*, 1949, *18*, 171–179.

33. McClelland, D. C., and J. W. Atkinson.   The projective expression of needs: I. The effect of different intensities of the hunger drive on perception, *J. Psychol.*, 1948, *25*, 205–222.

34. McClelland, D. C., and A. M. Liberman.   The effect of need for achievement on recognition of need-related words, *J. Personal.*, 1949, *18*, 236–251.

35. McGinnies, E. M. Emotionality and perceptual defense, *Psychol. Rev.*, 1949, *56*, 244–251.

36. Merkel, J. Die Zeitlichen Verhältnisse der Willensthätiskeit, *Phil. Stud.*, 1883, *2*, 73–127.

37. Murphy, G., L. B. Murphy and T. M. Newcomb. *Experimental social psychology.* New York: Harper, 1937.

38. Perkins, F. T. Symmetry in visual recall, *Amer. J. Psychol.*, 1932, *44*, 473–490.

39. Postman, L., and J. S. Bruner. Multiplicity of set as a determinant of perceptual organization, *J. exp. Psychol.*, 1949, *39*, 369–377.

40. Postman, L., J. S. Bruner and E. McGinnies. Personal values as selective factors in perception, *J. abn. soc. Psychol.*, 1948, *43*, 142–154.

41. Postman, L., J. S. Bruner and R. D. Walk. The perception of error. Paper read at Eastern Psychological Association, 1950.

42. Postman, L., and G. Murphy. The factor of attitude in associative memory, *J. exp. Psychol.*, 1943, *33*, 228–238.

43. Proshansky, H., and G. Murphy. The effects of reward and punishment on perception, *J. Psychol.*, 1942, *13*, 293–305.

44. Sanford, R. N. The effect of abstinence from food upon imaginal processes, *J. Psychol.*, 1936, *2*, 129–136.

45. Schafer, R., and G. Murphy. The role of autism in a visual figure-ground relationship, *J. exp. Psychol.*, 1943, *32*, 335–343.

46. Sherif, M. A study of some social factors in perception, *Arch. Psychol.*, 1935.

47. Tolman, E. C., and E. Brunswik. The organism and the causal texture of the environment, *Psychol. Rev.*, 1935, *42*, 43–77.

48. Wallach, H. Some considerations concerning the relation between perception and cognition, *J. Personal.*, 1949, *18*, 6–13.

49. Watson, W. S., and G. W. Hartmann. The rigidity of a basic attitudinal frame, *J. abn. soc. Psychol.*, 1939, *34*, 313–335.

50. Woodworth, R. S. Reenforcement of perception, *Amer. J. Psychol.*, 1947, *60*, 119–124.

51. Wulf, F. Über die Veränderung von Vorstellungen, *Psychol. Forsch.*, 1922, *1*, 333–373.

52. Yokoyama, M., as reported by E. G. Boring. Attribute and sensation, *Amer. J. Psychol.*, 1924, *35*, 301–304.

CHAPTER 11

⊓⊔⊓⊔⊓⊔⊓⊔⊓⊔⊓⊔⊓⊔⊓⊔⊓⊔⊓⊔⊓⊔⊓⊔⊓⊔⊓⊔⊓⊔⊓⊔

Scales of Judgment and Their Implications for Social Psychology

JOHN VOLKMANN

Mount Holyoke College

This account of the experimental psychology of judgment will offer only the simplest and most basic functional facts. These facts will lead to a very broad application to problems of social psychology. This chapter will not be a critical review of the literature, or an account of the research in judgment that is now going on in American laboratories. In the field of judgment, the facts to be emphasized are still the older and the simpler ones. They have been well applied by Sherif and his co-workers, but most social psychologists have not yet followed the example.

The field of application chosen for this chapter is educational theory. This choice may be surprising; education is not commonly regarded as a special part of social psychology. But even the political scientists are now aware that the creation of a democratic society and an orderly world depends upon the education of the world's inhabitants. The social psychologist will want to go even further than that, and will eventually want to specify the particular ways in which people should be educated if they are to live together happily in the modern world. This is the sense in which education becomes a proper part of social psychology.

American colleges are showing very dramatically the confused state of educational theory. Similar confusions exist in ideas about education in general, but we can begin with the colleges. Inside the ivy-covered walls, the notion of *formal discipline* may be dying, but it is certainly not yet dead. Educators are still trying to strengthen the powers of the mind, even though there are no powers, there is no mind, and the strengthening is not easily demonstrated. Education by *ideological indoctrination* loads the student with descriptive models in a job lot—if he takes one, he takes them all. In another noble experiment, some colleges attempt to educate through the study of *great books and great men*. The books and the men are often intrinsically interesting, and primary sources are often better than secondary sources. But the books and the men cannot escape the limitations of their time, and they often present exactly those confusions that the educated man should avoid. The progress of the last hundred years has been intellectual as well as technological. It is not much more feasible to learn logic from Aristotle than to learn city planning from St. Augustine.

Fortunately there are more enlightened ideas about education. Some colleges have practiced what might be called *cultural immersion*. This may consist, for example, of an entire semester devoted to the culture of Periclean Athens, or to a close sociological study of the community in which the college is located. Probably a great deal is accomplished in this way, but it becomes a little hard to say just what it is. Cultural immersion is a special application of the *project method*.

Probably we have all taken *survey courses* at one time or another, and some of us have even taught them. In these courses the lecturer races through the corridors of time at a century a week. With skill and good luck, he can transmit a lot of a little. Without the skill or the good luck, the students lose the race, and the teacher fails to win it. Probably the most interesting development, related to the survey courses, is the *combined course*. For example, there are now combined courses in Western culture to which historians, economists, political scientists, and philosophers contribute quite effectively.

This is not a photographic likeness of educational theory and practice, it is a caricature. Nevertheless, there is a good deal of confusion in education, and perhaps at least one of the areas of confusion can be cleared up by the psychologists. Most of these educational procedures try to produce in the student a better or broader *perspective* to alter his view on some parts of the world. In ordinary language, the world is made to look very different to the educated man. In the language of objective psychology, the discriminatory responses of the educated man are (or can be) very different from those of the uneducated man.

How do we gain perspective? The first job is to find by abstraction a number of particular discriminable aspects. In short, we must first find what we are going to discriminate—in what relevant ways the objects of our discrimination differ among themselves. Now one of the conditions for finding a discriminable aspect is a moderate amount of heterogeneity among the stimulus-objects. In a most casual experiment performed in the laboratory at Mount Holyoke, Oppenheimer and Wells (1) presented simultaneously pairs of visual figures; they asked a group of subjects in what ways these figures were alike, and in what ways they were different. The figures were in one series combinations of geometrical shapes, in another series butterflies, and in another series Kilroy-faces ("Kilroy was here"). The paired patterns were at first identical, and were then made to differ in certain ways, and to differ by increasing amounts in the successive presentations. Kilroy's nose got longer, for example, and his eyes got farther apart. The discriminable aspects could be reported either as likenesses or as differences. The frequency with which they were reported by the group of subjects increased with the heterogeneity of the stimulus-patterns, until the two figures were made very different indeed; then the frequency of reporting tended to decrease again.

There are other conditions that favor the finding of discriminable aspects. The most obvious one is, of course, the verbal instruction to look for one or more given aspects. Various kinds of verbal instruction are used in the classical abstraction experiment, in most experiments on human discrimination, and indeed in any lecture or text or conversation in which somebody is talking analytically. There are people who think that there must be an indefinitely large number of discriminable aspects in any situation; they therefore hesitate to proceed analytically at all. Surely the experience of practicing scientists does not favor this view; there may be a large number of possible aspects, but only a few of these are relevant to one's purposes in describing, and an excellent description of the situation can eventually be given in terms of these few. We need to be able to find the relevant aspects, and to shift with flexibility from discriminating one to discriminating another. In educating, we want to prepare people to do exactly this.

The process of finding discriminable aspects is not easy. Most people in the world are probably object-bound most of the time. They see objects, but do not find the variables in terms of which these objects can be described. Their vocabularies may not even include the word *variable* or its equivalent. There may even be psychologists who in some obscure way do not seem to know what a variable is. How can one produce perspectives when so many people regard the world as if it were composed of unanalyzed differences: *a* is *a,* dogs are dogs, men are men, women are women, and there are no variables? A world like that is doomed to be chaotic; it simply will not make sense. To produce perspectives in our fellow men, we shall need to offer some heterogeneous stimulation, and to do a lot of very pointed talking about the particular, relevant ways in which things differ—children's workbooks in arithmetic take pains to distinguish the numbers "two" and "six" from two oranges or six policemen. Perhaps we need similar workbooks for adults.

Some failures in judgment come, then, from an original failure to find the relevant discriminatory aspects. The visitor to a picture gallery will probably not find his ideal of a good-looking girl in the work of Rubens, or Picasso, or Braque. If he looks for strength and subtlety of composition, however, he will find them in all three.

Some disagreements between people who are discriminating in the same stimulus-situation occur when one person discriminates one aspect, and another person a different aspect. This is another prominent source of disagreement in judgments, as has been pointed out by Pratt (2). He showed that when subjects are instructed to discriminate total fusion, they may actually go on to discriminate one or more of at least four quite different aspects: smoothness-roughness, analyzability, adjacency-remoteness, and pleasantness-unpleasantness. Part of the problem is obviously semantic; in educating, we must use language that not only leads people to find an aspect, but also makes sure that they will find the one that we are talking about.

Suppose that a given discriminable aspect has been located by a discriminating person. What is the next thing that determines that person's discriminatory responses? The answer is simple: it is the particular range of stimuli that is offered for discrimination. Here it will be necessary to introduce some notions taken from psychophysics.

Figure 1 (upper part) shows a schema of a two-category absolute scale of pitch. The upper line represents the scale, which consists of the two categories of judgment "low" and "high." The lower line represents a correlated stimulus-variable, auditory frequency in cycles per second.

The particular set of stimuli to be judged ranges from 300–400 cps, and the difference between these of 100 cycles is the stimulus-range L_{rn}. The stimulus-center, R_c, is in this case 350 cycles. The dividing line between the two absolute categories "low" and "high" is the category-thresholds. It is measured in terms of the stimulus (345 cycles), and is defined as

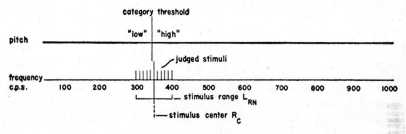

A two-category absolute scale of pitch.

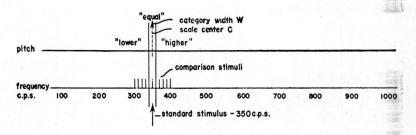

A three-category comparative scale of pitch.

FIGURE 1. Schemas to illustrate a two-category absolute scale, and a three-category comparative scale.

that stimulus-value at which the probability of a judgment "low" equals the probability of a judgment "high."

The lower part of Figure 1 presents in terms of the psychology of judgment a more familiar psychophysical example, a 3-category comparative scale of pitch. (Pitch is used as a typical discriminable aspect in this figure and in most of the succeeding ones. The applications to social psychology will follow shortly.) For purposes of the figure only, the comparison stimuli are shown as ranging from 300 to 400 cycles. There has been added a standard stimulus at 350 cycles. There are in this example 3 categories: "lower," "equal," and "higher," and consequently two category-thresholds rather than one. The stimulus-differ-

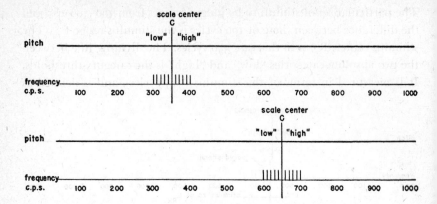

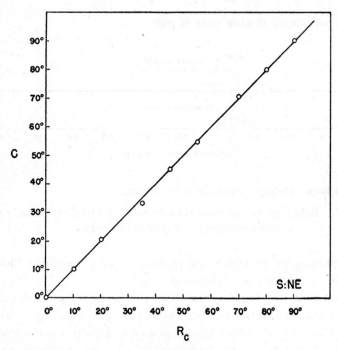

FIGURE 2. A schema to illustrate the dependence of the center of a two-category absolute scale on the center of the stimulus-set. Also, a graph of experimental data that show this dependence.

ence between the two thresholds represents the width W of the "equal" category. The center C of the 3-category comparative scale might be taken as the middle of the "equal" category. So much for terminology.

The first fundamental relation that we should consider is the dependence of the center of an absolute scale upon the stimulus-center. The schema in Figure 2 shows two different, two-category absolute scales of pitch, one centered about 250 cycles and the other about 650 cycles. This schema presents a perfectly obvious fact: that what the subject in an experiment of this kind calls "low," and what he calls "high," depends upon the particular range of stimulus-frequencies that he is given. If he is given frequencies from 600–700 cycles, he will call 600 cycles "low." If he has been given 300 to 400 cycles, he will call even 400 cycles "high." It is not so obvious, however, that the dependence of the scale-center upon the stimulus-center is as thoroughgoing as experiments show it to be. The graph in Figure 2 presents a handsome rectilinear relation between these two variables in the discrimination of visual inclination. Experiments on visual extent, visual duration, and kinesthetic extent all show the very same relation. Human scales of discrimination are very flexible indeed, and this is one of the ways in which they are most flexible. In one discriminable aspect only is the flexibility known to be limited: pleasantness and unpleasantness (3). This is not in any way a surprising exception.

To avoid misunderstanding, a few things should be noted about the relation shown in Figure 2. The data came from experiments in which the subject was instructed to make his judgments relative to the particular range of stimuli that he was being given in the experiment at the time. Very similar data have been obtained, however, under a very different set of instructions. Note also the extreme terminological unhappiness with which we call a scale "absolute," when the subject has been instructed to make it *relative*.

The next fundamental relation is the dependence of the width of a category (or of an entire scale of categories) upon the stimulus-range. The schema of Figure 3 contrasts a relatively narrow 4-category absolute scale with a relatively wide one. The names of the categories in order are the numerals "one," "two," "three," and "four." The stimulus-range runs in one example from 440 to 560 cycles; in the other, from 150 cycles to 850 cycles. The stimulus-center is the same: 500 cycles. The graph of Figure 3 shows that over a wide range the width of absolute

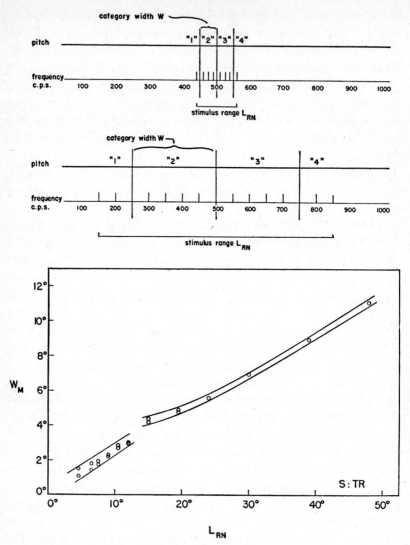

FIGURE 3. A schema to show the dependence of category-width upon stimulus-range. Below, a graph of experimental data that show the form of this dependence.

categories (or of the entire scale) varies in rectilinear fashion with the stimulus-range. This is still another way in which scales of judgment are very flexible indeed. The flexibility reaches a limit at some low stimulus-range, however; the categories are not indefinitely compressible; their width cannot be decreased beyond a certain value. If the stimulus-range is still further decreased, there results a "broken scale"; the subject may use the top categories and the bottom ones, but he cannot also use the middle categories. The data plotted in Figure 3 repre-

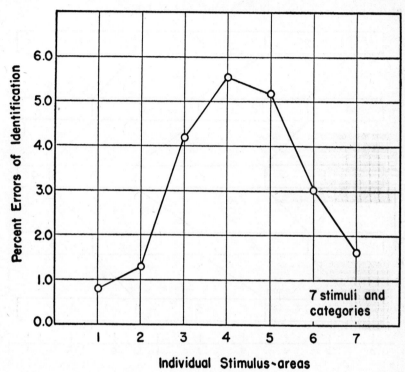

FIGURE 4. A curve relating the percent-error of identifying 7 visual stimulus-areas to the particular area to be identified. The errors pile up on the middle stimuli.

sent the discrimination of visual inclination, but there is no reason to think that they could not be duplicated with any other stimulus-material.

In order to learn more about how a scale of judgment works, we might look next at a curve that shows the percent-error of identifying each of a number of visual stimuli, plotted against these stimuli (Fig. 4). In this experiment, the subjects looked across an auditorium at a large screen, and saw appear there one at a time a series of triangular forms. These forms were constant in shape and brightness, and varied only in area. There were seven stimulus-areas and seven absolute categories. In short, the subjects wrote down whether they thought that the particular triangle being shown was the smallest one of the set ("1"), the largest one ("7"), or some one in between. Figure 4 shows that the errors pile up on the middle stimuli and middle categories.

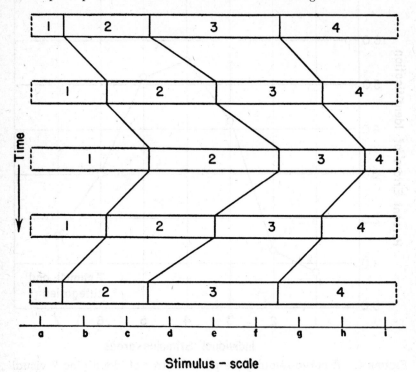

FIGURE 5. A schema to explain the curve of Figure 4. The absolute scale oscillates between its ends, making the judgment on the middle stimuli most variable and most open to error.

Figure 5 offers a schema to explain this result. The absolute scale undergoes marked changes in time; one of the changes is an oscillation between the region of the top stimulus and the region of the bottom one. For simplicity, the schema shows a 4-category scale instead of a 7-category scale. The bottom stimulus will be called "1" without error, and the top stimulus will be called "4" without error. Some of the middle stimuli, however, will sometimes be called "2," and sometimes "3." There is thus an increased variability of judgment in the middle of the scale. In an experiment that calls for the identification of particular stimuli, like the one just described, there will consequently be a higher frequency of errors in identifying the middle stimuli.

The experiment has something else to tell us, however: it is primarily the *end-stimuli* that control the oscillations of the absolute scale. The center of the stimulus-range has no special functional significance whatever. It is merely a convenient numerical value: the mean of the two end-stimuli. This is the way that it was used in Figure 1. We should not make the mistake of thinking that the operation of an absolute scale requires some implicit or averaged value equivalent in its effect to a standard stimulus. Indeed, the graph of Figure 4 shows that the judgments are most variable (and consequently most likely to be in error) on the middle stimuli, exactly where an implicit standard might be located. Apparently it is not there.

If it is in fact the end-stimuli that control the principal properties of the absolute scale, it should be possible to intensify their effect. This we can do by presenting an auxiliary stimulus equal to the bottom judged stimulus, and by telling the subject that this stimulus is to represent the bottom category of his scale. This is a special case of *stimulus-anchoring*. The top category is anchored in a similar way, and we may call the whole procedure *end-anchoring*. The schema of Figure 6 represents end-anchoring, and the graph in Figure 6 shows what happens to category-width when end-anchoring has been provided. The width of the various absolute categories is drastically reduced; that is to say, the discrimination becomes much finer. The actual experiment called for judgments in 8 absolute categories. Without end-anchoring, it was possible to determine from the data only 4 category-thresholds (and the width of 3 categories). With end-anchoring, it became possible to determine 6 category-thresholds and the widths of 5 categories. The stimulus-material was a set of visual inclinations; the stimulus-range was relatively short, 16° to 37°. Although the data are fragmentary, there is no reason to suppose that they could not be paralleled under a wide variety of stimulus-conditions.

What happens when we use a single anchoring stimulus, and take it out of the range of judged stimuli? The experiments of Rogers (4) and of McGarvey (5) have told us. Rogers used discriminations of visual inclination and lifted weight; he first inserted an anchoring stimulus equal to the highest judged stimulus and then, in subsequent parts of the experiment, displaced it upward by increasing amounts (see Fig. 7). The first effect that he observed was an approximately rectilinear extension of the absolute scale in the direction of the anchoring stimulus. The extension was partial rather than complete; the scale apparently did not extend far enough to actually include the anchoring stimulus

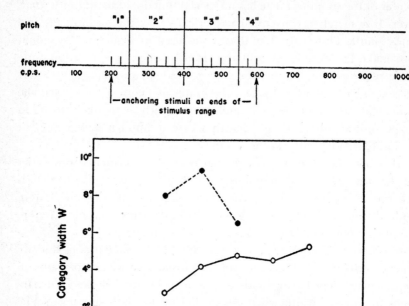

FIGURE 6. A schema to illustrate end-anchoring. Below, a graph of experimental data, showing that end-anchoring reduces the width of absolute categories.

in the center of its top category. The next thing that happened, when the anchoring stimulus had already been considerably displaced, was a failure in the anchoring effect. The scale tended to pull loose either from the anchoring stimulus, or from the judged stimulus located at the bottom end of the scale. Apparently an anchoring stimulus does not retain its desired effect if it is too far removed from the set of judged stimuli. The schema of Figure 7 shows the partial extension of a 4-

category absolute scale in the direction of a remote anchoring stimulus. The graph of Figure 7 is taken from Rogers' data; it shows the approximately rectilinear extension of the scale up to a point, and the abrupt decrease in the extension of the scale at that point.

All of the examples used so far have been psychophysical in a narrow sense, that is, they have been drawn from the discrimination of visual

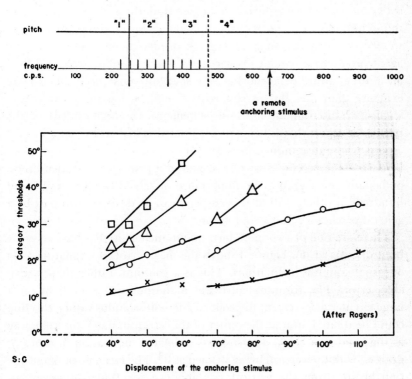

FIGURE 7. A schema to show that a remote anchoring stimulus extends an absolute scale. Below, a graph of Rogers' experimental data, which describe the anchoring effect of a function of the displacement of the anchoring stimulus.

or auditory stimuli. Perhaps it has been hard enough to make the point that there are some fundamental ways in which the discriminations of pitch, loudness, inclination, area, and brilliance are all alike. In fact, they may be described by the same quantitative regularities. But it is still more important to say that these regularities also apply to the discrimination of *nearly any aspect at all*. In experimenting, we may use physically calibrated stimuli and a classical psychophysical technique, as Rogers did. Or we may use verbal materials and carefully constructed psychological scales for measuring them, as McGarvey did. Her subjects discriminated the undesirability of various crimes and offenses in one part of the experiment, and the social prestige of trades and professions in the other part. She constructed separate psychological scales for each of her subjects, and chose from these scales verbal items to use in the place of judged stimuli and anchoring stimuli. Her results were very much the same as Rogers': displacement of the anchoring agent produced a regular displacement of the absolute scale and then an abrupt failure of anchoring. We shall of course need much more evidence than this, but psychologists should be looking forward to a science of discrimination whose statements are independent of the particular aspect that is being discriminated. This means that all of the aspects whose discrimination is relevant to social stimulation or social behavior—the acceptability of a slogan or a principle, the friendliness or hostility of a group, the importance or triviality of an issue, and hundreds of others—all of these aspects can be dealt with in part by a general psychology of discrimination.

There are one or two more facts about anchoring that have recently been discovered (6). Figure 8 shows the mean error of estimating a set of visual stimulus-inclinations. This is a constant, rather than a variable, error. The stimulus-figure was a stationary line of light on a large circular glass screen; to produce different stimulus-values, this line could be rotated around the center of the screen in much the same way as the hand of a clock. The subjects estimated inclination in terms of degrees, with the vertical being defined as $0°$. The mean error of estimation at $30°$ from the vertical was about $+6°$. When, however, an auxiliary line of light was placed on the screen at $30°$, and the subjects were told that it was intended to mark $30°$, the mean error of estimation naturally decreased to zero. It is more important that the errors of estimation decreased over a quite wide range of inclinations: from $5°$ to $40°$. Above $40°$, however, the amount of this constant error was actually increased. An experiment by Reed and Safford (7) on the anchoring of estimates of number has given parallel results. A single anchoring stimulus can therefore be expected to increase accuracy over a considerable range, but it can also be expected to decrease accuracy outside this range, unless it is supplemented by other anchoring stimuli.

Single anchoring stimuli produce some other important effects. Variability within the successive judgments of one subject is reduced over a relatively wide range of stimuli. The variability between subjects is also greatly reduced: one very effective way of bringing people to agree is to offer them the same anchoring stimuli. For another fact: Chapanis (8), working at Johns Hopkins, has recently shown that an anchoring

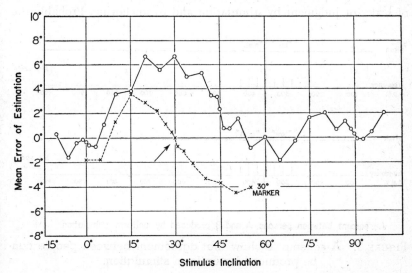

FIGURE 8.   A graph of data from an experiment on the estimation of visual inclinations. Inserting an anchoring stimulus at 30° decreases constant errors of estimating from 5° to 40°, but increases them outside that range.

stimulus increases the number of absolute categories that the subject is willing to use (the fineness of discrimination that he attempts), and consequently decreases the tendency to judge in round numbers. The data from experiments at Mount Holyoke are in complete agreement on this point. An anchoring stimulus at 30° of inclination, for example, leads the subject to use 1°-steps in estimating, (28°, 29°, and so on) instead of 5°-steps. If the number of categories were to be held constant in an experiment of this kind, two further effects of an anchoring stimulus could probably be demonstrated: an increase in the *speed* of judgment, and an increase in the *confidence* with which the judgment is given. As a final fact, anchoring can be achieved by appropriate verbal instructions, without the use of anchoring stimuli (9).

The psychology of judgment does not stop here, either in the present state of its information or in its plans for research. But enough has been said to point the way to an improved psychology of judgmental *perspective.*

Once the abstraction of the relevant discriminable aspect has been achieved, the problem of perspective is reduced to the determination of scales of judgment by stimulation and by anchoring. Probably the

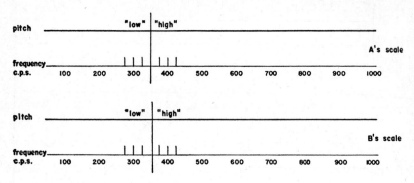

Agreement between persons A and B produced by uniform stimulation.

FIGURE 9.   A schema to show that agreement between people can be produced by uniform stimulation.

most common case is the one in which a relatively narrow range of stimulation leads to a very limited perspective (or, as one might say, no perspective at all). If two or more people are given the same narrow range of stimulation, and are given no external anchoring agents, their judgments can be expected to agree. Figure 9 presents a schema of this case. This is one way in which homogeneity of the culture, when realized in actual stimulation, leads to homogeneity of attitudes. An experiment using weight-discriminations (10) has shown that the absolute judgments of different people can rather quickly come to agree in the face of common stimulation. The stimuli can be social or non-social; the basis of agreement, which lies in the principles of discrimination, is the same.

Quite obviously, people can be led to give different judgments (and, in effect, to disagree) by presenting them with ranges of stimuli that are limited but are different (see the schema in Fig. 10). Person *A* would call 400 cycles "high" and person *B* would call it "low." If this were

any example other than a psychophysical one, we would probably say
that they both lack perspective.

A situation of disagreement like this one can obviously be improved
by extending the scale of person *A* in one direction, and the scale of

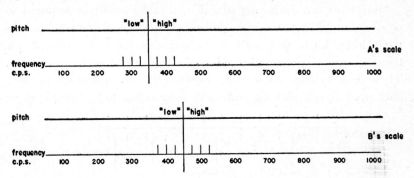

Disagreement between persons A and B produced by non-uniform stimulation.

FIGURE 10.   A schema to show that disagreement between people
can be produced by non-uniform stimulation. Contrast with Fig. 9.

person *B* in the other direction (see Fig. 11). In order to do this, anchoring stimuli can be placed at or above the top end of *B*'s scale and at or
below the bottom end of *A*'s scale. For the sake of simplicity, assume
that the same anchoring stimuli are presented to *A* and to *B*. Because

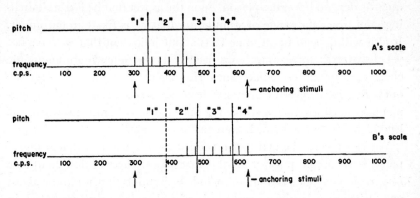

Increased agreement produced by uniform anchoring.

FIGURE 11.   A schema to show that people can be brought closer to
agreement by giving them the same anchoring stimuli.

an anchoring effect of this kind is only a partial effect, the scales of *A* and *B* will not completely coincide, but they will at least approach each other. Common anchoring tends to produce agreement among the judgments of different people.

More than two anchoring stimuli will undoubtedly be required to produce a well-anchored scale, however, especially if the scale is relatively long. There must still be anchoring at the two extremes, but there must also be a small number of intermediate anchoring agents. These should enable the scale to extend in the direction of the extreme anchoring agents, without pulling loose at either end. Probably there

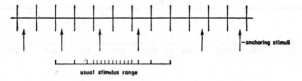

An extended, well-anchored scale.

FIGURE 12. A schema that presents a possible arrangement of anchoring stimuli. The arrangement is designed to produce an extended, well-anchored scale.

should be additional anchoring agents in the range in which stimulation is likely to be encountered by the particular person who is holding this scale. The optimum arrangement of anchoring agents will consequently depend upon the person, upon the aspect that he is discriminating, and upon the range of stimulation that he is likely to encounter. It also will depend upon some facts about judgment that we have not yet discovered; for example, we need to know much more about the effect of using intermediate anchoring agents in addition to remote ones. But it is nevertheless possible to suggest some sample arrangements of anchoring agents, like the one shown in Figure 12, where the legend reads "an extended, well-anchored scale."

We can now make a list of certain desirable features that scales of perspective might possess. In the first place, these scales should be *long,* as long as they can be, to include everything that we know about or can imagine. In the second place, they should be *well-anchored,* in the sense of the preceding paragraph. Thirdly, they should, if possible, include an adequate representation of the discriminating person himself, and of features of his own culture. In ordinary language, this would enable a man to see himself and his culture in relation to the known universe at large. Fourthly, the scales should be flexible in the following respect: at different times, different anchoring agents could be selected to determine the position and the width of the scale. The man who has a long, well-anchored scale should be able to shorten it for a particular purpose of discrimination. In this way man *A,* who has a long scale, can make the same discrimination as man *B,* who has a short one; in this sense he can "understand" the attitude of man *B.* Temporarily, he shares his discriminations. This is a very interesting case; it might be called *displaced perspective.* Conflict between groups frequently calls for the exercise of displaced perspective. Note, however, that only those people with relatively long scales have the privilege of shortening them. Displaced perspective is an achievement in which most people on earth do not share.

What kinds of perspective would we like to produce, in educating college people or any people? The list is long and varied, and it suggests some of the combined courses in general education that are now being offered. One would like to institute a *time*-perspective to which the astronomers, geologists, archeologists, historians, and physicists could contribute. Likewise a *space*-perspective: the cosmologists, geophysicists, geographers would do the talking here, and they would preferably be supplemented by the people who know intimately the home state and the home town. There is *evolutionary* perspective, to be gained by listening to the paleologists, the zoologists, and the anthropologists. We would like to have perspective upon *groups* and *peoples,* from the sociologists and the physical and social anthropologists. Obviously there is a whole series of *cultural* perspectives, dealing with family-structure, class-structure, mores and folkways, values and tastes, economic practices, and features of the material culture.

Finally, we should note a class of perspectives in which the psychologists would be especially interested. The wide range of individual differences in abilities, in temperament, and in attitudes can be opened up to each individual. In most of the scales that establish perspective, there is an opportunity to place the individual himself and his conditions of life; his time and his place, his species and his skin-color, his class and his family, his intelligence-test score and his somatotype, his place in Kinsey's tables. The view that this gives him will not always be encouraging, but the action to which it leads can at least be realistic.

Placing the individual in various scales of perspective is useful for another reason also. It gives a good answer to the freshman or layman who
is puzzled and repelled by organized learning, and who asks, "What
does all this have to do with me?" This is a perfectly proper question,
and it deserves a better answer than it usually gets.

What would the institution of these perspectives do for us and our
fellows? In the first place, our judgments would become more stable—
less open to transitory pressures and the accidents of stimulation. In
the second place, we and our fellows would agree more often, and could
take action on the basis of that agreement. Discussion is splendid but
disagreement is not; nobody (maybe not even a lawyer) wants to spend
the rest of his life arguing. The flexibility that allows displaced perspective will in the long run favor agreement. Lastly, perspective has
a protective function. It tends to protect a man against his own residual
small-mindedness, and against domination by small-minded people.

Almost all of the educational procedures referred to at the beginning
of this chapter can contribute in some way to the growth of perspective.
Naturally some will contribute more than others, and they all have
other things to do beside instituting perspectives. People who are offering survey and combined courses might decide first which particular
perspectives they want to institute; having done this, they can then
make a more economical selection from among their materials. They
can follow our knowledge that a very high density of anchoring agents
is not required; each anchoring agent acts over a considerable range.
The people who are practicing cultural immersion can be encouraged,
especially when the culture studied is the student's own culture. After
all, this probably is the culture that he will have to live in. In order to
bring about a proper perspective, however, some very different cultures
should also be studied, and a few that are not so different. Even the
great books and the great men can be fitted with some difficulty into
historical perspectives, and they will in turn contribute to these perspectives.

Many of us have thought that the psychology of judgment and perspective could be important for social change, and for the construction
of an orderly society. To reach these goals, human beings will not have
to agree on every issue. They *will* have to agree on a few things, including this one: what kinds of social behavior they will struggle for and
retain, and what kinds they will tolerate. One of the basic problems of

our time is how to bring about this required minimum of agreement. It is partly a problem of building perspectives. The argument of this chapter holds that the solution to such problems lies in providing heterogeneity of stimulation, in pointing out which discriminable aspects are relevant, and in providing anchoring stimuli and anchoring instructions. That is what the psychophysicist says that the educator is already doing in building perspectives, or what he might preferably do.

We have noted that the restricting of stimulation to a narrow range can lead to agreement or attitudinal uniformity within a group of people. Within this group the underlying discriminable aspect may not even be seen; if it is seen, the agreement will rest only upon the fact of common stimulation. Repressive social forces (of any political complexion) act characteristically by restricting stimulation. The effort of rigid censorship to produce uniform opinion by restricted stimulation may fail, however, because of the many channels of communication that modern technology has already produced. Some basic perspectives may arise, and bring some basic agreements with them, whether or not the censors go on censoring, or the professors go on talking in opposition. This is a slim chance, and nobody should depend upon it.

Enlightened education has other things to do beside producing perspectives. It aims to teach *scientific method*. People have at last found out how to find out about things; there can hardly be any information that is more important than that. Education also provides the student with some well-tested *descriptive models,* the result of the thoroughgoing application of scientific method. To the incredibly precise and dependable models of physics will sometime be added a model of human behavior. Finally, enlightened education will favor the acquisition of useful *skills*.

The psychology of judgment does not provide social psychology with what it needs most, that model for human behavior just mentioned. Indeed, the psychology of judgment can serve best right now in illuminating particular, large problems like those of perspective and agreement among people. We want the psychology of judgment to become incorporated as soon as possible in a modern science of discrimination, which is in turn an integral part of a science of behavior. Because this science of behavior is already well under way, and because there is much more agreement about it than there is commonly supposed to be, we shall see it emerge before long. In seeking out this basic science of behavior, however, the social psychologists should be not among the last people but among the first. They have, after all, the greatest need for the basic science, and the world is waiting.

REFERENCES

1. Oppenheimer, J., and Wells, J. A. The discovery of reputable aspects. (Unpublished.)
2. Pratt, C. C. Some qualitative aspects of bitonal complexes. *Amer. J. Psychol.*, 1921, *32*, 490–518.
3. Beebe-Center, J. G. The law of affective equilibrium. *Amer. J. Psychol.*, 1929, *41*, 54–69.
4. Rogers, S. The anchoring of absolute judgments. *Arch. Psychol., N. Y.*, 1941, No. 261.
5. McGarvey, H. R. Anchoring effects in the absolute judgment of verbal materials, *Arch. Psychol., N. Y.*, 1943, No. 281.
6. Rogers, S., Volkmann, J., Reese, T. W., and Kaufman, E. L. Accuracy and variability of direct estimates of bearing from large display screens. Psychophysical Research Unit, Mount Holyoke College. Report No. 166–I–MHCl. 15 May 1947.
7. Reed, E. C., and Safford, K. The effect of anchoring on the visual discrimination of number. (In press.)
8. Chapanis, A. Number Habits and Visual Displays, *Minutes and Proceedings of the Armed Forces NRC Vision Committee,* 25th Meeting 17 to 18 February, 1950, p. 145.
9. Volkmann, J. The anchoring of absolute scales, *Psychol. Bull.*, 1936, *33*, 742–743. (Abstract.)
10. Tresselt, M. E., and Volkmann, J. The production of uniform opinion by non-social stimulation, *J. Abnorm. & Soc. Psychol.*, 1942, *37*, 234–243.

Part Five

Group Structures and Individual Roles

CHAPTER 12

⊓⊔⊓⊔⊓⊔⊓⊔⊓⊔⊓⊔⊓⊔⊓⊔⊓⊔⊓⊔⊓⊔⊓⊔⊓⊔⊓⊔⊓⊔⊓⊔⊓⊔

Small Groups and Large Organizations

WILLIAM FOOTE WHYTE
Cornell University

Studies of groups, I feel, need to be placed in a perspective of larger organizational structures. Ours is a society of large and complex organizations. The most difficult human relations problems are found within these organizations. We cannot afford to lose sight of the small group, but neither can we afford to study it in isolation.

Early studies of autocratic and democratic leadership in small groups seem to me to illustrate this problem. In terms of research strategy, it makes good sense to do intensive work on the simple and the small scale first. In fact, that was my own experience in the study of street-corner gangs. However, we simply cannot extrapolate conclusions from the small group studies when we are dealing with groups in large organizations.

Suppose, for example, we are dealing with a foreman and a group of workers. To what extent can the foreman develop worker participation in decision making? While there are certain opportunities, it is clear that they are much more limited than is the case in an autonomous group.

I do not mean to say, as do some businessmen, that group dynamics has no relevance against the hard realities of business life. I feel that important work has been done on small groups. I simply feel that we need to learn how to tie our small group and large organizational studies together in the same general framework of theory.

METHODS FOR STUDYING GROUPS

My work has involved studying group structures. In simpler language, this involves the study of *leader-follower relations*. Now nearly everyone is interested in studying "leadership." The field seems to me in a deplorable state of confusion because quite different phenomena are often lumped together under this same heading. Let us see if we can sift out some of these differences.

At least four distinctions can be made:

1. *Operational leadership.* We observe that individual X commonly initiates action for individuals A, B, C, D, E, and F. X can therefore be called the leader of this group of seven men.

2. *Popularity.* The fact that individual Y was elected president of his club tells us something about his popularity with the members. However, it does not tell us that he is an operational leader. He may commonly initiate action for the other members—but he also may not. All of us can recall cases of elected officers who were merely pleasant figureheads, while other men initiated action within the organization. Now, popularity is worth some study, but we must begin by recognizing that it is definitely not the same phenomenon as operational leadership. The operational leader is likely to be popular, but many popular people are not operational leaders.

3. *The assumed representative.* Members of group A choose Z, a "prominent" individual in group B, to work with them in gaining the support of group B. If the choice is to be effective, they will choose an operational leader in group B. However, if differences of status and culture separate the two groups, the chances are overwhelming that group A will choose a man who is prominent in the "right" way—that is, a man who is close to them in status and culture. This means that he will already have alienated himself from group B and will have no influence there.

For example, the director of a settlement house in an Italian-American slum district picks a group of Italian-American "leaders" as an advisory committee to gain him greater community participation. These "leaders" are all business and professional men. Some of them have not even been heard of by the people in the neighborhood, and there is not a single one on the advisory committee who has a local following.

Or take this one. The powers in the political organization wish to

win more Jews to their party. For this purpose, they nominate a prominent Jew for one of their offices. But this man left the Jewish religion
some years ago, and he no longer participates in any Jewish activities.
In the Jewish community he is regarded as a turncoat. He is almost
getting himself accepted by the non-Jewish business and professional
people, but he can no more line up the Jewish vote than can Tim
Flaherty or Frank Luongo.

4. *The prominent talent.* Sergei Popoff is considered one of -the
greatest violinists in the world. He is sometimes referred to as "a leader
of the musical world." But Sergei Popoff is also a lone wolf socially who
does not consistently originate action for any group of people. Clearly,
if we refer to him as a "leader," we are talking about a phenomenon
quite different from operational leadership.

The distinction between talent and operational leadership would
seem so obvious that I hesitate even to mention it, but I recently read
a monograph summarizing some of the latest leadership studies in social
psychology, and I found there this confusion prominently represented.
For example, the author reported a study of "leaders in six types of
school activities." In none of the cases was any evidence furnished that
the individuals were operational leaders and not simply popular people. One category, "staff members of school magazines," seems clearly
to represent talent with no necessary connection with operational leadership.

Now, I don't object to people studying the popular man, the assumed
representative, or the artistically talented individual, but I do urge that
the researcher not get these phenomena mixed up with operational
leadership.

It is only leadership of the first definition that I am interested in. For
want of a better term, I call it "operational leadership" because the research operations to identify it can be clearly specified.

Since I described these research methods in a paper some years ago
(1), I shall simply summarize what to me seem to be the main points.[1]

The primary method involves the *observation* of overt behavior. For
studies of leadership or group structure, this involves particularly two
sorts of observations.

1. *Spatial observations of groupings.* How often is A observed to-

---

[1] The six paragraphs that follow are used also in my technical appendix for the
forthcoming volume: *Research for Action.*

gether with B, C, D, and E? For this purpose, it is not necessary to record the content of conversations. We only need to record that certain men were seen interacting together on the street corner, around a card table in a club room, and so on. Repeated observations of this sort soon yield a definite pattern in which men fit together most closely, which are less regular participants, and which are on the periphery of the group. But to determine leadership patterns, we need to make the observations noted below.

2. *Changes in group activity.* We observe here the interaction, including conversation, through which there is an objective change in the pattern of group activity. These examples will serve as illustrations:

A. Seven men are standing in the club room, in groups of two, two, and three. Individual X comes in and the three little groups immediately reform into one larger group, with the seven men remaining silent while X talks and each man seeking to get the attention of X before he himself speaks.

B. X says, 'Let's take a walk." We then observe the group setting out for a walk. Or A says to X, "Let's go to the Orpheum." X says, "Naw, that picture is no good." No change in group activity. Then B says to X, "Let's go to the State." X says, "O.K." The group is then off to the State.

C. Some of the fellows are sitting around a table in a cafeteria having their evening coffee-ands. A leaves the group to sit down for a few minutes with people at a nearby table. X remains at the original table, and the conversation continues much as it did when A was present. On another occasion, the same people are present in the same spatial arrangement in the cafeteria, but this time it is X who gets up and goes over to another table. The conversation at X's former table noticeably slows down and perhaps breaks up into twos and threes. The men talk about what X could be doing over at the other table. If X stays away beyond a given point in time, we may observe his friends picking up their chairs and moving over to the other table with him.

Observations along these lines establish that X characteristically initiates action for this group, that he is the leader of the group.

Observation is a very time-consuming method. It is indispensable, but it can be supplemented and enriched by interview data. What do we want out of an interview? We want an account of the individual's experience in interpersonal events. The interview can serve to give us such a record—to give us an account of events that we ourselves could have observed had we been present. In this way, interview and observational data can be fitted together.

We follow, in general, the non-directive interviewing technique developed in the Western Electric research program and in Carl Rogers' counseling work, but we modify the technique so that it serves the needs of research rather than those of therapy. We aim to get the informant to talk fully and freely about his experience and the problems that concern him. At the same time, we ask the informant to discuss with us the various areas of human relations in which he participates, whether or not he voluntarily steps into each area that interests us. (Naturally, to build and maintain rapport, we cannot push into areas of resistance. The aim is to provide a permissive atmosphere in which the informant will take an interest in exploring these areas with us. We do not expect to get much such information on the first interview. That is used primarily to get the informant used to us and to pave the way for further interviews. With further contacts, we are able to get a more intensive picture.)

For example, if we were studying a work group in a factory, we would interview the individual worker upon his experience in the following areas of relations: within the informal work group; with foremen and other ranks of supervisory management; with time-study men, inspectors, personnel men, and other men from staff or control agencies; with union steward and other union officers. We would seek to get some general background upon family and community life; how far we would go into this would depend upon the definition of our research problem.

All these data would be developed with special attention to the *time* dimension. We want to know what events happened in what order. If we are to predict and control inter-personal relations, *a static picture is of no use to us*. We need to study the sequence of events.

The interviewing method I have described in itself suggests our interest in research data. It is sometimes said that people's perception of social situations, as expressed to us in their words, provides us with scientific data, whether or not the report of events is factually correct. This is true. But sometimes the inference is drawn from this that it makes no difference what "actually happened"; the important thing to study is people's perceptions of these realities. That view I categorically reject.

Of course, we want to know how people perceive situations and what sentiments they have toward these situations, but we also want to know what "actually happened" in those situations. Only if we have such reality data can we discover why people perceive situations as they do.

But how are we to discover such reality data? Here we must distinguish sharply between *descriptions* of events and *interpretations* of events. I have had a good deal of experience in studying conflict situations where the interpretations given me by participants were sharply at variance with each other. Yet, even in such situations, I have had little difficulty on the level of description of events: just who was present, who initiated action for whom, what was said (at least in a very general way). Such descriptive data from different sources generally fit together surprisingly well, even when the informants disagree most extremely in their interpretations of the events.

It is important to establish the nature and sequence of these events, for such data help to explain why people make the interpretations they do of the events. Science cannot develop simply by studying differing individual perceptions of situations.

There is a further conclusion implicit in this statement on interviewing method. It involves a viewpoint regarding the nature of the group. We may ask: what is a group? And, how do we know who is in the group and who is not in?

As I see it, the group should be studied in terms of frequency of interaction. That way there is no problem in determining, for example, whether Jack and Tom are both members of the group when Jack spends one hour a day with the others every day and Tom spends an average of one hour a week. If we try to determine who is in the group and who is not in it, we get into all sorts of difficulties with borderline cases. If, on the other hand, we simply think in terms of a range of frequency of interaction, the problem does not arise.

To put it in another way, there is a tendency in many studies to reify the group, to treat the group as a tangible object—though of course no one would claim to be dealing with a "group mind" or any such phenomenon. The sounder approach is to think in terms of a pattern of interaction that tends to recur among a number of individuals. That way all the interactions among a given number of people who frequently see each other can be counted, and the individual who interacts relatively infrequently with others in the group is as readily handleable in our data as the individual who has large numbers of interactions.

I have already emphasized the *time dimension* in research. Here I want to point out that studies of interaction are peculiarly suited to development in the time dimension. If we discuss the group as a group in general, descriptive terms, we have no convenient means for coping with changes in group structure. When we deal with frequencies of interaction, we have the tools necessary for studying dynamic processes.

Furthermore, the interaction framework allows us to take a more flexible and realistic view of group processes. *Most individuals in a complex society do not limit their participation to a single group.* Now, it may be scientifically wise in the early period of research to focus all our attention upon the internal relations of a particular group, but we must be wary of the general conclusions we draw from such a study.

This problem is particularly important when we are studying a complex organization, even if we are focusing our attention upon the people in a given department of that organization. For example, let us assume that we are studying the workers in one department of a factory. We are interested in their group life—but what does that mean? Are we studying the groups that congregate in the washrooms or in the cafeteria during breaks in the work? Are we studying the relations that develop among workers in the actual performance of their work? And how about the various officials with whom these workers have contacts connected with their factory life: foreman, superintendent, inspector, time-study man, engineer, steward, other union officials, and so on? Are these people considered to be in the group? If we think of THE GROUP, any answer to that question is simply arbitrary.

Instead, we should think of a number of *mutually dependent* sets of relations. That means, for example, that a change in the relations between foreman and workers can be expected to be accompanied by a change in the relations among the workers. Therefore, our problem is to study the sequence of changes in these various interrelated sets of relations, so as to discover how a change in one set is necessarily followed by changes in other sets.

Incidentally, this point of view involves a breakdown of the distinction between formal and informal organization. If by "formal organization" we simply mean the blueprint chart of organization that hangs on the wall in the executive offices, then that is a real and objective item of data. But, if we mean the interactions that actually take place in conformity with the blueprint lines of organization, then those interactions are subject to observation and measurement with the same research methods we apply to relations not specified on the organizational chart. It is quite misleading if we separate them into categories of formal and informal. In fact, I have had some experience in trying to make such a separation with data from field observation, and I can testify that there is a very broad area of behavior where it is impossible to make any objective differentiation.

I am not assuming that studies of leadership or group structure are complete when we have got a quantitative record of interactions, over a period of time. Many significant questions can be asked when that point is reached. Why do some individuals interact in this pattern much more frequently than others? Why does individual X interact frequently with A, B, C, D, E, and F and rarely with N, O, P, Q, and R? Why do the individuals respond to this particular leader? What factors account for changes in the interaction pattern?

Those and many more significant questions could be asked, but let us base them upon some systematic record of behavior directly observed and inferred from interviews. The task of science is then to relate together the observed pattern of *interaction,* the *actions* people perform with physical objects, the *symbols* people express to each other, and the *sentiments* we attribute to them on the basis of what they say and what they do. How this should be done is a problem in theory, which is beyond the scope of this paper.

This approach seems to me in accord with current trends in social psychology. Newcomb has rightly emphasized the cleavage between the psychological and sociological approaches to social psychology (see pp. 31–49). The psychologically trained tend to delve into individual mental and emotional processes, quite removed from culture and social organization. The sociologically trained tend to treat the individual as a neutral, empty vessel, into which the culture is poured.

Individual mental and emotional processes and culture and social organization cannot be effectively related together in static terms. For example, we may find that most individuals holding a given status in society tend to have certain attitudes and sentiments in common, to vote for the same political party, and so on. But correlation is not explanation. Such correlations only pose the problem for us; they do not tell us how such conformity arises.

We must learn to cope with the relationship between the individual and his society. This can only be done through studies *in the time dimension* in which we follow through a process of change. Sherif's summer-camp experiment presents an impressive example along this line (see pp. 388–424). There we see changes in individual sentiments and behavior directly related to changes in interaction among the campers. Research along this line enables us to bring to bear most effectively all we know about psychology, sociology, and anthropology.

THE DESIGN OF ORGANIZATION

I wish now to bring this point of view to bear upon the problem of studying groups in relation to larger organizations in which we find them.

If, instead of thinking of THE GROUP, we think of a network of interpersonal relations, we can examine the relationship between small group and large organization. And examine it we must, for that, I feel, is one of the great problems of our industrial civilization.

All of us who have worked in industry have learned that little can be done to effect human-relations improvements by working directly upon workers or even upon foremen. All too often, higher management makes the foremen the scapegoats for whatever difficulties arise and feels that problems may be solved through foreman training. Actually, we find that people up toward the top of the organization tend to set the pattern for the relations that develop down the line—and, of course, more by the way they act than by the written policies they promulgate.

We can approach the problem through studying the personalities of the higher executives—an interesting topic but one outside my field of competence. We can also approach the problem through observing that the overall pattern of organization, which these men build up, has most definite effects upon group behavior right down to the worker level in the factory. This suggests that the relationship between organizational structure and group behavior should be given intensive study.

The most significant work along this line has been done by Burleigh

Gardner and David G. Moore (2), James C. Worthy (3), and by F. L. W. Richardson, Jr., and Charles Walker (4).

Their findings all point in the same direction. They contrast long, narrow hierarchies, having many levels of authority, with broad or flat hierarchies, having few levels of authority for large numbers of people.

Organizations differ strikingly in this respect. Take, for example, a certain automotive plant of 12,000 employees which had, several years ago, *ten* positions between workers and operating executive of the plant. (There were several more levels up to the top of the company.) Compare this with Sears, Roebuck and Co. which has only *four* levels of supervision between the President and the 110,000 employees in the retail division.

Our evidence suggests that a manufacturing organization tends to require more levels of authority than a retail organization of the same size, although that would by no means account for the contrast cited above. In any case, we are not here examining the differences between manufacturing and selling. Instead, we are examining the effect of the structure upon the people inside it.

The long, narrow hierarchy seems to grow directly out of men's inability to win the co-operation of other men. The organization gets into difficulties. Top management introduces another link in the chain of command—puts in another man to watch, check, and control. And top management sends in bodies of staff specialists to devise systems of control so that people will be coerced into following procedures dictated from the top. These controls themselves further undermine co-operation and therefore suggest the need for more people to exercise supervision and devise more detailed controls.

It is hardly surprising, then, to find that these top-heavy organizations are relatively low both in economic efficiency and in employee morale. But, before we explore the problem further, let us note the conflict between these findings and the orthodox "principles" of administration. One of these principles is known as the "span of control." This simply points out that the number of men who can be closely supervised by any given individual is strictly limited. Stated in that general way, the principle is simply a truism. But the conclusion drawn from this truism is that the ratio of supervised to supervisor should be kept at a minimum—and this does not logically follow at all.

The conclusion follows only if we assume that men must be *closely* supervised. An alternative approach would be to give each manager so many people to supervise that it is impossible for him to supervise them closely. In that situation, he will have to give them a good deal of freedom to exercise their own initiative, and he will have to learn to trust their judgment. He will expect them to make mistakes but also to learn from those mistakes. He will have to become more interested in developing his people—or in helping them to develop themselves—than he is in trying to get each job done just exactly as he would do it himself.

On the other hand, in a structure so designed that a supervisor has only a small number of people reporting to him, he tends naturally to give them close attention; where else can he give that attention? When subordinates are in doubt, they refer problems to the boss, and he gives them the answer. He prevents them from making mistakes, *but* he also prevents them from discovering what their strengths and weaknesses are. They may get some satisfaction from pleasing the boss, but they don't get the greater satisfactions of feeling that they themselves have really mastered their job. They work in a situation where men's capacities can only be partially developed.

These findings, I feel, are of the utmost importance both for our society and for social research.

If we wish to apply our research so as to strengthen and support the values of democracy, let us not take too narrow a view of that task.

Some social psychologists seem to see in group decision or group participation in decision-making the basic process of democracy. Now, the group-decision experiments seem to be most impressive, and I would not quarrel with anything except the implications that are sometimes drawn from them: that the values of democracy and individual liberty can only be strengthened as group participation increases.

By all means, let us have increased participation of working groups in deciding what they will do, but let us recognize that individual liberty is not to be preserved only through getting into a huddle on all our problems. It can also be preserved through building organizations in which individuals are given the widest possible latitude to make their own decisions.

I am not suggesting that group decision and individual initiative are incompatible. On the contrary, they may fit together very well, and the wise manager will seek to strengthen both. He will explore to discover the situations in which group decision can most effectively be used and those in which he should rely upon giving scope to individual initiative. He will not take a doctrinaire point of view in favor of one or the other.

Without minimizing the importance of group participation, I should like to explore with you the possibilities of supporting individual initiative in our large organizations.

The issue is one of centralization versus decentralization of control of human activity. David E. Lilienthal puts the problem in this way:

> Overcentralized administration is not something simply to be made more palatable, more efficient, and better managed. It is a hazard to democracy. It is a hazard to freedom. Centralization at the national capital or in a business undertaking always glorifies the importance of pieces of paper. This dims the sense of reality. As men and organizations acquire a preoccupation with papers, they become less understanding, less perceptive of the reality of those matters with which they should be dealing: particular human problems, particular human beings, actual things in a real America—highways, wheat, barges, drought, floods, backyards, blast furnaces. The facts with which a highly centralized institution deals tend to be the men and women of that institution itself, and their ideas and ambitions. To maintain perspective and human understanding in the atmosphere of centralization is a task that many able and conscientious people have found well-nigh impossible (5).

Lilienthal's comments, I feel, simply apply some basic principles of social psychology to administration. People naturally tend to respond to the people with whom they are in most frequent interaction and to the symbols to which they are most commonly exposed. Centralized administration builds up a main office of people who come to respond to the symbols of information from the field in terms of human relations within the main office. Thus the controls imposed from the top are necessarily poorly adapted to the field situation.

Such bureaucratic rigidities are customarily associated with large-scale organization, but the two need not necessarily go together. I have mentioned Sears, Roebuck and Co. as an example of a large-scale organization that has escaped the repressive effects of bureaucracy. There are other impressive examples at hand.

Unilever Co. Ltd. is an organization having over 600 factories scattered throughout the world—big business on a colossal scale. Yet during the war, the management of the Toronto plant was able to work out with its local of the International Chemical Workers Union a highly elaborate plan whereby working hours were reduced from 48 to 40, while labor costs to the company and take-home pay to the workers remained the same. This is one of the most impressive examples of union-management co-operation on record. The problem was highly complex. It could only have been worked out by people on the spot, who were free to make their own decisions (6).

Inland Steel Container Co. is a subsidiary of Inland Steel Co., a completely integrated company of some 25,000 employees. I have been studying the Chicago plant of the subsidiary, tracing out a most remarkable transition from conflict to co-operation. There is no simple explanation for the change that took place in this case, but any explanation would point to the importance of local autonomy. The key union and management men concerned with this plant were free, within very broad limits, to make their adjustments to the problems of the plant, as they had personally experienced them. No directives from main office of union or management would have solved these problems.[2]

The examples I have cited so far are in private industry, but I want to make it emphatically clear that this is not simply an issue of government versus private ownership. I could name for you in private industry examples of rigid bureaucracies to match anything we find in government. On the other hand, while many of our governmental organizations fit the bureaucratic stereotype very well, we must also note outstanding exceptions such as the Tennessee Valley Authority.

A basic decision was taken at the very start of T.V.A.: the main offices were located not in Washington but in Knoxville. The executives would be exposed primarily to the Tennessee Valley and its people. Also, from the outset, the builders of T.V.A. administration undertook to decentralize in so far as it was possible. Their viewpoint was that the power of decision should be located with the people who were in close touch with the problems requiring decision. Our research has found in T.V.A. a remarkably high level of morale and of co-operation between union and management, which we attribute in part to this grass-roots approach to problems.[3]

---

[2] A book on this case is now in preparation.
[3] Research conducted by Orvis Collins. Book now in preparation.

This seems to me a problem of the design of organizations. Can we design organizations that will stimulate a high degree of co-operation, that will be flexible in adapting to new situations, that will develop the initiative of participants, and that will provide rich personal satisfactions for their members?

The field is too uncharted to provide us with a blueprint now, but we can at least seek to state the problem in a way that makes fruitful research possible.

First, we must recognize that the over-all structure of the organization has an important impact upon all group activity within it. Second, we note that, while size of organization is important, it is not necessarily the controlling factor. There is a broad range of possibilities within organizations of the same size.

The examples I have given do not, of course, prove anything except that such a range of possibilities exist. We may speak glibly of decentralization of control, but we should recognize that it is a rather vague and general term. Let us define the term by pointing to the sorts of questions we would ask about an organization.

How many levels of authority are there, in relation to the total number of personnel involved? A centralized organization necessarily involves a greater number of levels of authority in order to provide close supervision.

How large are the operating units of the organization? A company with a number of small operating units tends to allow more freedom of action to those units than is found in a company having a fewer number of larger units. Given problems of time and travel, there is more likelihood that the small number of large units will be closely supervised.

We need to examine the frequency of interaction between main-office executive and executive of the operating unit. Are they in frequent contact with each other? Or is the operating executive left alone except for general directives and occasional visits?

How many levels of authority must be involved in a sequence of interaction before a given action is completed? For example, can a problem involving workers be decided by the foreman, or must it be channeled up to the superintendent, manager, and so on up? Here we should observe not only problems confined to one department but also problems that cross departmental lines. In some organizations, we see that such problems are hardly ever resolved until they have been referred up the line to an officer who has authority over both departments. In other organizations, the people immediately involved are able to adjust their differences without carrying the problem on up the line. We have seen enough to be confident that these differences are not due primarily to personality differences; rather we see different personalities adapting themselves to the over-all organizational pattern.

I mention these points simply to suggest that the centralization-decentralization problem can be studied in terms of objective and quantitative data. We still know very little indeed about the conditions that limit or promote the possibility of decentralization of control. We have observed some of the morale benefits of decentralization, but as yet we can only offer the most general advice to the executive who wishes to decentralize. We need to focus research on this problem. As we study cases of successful decentralization, we may learn how it can be done on a more general scale.

Such research would seem to take us into the area of research on principles of administration. Call it poaching if you will, but such an invasion is vitally needed. The alleged principles of administration are a curious mixture of folklore and fact. The one I have cited—the "span of control"—is typical; it is a principle which holds *under certain conditions,* but the conditions are not specified.

CONCLUSION

This paper has taken us far afield, from small group studies to studies of large organizations.

Studies of small groups and of large organizations should necessarily fit together. There is no point to studying the over-all organizational structure unless we can trace out its impact upon particular individuals and groups. *Nor is there any point in studying the small group as if it operated in a vacuum.*

How can we fit the two sorts of studies together? Probably we can expect a given research man to be primarily interested in one type of study or the other: in the small group or in the over-all organizational pattern. That may make for a reasonable division of labor, but the researches must not proceed in hermetically sealed compartments.

The social psychologist interested in small groups must be fully aware of the work going on in the larger structures. Otherwise he will attribute to factors within the group influences that really impinge upon the group from outside. Similarly, the specialist in organizational studies needs to be aware of the dynamics of group behavior in order to bring his research to bear upon the most significant problems.

If research proceeds simultaneously in both areas, we will learn that certain characteristic forms of organizational structure are associated with certain specified types of behavior in small groups within that structure. Then, if we wish to modify behavior within the group, we will recognize that it will sometimes be necessary, in order to effect significant modifications, to make changes in the over-all structure of the organization *first*.

REFERENCES

1. Whyte, William F. "Corner Boys: A Study of Clique Behavior," *American Journal of Sociology,* March, 1941.

2. See their forthcoming second edition (fall, 1950) of Burleigh Gardner's *Human Relations in Industry.* Richard Irwin & Co.

3. Worthy, James C. "Factors Influencing Employee Morale," *Harvard Business Review,* January, 1950, and "Employee Morale and Organizational Structure," *American Sociological Review,* April, 1950.

4. Richardson, F. L. W., Jr., and Walker, Charles. *Human Relations in an Expanding Company,* Labor-Management Center, Yale University, 1948.

5. Lilienthal, David E. *This I Do Believe,* Harper & Brothers, New York, 1949, p. 90.

6. Whyte, William F. "Union-Management Cooperation: A Toronto Case," *Applied Anthropology,* Summer, 1947.

CHAPTER 13

⎍⎍⎍⎍⎍⎍⎍⎍⎍⎍⎍⎍⎍⎍⎍⎍⎍⎍⎍⎍⎍⎍⎍⎍⎍⎍⎍⎍⎍

Work and the Self

EVERETT CHERRINGTON HUGHES
University of Chicago

There are societies in which custom or sanctioned rule determine what work a man of a given status may do. In our society, at least one strong strain of ideology has it that a man may do any work which he is competent to do; or even that he has a right to the schooling and experience necessary to gain competence in any kind of work which he sets as the goal of his ambition. Equality of opportunity is, among us, stated very much in terms of the right to enter upon any occupation whatsoever. Although we do not practice this belief to the full, we are a people who cultivate ambition. A great deal of our ambition takes the form of getting training for kinds of work which carry more prestige than that which our fathers did. Thus a man's work is one of the things by which he is judged, and certainly one of the more significant things by which he judges himself.

Many people in our society work in named occupations. The names are tags, a combination of price tag and calling card. One has only to hear casual conversation to sense how important these tags are. Hear a salesman, who has just been asked what he does, reply, "I am in sales work," or "I am in promotional work," not "I sell skillets." School-teachers sometimes turn schoolteaching into educational work, and the disciplining of youngsters and chaperoning of parties into personnel work. Teaching Sunday School becomes religious education, and the Y.M.C.A. Secretary is "in group work." Social scientists emphasize the science end of their name. These hedging statements in which people pick the most favorable of several possible names for their work imply an audience. And one of the most important things about any man is his audience, or his choice of the several available audiences to which he may address his claims to be someone of worth.

These remarks should be sufficient to call it to your attention that a man's work is one of the more important parts of his social identity, of his self, indeed, of his fate, in the one life he has to live, for there is something almost as irrevocable about choice of occupation as there is about choice of a mate. And since the language about work is so loaded with value and prestige judgments, and with defensive choice of symbols, we should not be astonished that the concepts of social scientists who study work should carry a similar load, for the relation of social-science concepts to popular speech remains close in spite of our efforts to separate them. The difference is that while the value-weighting in popular speech is natural and proper, for concealment and ego-protection are of the essence of social intercourse. But in scientific discourse the value-loaded concept may be a blinder. And part of the problem of method in the study of work behavior is that the people who have the most knowledge about a given occupation (let us say medicine), and from whom therefore the data for analysis must come, are the people in the occupation. They may combine in themselves a very sophisticated manipulative knowledge of the appropriate social relations, with a very strongly motivated suppression, and even repression, of the deeper truths about these relationships, and, in occupations of higher status, with great verbal skill in keeping these relationships from coming up for thought and discussion by other people. This is done in part by the use of and insistence upon loaded value words where their work is discussed.

May I, to illustrate the point that concepts may be blinders, tell you briefly of my own experience in the study of occupations. Maybe one reason we social scientists fall into their trap so easily is that many such occupations have higher status than our own.

My first assay into the field was a study of the real-estate agents in Chicago. These highly competitive men were just at that point in their journey toward respectability at which they wished to emphasize their conversion from business-minded suspicion of one another to the professional attitude, with confidence in each other and with a demand for confidence from the public. I started the study with the idea of finding out an answer to this familiar question, "Are these men professionals?" It was a false question, for the concept "profession" in our society is not so much a descriptive term as one of value and prestige. It happens over and over that the people who practice an occupation attempt to revise the conceptions which their various publics have of the occupation and of the people in it. In so doing, they also attempt to revise their own conception of themselves and of their work. The model which these occupations set before themselves is that of the "profession"; thus the term profession is a symbol for a desired conception of one's work and, hence, of one's self. The movement to "professionalize" an occupation is thus collective mobility of some among the people in an occupation. One aim of the movement is to rid the occupation of people who are not mobile enough to go along with the changes. There are two possible kinds of occupational mobility. One is individual. The individual makes the several choices, and achieves the skills which allow him to move to a certain position in the occupational, and thus—he hopes—in the social and economic hierarchy. His choice is limited by several conditions, among which is the social knowledge available to him at the time of crucial decision, a time which varies for the several kinds of work.

The other kind of occupational mobility is that of a group of people in an occupation, i.e., of the occupation itself. This has been important in our society with its great changes of technology, with its attendant proliferation of new occupations and of change in technique and social relation of old ones. Now it sometimes happens that by the time a person has the full social knowledge necessary to the smartest possible choice of occupations, he is already stuck with one and in one. How strongly this may affect the drive for professionalization of occupations, I don't know. I suspect that it is a motive. At any rate, it is common in our society for occupational groups to step their occupation up in the hierarchy by turning it into a profession. I will not here describe this process. Let me only indicate that in my own studies I passed from the false question "Is this occupation a profession?" to the more fundamental one, "What are the circumstances in which the people in an occupation attempt to turn it into a profession, and themselves into professional people?" and "What are the steps by which they attempt to bring about identification with their valued model?"

Even with this new orientation the term profession acted as a blinder. For as I began to give courses and seminars on occupations, I used a whole set of concepts and headings which were prejudicial to full understanding of what work behavior and relations are. One of them was that of the "code of ethics," which still tended to sort people into the good and the bad. It was not until I had occasion to undertake study of race relations in industry that I finally, I trust, got rid of this bias in the concepts which I used. Negro industrial workers, the chief objects of our study, performed the kinds of work which have least prestige and which make least pretension; yet, it turned out that even in the lowest occupations people do develop collective pretensions to give their work, and consequently themselves, value in the eyes of each other and of outsiders.

It was from these people that we learned that the common dignifying rationalization of people in all positions of a work hierarchy except the very top one is, "We in this position save the people in the next higher position above from their own mistakes." The notion that one saves a person of more acknowledged skill, and certainly of more acknowledged prestige and power, than one's self from his mistakes appears to be peculiarly satisfying. Now there grow up in work organizations rules of mutual protection among the persons in a given category and rank, and across ranks and categories. If one uses the term "code of ethics" he is likely not to see the true nature of these rules. These rules have of necessity to do with mistakes, for it is in the nature of work that people make mistakes. The question of how mistakes are handled is a much more penetrating one than any question which contains the concept "professional ethics" as ordinarily conceived. For in finding out how mistakes are handled, one must get at the fundamental psychological and social devices by which people are able to carry on through time, to live with others and with themselves, knowing that what is daily routine for them in their occupational roles may be fateful for others, knowing that one's routine mistakes, even the mistakes by which one learns better, may touch other lives at crucial points. It is in part the problem of dealing routinely with what are the crises of others. The people in lower ranks are thus using a powerful psychological weapon when they rationalize their worth and indispensability as lying in their protection of people in higher ranks from their mistakes. I suppose it is almost a truism that the people who take the larger responsibilities must be people who can face making mistakes, while punctiliousness must remain in second place. But this is a matter which has not been very seriously taken into account, as far as I know, in studies of the social drama of work.

Of course, the rules which people make to govern their behavior at work cover other problems than that of mistakes. Essentially the rules classify people, for to define situations and the proper behavior in situations one has to assign roles to the people involved. Thus among the most important subject matter of rules is setting up of criteria for recognizing a true fellow-worker, for determining who it is safe and may be even necessary to initiate into the in-group of close equals, and who must be kept at some distance. This problem is apt to be obscured by the term "colleague-ship," which, although its etymology is perfect for the matter in hand, carries a certain notion of higher status, of respectability. (In pre-Hitler Germany the Social-Democratic workers called one another "Comrade." The Christian trade-unions insisted on the term "Colleague.")

Allow me to mention one other value-laden term which may act as a blinder in study of the social psychology of work, to wit, "restriction of production." This term contains a value assumption of another kind—namely, that there is someone who knows and has a right to determine the right amount of work for other people to do. If one does less, he is restricting production. Mayo and others have done a good deal to analyze the phenomenon in question, but it was Max Weber who—forty years ago—pointed to "putting on the brakes," as an inevitable result of the wrestling match between a man and his employer over the price he must pay with his body for his wage. In short, he suggested that no man easily yields to another full control over the effort, and especially over the amount of physical effort he must daily exert. On the other hand, there is no more characteristically human phenomenon than determined and even heroic effort to do a task which one has somehow taken as his own. I do not mean to make the absurd implication that there could be a situation in which every man would be his own and only taskmaster. But I think we might understand the social interaction which determines the measure of effort if we are to keep ourselves free of terms which suggest that it is abnormal to do less than one is asked by some reasonable authority.

You will have doubtless got the impression that I am making the usual plea for a value-free science, that is, for neutrality. Such is not my intention. Our aim is to *penetrate more deeply* into the personal and social drama of work, to understand the social and social-psychological arrangements and devices by which men make their work tolerable, or even make it glorious to themselves and others. I believe that much of our terminology and hence, of our problem setting, has limited our field of perception by a certain pretentiousness and a certain value-loading. Specifically we need to rid ourselves of any concepts which keep us from seeing that the essential problems of men at work are the same whether they do their work in the laboratories of some famous institutions or in the messiest vat room of a pickle factory. Until we can find a point of view and concepts which will enable us to make comparisons between the junk peddler and the professor without intent to debunk the one and patronize the other, we cannot do our best work in this field.

Perhaps there is as much to be learned about the high-prestige occupations by applying to them the concepts which naturally come to mind for study of people in the most lowly kinds of work as there is to be learned by applying to other occupations the conceptions developed in connection with the highly valued professions. Furthermore, I have come to the conclusion that it is a fruitful thing to start study of any social phenomenon at the point of least prestige. For, since prestige is so much a matter of symbols, and even of pretensions—however well merited—there goes with prestige a tendency to preserve a front which hides the inside of things; a front of names, of indirection, of secrecy (much of it necessary secrecy). On the other hand, in things of less prestige, the core may be more easy of access.

In recent years a number of my students have studied some more or less lowly occupations: apartment-house janitors, junk men, boxers, jazz musicians, osteopaths, pharmacists, etc. They have done so mainly because of their own connections with the occupations in question, and perhaps because of some problem of their own. At first, I thought of these studies as merely interesting and informative for what they would tell about people who do these humbler jobs, i.e., as American ethnology. I have now come to the belief that although the problems of people in these lines of work are as interesting and important as any other, their deeper value lies in the insights they yield about work behavior in any and all occupations. It is not that it puts one into the position to debunk the others, but simply that processes which are hid-

den in other occupations come more readily to view in these lowly
ones. We may be here dealing with a fundamental matter of method
in social science, the matter of finding the best possible laboratory animal for study of a given series of mechanisms.

Let me illustrate. The apartment-house janitor is a fellow who, in
making his living, has to do a lot of other people's dirty work. This is
patent. He could not hide it if he would. Now every occupation is not
one but several activities; some of them are the "dirty work" of that
trade. It may be dirty in one of several ways. It may be simply physically disgusting. It may be a symbol of degradation, something that
wounds one's dignity.

Finally, it may be dirty work in that it in some way goes counter to
the more heroic of our moral conceptions. Dirty work of some kind is
found in all occupations. It is hard to imagine an occupation in which
one does not appear, in certain repeated contingencies, to be practically compelled to play a role of which he thinks he ought to be a little
ashamed morally. Insofar as an occupation carries with it a self-con-
ception, a notion of personal dignity, it is likely that at some point one
will feel that he is having to do something that is *infra dignitate*. Janitors turned out to be bitterly frank about their physically dirty work.
When asked, "What is the toughest part of your job," they answered
almost to a man in the spirit of this quotation: "Garbage. Often the
stuff is sloppy and smelly. You know some fellows can't look at garbage if it's sloppy. I'm getting used to it now, but it almost killed me
when I started." Or as another put it, "The toughest part? It's the
messing up in front of the garbage incinerator. That's the most miser-
able thing there is on this job. The tenants don't co-operate—them
bastards. You tell them today, and tomorrow there is the same mess
over again by the incinerator."

In the second quotation it becomes evident that the physical disgust
of the janitor is not merely a thing between him and the garbage, but
involves also the tenant. Now the tenant is the person who impinges
most on the daily work activity of the janitor. It is the tenant who interferes most with his own dignified ordering of his life and work. If it
were not for a tenant who had broken a window, he could have got his
regular Saturday cleaning done on time; if it were not for a tenant
who had clogged a trap, he would not have been ignominiously called
away from the head of his family table just when he was expansively

offering his wife's critical relatives a second helping of porkchops, talking the while about the importance of his job. It is the tenant who causes the janitor's status pain. The physically disgusting part of the janitor's work is directly involved in his relations with other actors in his work drama.

By a *contre coup,* it is by the garbage that the janitor judges, and, as it were, gets power over the tenants who high-hat him. Janitors know about hidden love-affairs by bits of torn-up letter paper; of impending financial disaster or of financial four-flushing by the presence of many unopened letters in the waste. Or they may stall off demands for immediate service by an unreasonable woman of whom they know from the garbage that she, as the janitors put it, "has the rag on." The garbage gives the janitor the makings of a kind of magical power over that pretentious villain, the tenant. I say a kind of magical power, for there appears to be no thought of betraying any individual and thus turning this knowledge into overt power. He protects the tenant, but, at least among Chicago janitors, it is certainly not a loving protection.

Let your mind dwell on what one might hear from people in certain other occupations if they were to answer as frankly and bitterly as did the janitors. I do not say nor do I think that it would be a good thing for persons in all occupations to speak so freely on physical disgust as did these men. To do so, except in the most tightly closed circles, would create impossible situations. But we are likely to overlook the matter altogether in studying occupations where concealment is practiced, and this gives a quite false notion of the problems which have to be faced in such occupations, and of the possible psychological and social by-products of the solutions which are developed for the problem of disgust.

Now the delegation of dirty work to someone else is common among humans. Many cleanliness taboos, and perhaps even many moral scruples, depend for their practice upon success in delegating the tabooed activity to someone else. Delegation of dirty work is also a part of the process of occupational mobility. Yet there are kinds of work, some of them of very high prestige, in which such delegation is possible only to a limited extent. The dirty work may be an intimate part of the very activity which gives the occupation its charisma, as is the case with the handling of the human body by the physician. In this case, I suppose the dirty work is somehow integrated into the whole, and into the prestiginous role of the person who does the work. What role it plays in the drama of work relations in such a case is something to find out. The janitor, however, does not integrate his dirty work into any deeply satisfying definition of his role that might liquidate his antagonism to the people whose dirt he handles. Incidentally, we have found reason to believe that one of the deeper sources of antagonisms in hospitals arises from the belief of the people in the humblest jobs that the physicians in charge call upon them to do their dirty work in the name of the role of "healing the sick," although none of the prestige and little of the money reward of that role reaches the people at the bottom. Thus we might conceive of a classification of occupations involving dirty work into those in which it is knit into some satisfying and prestige-giving definition of role and those in which it is not. I suppose we might think of another classification into those in which the dirty work seems somehow wilfully put upon one and those in which it is quite unconnected with any person involved in the work drama.

There is a feeling among prison guards and mental-hospital attendants that society at large and their superiors hypocritically put upon them dirty work which they, society, and the superiors in prison and hospital know is necessary but which they pretend is not necessary. Here it takes the form, in the minds of people in these two lowly occupations, of leaving them to cope for twenty hours, day in and day out, with inmates whom the public never has to see and whom the people at the head of the organization see only episodically. There is a whole series of problems here which cannot be solved by some miracle of changing the social selection of those who enter the job (which is the usual unrealistic solution for such cases).

And this brings us to the brief consideration of what one may call the social drama of work. Most kinds of work bring people together in definable roles; thus the janitor and the tenant, the doctor and the patient, the teacher and the pupil, the worker and his foreman, the prison guard and the prison, the musician and his listener. In many occupations there is some category of persons with whom the people at work regularly come into crucial contact. In some occupations the most crucial relations are those with one's fellow-workers. It is they who can do most to make life sweet or sour. Often, however, it is the people in some other position. And in many there is a category of persons who are, so to speak, the consumers of one's work or services. It is probable that the people in the occupation will have their chronic fight for status, for personal dignity with this group of consumers of their services. Part of the social psychological problem of the occupation is the maintenance of a certain freedom and social distance from these people most crucially and intimately concerned with one's work.

In a good deal of our talk about occupations we imply that the tension between the producer and consumer of services is somehow a matter of ill-will or misunderstandings which easily might be removed. It may be that it lies a good deal deeper than that. Often there is a certain ambivalence on the side of the producer, which may be illustrated by the case of the professional jazz-musicians. The musician wants jobs and an income. He also wants his music to be appreciated, but to have his living depend upon the appreciation does not entirely please him. For he likes to think himself and other musicians the best judges of his playing. To play what pleases the audience—the paying customers, who are not, in his opinion, good judges—is a source of annoyance. It is not merely that the listeners, having poor taste, demand that he play music which he does not think is the best he can do; even when they admire him for playing in his own sweet way, he doesn't like it, for then they are getting too close—they are impinging on his private world too much. The musicians accordingly use all sorts of little devices to keep a line drawn between themselves and the audience; such as turning the musicians' chairs, in a dance hall without platform, in such a way as to make something of a barrier. It is characteristic of many occupations that the people in them, although convinced that they themselves are the best judges, not merely of their own competence but also of what is best for the people for whom they perform services, are required in some measures to yield judgment of what is wanted to these amateurs who receive the services. This is a problem not only among musicians, but in teaching, medicine, dentistry, the arts, and many other fields. It is a chronic source of ego-wound and possibly of antagonism.

Related to this is the problem of routine and emergency. In many occupations, the workers or practitioners (to use both a lower and a higher status term) deal routinely with what are emergencies to the people who receive the services. This is a source of chronic tension between the two. For the person with the crisis feels that the other is trying to belittle his trouble; he does not take it seriously enough. His very competence comes from having dealt with a thousand cases of what I like to consider my unique trouble. The worker thinks he knows from long experience that people exaggerate their troubles. He therefore builds up devices to protect himself to stall people off. This is the function of the janitor's wife when a tenant phones an appeal or a demand for immediate attention to a leaky tap; it is also the function of the doctor's wife and even sometimes of the professor's wife. The physician plays one emergency off against the other; the reason he can't run right up to see Johnny who may have the measles is that he is, unfortunately, right at that moment treating a case of the black plague. Involved in this is something of the struggle mentioned above in various connections, the struggle to maintain some control over one's decisions of what work to do, and over the disposition of one's time and of one's routine of life. It would be interesting to know what the parish priest thinks to himself when he is called for the tenth time to give extreme unction to the sainted Mrs. O'Flaherty who hasn't committed a sin in years except that of, in her anxiety over dying in a state of sin, being a nuisance to the priest. On Mrs. O'Flaherty's side there is the danger that she might die unshriven, and she has some occasion to fear that the people who shrive may not take her physical danger seriously and hence may not come quickly enough when at last her hour has come. There may indeed be in the minds of the receivers of emergency services a resentment that something so crucial to them can be a matter for a cooler and more objective attitude, even though they know perfectly well that such an attitude is necessary to competence, and though they could not stand it if the expert to whom they take their troubles were to show any signs of excitement. I have not worked out in any full or systematic way all of the problems of this routine vs. emergency drama. Nor, for that matter, have I worked out systematically any of the problems mentioned in this discussion. My aim has been to call attention to certain problems which lie, it seems to me, on the margin between sociology and psychology, problems on which people of these two disciplines should be working jointly.

ЛЛЛЛЛЛЛЛЛЛЛЛЛЛЛЛЛЛЛЛЛЛЛЛЛЛЛЛЛЛЛЛЛЛ

Behavior and Organization:
Industrial Studies

CONRAD M. ARENSBERG
Barnard College, Columbia University

One of the central problems of social psychology—as of the other social and psychological sciences—has been the understanding of group behavior and the determination of individual behavior in group situations. Much work has been devoted to the discovery of the properties of the social group, usually defined for experimental control as the small group. The evidence from the study of industrial behavior and industrial relations seems to indicate that building theory upon research concentration on the small group may be mistaken, however experimentally justifiable as an object of research the small group may be. The individual behavior that psychology seeks to explain seems to be less a property of groups or the group in particular than one of processes of social interaction in general, inclusive of both large and small groups.

The mounting evidence from studies of industrial behavior is to be understood, in large part, not so much then as a set of properties of groups in any system of small-group dynamics *per se,* but rather as a class of social by-products, resultant from changes within the mutually dependent basic interpersonal relationships making up organization.

The evidence is so far empirical, but the conclusion lends itself to further experimental check. Much of the individual behavior social psychology seeks to explain is a by-product of changes within the larger organizations—themselves networks of interpersonal role adaptation—of which the small groups so far studied are but minute parts. Small-group dynamics is a dependent, not an independent variable.

Over the past twenty years or more there has been a great deal of study of industrial behavior. A great deal of it has been intentionally focused upon small groups—workrooms, departments, single companies, and their local unions. The study of such small groups in their real-life daily activity has meant a new realism, objectivity, and fidelity to fact in the social and psychological sciences.

Most of these studies have sought to explain particular "problem" behaviors. Some of these have been: changes in output (productivity), complaints against working conditions, against fatigue and monotony, grievances in general, labor turnover, absenteeism, losses or gains in "morale," restriction of output, evasion of industrial disciplines, walk-outs, "wild-cats" and strikes. These are manifestations of human behavior under real workshop conditions of modern industry or business. There have also been studies, though fewer, of unions, too, paralleling these.

There have been many particular discoveries within this body of field study, but more noteworthy, I think, is the general conclusion to which they all seem to lead. Most of these *explicanda* have turned out to be in one way or the other emergent products of shifts in organization, acknowledged or unacknowledged. These shifts have been, most often, quantitative changes in the classes of interpersonal interaction (social activity) constituting the basic relationships of the industrial institution of our age. The *explicanda* are thus clearly enough by-products of change in the "total situation" in which the daily life and work of in-plant or other small-scale work groups is passed. But the evidence from industrial studies also points out how such "total situations" are definable as parts of organization in mutual independence and opens up for us the possibility of following the dynamics of large-scale human organization. The evidence leads not to a small-group dynamics, but rather to an ever more rigorous and inclusive "institutional analysis" (or "organizational dynamics," if one prefers).

The study of small-scale work-groups has undoubtedly yielded fruitful particular results for social and psychological theory as well as information of practical use in management and industrial relations. But it seems more important, in the present article, to deal with what it has shown us about the general process by which social by-products, in the shape of the "problem" behaviors to be explained, occurs.

To restate the matter at the risk of repetition, it is pretty clear, empirically, what the process is. It is a series or sequence of shifts within the adaptations of one another of the people united to one another within the structure of a single institution, "the factory system," or "mass production," or "business organization." The institution is itself a cultural and social system, a system of status and roles of reciprocal force, of differentially shared social norms, converging or overlapping, though certainly not "common" goals, and derived personal motives of compelling and coercive force. Shifts within the interaction of these roles and their differential evocation of these norms are the dynamic element of the whole complex, and we shall try to follow them in detail.

Why shifts of social interaction within the institution have their effects upon individuals, bringing about the changes in attitude and forcing the evolution of the derived motives which lead to the emergence of the new by-products of individual and collective behavior so carefully charted in this field, is a psychological question. Investigators are going to have to appeal to psychologists and clinicians for an answer. Nevertheless, even without an answer, sociologists can continue to use the field of industrial behavior to explore the regularities of correlation between variables of the environmental field of the individual worker and the variables of group attitude and group-member performance. How these regularities are mediated in individual psychological and physiological processes within each person is a matter outside their competence.

Jurisdiction apart, however, the observed regularities raise many suggestive problems of social-psychological kind. What tensions do these shifts in interaction within institutional relationships create? What are the thresholds over which the tension will spill into the observed new activity? What are the mechanisms of discharge and displacement of such tensions, the directions of discharge, the choice of targets, the cumulations of feeling, the individual differences of reactivity, etc.?

To claim as an empirical discovery the existence of a general process of the production of group behavioral by-products within organization, from the evidence of industrial studies of the "human factor," is perhaps rash, but it is by no means premature. The body of observational data on industrial groups is by now quite large. It comes from observers of many different schools, working with many different conceptual schemes and canons of description. The diversity itself lends weight to an assertion that the generalization of a common process from the studies reflects a regularity of the facts rather than a common bias among the observers.

Perhaps the chief objection that will be raised to the generalization of a common process from the diverse studies' facts will be disbelief in the order of determination among the variables it specifies. In social psychology, and in the other social sciences, it is often insisted today that attitudes, norms, and sentiments determine behavior, in that order of causal determination, or else, failing such bold statements, behavior is the product of a "total situation," is of multifactorial origin. And so it often is. But here it is claimed that the attitudinal concomitants of behavior in small-scale situations in industry, within the limits of real events, show us quite another order of dependency. The attitudes which lead to the behavior-to-be-explained are dependent variables. They are responsive to changes in interactive adjustment within the basic relationships of organization. To say it differently, the empirical generalization to be drawn from studies of industrial work is that individual behavior changes in kind and degree *after* individual and collective attitudes undergo change, and that these in turn change *after* prior shifts in basic social relationships.

It might indeed be said in many other ways; the field is an arena for many contending vocabularies. Put most colloquially and narrowly, the generalization holds that people work well or ill according to the "nature" of the "human relations" in which they pass their working time. These human relations are nothing mysterious. They are in fact the particular, going patterns of interpersonal interaction uniting people at work to their fellows of each role, rank, duty, office, and kind, with whom they are in enduring contact. As such, therefore, these "human relations" can be classified, compared, assessed for their internal connections among their classes, counted present or absent in whatever degree in each situation, and their "nature," better: their "force," made clear for any time, place, and human group.

To summarize the work of the last twenty years upon small-group behavior in industry takes us through the recorded observational data to be found in the first-hand reports of all the various schools of industrial sociology and social psychology. It is not enough to use their authors' conclusions. Apart from findings claimed by the authors, apart again from differences in conceptual bias and vocabulary of description, we can compare the reports (and sometimes the field notes behind them) to ask for each case exactly what happened in the course of observation and experiment. We can reascertain just what the authors saw and did, and just how and when each of the human subjects spoke and acted, and just what events took place in each case in exactly what order of occurrence.

Granted that temporal sequence is not causality, certainly ordering the data of observation in the real order of their occurrence is the first step in searching causality out. And comparing data for common orders of occurrence is the first operation of scientific discovery of regularity of relationship among them. In all these first-hand reports the important question becomes: did similar events involving similar activity of similar people happen with similar results in similar sequence in similar periods of time?

It is the contention of this paper that the various studies of industrial small-group behavior whose first-hand data have been reported over the last twenty years or more do so agree. Despite differences in era, in place, in personnel, in kind of work performed, in authors' concepts and observers' biases, in formality or informality of organization, etc., etc., the descriptions do agree in showing such similarities. The groups observed by the Mayo school, by the Bakke group and others such as Charles Walker at Yale, by the workers in group dynamics descended from Kurt Lewin, by the followers of Lloyd Warner and the Chicago Committee on Human Relations, by sociometrists of the Moreno school, by persons such as Whyte, Richardson, Chapple, and myself associated in the Society for Applied Anthropology, by the occupational sociologists, by labor economists and business scholars outside sociology and social psychology together, show common features.

For the persons in and out of social and psychological science who have not specialized in industrial behavior, the fact that so many different schools of inquiry already exist in an area that used to be divided simply enough between industrial psychology and labor economics will be unexpected and confusing. The fact is that there has been a general movement of the social sciences into this once little-cultivated area, formerly given over mostly to psychological testing, to application of theories of motivation to the design of industrial incentives, or in economics to the testing of wage theory against the realities of the labor market and employment contract bargains. Social psychologists have become familiar with the work of Mayo, of Roethlisberger and Dixon in *Management and the Worker;* they know something of the group dynamics and survey approaches to labor and industrial relations, especially since the participation by Michigan social psychologists in the 1949 conference at Denver of the newly formed national Industrial Relations Research Association; they may know something of the "theory of adaptive human behavior" used in industrial research by E. Wight Bakke at Yale, founded as it is upon the Dollard-Miller theories of learning. They are less likely to be well-informed, I believe, about the other efforts at describing group behavior in industrial situations.

Before embarking, then, upon the voyage of discovery leading to the generalization of a common process among the first-hand reports of the many schools, it may be well to say something about the present state of the field. There seems to be the greatest misapprehension about it upon the outside. The field, indeed, has as yet no agreed-upon common name.

Economists, business theorists, and engineers, for example, all of whom deal traditionally with organization and with human behavior in it, speak of a generic "human relations approach." They lump all the workers in the field into a single school of human relations research. For reasons of their own, they mistake "human relations"—as they name the study of groups and organizations as systems of social (interactive, interpersonal) relationships—for "communications." They think of the field as the study of the internal communications of business companies, factories, and other hierarchic institutions. As an experimental simplification of the problem the confusion has some justification. There exists already a good deal of theory in engineering yielding models for the design and manipulation of communications networks. Much of this is a fruitful source of analogy for the study of social systems, but the fact remains that the field is not a study of communications, unless the word is stretched to cover every kind of interpersonal stimulation, as is sometimes done in zoology.

It is equally inadequate to think of the field as a further evolution of industrial psychology. Morris S. Viteles has done so recently, if perhaps only by implication, when he said: "It is commonly recognized that the most significant development in industrial psychology during the past ten or fifteen years is the growing concern with the feelings and attitudes of workers, supervisors, and managers, and with the interplay of people in the social organization of an industrial enterprise." The statement is accurate enough. But it neglects to specify that this enrichment of industrial psychology has come from outside, and, in fact, precisely from this very field of social-science convergence we find so hard to name. It came out of the social sciences, sociology and anthropology, and out of institutional economics, and the concern with attitudes and the interplay of persons Viteles mentions was no contribution of psychologists.

But it would be unfair to call the field, as many universities now do, simply "the sociology of industry." In addition to the new concerns above and beyond problems of individual work motivation, the new activities in the workplaces of business which the field seeks to explain, e.g., fluctuations of productivity, restrictions of output, complaints against machine installations, protests against discipline, collective bargaining, grievance procedure, walk-outs, local strikes, etc., are all of them of natural interest to the psychologist, as individuals display the activity involved. They are of equal interest to the labor economists who must understand the behavior of labor just as much as that of capital or the market. The fact that such activities are shared activities, products of group life, does not give the sociologist exclusive jurisdiction. The field is multidisciplinary. It is in reality one chief proving ground for social science.

The best common description of the field, then, is the historical one: scientific study of the sources of unrest in labor and management relations, that is, the study of the problems of industrial relations. All the schools we shall name are alike in that they have brought concepts, derived from whatever source, to bear upon the study of working groups in modern industry in order to discover something significant about the old "sources" or "causes" of labor "unrest." They have all wanted to learn something practical about the conflicts, the troubles, the pains, the protests of persons manning the factory system. In this they are direct descendants, either philosophically or pragmatically, of the early humanist and artistic protesters against "the machine." Most of them today have come to accept the factory and the machine and want to advise its masters how better or more humanely to run it. Many of them have thus opened themselves to the charge that they are "managerial sociologists," acquiescing in the manipulation of men by the powers which control the factory system. The charge need not delay us; science does not make the world and it can be used for any purpose by any power. Ethical choice is still free in the western world; one is free to elect to make a present "system" "better." It is more useful to remember that the many schools are alike in their going to the realities of present western-capitalist, technically planned industrial production or distribution for their setting in which to ask questions, make observations, and think about cause and effect in human behavior.

What unites the schools, then, is their interest in a set of *explicanda*. Even when, as lately, they study the "causes of industrial peace" or the attainment of "constructive and co-operative industrial relations," it is because these things are the antithesis of the "industrial unrest" with which they began.

Another trait which unites the schools is that they all, with or without announcement, want to "look at the situation whole." They agree that the *explicanda* are to be understood against the "whole situation," the full complexity of the real conditions of group life in real workrooms in real plants. It makes no difference whether they conceive the whole as a Gestalt, a total situation, a social setting, a cultural milieu, a universe of persons and attitudes; they all must abstract data relevant to an explanation and justify the abstraction.

It will be useful here, if certainly grossly unfair, to characterize the various schools and the various ways they have of looking at the "whole situations" in which real persons do real work in real business.

One can distinguish first a school of psychologistic studies. They are alike in that in them the attack on the problems of unrest and dissatisfaction in industry is conceived as a search for "human relations" capable of providing fuller satisfaction of human wants. "Good human relations" provide such satisfaction; bad ones deny it, unrest being the sign of such denial.

The nature of the wants better to be satisfied depends upon the psychology one subscribes to. In the managerially sponsored studies of human relations and in the many current non-academic pleas for "better" human relations, emphasis is usually placed on better manners, better treatment of employees, fuller courtesy, recognition of personal dignity, more warmth, etc., in personal contacts. The concealed theory seems to be that industrial unrest comes from denial of basic needs of the human "ego," i.e., from industry's too great impersonality.

The more academic studies coming from psychology are by no means so simplicistic. Thus the school of E. Wight Bakke at Yale seems to conceive the problem of industrial unrest to be one of seeking out all or any as-yet-unidentified basic needs, wants, or wishes of human beings presumably now being denied. They think of good or bad human relations as denial or satisfaction of such basic wants. If one can find, they reason, the worker's real wants, and then better satisfy these, one will have cleared up the sources of unrest. They define their task, therefore, as one of probing the worker for his real wishes, by interview, uncovering in his actual experience the real sources of his satisfaction and dissatisfaction. The definition is one they share with the followers of the "survey approach" and the sociologists of social-psychological orientation who study "levels of aspiration."

The Bakke school, at least, is carried into the study of small groups by the force of its own discoveries. They find, to summarize a long course of attitude study, that the sources of expressed satisfaction and dissatisfaction lie very close to home, oftenest in the workplace itself. Somewhat to the surprise of businessmen, the worker today in America seems more concerned with security and recognition in his particular present job and company, with freedom from tyrannical supervision and with rewarding personal relationships with his fellow workers and supervisors than he is with other, larger, out-of-plant, off-the-job issues, including the size of his pay check.

These schools out of psychology—alike in their devotion to attitude study and interviewing schedules—are useful to us here in that they give us our first step toward our generalization. They show us we must look to the small groups of the workplace for the source of attitudes lying behind the problems of industrial unrest. They remind us that the small groups of the workplace include, not only fellow workers, but supervisors and other superiors as well.

Three other schools, or bodies of students of the field, combine psychologistic concepts with a ready-made choice of the basic human want they feel is most denied. One has theoretical inspiration; two of them have pragmatic origins. The basic human want they think of first importance is the desire for participation.

In this, they echo a nearly century-and-a-half-old accusation, common alike to humanists, artists, democrats, socialists, and communists, and agreed upon by impartial observers whatever their political complexion: "The Machine" has most drastically deprived the individual worker, be he assembly-line interchangeable "hand," lower supervisor, or engineer, of any individual part or weight in the decisions setting up the hourly, daily, long-term conditions and controls of his working life. If for "The Machine" (or any other symbolization of the modern productive system) we substitute the disciplines attendant upon an ever more minute and technical division of labor temporally co-ordinated for simultaneous manufacture of interchangeable parts destined for a planned final assembly of finished products—the essence of machine technology—we can see the justice of the accusation, and we can move on to the problem of taming the new reality for Man.

The theory that good and bad human relations are developed or denied participation has a long history. The theory, holding that one chief source of the unrest of labor lies in the frustration of the desire to take part in the making of the decision ruling one's life, rests upon many philosophic bases in the democratic, republican, populist, and socialist traditions. It gets support today in newer physiological and psychological doctrines putting a high adaptive, even a survival, value, upon spontaneity, autonomy, and free activity. Its chief documentation, however, is to be found in the very few small-group studies made in recent years in which participation has been systematically correlated with differences in attitude, organization, and new behavioral product.

Working on the model of the original Lewin child-study experiments, and with "topological" concepts, Alfred Marrow and others have attempted to follow in a few industrial plants the consequences of varying the amount of participation workers are permitted in decision-making. The latest effort is "a practical effort in a garment factory of how best to introduce technological changes in job methods to avoid the usual strain between management and workers and the accompanying drop in efficiency [productivity]." Three matched groups of employees were introduced to similar changes in job methods in three different ways. The first, called "non-participating," were merely ordered to make the change; the second "participated" through representatives with whom they elected to meet, discuss, and plan the changes with management; the third group were given "total participation" in that they all personally acted directly as the representatives had done. We are told of the findings as follows: "The degree of morale . . . [presumably, satisfaction] was proportional to the degree of participation. . . . Aggressive criticism . . . against management was highest in the non-participant group . . . low in the . . . representative . . . no(ne) under total participation. . . . Turnover and absenteeism highest in the non-participation . . . lowest in the total participation. . . . In terms of production . . . the non-participants never did recover . . . their previous production . . . the representative group recovered . . . (theirs) in two weeks . . . the (total-participators) recovered in a (mere) several days and went on improving."

Here is the outline of the generalization with which we wish to work. It was of course foreshadowed in the original experiments of Kurt Lewin. Change some basic condition of group organization, in Lewin's experiment "leadership," here the form of supervision and decision making, and you change situational products; you change attitudes, as here hostility to management, and you elicit new behaviors, here the rise in output, or lesser absenteeism, in Lewin's cases, e.g. scapegoating. The order among the changes is clear. The question remains: what are the basic, independent conditions of group organization which thus change first? Leadership, supervision, participation in the process of making decisions are alike in that they are classes of events of interpersonal, interactive, social relationship basic to the factory system and common to group life, small groups included. What have they in common, how do they vary in these changes, how can we connect them and their variations in detail, faithful to the observed real-life conditions of group behavior and factory work, with the observed shifts in attitude and the observed emergences of new behavior? It is not enough to label these connections shifts in a topological field-of-forces; what forces existed before Lewin experimented? What change in the value of the forces did their experimenting bring?

Other small-group studies of psychologistic bent but of more pragmatic inspiration come from both labor and management scholarship. Ruttenberg and Golden reported from the Steelworkers' Union similar changes in morale and performance, with similar new emergences of new behavior, in a union-sponsored plan of management-encouraged consultation and experimentation over details of workers' individual machines, job-operations, and conditions of work, bringing "participation" to the individual worker at the level of decisions about his own job, a realm usually reserved for engineers and foremen. Here the new emergent behavior was an unexpectedly rich and lively inventiveness and ingenuity on the part of supposedly "dumb" or "uninterested" workers.

On the management side, there is still in existence the unsurpassed study of Eliot Dunlap Smith of technological change in the textile industries during the 'twenties and 'thirties. It was a piece of systematic, comparative analysis of real events, a good piece of social psychology, though nearly devoid of any but the most popular then-current psychological notions. There Smith shows us that those managements that made the new loom installation of the "stretch-out" in such a way as to allow participation to develop *during* and especially *after* an installation, both in planning and executing and in working out readjustment and redress afterwards, won the "confidence" of their workers. They got through the change to acceptance of the new methods and machines, suffered no work stoppage and strike. Those others that did not do so got instead resentment and resistance, stoppage and strike. Smith needed no elaborate topology for this demonstration of the interdependence of variations in basic relationships, attitudes, and performances. It is perhaps unfair to call the work psychologistic at all; I do so only because Smith stressed so heavily the psychological variables "understanding" and "confidence" so dear to businessmen. He saw these as causes of acceptance or non-acceptance of management's technological innovations. But his evidence showed these attitudes to be dependent upon variations in management procedure; they had to be "won."

The emergence of "industrial sociology" narrowly defined seems to have taken place quite independently, with little reference to these psychologistic studies of small-group behavior in or out of industry. It represented the invasion by social anthropology, sociometry, and sociology, of the study of industrial behavior; where psychology had a part, it was a psychology of the "clinical" variety.

Three main currents of theory have been in competition here. One of them comes from occupational sociology, largely on inspiration from Max Weber and his doctrine of types. It has not till lately concerned itself with the study of (localized) groups. It has sought instead to describe whole professions. But it has been important in stressing that the social norms of persons filling various offices in the workplace are shared beyond the workplace "horizontally" among the members of an occupation; the cultural, social, or economic definition of occupation being one limit of variability of behavior in the workplace.

Another current of theory comes from Moreno's sociometry, itself in part out of psychiatry. It is, of course, most significant for its invention of the sociogram, a basic tool for systematically charting networks of social relationship, paralleling the kinship chart, the organization chart, the flow chart, the village plan, and the population pyramid, in other social sciences. But Moreno's concept of *spontaneity* is equally important.

Neither of these schools has given us much first-hand reporting of industrial groups. The Weberians have been important as a source of criticism, sharpening our realization of the class and occupational character of the "symbolic logics" used by various personnel of industrial groups. Moving, too, from a study of the bureaucrat, as a human type, to the study of bureaucracy, they have also contributed an understanding of much individual and small-group behavior within organization as a typical bureaucratic conversion of rationalist means into ends-in-themselves.

It is thus really the third main current which has made "industrial sociology." It sets the tide, too, into which the other psychologistic schools have been swept: "the human relations approach" of outsiders to the field. It has also been called, wrongly, the Mayo school, as Elton Mayo was historically the first person to make studies of industrial behavior in which insights and methods from the functional school of social anthropology were combined with those from clinical psychology. Today the third main current has divided into three main subschools, only one of which in any way follows the original doctrines of Mayo. Nevertheless, the personnel of all three subschools were nearly all of them in one way or another students of Mayo or exposed to him when they were young. All of them take off from the book *Management and the Worker* and the Hawthorne studies now so widely publicized.

What unites the three subschools is their theoretical debt to social anthropology and the formal sociologies of Durkheim, Simmel, and Pareto, and their common use of participant observation, free-association interviewing, and techniques of observation derived from anthropological field-work. They conceive interviewing not merely as a sounding of individual minds as with workers with attitudes coming from psychology; they use it as a supplement to direct observation in a search, like that of the seeker of culture patterns, for the regularities of actual social behavior. They all agree, with other naturalists, that one gets primary data about behavior of even so talkative an animal as man from what one sees men do; they do not feel happy with those psychologists of social science who seem to be interested only in what men say. They concede meanings to be important, but they insist meanings are interpretable only against the background of behavior.

This naturalist's concern with observation makes these subschools' observation of industrial groups very different from that of researchers whose training is psychological. Yet their published reports all point to the same generalization. The *explicanda*, performances, and emergent new behaviors of industrial workers they have observed, arise out of changes in attitude which are in turn responsive to changes in the basic interpersonal relationhips within the organizations in which they do their work.

Let us take up these three subschools in the order of their historical appearance. Mayo, himself, gave us the first industrial case: the mule-spinning room. Mayo was, of course, a clinical psychologist, conversant with physiological studies of factory work conditions. But he was greatly influenced by the functional anthropologists, Malinowski and Radcliffe-Brown, who were reworking ethnology in the direction of comparative sociology, asking questions about the function of social life and custom for all men and all human groups.

The problems of the mule-spinning room were low output, high turnover, complaints of fatigue, and "oppressive reveries" in the bitter, low-morale workers who did stay. These were classic signs of industrial malaise, Mayo's "anomie" after Durkheim, in a day—1927 in Philadelphia—of maximum rationalization of industry, minimum security, incentive pay schemes, and no unions. Mayo introduced an ambulatory nurse to whom the men might pour out their "reveries" in order to achieve catharsis. He gave them rest periods to combat "fatigue." After a time he let them first discuss and then decide among themselves upon the allocation of their own and their fellows' permitted periods of rest. Simple as these innovations seem, they nevertheless worked progressive change. Men who had had no contact with one another in the long, noisy workroom began to interact, then to "participate" to a minor degree. With each innovation they moved progressively, first to lose their pessimistic reveries, next to find themselves no longer fatigued, then to suffer a change of heart from the abysmally low morale of the place, lastly to produce better and better, to stay on longer and longer. Mayo concluded that the emergence of a social life, an "informal group," worked the effect. Perhaps it did, but where did it come from in its turn? Mayo tells us nothing of that, but the record he gives us speaks for itself. Changes in the basic relationships in which they passed their working time came first, for these men. They stopped and spoke to a nurse on their own whim, at their own time; they spoke with and to their fellows as they had not before; they directed each other to the rest time decided upon by themselves jointly; they informed the supervisors of these decisions and thus affected their decisions over the working day.

If one cannot accept the generalization and the relevance of these facts just named, as Mayo, who recorded them, could or did not, look a moment at the rest of Mayo's case record. Mayo, himself, tells us that the new morale and the new increasing output held up until a higher supervisor, in an excess of zeal, reversed the whole process. He ordered that the men must henceforth earn the rest periods they had been allocating among themselves. Their initiative, small as it was, should be stripped from them, and their foreman decide here too. From that point on, nurse or no nurse, catharsis or no catharsis, morale and output took a nose-dive, the reveries recurred, fatigue came back, and the situation Mayo had doctored quickly reverted to its former state. But even that turn of events does not end the case's demonstration of the dependence of morale and performance upon basic interpersonal relationships. Mayo faithfully records what happened next, though he seems to have drawn no theoretical inference from his own record. He appealed over the zealot's head and got the company's president to countermand him. With the restoration of the new activity, the new changes recurred; morale first, and then output, climbed upward again.

As I have said, Mayo attached little importance to his own faithful record of this first industrial case of the dynamics of small-group behavior. He had other theories to serve. He saw only the catharsis of the interview and the effect of building up worker-to-worker social relationships, where none had existed. Out of the sociology of Durkheim and functional social anthropology there was at hand the notion that the function of social relationships is to bolster the individual, to let him healthily act out his feelings, rather than, sickly, to bottle them up or invert them, to give him motivation, identification and willingness to accept the tight new rationalist controls over work, imposed by taskmasters, now taking the place of older but now dead customary controls. Out of Mayo's watching these worker-to-worker relationships of a new sort unite the lonely, embittered, apathetic workers of the mule-spinning room, the doctrine of "informal organization" or "teamwork" seems to have been born.

The orthodox followers of Mayo, who remain behind him at the Harvard School of Business Administration, have elaborated the doctrines very far. Their painstaking studies of teamwork and informal organization are so complete that they too can be re-examined, like Mayo's work, both for what they tell us and what they fail to tell us, even though their own records show it to exist. Three of their best-known studies document the generalization we are drawing and show something of the range of variability of the correlations between changes in basic relationships, in attitudes, and in new performance or situational product.

Thus the famous five girls of the Relay Assembly Test Room of the Hawthorne plant study show us how the output of a workroom rose progressively over five years because an esprit de corps grew up out of the emergence of a structure of informal organization and leadership, and demonstrated that, at least within the limits of ordinary working conditions, not physical or physiological or individual capacity factors, or even financial incentives, but rather social factors, determine worker morale and productivity. The equally careful study of the Bank Wiring Room documented the fact the "steady plateau" of ordinary performance in factory work represents a "restriction of output" expressing a secret, underground, defensive, and evasive social organization of workers in opposition to the industrial controls set over them. The wartime studies of turnover and absenteeism in the airplane industry of California show us the dependency of these behaviors on teamwork and group identification.

But here again one has the feeling that the orthodox inheritors of Mayo's mantle fail to ask questions of their own, so faithful, records. They say that the cases they observe, like these three, can only be diagnosed whole; they are not instances of any larger class. Each must be treated as unique, as a skilled doctor, steeped in his practice, treats the unique configuration that is each patient. They chart out the custom of informal organization, show it to be auxiliary or opposed to the rules of formal organization, list for us the symbols which operate, interpret them for us, interview personnel and assess the state of their minds, in very thorough documentation, but they insist that no connection can be guessed among these things, and that all of them are part of a configuration without internal process or structure. Such devotion to the intuitive summations of medical diagnosis is commendable indeed in a general practitioner—and such is their role vis-à-vis the business administrator—but it is lamentable in science.

Yet if one goes back to their records of participant observation and interview, what a different picture of small-group behavior appears! One has merely to ask the simple scientific questions they do not seem to have asked: where does teamwork come from? What is the order of events in these cases? How do the cases compare among themselves?

If we simply rearrange the evidence in the order of the occurrence of the phenomena (or the factors) noted, we see some new relationships. The five girls of the Relay Assembly Test Room developed their vaunted teamwork *after* they were segregated by management as an experimental group, *after* their segregation brought them into much more nearly exclusive contact with one another, *after* they came into contact, consultation, and even veto-power relation with their supervisors, *after,* as they testified themselves, "we have no boss." All this makes a continuous change away from impersonal and authoritarian supervision—a very sweeping shift in a basic relationship of modern industrial work—in the direction of greater "participation." This change preceded, in correlation, the growth of special identification, of interworker teamwork and leadership, of upward rise in output. Teamwork did not come from the girls alone, whatever their sentiments. It came *after* and thus perhaps *from* a sweeping change in supervision. The girls' "experimental" workroom had a structure only initially like that of other departments of modern industry. Their strange new morale and stranger new output behavior were products of a process-in-structure; they were situational products, but the situation has parts and connections among the parts capable of orderly change.

The other workrooms of the cases of the Mayo school bear similar witness. The Bank Wiring Room shows us the correlated constancies among the variables. A durable, constant, and long-continued basic supervision and its tight industrial discipline correlates, by the record, with a constant, durable, long-term flow-of-work (here as yet undisturbed by the engineers who must improve it), and these with a constant, long-term, durable interworker "informal organization" or clique structure, a body of custom or teamwork in opposition to management's controls, inclusive enough to ensnare in equal constancy the relations between lower-ranking supervisors and the men, for foremen are also caught in the secrets of informal organization and restriction. To these constancies of basic relationship are correlated also equally durable long-term attitudes and beliefs, a fair day's work, a fear of rate-cutting, a constant "morale." To these again is correlated, too, a steady and durable production, the normal straight-line output curve of ordinary work-conditions. The situation in which small-group behavior is determined is a whole again, but the parts have connections among themselves which allow comparisons between this case and the last.

The second subschool of industrial sociologists, those grouped with Lloyd Warner's erstwhile Committee for Human Relations in Industry in Chicago, or sharing Chester Barnard's and George Homans' view of an organization as a social whole, have a theoretical position which recognizes this complexity of correlated variables in the observed data of industrial small-groups, companies as well as workrooms. They call the whole configuration of organization, informal and formal together, and the products of sentiment, group custom, and individual performance, a "social system" or a "co-operative system." But they are more concerned with description of such systems and their static properties than with their analysis and dynamics.

Their concern with "social systems" and their statics is widely shared today. It was already foreshadowed in *Management and the Worker* and in the Counseling Programs which grew out of it. It is fruitfully wedded in the work of Chester Barnard and Herbert Simon to the traditional theories of organization coming out of political science. Gardner, Whyte, and Everett Hughes, as well as Warner and Low, have used it in studies of industrial behavior. George Homans has given a good account of its origins in older sociological theory in the work of Pareto and its elaboration by L. J. Henderson, where the formal connections between attitudinalized beliefs (myths, derivations), sentiments, organized social relationships, and personal behavior, as a "social system" were schematized.

The other origin of the doctrine is, of course, the functional social anthropology to which all Mayo descendants, of whatever subschool, are indebted. Outside industrial sociology altogether, Warner and his followers have elaborated the doctrine into a formal, positional sociology, mapping out very precisely the class structure, statuses, and role enactments of American communities. Theirs is, of course, a comparative sociology, or a sociography, interested first and foremost in documenting how individuals act and feel and think of their positions within social structure, and in comparing social structures around the world. It is related to social anthropology in that it holds that individual behavior, in large part, end social custom (and other collective behavior) completely, expresses such social position, "functioning" to create, affirm, reiterate, police, etc., the sentiments necessary to motivate the individual's learning and exercising behavior appropriate to his status and role in social groups of every size. Culture patterns—this appropriate behavior—in their turn arise and take their form in the process of integrating and making consistent, not only some individual needs of the culture-bearers alone, but also group needs for solidarity, for superordination and subordination, internal order, preconciliation of antagonism, cohesion, etc.

In individual studies, the use of concepts of a "social system," however statically conceived, has also contributed toward our generalization. Warner and Low have told us how a strike in Yankee City's shoe industry came about as a response to changes in industrial organization—ownership, supervision, technological structure, etc. They show these changes to have been destructive of the older craft skills, the older master-and-apprentice relationships, upsetting the connections of these with the customs and sentiments of age-grading, destroying worker status identification through loss of respect for local community business leaders now become an elite without power. Here the changes were a continuous process ending in explosion when the depression came. The case documents beautifully, nearly one hundred years later, on another continent, the social changes studied by the engineer-sociologist Le Play during the early industrialization of Europe. Everett Hughes has shown for Canada and Chicago how the in-plant behaviors of the workplace reflect the social customs of the community under the distortion imposed by industrial organization. Miss Herring in the South, Frederick L. W. Richardson for the Pennsylvania coal patches, I for the New England factory-town mills have all reported like findings. Burleigh Gardner has shown us, along with others, the disastrous lag between old custom and self-appraisal and present industrial relation realities in the position of the foreman. Whyte has shown us the effect of prestige evaluations of foods on status and job adjustment among restaurant workers.

It is specifically not true, as Blumer, Shephard, Moore, Dubin, and many others have claimed, that industrial sociology has not traced out the influence of out-of-plant, larger factors—economic and social—upon in-plant behavior. Since my original warning that it must be done, and suggestions for doing it, many persons have undertaken the task. Goode and Fowler have done it in feeder plants in Detroit; Harbison and Dubin have done it in contrasting the industrial relations of General Motors and Studebaker, where they show that management, in a small city and company, where the heat of making national wage-bargain decisions does not impose blockages to interaction over conflict of principle and interest, can and does find in itself a far easier receptivity to initiative from "below" among workers and through their union. Both cases correlate psychological and behavioral by-products with the internal organizational difference. They differ from the other industrial sociologists, whom they criticize, merely in extending the chain of causation back a step into the larger environment. The by-products are very different—workers driving workers, on the one hand, and "cooperative industrial relations and industrial peace," on the other—but they are both clearly members of the class of products of variability in basic relationships within the generalization with which we are dealing.

It can also be insisted, *en passant*, that industrial sociology has by no means shown a neglect of unions, as they have been accused of doing. The unions are a vital part of the "social systems" or "co-operative systems" of this subschool; companies and their particular unions are also small groups. Whyte and I have made many studies of extant literature and case materials on union-management co-operation; C. W. M. Hart has given us a magnificent study of the reworking of the new "union towns." These studies, too, support our generalization. "Co-operation" or "no co-operation," strike and conflict and industrial peace and continuance of stable relations between union and management, are likewise determined in great part—how great we do not yet fully know—by changes within the balance of interpersonal relationships within company, within union, and between them.

The last subschool of the "industrial sociologists" devotes itself head-on to this generalization of process, balance, and change within the interconnected interpersonal relationships of "such social systems" which are the whole situations of which small groups are reactive parts and small group behaviors by-products. The subschool is best identified as the group of persons associated in the Society for Applied Anthropology. They are again an offshoot, a dissident branch, trying to carry the proving of social science in the field of the problems of industrial relations a step further. One could name Whyte, Chapple, Richardson, Coon, Oliver, and some younger persons in industrial sociology itself; Loomis, Mead, Erick Lindemann, Saslow, some others in sociology, anthropology, or social psychiatry, have shown receptivity to the newer concepts.

We could be called, I suppose, interactionists or, were it not such a fighting word in science today, operationalists. We work within the framework of a theory and method first published by Chapple and myself in 1940, repeated in 1942 by Chapple and Coon, and in various articles of mine, restated by Whyte in various places. It holds that group life is the outcome of interaction (communication in biology) among animal organisms (including men). These interactions (communications) are events of stimulation and response between one animal and the next, taking place in time, one animal initiating or originating (either in reaction to the environment or acting spontaneously from internal physiological stimulation) the behavior of such an event, the other(s) responding to the prior behavior, thus "terminating" the event with behavior of his own. Such events give one one's definition of the social; they are thus a particular class of happenings in the life of living beings, conditioned by the properties of the organisms and their environments, but still a demarcatable class of natural phenomena.

These events have properties which yield universal operations for describing and comparing them. The simplest and most general of such operations, thus the basic ones of social science, are: (1) *identification and enumeration of the actors;* (2) *the establishment of the order or sequence of the activity in the event among them* (whether the one or the other(s) acted first, or second, in time); (3) *statement of the frequency through the time of observation with which the events, or the orders, took place.* It is claimed, further, that these basic operations are in fact in universal use in the social sciences and that it is only good scientific method to recognize the not-yet-perceived fact and build one's concepts upon the basic ways by which data are in fact gathered, compared, and assessed, by others as well as by oneself.

It is further held, in this subschool, that scientific method requires that taxonomy, i.e. classification of the various kinds of natural phenomena here defined as social, be attempted, not *a priori* or nominally, but by reference to common properties exhibited by the recorded events of observed social activity, as these are compared (measured) in terms of the basic operations of description. Using one's operations of description, one must erect that minimum classification of the events described which allows one to make clearer the observed or inferred connections between them, justifying the choice progressively against its usefulness in allowing us to follow the regular occurrences of those connections in the real happenings (situations) of nature.

This is the method of natural science and the discovery and statement of natural law. It is claimed that the social sciences offer no differences, once relevant and appropriate operations, definitions, and rules for notation and abstraction have been invented empirically. It is the contention of this subschool that classification of social phenomena is still only nominal (e.g., co-operation, authority, etc.) and has been, and is being, attempted prematurely, in advance of the discovery of universally usable common operations of description.

The theory holds, out of the evidence of psychology and anthropology, that the properties of the physiological facts of interpersonal stimulation in events of interactive (communicative) behavior are both wider spread and more general, ontogenetically as well as phylogenetically, than are those of the occurrences of language, words, meanings, signs, symbols, and attitudes, now appealed to in definitions of the social and attempts at interpretation of social behavior. These latter, then, should be subordinated in description and interpretation to the former; and they are to be understood, ultimately, only in their semantic connection to the events of interpersonal interaction.

Such a theory is obviously a reworking and a unification of the social sciences in the direction of natural science. How does it relate to the problem of small-group behavior in industry?

Some years ago I suggested an empirically relevant minimum classification, upon operational criteria, of the social action to be found in all factories, part of industrial production everywhere.

The first of these are the social events of the flow of work. The class is defined sociologically. That is, it is the sum of events comprising the activities of the persons known to stimulate one another in the *order* of their contacts during their transmission of product or material from one process to the next in its technical conversion into final, finished form. Usually one group of persons stands nearest to the physical process of manufacture, at the lowest level of organization, as a rank-and-file of "workers" in a supervised co-ordinated division of labor. They share a common propinquity to materials and machine processes, but it cannot be said to give them any social or group activity unless they can be seen to act upon one another. By such observation one learns they are in a tight, repetitive, frequent contact, man-to-man, "up" and "down," this line of flow or "assembly line." It is the order of interaction among the persons, not the flow's environmental position, nor its accidental properties, that defines this basic class of events and relationships. The flow is a definite sequence of human communications describable by its general occurrences among identifiable persons, in identifiable space and time. The particular technique or operation any one worker is carrying out is a cultural product, of course, but it is not part of a present social structure if it is performed in isolation. Even in the flow of work, any individual worker stands not only in a man-machine relation but also in at least two man-to-man relationships, that with the man above him, that with the man below him, in the flow. If one is to deal with "human relations" within which work is done, one must count these relations too. And many a "source of labor unrest" has had its cause within these real, if neglected, relationships.

The second minimal basic class of social events, behaviors, or activities of the small group in industry is that of supervision, or line authority. Here again one can make the definition of the relationships of the hierarchy of supervision or authority operational and sociological. It need not remain nominal, *a priori,* deductive, or imprecise. Supervision is therefore reducible to the sum in time of those events in which initiative and response have taken place, among the persons of the group, in the order or direction leading "downward," pair by pair, or through combinations of single initiant and simultaneous respondents (set-events), from an initial activity by the person who has the widest co-ordinate, simultaneous response out of the persons of the group already shown to be united by the flow-of-work relationships of the group. That latter person who co-ordinates the others is, of course, the "pinnacle of authority," the chief executive. Identifying him establishes one end of the flow of supervision; identifying the co-ordinate-responders of the flow-of-work, the "lowest level workers," establishes the other. Supervisors and supervisees of all ranks in between group themselves into hierarchical position along this order of sequence of human communication. Here again, no external attribute of the relationship defines it, either formality or informality, status ascription, or personal achievement of ascendancy. Like "work," "supervision" is a class of real events of interpersonal interaction, of whatever content or antecedence. As such, like "flow of work," it is defined now with reference to concrete occurrence among identifiable persons in real space and time. It can be compared with, and measured against, "work." One can establish there to be more or less of it from place to place and time to time. One can relate it concretely to changes in attitude and, in special, narrower-defined behaviors.

Supervision "line authority" is thus a basic, universal class of social events in any industrial group of any size, as well as in any other organized group. It is that class of events among the personnel of the group defined by the order among the personnel in which initiation of response flows "downward" through successive co-ordinations, running from those of the one person able to win the most frequent, widest co-ordinate response out of the workers of the flow of work, down to those of the foreman and his immediate gang. The successive co-ordinations give us the "structure," the hierarchy of organization. But the class contains numerous pair-events at every level, too. These are commands from one subordinate to a subordinate because they follow in the pair relationships the order of the co-ordinations.

The definitions are of more than theoretical interest. They perform a useful function in showing the interconnection of flow-of-work and supervision, two basic classes of universal interpersonal relationships uniting the human beings of the modern factory institution tightly and immediately. It is not the machine itself which is coercive in modern industry. The distinguishing feature of the factory system is another, not too often noticed, fact.

Neither the use of machines in production, nor the minuteness of our modern division of labor, nor labor saving by machines themselves, is new in human history, unexpectedly and immensely ingenious, powerful, and productive as our machines have come to be. What is new is rather a social invention. The social invention harnesses men and the saving of time to machine sources of power through preplanning and scheduling. What is new is the mastery of simultaneity in the division of labor, the co-ordination of simultaneous manufactures of interchangeable parts. The ever-increasing precision, standardization, and repetitiveness which make for efficiency in today's production are attributes of interchangeable hands making ever more and more minutely diverse interchangeable parts on more and more tightly predetermined and controlled schedules of time, tempo, and speed of completion, designed the better to bring such parts together the more neatly and the more quickly in common final assembly. In all this, vast armies of industrial workers come to work to jobs already set up in minute detail on the drafting board. Every gain in detail of interchangeability is a gain in competitive speed of completion and in reduced labor cost, but it is also an increase in the minuteness of control in the flow of work and in tightness of co-ordinating supervision for the interchangeable human "hands" of the process of manufacture. It is quite clear that machines are better suited for the kinds of control here necessary than are men. Some day fully automatic processes, already existing today in a few plants, may make the whole flow of work and most of co-ordinating supervisory control itself automatic. But our paper deals with the conditions still extant. Under them, men still work in such relationships with one another. Under such conditions both aspects of organization, however, formal, tight, rational, efficient, logical, and necessary they become, are still classes of social, interpersonal adaptation, among fallible human beings. To neglect these basic and different adaptations in a treatment of "human relations," in a work group of any size, is a most unreal distortion.

The brief diversion we have just made into production engineering serves to introduce a third class of social relations of the working group in industry. This is the class of staff-line events: initiations and responses made by and to staff men, chiefly engineers. These men are the planners and policers of the controls upon production, supervision, and flow of work. Staff-line relationships are a formal category of organization behaviors. We can redefine them operationally as we have the other formal categories, keeping in mind that staff men act upon workers and supervisors in all the workrooms and work levels of industry, with greater or lesser pressure whatever the formal rules governing their activity may be. Again we can state the pressure comparatively in terms of specific events of specific persons in identifiable orders of stimulation, in space, and in time. Engineers, in particular, initiate action for foremen and supervisors in making studies, in advising new plans, in inspecting old ones, in directing technical innovations; they push workers into new responses through time-study, through rerating, through machine-checks, and in a hundred, often fateful, ways. That they do all this in the interest of efficiency or the performance of machines does not make their activity any the less social, in our terms, nor the coercive force of their initiation of responses from workers and supervisor any the less great.

The next basic general class of relationships is comprised of events of "up-the-line" activity. Again it is a sum of initiations and responses in a direction among the personnel: namely, those activities originating with the workers and involving responses from supervisors in an order reverse to that of "supervision." Sometimes called formally "reporting" in higher levels of organization theory, or cited as a necessary part of "two-way-communication" by the alert in management, it is not usually recognized that events of this class, representing the initiative or "spontaneous" activity of the governed, are universal components of the workplace or of any other hierarchical human institution. Often it is only when such initiative from below is blocked that it is first apparent that such basic relationship is failing, and it becomes clear that the blockage is having marked emotional consequences in the frustrated initiants-from-below. Defining it as we do, however, and counting as always both the instances of the class, which by definition involves only the successful examples in which communication from below is completed by a responsive action on the part of the higher-placed communique, and the instances of blockage, where no such successive response is noted, we can follow this basic relationship, too, for its relative role in the dynamic short-term history of the group.

This class of "up-the-line" events of social relationship is what usually goes by the name of "participation" in industrial studies, it seems. Particularly is this so in the group-dynamics studies of the Lewinians, who seem also to be exploring its connection with supervision when they study "democratic leadership." But even where no channel for expression of initiative from below exists, some such activity seems always to be present or attempted.

Thus "up-the-line" activity includes all manner of informal "pull," indirect influence, protest, complaint, grievance, etc., and the class is a universal basic relationship of groups whatever the state of its blockage and diversion. Blockage and diversion show us the evolution of intermediaries in some, usually the lower, steps or the relationship "up-the-line" of command from worker to decisive supervisor. Sometimes such action through an intermediary is directly redressive, in reaction to supervisory or staff pressure; sometimes it is representative, bringing up new matter from workers for supervisors' decisions.

In either event, intermediary or none, such activity is still of this basic class, involving initiation by workers and response by supervisors. We have some admirable studies in the personnel field, notably by Paul Pigors, showing us that in companies having no unions, attempts to get personal redress, to win complaints referral, to exert influence from below on persons of authority will take any handy channel in local community custom or informal interpersonal ties. In Pigors' study the personnel man of an ununionized company, the captain of the company baseball team, the mayor of the town, the welfare head, the company stenographers, were all used sooner or later by one worker or another as intermediaries in an effort to reach and influence a supervisor.

The function of the unions as a channel for such redress is perfectly clear and very abundantly documented. The crucial daily activity of a working union is its grievance machinery. Unions of the Anglo-Saxon countries are representative institutions, their constituents are the members of shop-committees and locals, who are also the workers of the shops and the companies' sociologists of industry study. Contract negotiation is a great annual ceremonial, in which officers must "get something for the boys" or lose their votes. But week in and week out, a shop-steward at the level of the foreman and a business agent at the level of his superiors handle and usually settle grievances, under the contract. These make up a sequence of interactions, a channel of referral and decision or blockage and appeal higher, carrying out into action the wishes of individual workers, communicating them *upward* through the successive steps of the ranks of his union, *over* to the appropriate supervisor, *down* into a new decision over the matter in which the individual feels himself "aggrieved." Blockages—unsettled grievances—have explosive emotional consequences here, as well as in the company's internal "up-the-line" referrals. The dynamics of "co-operative industrial relations" are as rapid and decisive in their sensitivity to balance of relationships here, in union and between union and company, as are those of in-plant morale, and involve many more people with much greater stake in principle.

Lastly, then, among basic classes of social events in industry, worker-worker relations of informal kind, the teamwork of Mayo, the inter-worker participation of the Lewinians, the supposed sole source of good "human relations" and "high morale" of many too-quick commentators on the impersonality of the modern industrial scene, is simply a residual basic relationship. Definable as those events of interpersonal stimulation among members of the flow of work *outside the order* of communication of the other relationships, it is merely one part of the situation in which workers pass their working time. Great as the importance of warm human surroundings may be, compelling as the customs of worker solidarity can be, they are merely one among the basic relations of the workplace. One can see why, then, they are so responsive to the state of the other relationships. They are a universal class of social activities, too—witness the comradeship of soldiers, the underground resistance of concentration camps, the grapevines of prisons, student life, the growth of congregations into dissident sects, etc., etc. "Informal organization" as a form of group life is no more an independent variable than are these.

The last subschool, or the latest, among the students of small-group behavior in industry are the "interactionists" or "operationalists." They make the generalization I have documented on this paper; they try to deal with it by developing empirical methods for following in real-life detail the connections between the basic relationships of the industrial system as they appear in the situations of small groups in industry, observed changes in worker attitudes reported in these situations, observed emergences of new behavior—products of group life, observed variations in individual performances.

Many fruitful hypotheses about the dependency of particular collective behaviors and emotional results in individual members of organized "co-operative" systems of every kind—the great associations or institutions of society—upon the internal connections of the classes of interpersonal communication (interaction) have already emerged. Significant similarities between group behavior, organization at all levels, multiple and individual membership roles and role-effects are suggested by the generalizing concepts here advanced. It remains to report the observational and experimental testing of such hypotheses by the methods so far invented and to continue further testing and discovering and further innovation of operational methods of analysis and adaptation of modes of synthesis. It is clear, however, as from the review of work in industrial small-group behavior summarized here, that the task is one, not for any single traditional narrow discipline in psychology, physiology, sociology, or anthropology. They are tasks for a unified natural science of human life.

Part Six

Human Behavior in the Social Psychological Frame of Reference

CHAPTER 15

⊓⎍⊓⎍⊓⎍⊓⎍⊓⎍⊓⎍⊓⎍⊓⎍⊓⎍⊓⎍⊓⎍⊓⎍⊓⎍⊓⎍⊓⎍⊓⎍

Conceptions of Role and Ego in Contemporary Psychology[1]

S. STANSFELD SARGENT

Barnard College, Columbia University

One sign of growth and, we trust, of progress in a field of study is the development of new concepts. Two of the most provocative and potentially valuable new concepts in contemporary psychology are "role" (or "social role") and "ego." I propose to describe briefly major formulations of the role concept, then present my own social psychological interpretation, and conclude by discussing the relationship between role and ego.

Let us deal first with roles. The first serious psychological treatment of roles, so far as I know, was given by Woodworth in 1934 in the third edition of his general text (55). Woodworth had been stimulated but somewhat troubled by the efforts of several Chicago sociologists (Park, Faris, and Thrasher) to show that the individual's personality is the product of his social role. "My effort in the third edition (and later)," wrote Woodworth recently, "was to show that this environment factor was only part of the basis of personality, the individual's inherent traits being the other factor" (54). Woodworth agreed that two important social influences, the code and the role, operate significantly in personality development. "The individual adopts the code of his group; and he finds or makes a role for himself in the group (56, p. 135). The available roles are determined only in part by group organization, continues Woodworth; in the main "each individual gravitates

---

[1] I am indebted to John and Ruth Useem, Conrad Arensberg, and Roland L. Warren for many helpful suggestions incorporated in this paper.

toward a role that suits his own characteristics, . . . he finds his role
or makes it rather than having it thrust upon him by arbitrary group
action" (56, p. 138).

Guthrie, in his *Psychology of Human Conflict* (11), dealt at length
with roles, treating them as an enduring aspect of personality. He
found role-taking is almost universal: "We recognize a description of
ourselves, acknowledge our attributes or our membership in a class,
and appropriate behavior follows the thought. . . . A man who has
been mentioned in the local newspaper as a prominent citizen may be
changed for the rest of his life by that chance paragraph. He now begins to reject actions which are not the actions of a prominent citizen.
He now buys his theater ticket for an orchestra seat because prominent
citizens do not sit in the gallery. At the haberdasher's a new verbal formula enters into his choice of clothing. "Is this a suitable hat for such
a person as he is?" (11, p. 139).

Besides stressing the significance of a person's awareness of his role,
Guthrie emphasized the importance of role conflicts in maladjustment.
"The man who thinks of himself as an open-handed host loses his income and his social adjustment is thrown completely out of gear by his
persistence in that role" (11, p. 141). Likewise, an unfortunate mar-
riage may result in role conflict if the spouses continue to pretend in
public that all is well. Guthrie (in contrast to Woodworth) seems not
to have been influenced by the sociologists in working out his interpretations of role.

For many years, psychologists did not follow the leads provided by
Woodworth and Guthrie in their discussions of personality and abnormal behavior. However, a few psychologists writing books on social
psychology did show an interest in roles. Katz and Schanck, for example, noted that clinicians often miss the importance of role behavior. "If we consider the effects of a man's behavior upon his fellows it
is often not necessary to know his personality. His action may be
deeply interiorized within him, or it may not be at all characteristic of
him. But its effect upon his fellows may be the same. At an auction the
enthusiastic bidder who bids first and who keeps bidding up the price
of an article may be planted there for that purpose by the auctioneer.
Or he may be there because he loves auctions. Nevertheless, he plays
the role of the enthusiastic bidder and affects the bidding of other people, regardless of his motive. In many situations of life, role behavior

of this sort is of first importance" (**20,** pp. 394–395). Following the emphasis of anthropologists and sociologists, Katz and Schanck also dealt, as did Krout, (**22**) with age, sex, occupational and class roles as factors affecting the patterning of social interaction.

In his study of attitudes and personality at Bennington College, Newcomb found that community roles, of typically negativistic or cooperative character, seemed to mediate between social attitudes and other personality characteristics (**31**). He found that *objective* roles were assigned by members of the college community on the basis of observable personality characteristics. In addition, *subjective* roles were self-assigned, on the basis of other personality characteristics.

Beginning in 1947, psychological interest in roles has mushroomed. Murphy, for example, devotes a chapter to "Social Role" in his volume on *Personality* (**30**). He treats role as "a social task or function carried out by the individual"; he notes the reciprocal interplay of roles and the part played in their production by both social requirements and individual needs. Newcomb and Hartley have a sizeable section on "Role and status" in their *Readings in Social Psychology* containing several sociological contributions (**34**). Cameron, following G. H. Mead, discusses roles from the standpoint of communication and social adjustment in his *Psychology of Behavior Disorders*. For example, he says:

. . . by taking this role or that in fun, children learn incidentally to see things from something approaching the diverse standpoints of all the social persons whom they pretend to be. Each child finds out, in each role he plays, what he can look for in the behavior of children playing dominant, dependent or other reciprocal roles, and what he must do to meet, accept, resist or evade others' demands in those roles (**4**, p. 92).

Other evidences of increasing psychological interest in roles can be cited. Sherif and Cantril refer to the subject frequently in their study of ego-involvments (**45**). A social psychologist and sociologist collaborated in a paper on roles presented to the Eastern Psychological Association in the spring of 1948 (**43**), and a few months later an APA symposium on the subject brought together contributions from two social psychologists, an anthropologist, a sociologist, and a psychiatrist-psychologist (**35**). Two 1950 texts in social psychology, by Newcomb and by Sargent, give considerable emphasis to roles (**33, 40**), as does another by the Hartleys scheduled to appear in 1951 (12). Nor should one overlook the books by Kimball Young (57, 58), Lindesmith and Strauss (24), and Coutu (8), which reflect the earlier and continuing sociological interest in roles.

I would be remiss in failing to mention also the work on psychodramatic roles done by J. L. Moreno and his followers, which is well known to many psychologists and social scientists (e.g., 29, 39, 23). Psychodramatic emphasis, however, is placed upon voluntary role-taking and its therapeutic value, whereas the primary interest of social psychologists must be, I believe, clarification of the role concept and understanding of roles as they operate in our daily social life.

Why have psychologists suddenly become so interested in roles? We lack knowledge, but a few hypotheses may be in order:

First, psychologists have become increasingly aware of "situational" influences, such as age, sex, and economic status, occupational and social group membership, as well as of more specific influences of one's family and various other membership and reference groups. They are finding traditional psychological concepts such as personality traits, conditioned responses, and attitudes inadequate tools for describing the effects of these social influences upon the individual or for making possible prediction and control of social behavior.

Secondly, psychologists have never been enthusiastic about the orthodox sociological treatment of social interaction, i.e., the Park and Burgess categories of competition, conflict, accommodation, and assimilation, with co-operation thrown in for good measure (37). Nor, if acquainted with them at all, have psychologists been partial to the more extended classifications of interactional processes such as those offered by Von Wiese and Becker (48), or, at the other extreme, to the treatment of interaction in terms of number and duration of interpersonal contacts, as proposed by Chapple, Arensberg, and McGregor (6, 2).

In contrast with these formulations, it seems to me, role appeals to psychologists as an interactional concept, with a patterned Gestalt-like quality. A given role often includes basic elements of competition, co-operation, and the like. But it typically includes much more, depending upon the specific social situation and the personalities involved.

A third hypothesis to account for increasing psychological interest is the fact that the role concept provides a bridge for interdisciplinary co-operation. The "situational" emphasis of social scientists and the "personality" emphasis of psychologists and psychiatrists still exists, but all of us are groping toward synthesis. Now a role is linked to a particular social situation or type of situation. At the same time, roles are learned and perceived by individuals, and may be conceptualized by them. Hence "role" has excellent potentialities as an integrational concept in present-day social psychology.

But, one may well ask, do psychologists have a well-defined role concept which will answer the needs and hopes just mentioned—and also make possible fruitful research? So far, social psychologists have tended to husband and wife, host and guest, teacher and student, employee and employer, for example. Consider the host-guest role in middle-class American society. Cultural prescription demands that the host welcome his guest, introduce him to other guests, make him comfortable, furnish him with food and drink. Reciprocally, the guest greets his host, converses with other guests (rather than retiring to a corner and reading), and thanks the host, on leaving, for his hospitality. Within these limits, however, a good deal of variation is permitted, depending on subcultural and personal factors.

Situational roles derive, still more clearly, from personality variables. An insecure person, with great need for recognition, let us say, plays the role of a "man of the world," or perhaps a "woman of sophistication." The bully, flirt, lady-killer, and life-of-the-party are other examples of situational roles; all these have a skeleton of cultural definition, but their precise character as well as the time of enactment depends upon personality trends and perceptual interpretations.

In other words, I suggest that those patterns of social behavior which may reasonably be called "roles" have ingredients of cultural, of personal, and of situational determination. But never is a role *wholly* cultural, *wholly* personal, or *wholly* situational. A given role, as conceptualized and as enacted, is affected by differing degrees of these three components.

One reason sociologists have failed to agree upon a concept of role is that some have approached role as an objectively defined aspect of the culture pattern which can be considered apart from the persons who actually enact or play the roles. Other sociologists include personal variables in their concept. The social psychologist, always concerned with individuals, naturally leans toward the latter type of conceptualization. His problem is to frame a concept of role which is broad enough to cover such cases as those just mentioned, yet specific enough to have meaning. Can we then define role so as to embrace cultural patterning and personal modifications, including that elusive but very important individual perceptual factor?

With these considerations in mind, I venture the following definition: *A person's role is a pattern or type of social behavior which seems situationally appropriate to him in terms of the demands and expectations of those in his group.* Let me comment briefly on a few points of this definition.

"A person's role" is used to underline the fact that roles are always enacted by individuals—and that the roles of two individuals are not identical.

"Pattern or type" of social behavior suggests that most roles are not predetermined like the words and actions of the characters in a play. Roles are culturally and socially defined delimitations of behavior, or patterns of permitted alternatives, within whose bounds much variation is possible.

"Social behavior" is used because roles constitute an aspect of social interaction; they have no meaning except in terms of interpersonal relationships.

"Situational appropriateness" indicates the importance of perception. One does not respond to a situation as defined objectively, but rather as he perceives or interprets it. One behaves in a way that is congruent with his subjective definition of the situation. Thus an individual who decides that a party is "dying on its feet" may try to resuscitate it by becoming the "life of the party," whether or not others consider such behavior necessary.

The "demands and expectations" of others, learned through one's social experience, give a role its basic character. Most roles are reciprocal; their structure is patterned through the mutual expectations of group members—e.g., husband and wife, parent and child, teacher and pupil, employer and employee, leader and follower.

"Group" may refer to a small, closely knit, social unit like a family, club, or play-group, or to large, loosely structured collections of individuals such as a whole community, social class, or nation.

Roles depend upon the ability of the human organism to take and maintain a "mental set," thus facilitating certain kinds of behavior and inhibiting other responses. The guest at a polite dinner party doesn't even think of telling a dirty joke, nor does it occur to the man in church to light a cigarette. A good deal of experimental evidence exists (e.g., controlled association tests) to show how effectively behavior may be limited and channeled by mental set. Newcomb made much the same point in a recent paper when he spoke of "role attitude" as an intervening variable between a person's role as prescribed and the actual role behavior which occurs (32).

The social psychological conception of role presented above may be further clarified by describing certain dimensions of roles.

First, roles differ greatly in the specificity with which they are patterned. In a dramatic role, or in ceremonies like a formal wedding, a college graduation, or "changing the guard," the acts and words are definitely prescribed. (Nonetheless, a slight degree of latitude is permitted, as shown by two actors' interpretations of the role of Hamlet.) In many other roles, however, there is little or no prescription of specific acts or words; the latitude is great and conformity is demanded only within rather general categories of "musts" and "must nots." For example, a child must not be rude to or disobey his parents, a minister must not drink, swear, or go to burlesque shows; a doctor must treat all sick people to the best of his ability; and so on. But most behavior is left unregulated by the role and individual variation is permitted. The host-guest relationship sketched above is an example that falls between these two extremes. This role defines the general pattern of host-guest interaction, but does not specify the exact words to be spoken, the particular subjects of conversation, the food and drink to be served, or the hour at which the guests should depart.

Newcomb made a good suggestion in this connection—a distinction between *role* and *role behavior:* the actual role behavior is a function of an individual's role (and of others' reciprocal roles) along with various intervening variables deriving from personality and the characteristics of the specific social situation (32).

Second, as already suggested in comparing cultural, personal, and situational roles, we find great variation in breadth or extensiveness. A king or president must conform to his role in all public contacts; so must a monk or a nun. Other roles are more situationally-linked: a girl may be a "sophisticate" in only one social group; a man may be boss in his own office but by no means in his own family, depending on many personal factors and specific interactional relationships.

Similarly, roles differ in continuity or permanence. Cultural roles like man and woman, nobleman or outcast, are permanent within a society, though their pattern may change slowly over the years. Occupational roles endure after one chooses his vocation. Some roles last for a few years—those of debutante or eligible bachelor, for example. Still other roles are more transitory, like the presidency of a club, or situational roles such as those mentioned earlier.

Other aspects and variations of roles could be suggested—for example, prestige and importance, and the ease or difficulty in fulfilling a role. But more important, perhaps, is another consideration: integration or conflict among roles.

All of us enact several roles. A college boy may function as a student, fraternity member, campus leader, and as a son and brother as well, and may play a number of other occasional roles besides. Most persons succeed in carrying out their various roles without disorganization or conflict. Some persons, indeed, change easily and skillfully from one role to another, according to situational demands, like the suave diplomat, gracious hostess, or clever salesman. However, if the changes are quite abrupt and seem more dramatic than the situations warrant, an individual may be considered a chameleon-like personality, a poseur, or an opportunist.

Sometimes a person's various roles occasion conflict, especially if two roles derive from groups having different standards. When a boy from a strict, small-town home background goes away to a university, or to a big city, he finds that more sophisticated behavior is demanded if he is to be accepted socially. Conformity to these demands means learning roles and values incompatible with existing behavior patterns, and is very likely to result in emotional conflict.

A good illustration of such conflict is furnished by Komarovsky in a study of college girls (21). A large number, especially among the brighter and more serious students, reported conflict between the "feminine" role and that of the career or professional woman. One student's father wants her to get an "A" in every subject and to prepare for a profession. But her mother says, "That 'A' in philosophy is very nice, dear. But please don't become so deep that no man will be good enough for you." The student wonders how she is to pursue any course single-mindedly when those she loves and respects have such differing plans and expectations for her. Komarovsky found the college woman also in conflict about whether to be herself in relations with men or to play the expected feminine role—that of dependence and inferiority. Nearly half the informants had occasionally "played dumb" on dates—concealed academic honors, pretended ignorance, or allowed the man the last word in discussion. But they felt hypocritical, and decidedly unhappy about the conflicting pressures exerted upon them.

Is a person conscious of the social roles he enacts? The degree to which one is conscious of his behavior is, of course, most difficult to determine reliably. However, a few hypotheses may be in order—hypotheses based upon introspective and observational evidence.

For the most part people seem unaware that they are taking or playing roles. That is to say, they are not conscious of the way their behavior is patterned and delimited within particular social situations. The student and teacher seldom stop to ponder the kinds of behavior appropriate to the classroom; each has learned or worked out his role and his classroom behavior is congruent with it. Our customary life situations—in home, school, office and community—are well-defined and understood and our behavior within them is performed without reflection or conscious decision.

This is not true, however, for new and unusual situations. Here one's role is not clear and may be the subject of conscious consideration. A recent recruit into the armed services is acutely aware of the requirements of his new role. When a young woman sees her ex-fiancé coming toward her in a restaurant, she may decide rapidly whether to ignore him, to be courteous but distant, to act like an old friend, to behave as if things were on the same old basis, or to choose some other alternative. Unfamiliar, unexpected, and critical situations, it would seem, facilitate one's consciousness of his role.

Again, it seems that the higher the status associated with a person's role, the more likely he will be conscious of it. Thus a philanthropist, community leader, or noted scholar would be conscious of his major role but a ward politician, drunkard, or criminal would not. This hypothesis is supported to some extent by clinical evidence that criminals typically repress awareness of their status and rationalize themselves into a more favorable position. The question is related to ego-involvement and the self-image, which will be discussed later.

Consciousness of one's roles may also be related to individual differences in insight and self-awareness, or in anxiety. Horney's characterization of the neurotic as one who is acutely concerned about the way he appears to others exemplifies sharpened awareness of one's role (**17**).

The discussion thus far has treated roles as an aspect of social behavior—of interpersonal relations. Let us turn now to consider roles in relation to personality traits of the individual.

Personality tests are constructed upon the tacit assumption that the individual's social behavior is primarily a function of certain enduring and measurable traits or tendencies of personality. Most questionnaires, for example, contain items such as these:

> Would you rather spend an evening reading at home than to attend a large party?
> Are you inclined to keep quiet when out in a social group?
> At a reception or tea do you seek to meet the important person present?
> Have you found books more interesting than people?
> Do you argue over prices with tradesmen?
> Do you feel as if people are watching you?

Respondents answer several dozen questions by indicating "Yes," "No," or "?." The answers are scored and analyzed in order to show the degree to which each person is introverted or extroverted, dominant or submissive, neurotic, self-sufficient, and the like—i.e., to show generalized personality tendencies.

Those taking personality tests, however, find it difficult to answer such questions. They wonder which social group is meant—which important person, which book, which tradesman? They realize, albeit dimly, that their behavior cannot be described in general terms, but that they do have roles in specific situations.

The distinction between roles and personality traits was shown strikingly by Cottrell (**7**). He read two brief case studies to a class and asked for personality trait ratings. One case was a child who was a difficult problem in the home—who sulked, fought, bullied younger children, and refused to co-operate. The second was a timid, submissive child, bullied by his schoolmates, a daydreamer in class, etc. The members of Cottrell's class rated the first child high on aggressiveness, hostility, and stubbornness; the second child low on these traits.

Then Cottrell informed them that the two cases were one and the same child! It was simply a youngster who showed more than average variation between home and school behavior—a type of case well-known to the clinician. The college students found it almost impossible to estimate the child's personality traits on the basis of such conflicting data.

Whether or not "personality" varies from one situation to another, considerable evidence shows that social behavior does so. Recent studies of leadership, for example, emphasize the important function of the particular social situation in determining leadership behavior, along with personality characteristics (e.g., 19, 15). The author and a colleague devised an ascendance-submission test in which questions centered about one or another of six social situations: classroom, group of friends, groups of strangers, boy-friend, girl-friend, and salespeople and waiters. Within some of these situations, college students showed fairly consistent reactions which differed from their behavior in other situations. Toward strangers, for example, they tended to be submissive, whereas with close friends they were more likely to be ascendant (42).

Since personality is inferred largely from social behavior, such data cast doubt upon the constancy of personality traits in general. It may well be that some aspects of personality are quite consistent from one situation to another, while others show great variability. Or it may be that some individuals change little or not at all, while others adapt themselves to different situations. Further research is necessary. In all probability either the "trait" or the "situational" interpretation, by itself, will be found extreme. The role concept should be a useful tool, along with the trait concept, for studying the relationship between changing situational demands and enduring personality trends.

Before describing recent research on roles, a word of caution is in order. As we have seen, the role concept is finding favor among psychologists, particularly social psychologists. Is there danger that it may be pushed too far? Is there social behavior which does *not* have role character?

Certainly most social interaction has a considerable degree of role character, particularly that which occurs in institutionalized settings like home, school, office, and church. When a social situation is not highly "structured," in the sense of regulation by established norms, role factors are less clear; for example, when asking street directions of a stranger. But when social interaction is less casual and more sustained, roles come into play. If two strangers continue to chat, they begin to define their relations to each other. Perhaps they discover they were both born in the same town, that they have mutual friends, that they are both parents of small children, that one was an officer and one a private in the last war. Here friendly or hierarchical kinds of relationship emerge and roles begin to operate.

Again, roles appear to be minimal in emergency situations. Established social norms and relationships break down in the face of fire, riot, or panic, or under conditions or prolonged deprivation, insecurity or crisis, as Sherif has noted (44, p. 401).

Though research on roles has not yet progressed very far, a number of studies can be cited. The conformity behavior studied many years ago by Floyd Allport and his associates can be considered role behavior (1). Motorists stopping for a red light or Catholics performing the holy-water ceremony are exemplifying expected behavior with penalties for non-observance.

Probably the first extensive observational and clinical study of roles was done by Waller; in his *Sociology of Teaching* he described and illustrated major aspects of teacher and student roles in our society (49, 50).

Several investigators have studied the role of the bureaucrat, notably Merton (28) and Watson (52). Reissman recently reported on the characteristics and attitudes of civil servants in a midwestern state (38) and Henry has described personality characteristics important to the role of the business executive (16).

Studies of leadership sometimes focus attention on roles, e.g., the assessment procedures of the Office of Strategic Services during the recent war (36). Similarly, research in group discussion has disclosed the operation of various roles, such as "group task," "group building," and "individual" roles (3).

More experimental approaches have also been employed. Hartley and others used pictures and interviews to show that quite young children identify themselves with ethnic group symbols and can distinguish between various adult roles (13, 14). The author found that questionnaires could be used to discover patterns of approved and disapproved behavior in a college community (41).

A number of investigators have studied role-taking from a more clinical standpoint, notably Moreno and his associates (29, 39, 23). Dymond and McClelland have reported on personality correlates, respectively, of empathy and of role-playing ability (9, 10, 26).

A few comments are appropriate in conclusion, as to the relationship between role and ego or self. In their *Psychology of Ego-Involvements,* Sherif and Cantril define the ego as a cluster of constellation of attitudes related to what the individual considers "I," "me," or "mine." These attitudes are affectively charged, they point out, largely because many of them "prescribe the individual's relationship, status, or role with respect to other individuals or groups." That is to say, "attitudes related to role or status are ego-involved" (45, p. 134).

If one conceives role as closely akin to status, the relationship between role and ego-involvement is clear. But if role is defined in broader terms, as patterned forms of social interaction, the connection seems less obvious. Is a person, for example, ego-involved with his role as father-of-a-family, student, or employee, or with his occasional roles as host, guest, or committee member? It seems likely that in so far as the activities constituting a role yield rewards or punishments (e.g., prestige, power, disapproval, ostracism), the individual will tend to become ego-involved with that role. But if a role brings no particular satisfaction or dissatisfaction, ego-involvement will not occur.

Another aspect of the ego, the "self-image," is definitely based upon roles. The individual's more or less consciously formulated idea of himself depends upon his "subjective" roles—his conceptualization of his relationship to others. It may be well that a person has several self-images, depending on his major group affiliations and attendant roles (see 18, p. 294; 46, p. 170). Furthermore, it is quite possible that the clearer and more articulate a person's self-image, the more he becomes ego-involved with the included roles. Thus the young lady who thinks of herself as the campus queen is upset when she is referred to as merely "good-looking." Or the professor, who fancies himself as a carpenter and handy-man-about-the-house, is delighted when someone praises his craftsmanship. These comments, however, should be considered hypotheses. Greater clarification of the concepts of role and of ego (self) is necessary before their relationship is well understood.

In conclusion: Major conceptions of role have been reviewed in this paper, and an attempt made to present a definition of role which is useful to social psychologists. Such a definition, it was suggested, must recognize the cultural framework of roles, and the personal variations (especially the perceptual) on this central cultural theme. This is to say, it extends the social scientist's "objective" cultural roles in a social psychological direction.

Roles are linked to social situations, but are learned, perceived, and often conceptualized by individuals. Their situational character makes roles a valuable supplement to, if not a corrective of, personality-oriented interpretations of social behavior.

An adequate concept of role can provide needed integration among psychologists and social scientists who, with differing training and orientation, are working toward an understanding of human social behavior.

REFERENCES

1. Allport, F. H. The J-curve hypothesis of conforming behavior, *J. Soc. Psychol.*, 1934, *5*, 141–183 (Summary in Newcomb, T. M., and Hartley, E. L. (eds.), *Readings in Social Psychology*, Holt, 1947, pp. 55–67).

2. Arensberg, C. M., and McGregor, D. Determination of morale in an industrial company, *J. App. Anthrop.*, 1942, *1:2*, 12–34.

3. Benne, K. D., and Sheats, P. Functional roles of group members, *J. Soc. Issues*, 1948, *4*, #2, 41–49.

4. Cameron, N. *Psychology of Behavior Disorders*, Houghton Mifflin, 1947.

5. Carr, L. J. *Situational Analysis*, Harper, 1948.

6. Chapple, E. D. Measuring human relations, *Genet. Psychol. Monogr.*, 1940, #22, 1.

7. Cottrell, L. S., Jr. The analysis of situational fields in social psychology, *Am. Sociol. Rev.*, 1942, 7, pp. 370–382.

8. Coutu, W. *Emergent Human Nature.* Knopf, 1949.

9. Dymond, R. F. Personality and empathy, Paper delivered at Eastern Psychological Assn. meetings, April 21, 1950.

10. Dymond, R. F. A scale for the measurement of empathic ability, *J. Consult. Psych.*, 1949, *13*, 127–133.

11. Guthrie, E. R. *Psychology of Human Conflict.* Harper, 1938.

12. Hartley, E. L. and R. E. *Fundamentals of Social Psychology.* Knopf, to be published in 1951.

13. Hartley, E. L., and Krugman, D. C. Note on children's role perception, *J. Psychol.*, 1948, *26*, 399–405.

14. Hartley, E. L., Rosenbaum, M., and Schwartz, S. Children's perception of ethnic group membership, *J. Psychol.*, 1948, *26*, 387–398.

15. Hemphill, J. K. Situational factors in leadership, *Bureau of Educ. Res.,* Ohio State U., 1950.

16. Henry, W. The business executive—the psychodynamics of a social role, *Am. J. Sociol.*, 1949, *54*, 286–291.

17. Horney, K. *The Neurotic Personality of Our Time.* Norton, 1937.

18. James, W. *Principles of Psychology.* Holt, 1890.

19. Jenkins, W. O. A review of leadership studies . . . , *Psy. Bull.*, 1947, *44*, 54–79.

20. Katz, D., and Schanck, R. L. *Social Psychology.* Wiley, 1938.

21. Komarovsky, M. Cultural contradictions and sex roles, *Am. J. Sociol.*, 1946, *52*, 184–189.

22. Krout, M. H. *Introduction to Social Psychology.* Harper, 1942.

23. Lawlor, G. W. Role therapy, *Sociatry*, 1947, *1*, 51–55.

24. Lindesmith, A. R., and Strauss, A. L. *Social Psychology.* Dryden, 1949.

25. Linton, R. *The Study of Man.* Appleton-Century, 1936.

26. McClelland, W. A. A preliminary test of role-playing ability, Paper delivered at Eastern Psychological Assn. meetings, April 21, 1950.

27. Mead, G. H. *Mind, Self and Society.* University of Chicago Press, 1934.

28. Merton, R. K. Bureaucratic structure and personality, *Social Forces*, 1950, *18*, 560–568.

29. Moreno, J. L. *Psychodrama*, Vol. I. Beacon House, 1946.

30. Murphy, G. *Personality.* Harper, 1947.

31. Newcomb, T. M. *Personality and Social Change.* Dryden, 1943.

32. Newcomb, T. M. Role concepts in social psychology, Paper delivered at American Psychological Assn. meetings, Sept. 10, 1948.

33. Newcomb, T. M. *Social Psychology.* Dryden, 1950.

34. Newcomb, T. M., and Hartley, E. L. (eds.) *Readings in Social Psychology.* Holt, 1947.

35. Newcomb, T. M., Linton, R., Warren, R. L., Cameron, N. A., and Henry, W. E. Symposium: the value of "social role" for interdisciplinary synthesis, American Psychological Assn. meetings, Sept. 10, 1948.

36. Office of Strategic Services Staff. *Assessment of Men.* Rinehart, 1948.

37. Park, R. E., and Burgess, E. W. *Introduction to the Science of Sociology.* University of Chicago Press, 1921.

38. Reissman, L. The civil servant—a study of role conception in bureaucracy. University of Wisconsin M.A. Thesis, 1947.

39. Sarbin, T. R. The concept of role-taking, *Sociometry*, 1943, *6*, 273–285.

40. Sargent, S. S. *Social Psychology.* Ronald, 1950.

41. Sargent, S. S. Unpublished study.

42. Sargent, S. S., and Pease, K. Social roles and personality traits, to be published.

43. Sargent, S. S., and Useem, J. The psychological significance of social roles, Paper delivered at Eastern Psychological Assn. meetings, April 16, 1948.

44. Sherif, M. *Outline of Social Psychology*. Harper, 1948.

45. Sherif, M., and Cantril, H. *Psychology of Ego-Involvements*. Wiley, 1947.

46. Stagner, R. *Psychology of Personality*. 2nd ed.; McGraw-Hill, 1948.

47. Thomas, W. I. *The Unadjusted Girl*. Little, Brown, 1923.

48. Von Wiese, L., and Becker, H. *Systematic Sociology*. Wiley, 1932.

49. Waller, W. W. *The Sociology of Teaching*. Wiley, 1932.

50. Waller, W. W. The teacher's roles, Chap. 10 in Roucek, J. S., et al., *Sociological Foundations of Education*. Crowell, 1942.

51. Warren, R. L. Cultural, personal and situational roles, *Sociol. soc. res.*, 1949, *34*, 104–111.

52. Watson, G. (ed.). Problems of bureaucracy, *J. Soc. Issues*, 1945, *1:4*.

53. Wilson, L., and Kolb, W. L. *Sociological Analysis*. Harcourt, Brace, 1949.

54. Woodworth, R. S. Letter to the writer, May 10, 1948.

55. Woodworth, R. S. *Psychology*. 3rd ed.; Holt, 1934.

56. Woodworth, R. S., and Marquis, D. G. *Psychology*. 5th ed.; Holt, 1947.

57. Young, K. *Personality and Problems of Adjustment*. Crofts, 1940.

58. Young, K. *Social Psychology*. Rev. ed.; Crofts, 1944.

59. Young, K. *Sociology*. American Book Co., 1934.

CHAPTER 16

Psychological Problems of Multiple Group Membership

EUGENE HARTLEY
City College of New York

On being confronted for the first time only a very short time ago by
the full program for this series of meetings, it was clear to me that the
best use of the time available to us this afternoon would probably be to
attempt to extend the discussion of the paper of Professor Hughes to
which we listened last night. It occurred to me, however, that it might
be of some value to undertake an independent statement in order to
provide data for a comparison of how a Sociologist and a Psychologist
might approach the same problem; especially since one of our ob-
jectives for this conference is to observe the converging tendencies as
well as the gaps in the research frontiers of social psychology. (The
difference due to the fact that Professor Hughes dealt with substantive
material while I shall be completely theoretical should not make comparison too difficult.)

It may be worthwhile to establish at the outset the equivalence of
our topics (as printed in the program). Dr. Hughes addressed himself
to the topic "Problems produced by contradictory statuses and roles."
Roles and statuses stem from a functional differentiation of positions
within a social group. Since in any one social group, at any given time,
an individual validates but one position, unless I am quite mistaken,
the problems produced by contradictory roles and statuses must refer
back to the different reference groups from which those roles and
statuses have come, and therefore, to the problems produced by an
individual's functional membership in a plural number of groups.

At the risk of being repetitive, I will proceed with the development of my presentation counting on the attitude of polite and sympathetic tolerance which in our group is the norm for all variants of definition of the generic "seminar auditor" role. I should like to rationalize the incomplete nature of the theoretical presentation of the problems I am dealing with in order to avoid closure—to induce with respect to these problems a "Zeigarnik effect."

An examination of the psychological problems of multiple group membership in 1950 must have as its subtitle: An Agenda of Unfinished Business. The problems involved have been with us since the beginnings of human society and our professional literature has made explicit reference to them on many occasions. Nevertheless, psychologists have been relatively unresponsive and little more can be done today than to attempt to throw the spotlight on an important but generally overlooked research area.

The concept of the "marginal man" as developed by Park and by Stonequist has been a most productive source of data for the clarification of our problem. In his Introduction to Stonequist's classical study (1), Park stated: "The marginal man, as here conceived, is one whom fate has condemned to live in two societies and in two, not merely different but antagonistic, cultures" (2, p. xv), and a bit further on, Park continued: "From what has been said one may infer that the marginal man is an incidental product of a process of acculturation, such as inevitably ensues when people of different cultures and different races come together to carry on a common life" (2, p. xviii).

Stonequist's study of the marginal man focuses directly on the resultant of such membership in contrasting groups and similar additional data are readily found in the American Youth Commission studies of Negro youth (3); the Indian Education Research Project studies among the Navaho, Sioux, and Papago (4); the studies of the Nisei (5), the Italian (6), and other second-generation immigrant groups in "the melting pot," and many other forms of acculturation studies.

Such studies, however, take as their point of departure contrasting pervasive membership groups and provide insight into the general implications for the over-all personality of the individual who is confronted by the need to make appropriate adjustments. Today, we may go further.

Before we proceed, it may be well to re-establish the fundamentals of the social psychologist's approach to personality. To do this I should like to quote rather extensively from *The Principles of Psychology,* by William James—I am sure my friends in Sociology will pardon my ethnocentrism at this point, no disparagement nor neglect of Cooley and Mead is intended.

Properly speaking, *a man has as many social selves as there are individuals who recognize him* and carry an image of him in their mind. . . . But as the individuals who carry the images fall naturally into classes, we may practically say that he has as many different social selves as there are distinct *groups* of persons about whose opinion he cares. He generally shows a different side of himself, to each of these different groups. Many a youth who is demure enough before his parents and teachers, swears and swaggers like a pirate among his "tough" young friends. We do not show ourselves to our children as to our club . . . companions, to our customers as to the laborers we employ, to our own masters and employers as to our intimate friends. From this there results what practically is a division of the man into several selves, and this may be a discordant splitting, as where one is afraid to let one set of his acquaintances know him as he is elsewhere; or it may be a perfectly harmonious division of labor, as where one tender to his children is stern to the soldiers or prisoners under his command (7, I, 294).

And a bit further on, James considers the rivalry and conflict of the different selves thus:

With most objects of desire, physical nature restricts our choice to but one of many represented goods, and even so it is here. I am often confronted by the necessity of standing by one of my empirical selves, and relinquishing the rest. Not that I would not, if I could, be both handsome and fat and well dressed, and a great athlete, and make a million a year, be a wit, a *bon-vivant,* and a lady-killer, as well as a philosopher; a philanthropist, statesman, warrior, and African explorer, as well as a "tone-poet" and saint. But the thing is simply impossible. The millionaire's work would run counter to the saint's; the *bon-vivant* and the philanthropist would trip each other up; the philosopher and the lady-killer could not well keep house in the same tenement of clay (7, I, 309).

At this point I will stop the quotation for in his further development of the theme, James emphasizes the selection of a single self and the suppression of other possible alternatives. Essentially he resolves the problems of conflict among alternatives by assuming repression of all but one. Though his discussion starts, as we have noted, with an emphasis on the multiplicity of selves, in his elaboration he shifts to a more unitary conception.

An extract from Stonequist's report maintains the perspective a bit more consistently from our point of view:

> The concept of role in the group provides a frame of reference within which various traits play their parts both as causes and consequences of the role. Thus intelligence may help to make an individual into a leader, and the role of leadership in turn produces certain personality traits, such as self-confidence. But, since the individual usually belongs to several groups in each of which he has a role, his personality has multiple facets. Thence arises the problem of harmonizing and integrating his various selves, so that a stable character and meaningful inner life can be achieved. To the degree that the individual lives in a society where change is rapid, and where different codes of conduct exist, his problem of achieving a harmonious personality and a stable character is correspondingly increased (1, p. 210).

Here we have our problem somewhat more directly stated, first with respect to the "individual" in terms of multiple group memberships providing a multiplicity of roles which are to be integrated into a more pervasive personality or character (in James's terminology, the integration of the selves and the ego, the me's and the I), and second with respect to the societal and cultural factors which influence the establishment of obstacles to such integration.

Linton's restatement of this general approach in what is currently called "status personality" theory raises the problem again, but adds little to the phase that concerns us here. After offering redefinitions of the terms *status* and *role* and illustrating the multiplicity of roles as a function of the many statuses (or positions) the individual has, Linton states:

> The fact that the individual's various statuses are activated at different times prevents a head-on collision. . . .
>
> In the rare cases in which, through some accident, statuses whose roles are fundamentally incompatible converge upon the same individual, we have the material of high tragedy . . . (8, p. 80).
>
> Such conflicts rarely arise in primary societies or even within larger social groupings which have persisted for some time and developed well-integrated cultures. However, they may become fairly frequent under the conditions existing in our current society. Under the necessity of reorganizing our social structure to meet the needs of a new technology and of a spatial mobility un-

paralleled in human history, our inherited system of statuses and roles is breaking down; while a new system, compatible with the actual conditions of modern life, has not yet emerged. The individual thus finds himself frequently
confronted by situations in which he is uncertain both of his own statuses and
roles and of those of others. He is not only compelled to make choices, but
also can feel no certainty that he has chosen correctly and that the reciprocal
behavior of others will be that which he anticipates on the basis of the statuses
which he has assumed that they occupy. This results in numerous disappointments and frustrations (**8**, pp. 81–82).

Time after time we are led to the brink, but practically never does
the analysis flow over into the psychological processes involved. The
problem is not a minor one; practically, it concerns us all in very much
of our functioning. It is involved in daily incidents, not solely in critical events. Consider, for example, in my own case—when I was invited
to participate in this series of meetings, my decision involved the interaction of my professional and family group memberships. At the beginning of the fortnight I had scheduled for the preparation of this
paper, I was called for jury duty. My conflict did not involve ambivalence toward service, but rather the mutually exclusive requirements
of my college group membership, my conference group membership,
and my community group membership. (Oh, yes, I served.) At the
present moment, I am relating myself to you in a role defined by our
common conference group, though there is a strong temptation to yield
to the more informal friendship-group derived role which I have with
many of you and which I anticipate during the discussion period may
obtain.

At home, when my daughters raise questions about their school-day,
their teachers, their classmates, do I respond within the attitude and
value framework of my respectable middle-class position, my professional orientation, my teacher loyalties, my father role? Most, well, if
not literally *most,* certainly *many* social situations are potentially as
ambiguous, as capable of being structured and restructured in different
ways, as any ink-blot.

Lest we get the impression from the references to our contemporary,
rapidly changing society that conflict of group memberships is historically a new problem, let me cite a few illustrations from an earlier
day. The mutiny of the British fleet in 1797 offers many interesting
examples. The war with France had started in 1793 and by 1797 Eng-

land stood practically alone, her major allies defeated and Napoleon Bonaparte brilliantly victorious. The seamen, subjected to many abuses, after a series of vain efforts to secure improvement of their lot, finally organized and on the 16th of April, when Lord Bridport ordered the Channel Fleet to put to sea, the sailors refused. The Navy was in open mutiny, and in the midst of the prosecution of a war. This is not the place to go into a discussion of the events leading up to the mutiny nor the way in which it was resolved. For those interested, I can heartily recommend a perusal of "The Floating Republic" by G. E. Manwaring and B. Dobrée (9). Only two incidents are of particular interest to us here. The mutineers insisted that they were loyal Englishmen, loyal to their king and country, but that they were rebelling against the administration within the Admiralty. They announced publicly that they would maintain their ships in seaworthy condition, and if the enemy fleet set forth, they would sail to do them battle, but that otherwise they would not lift anchor nor obey the commands of the officers until their grievances were adjusted. On the 17th of April, the *Romney* and the *Venus* were detailed for convoy duty to Newfoundland, but their crews refused to set sail, preferring to stand by the mutineers. The General Assembly of Delegates, the central governing body of the mutinous fleet, however, expressed the "desire and earnest wish" that the two crews comply with the orders, and on the 20th they did (9, p. 40). Here the mutineers felt that their national group membership required a continuance of trade, as well as sympathy from the trading middle class for their cause—in effect they established common group membership with the populace while retaining their disciplined mutiny against the Admiralty.

The second incident I find even more startling as evidence of the operation of the national group membership functioning in the midst of what must have been a situation fraught with tremendous affect, that is membership of sailors mutinying in time of war. ". . . on Wednesday, [the] 19th the Prince of Württemberg—who was about to marry the Princess Royal—came to Portsmouth to receive its freedom, Lords Spencer and Bridport, with Sir William Pitt, Governor, took him round the Fleet in all the gay panoply of the commissioner's barge" (9, p. 54). Can you picture the situation . . . the First Lord of the Admiralty, the Admiral of the Fleet, and the Governor taking a distinguished foreign visitor on a tour of state through their Fleet in full mutiny; and—the sailors in full mutiny turning out to "salute the cruising dignitaries"?

The annals of mutiny and piracy are replete with material for analysis of multiple group membership, but I feel that for the present enough has been presented to establish the validity of looking to the reference groups of the individual to understand the role he assumes in structuring a social stimulus field.

IDENTIFICATION

As a first step in our analysis of the general problem, I would like to consider the nature of identification with a group. The infant, born into a family, plays a role in the group, but until in some way he establishes the boundary, develops a symbol which will serve to represent the family group as distinct from out-groups, or even a generalized not-family category, he can hardly be said to have developed a group identification. Often we find in developmental studies identification with a verbal symbol before the term is understood in a conventional way. The child who is taught a sex identification as boy or girl becomes attached to the word, ego-involved with the symbol, long before there is any appreciation of the social significance of the term. Studies of the development of identification as Negro, Jew, American show similar trends. By the time the child is 5 or 6 years old, in our society, he tends to have such ethnic identifications, but until he is 9 or 10 he is unable to deal with the sort of abstract concepts necessary to understand the full implications of these terms (10). Nevertheless, the group identification functions in his own age integration as well as for the perceptions of others in dealing with him as a social stimulus.

At the more mature level, not only does the individual identify with the verbal symbol for the group, but this process is reinforced through integration with the variety of denotational and connotational meanings which the symbol has for him. The person can articulate a consensually validated symbol for his group membership and be reasonably accurate in delimiting his fellow members and in identifying through appropriate tests who is and who is not a member of the group.

Where we are dealing with an individual whose affective organization involves rejection of a group membership, I would expect the same cognitive processes to be involved, that is, symbolization and delimitation, but integrated in a different fashion into the dynamics of the personality. Just as recent experimental studies have demonstrated that words with negative connotations require more illumination before the threshold for perception is reached than do neutral or positively toned words (e.g., 11) and by virtue of the significant resistance to response indicate that in some way the organism has perceived them; so might we assume that there is comparable unconscious perception of denied or rejected group membership.

GROUP ROLE

Systematic studies in social psychology generally conceive of roles as differentiations within the social aggregate which originated to facilitate the successful prosecution of the group tasks. Each role is defined in terms of its reciprocal relationships with other roles in the group. Each role-player, therefore, must function in terms of acceptable expectancies of other roles with which he is interrelated. The role is essentially defined by what the members of a group expect of an individual who occupies any given position in the group. As a member of the group, an individual shares with others, within the limits of the variability which might be expected under the general rubric of "individual differences," and expects this behavior of himself when he occupies a particular position. His general group membership thus establishes his performance goal, his ego-ideal for that particular function.

Varying with the size of the group, its complexity, the actual interaction of the individual members, the mobility within the group, each individual, though he plays but one role, shares in the definition of others through his expectancies which function as demands on those individuals playing the other roles with which he interacts. To this extent, the individual, while playing his role, is practising other roles and assimilates a mastery of the variety of the intra-group roles to which he has access. It should be noted that our emphasis here is on the role definition, what is expected of an individual in a given position. In actual practice, though he may share such expectancies, he may not have the skills required nor the temperaments appropriate for a successful performance in the role.

However, an individual often finds himself in a situation in which his role is that of a representative of a group. In the field of international negotiations, delegates from different countries will often have carefully designated roles. They will partake of a conference role as a national representative. When delegates are instructed, the factors governing much of their functioning within the conference are sufficiently obvious to require little attention from a psychologist. But what of the uninstructed delegate? What of the completely untrained group representative? The individual who is well integrated into a group, is thoroughly familiar with numerous intra-group role requirements, suddenly finds himself in a social situation with an out-grouper in which his role is essentially that of an uninstructed, untrained group representative. Let me illustrate this to provide a more concrete form for our thinking. When I talk with my colleagues at the City College in New York, my role as a member of the Psychology Department is reasonably precise and well-practised. When I talk with one of my neighbors who teaches History at another institution, I find myself speaking as a City College man. When I develop a social relationship with fellow psychologists, I am a social psychologist; if I find myself in other contexts, I may be an academician, a social scientist, a professional, an intellectual, a New Yorker, an Easterner or an American. In such cases my role is that of an undifferentiated representative of a group, a group role, rather than the social role we generally think of, a differentiation within a group.

GROUP STATUS

Just as we customarily think of role as differentiation within a group, so do we think of status as stemming from the hierarchical arrangement of positions within the group. But in a situation in which an individual plays a group role his status will stem from the group as a whole and not from his particular position in the group; he will have the group's status. When I, a teacher, talk with a successful businessman about living comforts, I have, essentially, a low status. When I, a City College person, talk with a representative of another college, to achieve high status, I'll talk basketball.

ETHNOCENTRISM

If the presentation to this point is acceptable, that is that group role and group status are valid concepts phenomenologically, then we must acknowledge the extension that the interaction of two individuals each playing a group role can only occur within the framework of some larger common group membership. Certainly group status is completely meaningless unless taken within the framework of a larger common group membership. My illustration of relating to the businessman is predicated on the comparative positions of teachers and entrepreneurs in the framework of earners; basketball is a determinant of status within the frame of reference of sport fans. Our group role, our group status are still differentiations within a larger, more inclusive group. BUT it may well be that the larger group is one for which we have little, if any, feeling of identification, and little, if any, experience in role-playing. The individual who plays a group role without awareness of and practice in the larger group cannot relate to others smoothly.

In the reference to the mutinous fleet at Portsmouth, earlier, to my relations with my children, and with the national delegate to the United Nations General Assembly or the Congressman or the State Legislator or the campus student-government members, the multiplicity of group memberships are expected, the alternate frames of reference clear, and the expectancies of interaction shared. The problem which may arise is the selection of a particular reference group which will structure the situation for the individuals. Where an individual is playing a group role and unaware of the requirements in the larger group context, he will tend to play it in accord with the unilaterally derived definition stemming from the group itself. Such a group role, unchecked by recognition of reciprocal responsibilities and needs to co-operate, to share in the goal strivings with other groups, will almost inevitably be one of exaggerated self-importance to which terms like conceited, overbearing, egotistical might be applied—in short, an illusion of perspective because only a single stimulus point is available without an anchorage point or an attendant frame of reference, in short, almost back to the autokinetic phenomenon. Failure to adjust to the multiple group membership, to a recognition of the common ground of a larger common group gives us ethnocentrism.

Illustrative of the ineffectiveness of certain forms of education to overcome ethnocentrism is the anecdote which concluded with the proof that English is the best language in the world—take knife for example. The Germans call it *Messer,* the French call it *canif,* the Danes call it *kniv,* while the English call it *knife,* and that's what it really is.

Ethnocentrism in one form or another is a major obstacle to the development of the sort of world we all seek. It is to be found as a component in all inter-group conflicts at the international and local levels. Individual A playing a group role A interacts with Individual B playing group role B. Unless there is recognition of the common group C within which each has a part, A will attempt to deal with B in the light of the norms of A, that is, ethno- or sociocentrically. Such behavior cannot be completely sensible to B if he is functioning without regard to A norms. Improvement in the relationship will arise as each discovers C, the common group, identifies with it, and learns his social role within this framework. Of course, some situations lead to an accommodation pattern in which, through a differential in power, B, for example, is absorbed into the A norms and plays a role defined by the dominant A norms. Experience with this form of adjustment in minority group relations, industrial relations and international relations would suggest that this rarely, if ever, is acceptable to group B individuals since the lowered status within A presents too great a contrast with the self roles which stem from B.

The analysis here is, of course, completely abstract, but I think there would be little difficulty in applying it to our major social conflicts. Developing suitable educational procedures might be very difficult when there is little tangibility to the larger common groups and little opportunity to practice the roles that would be appropriate for group representatives in such a context—but that is another problem.

To this point, regardless of how others may perceive it, I feel I am on relatively solid ground. But this changes as soon as I confront the problem: If A knows his via-C group relationship, why does he at times deal with B on the basis of A alone or of D? Why, during the war, did people interact so often on the basis of their national group membership, and since the war, revert to interaction on the basis of their various sub-group memberships? Why, in any one situation where several alternative frames of reference are equally valid, will one rather than another be selected? The problem is essentially similar to that which confronts the student of thinking—how and why does one rather than another mode of attack emerge to structure the field for an individual —except that more ego is involved in the social functions than in ordinary problem solving.

Since in my posing of the problem I am deliberately barring situational factors from being definitive, I am forced to turn for suggestions to learning theory, perception theory, motivation theory—in short, to fundamental personality theory.

Though from many points of view, particularly within the audience, the time allotted this paper is over-long—it does not permit even a beginning to be made in the development of a coherent synthesis from the wide variety of fundamental psychological theories that would have to be brought to bear on our problem, and of course, there are many others present who are far more competent to do it than I.

SELF AND EGO

Unwilling, therefore, to turn to general psychology at this time, I should like to continue the discussion within the same frame of reference I have been using. The emphasis on the multiplicity of organized social selves within the individual does not by any means imply a rejection of some basic principles of organization which may be referred to as a master self, an ego back of the selves, an "I" functioning along with many "me's." Consider the evidence for such an "I" in our tendency to recognize certain groups as appropriate for us and others as inappropriate. Some roles would be in conflict; others, congruent. The physician can not identify with undertakers any more than his patients could accept such a role combination. The scientist and thug, the prizefighter and beautician, these are incongruent roles, incongruent group memberships not only in our perceptions of others but in our perception of ourselves. Once group identifications have been established, we cannot identify with certain other groups and retain our integrity—that is, our integration.

Genetically viewed, the baby born into a family has its first social learnings within the family milieu, learns its role, develops a self-image in the light of its social treatment by parents and sibs. As the child grows and begins to establish relations in other social groups, the first approaches will tend to be on the basis of the child's previous experiences. The rejected child will expect rejection, the accepted child will expect acceptance, and each child will behave in accordance with his expectations. Within obvious limits, further, the child will be treated in accordance with his expectancies. This tends to establish a certain amount of consistency, but as experiences continue within an ever-expanding number of groups with norms derived from more varied sources, differentiation ensues and divergent selves may be seen. But before he can accept identification with a new group, it must be congruent with an old. Once in a group, his line of development might be quite different from what would have been expected from an out-grouper's perspective, but the original step was within the framework of a previously integrated pattern. Group memberships are not *all* ascribed, most are achieved, many at considerable cost. Why do people join clubs, go to college, train for professions? It is because of past group memberships that they wish to establish new ones.[1]

I would expect, therefore, that the dynamics of development as de-scribed by the clinician, whether directive or non-directive, would con-tribute to our understanding of the progressive differentiation of selves from ego, of me's from I, and the dynamic of the relation of the resid-ual ego to its parts and the development at times of resyntheses among the parts.

The functioning of master self-image in the determination of spe-cific group selves may be seen in the social psychology of status. Hy-man's brilliant study of subjective status not only introduced the con-cept of reference group but provided much empirical data concerning self-estimates of status. Among these substantive findings is evidence that there tends to be substantial agreement between self-rating on "general status" and the sum of the self-ratings on the major specific dimensions of status for his subjects (12). Does this mean that the sub-jective general status is simply the subjective summation of specific statuses? Far from it. Benoit-Smullyan suggested an equilibration hy-pothesis—that the individual anchors himself at the point of his high-est status in any one dimension and tries to bring his status in all other dimensions up to a comparable point (13). Corroborative data for the equilibration hypothesis have been obtained in an Honors study at the City College. This study used an adaptation of Hyman's scale and had the respondents indicate both their present and desired subjective gen-eral status in five different reference groups. The data thus permitted objectification, crude though it may have been, of both present posi-tion and aspirations in each of several different groups. As was to have been expected in accordance with the equilibration hypothesis, the

---

strivings of individuals in the reference groups in which they rated their status lowest was significantly greater than their strivings in the groups in which they rated their present status highest (14).

Such evidence would suggest that the individual has a generalized image of his self which serves as a goal, an aspiration level to define his behavior in the different reference groups.

I repeat, explanation of selectivity among the selves will in part come from analysis of the relation between the selves and the "I." I am aware that in this audience there may be considerable objection to the terminology I have been using. Ego, Self, integration have various con-notations. I am not ego-involved in the words, but I am in the con-cepts. If "functional relatedness" [of "selves"] is denotationally the same as "ego" in my use of the word, I would willingly make an ex-change. But I feel that an understanding of the dynamics of functional relatedness—the nature of ego—can in large measure be improved through genetic study, through examination of the life history of the individual.

A second approach to the study of the interaction of the functional group memberships of the individual is synchronic rather than dia-chronic. Gregory Bateson, in his analysis of the Naven ceremony among the Iatmuls of New Guinea, found that a useful concept was one which he names "schismogenesis" and which he defined as "a proc-ess of differentiation in the norms of individual behavior resulting from cumulative interaction between individuals" (15, p. 175). He identified two forms of schismogenesis:

(1) symmetrical in which each behavior calls forth similar but more intense forms of response, and

(2) complementary in which each behavior induces more intense manifestation of a polar form of response.

Illustrations of the symmetrical schismogenesis may be seen in the rivalry of two children, starting with "My father can lick your father" and going on to a fitting climax, and in the interaction among the Bulldogs and the Red Devils as it developed in stage three of Professor Sherif's exciting and stimulating study, the preliminary report on which was presented before us on Sunday. Complementary schismo-genesis is often seen in the interaction of two individuals, one slightly more dominant than the other. The submissiveness of one calls forth more dominance of the other which increases the submissiveness of the first which is stimulus for still greater dominance and so on.

Bateson's presentation outlines a considerable extension of the theory of schismogenesis, utlizing illustrations and suggesting applications in the field of inter-group relations, inter-individual relations, and intra-individual relations.

My preliminary explorations in search of a suitable methodology for testing some hypotheses about schismogenesis are still too feeble to permit discussing. I am convinced, however, that empirical, controlled studies can be fruitfully developed in this area and that the principles of interaction among the systems within the individual can be experimentally studied. Some of my colleagues with whom I have discussed schismogenesis informally confess to a certain distaste for the word. Again, I must insist on holding no brief for any particular nomenclature, but I do wish to emphasize the need for studying further the dynamic relationships among the group memberships, among the roles within the individual. Whether we elaborate and test the hypotheses of Bateson or use the Adlerian conception of compensation or some other, the problem *is* capable of analysis and warrants, even demands, attention.

On Sunday, Professor Sherif presented a preliminary account of some of the data of one of the most stimulating studies of inter-group relations I know of. We do not have the full details of the study available as yet. I should like to extend my remarks, if he will permit, along the lines of thinking stimulated by his presentation. You recall, of course, that two small groups of boys, completely comparable, organized the Bulldogs and Red Devils under experimental conditions. Competitive attitudes developed, and were fostered, between the groups. In the face of prospective defeat, the attitudes in one group became exceedingly bitter. When a frustration in the form of an apparent act of aggression by one group was introduced into the situation, hostilities broke out and open conflict ensued.

Before we proceed to elaborate studies of basic personality, of the forms in which aggressive impulses are customarily dealt with, of the frustration-aggression hypotheses, of the application of fundamental cognitive, learning or judgment theories, ought we not, as Professor Sherif suggested, develop an analysis of the influence of the alternate frames of reference? It seemed clear that the development of a pattern of physical violence indirectly and directly expressed might well refer back to the general peer culture mentioned in the discussion of Dr. Barker's paper on Monday and the stockpiling of ammunition back to the still more general American norm.

Ought we not in our researches be seeking for the shifts in applicable reference groups? If behavior is referred to group norms, if the individual has many group memberships, if the regnant norms may be that of a social group not physically present, I would search in such dimensions to account for changes in social behavior. I would expect that our tasks as social psychologists would be to elaborate descriptions in such terms before seeking the explanatory concepts of either general psychology or of institutional analysis. If this is our task, then social psychologists, whether drawn from anthropology, psychology, or sociology, have the same job, can use the same frame of reference and can supplement one another by elaborating different dimensions of explanatory concepts.

REFERENCES

1. Stonequist, E. V. *The Marginal Man; a Study in Personality and Culture Conflict.* New York: Charles Scribner's Sons, 1937.
2. Park, R. E. Introduction to E. V. Stonequist, *The Marginal Man* (see 1).
3. See summary volume: Sutherland, R. L. *Color, Class and Personality.* Washington: American Council on Education, 1942.
4. Indian Education Research Project publications to date:
    Thompson, L., and Joseph, A. *The Hopi Way.* Chicago: University of Chicago Press, 1944.
    MacGregor, G. *Warriors Without Weapons.* Chicago: University of Chicago Press, 1946.
    Kluckhohn, C., and Leighton, D. *The Navaho.* Cambridge: Harvard University Press, 1946.
    Leighton, D., and Kluckhohn, C. *Children of the People.* Cambridge: Harvard University Press, 1947.
    Joseph, A., Spicer, R. B., and Chesky, J. *The Desert People.* Chicago: University of Chicago Press, 1949.
5. Leighton, A. H. *The Governing of Men; General Principles and Recommendations Based on Experience at a Japanese Relocation Camp.* Princeton: Princeton University Press, 1945.

6. Child, I. L.   *Italian or American? The Second Generation in Conflict.*
New Haven: Yale University Press, 1943.

7. James, W.   *The Principles of Psychology.*   New York: Henry Holt and
Co., 1890.

8. Linton, R.   *The Cultural Background of Personality.*   New York: Apple-
ton-Century-Crofts, 1945.

9. Manwaring, G. E., and Dobree, B.   *The Floating Republic; an Account
of the Mutinies at Spithead and the Nore in 1797.*   New York: Harcourt,
Brace & Co., 1935.

10. Hartley, E. L., Rosenbaum, M., and Schwartz, S.   Children's use of ethnic
frames of reference: an exploratory study of children's conceptualizations
of multiple ethnic group membership, *Journal of Psychology*, 1948, *26*,
367–386.
Hartley, E. L., et al.   Children's perceptions of ethnic group membership, *Journal of Psychology*, 1948, *26*, 387–398.
Hartley, E. L., and Krugman, D. C.   Note on children's role perception,
Journal of Psychology, 1948, *26*, 399–405.

11. McGinnies, E.   Emotionality and perceptual defense, *Psychological Review*, 1949, *56*, 244–251.

12. Hyman, H.   The psychology of status, *Archives of Psychology*, 1942, No.
269.

13. Benoit-Smullyan, E.   Status, status types and status interrelations, *American Sociological Review*, 1944, *9*, 151–161.

14. Fenchel, G. H., and Monderer, J.   The manipulation of status and status
equilibration in the multiple reference groups of college students.   Unpublished Honors paper, Psychology Department, The City College, New
York, 1949.

15. Bateson, G.   *Naven, a Survey of the Problems Suggested by a Composite
Picture of the Culture of a New Guinea Tribe Drawn from Three Points
of View.*   Cambridge: Cambridge University Press, 1936.

C H A P T E R   1 7

A Preliminary Experimental Study
of Inter-Group Relations[1]

MUZAFER SHERIF

University of Oklahoma

The main aim of this paper is to give a summary report of a preliminary experiment dealing with inter-group relations. It may be relevant at the outset to state briefly the approaches leading to the formulation of the study and hypotheses to be tested. Naturally the design and the points which will be particularly stressed follow the leads from these approaches.

The topic of inter-group relations is the most complex, the most baffling of all social psychological problems. This statement is, of course, a confession of ignorance. The study of group relations on the psychological side alone necessarily involves all major topics of psychology—motivation, judgment, perception, learning, attitudes, ego-involvements, effects of social situations, etc. These major topics are each in themselves far from being settled matters; they are still controversial topics. Some psychologists seem to advocate that from a strictly scientific point of view it might be wise to postpone tackling the problem of group relations until the basic topics of psychology are more or less established beyond being merely so many points of view of different schools.

But in the present-day world of flux, tension, and conflict among human groupings, the concern over group relations has forced itself into the foreground. As a consequence, several universities and other

---

[1] The fuller account of the study will be included in the book being prepared by the author on group relations, to be published by Harper.

organizations are rapidly making provision for the study of group relations. An ever-increasing number of social psychologists and men in related fields are moving to concentrate their work in this area. Taking note of the feeble and helpless state of academic discipline of social science today in comparison to the startling new developments in physical sciences, an increasing number of writers point out the urgency of making rapid strides in the study of human relations.

Although the need is urgent, real progress in the study of groups is still impeded by the well-worn grooves of certain historical approaches which were based on insufficient data and hence were one-sided. The alternative on the positive side is not the creation of a vast new terminology. We can more safely proceed by following the leads of a few well-grounded lines of facts, which seem to be converging.

One such well-grounded line is the fact that the individual reacts differentially as a member of group situations as compared with individual situations. His judgments, his perceptions, and his motives in group situations are determined not only by the individaul characteristics that he brings into the situation, but also by the structural properties of the group situation and his particular place in it. By structural properties of group situations I mean simply the reciprocal functional relationships that operate between different parts in a given situation at a given time. This basic fact has become almost a truism in social psychology on the basis of experiments carried out during the last two decades. The differential effects of even transitory group situations on various psychological processes such as "association" and affectivity, etc., were almost without exception discovered in the experiments of the previous decades. The varied findings of this earlier period concerning such differential effects acquire more integrated significance when viewed in terms of the structural effects mentioned above, rather than as merely added or subtracted "social increments" and "social decrements." In short, the differential effect of group situations is not an additive process.

Such differential reactions do not pop up suddenly in group situations alone. The judgment of a stimulus within or outside of a scale, within limits, is not determined only by its individual properties, but also by its relation to other parts of the scale which set the limits, that is, the main anchoring points. Likewise, properties of a perception are determined by the reciprocal effects of all internal and external factors that operate at the given time, the totality of which constitute the *frame of reference* of the reaction in question. If even the perception of simple lines and circles is determined not only by their own properties in isolation, but as structurally affected by the presence of other stimuli at the moment, it is a sterile effort to try to build up the account of reactions of the individual members in social situations on the basis of the discrete accounts of the individual and stimulus situation. This consideration becomes even more imperative when we realize that social situations are more complex and at times more compelling than the presence of lines or other stimuli in the proximity, or than some experimentally introduced anchorages.

The above line of evidence was included in this chapter after some hesitation. It is stated and demonstrated in any elementary textbook. Yet the implications of this basic fact for our problem and certain historically important modes of approach are crucial.

For example, in his "Group Psychology and Analysis of the Ego" (1), Freud states: "From our point of view we need not attribute so much importance to the appearance of new characteristics. For us it would be enough to say that in a group the individual is brought under conditions which allow him to throw off the repressions of his unconscious instincts. The apparently new characteristics which he then displays are in fact the manifestations of this unconscious, in which all that is evil in the human mind is contained as a predisposition" (pp. 9–10).

It seems to me that the whole indication of the findings of the experimental work of the last fifteen years or so is in the opposite direction—that is, in the direction of emphasizing the major importance of *the new characteristics* generated in group situations. In the current attempts to eliminate prejudice, hostility, and other harmful attitudes, and to build up new identifications, the positive effects of the group situations are being brought into the foreground as perhaps the most effective method.

To be sure, there are cases of group situations which produce effects conducive to aggressive, cruel, and impulsive actions on the part of an individual member (e.g., a lynching party). These cases represent one kind of the differential effects of group situations. On the other hand, there are other cases of the differential effects of group situations which are conducive to behavior of a high degree of coöperation, solidarity, and, at times, self-sacrifice hardly possible if the individual stopped to calculate in isolation the pros and cons of the consequences.

Another example of such one-sided emphasis in dealing with group relations is represented by the attempts to solve everything through *leadership* alone. Of course leadership is important and exerts greater influence in the orientation of the group, for good or for bad, than do other parts of the group. But this influence of leadership is limited within certain bounds. Leaders who go too far beyond these bounds are repudiated. The leadership position is also within the hierarchical scale of positions of the group. The attempts based on the assumption of unlimited powers of leadership in the solution of group problems do not, therefore, promise solutions of lasting value.

Of course, the most flagrant illustration of misleading and, in this case, thoroughly untenable approaches is any *racist doctrine* which attempts to explain the gaps and conflicts among human groupings on the basis of alleged inherent superiority or inferiority of the groups in question. To this audience I hardly need mention the fallacy of race doctrines. Such doctrines are nothing but self-righteous justifications of the beneficiary groups for the purpose of perpetuating existing inter-group relationships.

The adequate line of approach to the problem of group relations is, then, the study of the experience and behavior of individuals in intra-group and inter-group relations as affected by the group situation and group membership. Therefore, it becomes imperative to study the individual's inter-group behavior on the level of differential experience and behavior as affected by his actual participation in the group activity in progress or as affected by his membership in his group when he is reacting alone to other groups or their members. This does not preclude the study of his special personal motives, attitudes, intelligence, and other individual capacities. On the contrary, the very notion of differential experience and behavior is meaningless unless two kinds of data are related to each other: (1) data concerning individual motives, attitudes, characteristics, and capacities of the individual, (2) data concerning products generated in the group situation.

In concrete terms this means the necessity for studying group relations on the group level. It is almost stupid to make tautological statements like this, but, unfortunately, the tenacity of outworn approaches forces one to make such statements. The extrapolation from the individual motives, attitudes, characteristics, traits, and capacities *alone* in explaining group phenomena have led us up blind alleys. As psychologists, even of the social brand, neither can we be satisfied by merely noting the characteristic features and trend of the group as a whole; we must make our observations in terms of the reactions of single individual members and as intensively as possible. Therefore, at this early stage, we, as social psychologists, can deal only with intra- and inter-group relations of small groups, whose individual members can be singled out and observed in space and time. Since small groups do possess at least the minimum structural characteristics or features of groups of any size, the likelihood is that we can more effectively extend the generalizations obtained from them to the inter-group relations of larger social units than has been the case heretofore.

The *informally* or *spontaneously* structured small groups such as cliques and gangs are particularly suited for our purpose. The *formally* organized small groups, such as an army squad or staff members of a university department, have features which make them unsuitable for such studies. In the formally organized groups there are too many outside pulls and pushes which are themselves highly complex. For example, in a formally organized small group, such as a small army unit, the statuses of members are assigned from without, as are the major rules and regulations.

In informally or spontaneously structured small groups, whatever status a member acquires, and the upward or downward shifts from it, are determined by the interaction of individual members within the group, each member with ascertainable personal motives, characteristics, and capacities. Even the leader himself is not appointed from without, with instructions to behave in specific ways. He achieves a position of leadership in the process of group interaction through personal characteristics that enable him to move to the top in that particular group. In such spontaneously structured groups, whatever decisions, standards, or norms are upheld and followed are the ones that either generate in the process of group interaction or are adopted by the group as their own. It seems to me that the inter-group harmony and alliance, friction and conflict, among these informally structured groups embody some crucial prototype illustrations of the inter-group relations of larger social structures.

With such considerations in mind, since 1936 I have been trying to learn as much as possible about these informally organized in-group structures. The works of such investigators as Thrasher, Zorbaugh, Clifford Shaw, and William Whyte are highly illuminating in this respect. The accumulating data on clique formation and functioning coming both from psychologists and sociologists are organically related to the work of these investigators. A survey of data dealing with other kinds of informally structured small groups will further elucidate these converging lines of research.

The social psychologist cannot help finding in the above works, accumulating since the 1920's, results which fit with the emerging trend of the last fifteen years or so in his own field. In the sociological works mentioned above, one finds concrete and recurring illustrations of the facts of differential experience and behavior, the rise of standardized group norms, the formulation of group decisions, the interdependence of the reactions of the individual members on functional reciprocal relationships within the group structure. This literature also offers ample evidence of the considerable determination of the behavior of individuals in inter-group relations on the basis of their group membership.

The survey of literature on informally structured small groups forces one to take note of certain features which are common to all such small groups. We take our lead to the study of inter-group relations from the implications derived from these features. (In this connection I am deliberately using the empirical and harmless word "feature" without putting any special conceptual significance into it. Each one of these features embody one or more basic topics of psychology, namely motivation, perception, judgment, learning, attitudes, ego-involvements, individual differences, etc.) The following *four* are certainly among the features that stand out in any of these informally structured groups. Here I can only cite them briefly. Elsewhere, I have said a little more about each one of them (2).

1. There are common *motivational* factors that bring the eventual group members into interaction and that determine the shorter or longer duration of this interaction. In the case of one group, the *dominant* motivational factor may be material deprivation, such as deprivation of food; in the second group the *dominant motivational* factor may be sex; in the third it may be *insecurity;* in the fourth it may be

recognition and *social prestige,* etc. It is factually erroneous, therefore, to posit any one single motive (such as Eros or sex, hunger, or some alleged ego-drive) as a sovereign instinct, drive, or need which holds groups together in every case.

The dominant motivational factor, whatever it may be, certainly is a weighty determinant of the direction of the particular activities of the group, the character of group products that will arise in time, and the determination of the special statuses and roles each member will occupy.

Once the statuses and group products become more or less stabilized for the group (as we shall see in features 3 and 4), the ways and means of satisfying even the dominant motive which was initially responsible in bringing the individuals together tend to be regulated in terms of the group structure.

2. Now a few words on the *second feature,* namely, the *differential effects of group interaction* on the experience and behavior of individual members. Not only motives, but all the psychological functions, feeling, perceiving, judging, thinking, and reasoning, etc., are modified in group situations. As we have said, the differential effects of group situations are not merely additive or subtractive affairs. Rather, they are *structural* changes which can be adequately understood in terms of their *membership-character* in relation to the total situation. This key concept of *membership-character,* so rightly stressed by Wertheimer, Köhler, Koffka, and Lewin, is indispensable for any understanding of group situations.

These structural changes, I must stress again, do not pop up only in group situations, as some leading sociologists like Durkheim and his influential school advocate. They are observed in the perception and behavior of the individual in any kind of situation in which new factors enter with a certain measurable degree of weight or compellingness.

3. Now I come to the *third feature,* and this embodies the promise of the starting point for a more adequate study of group relations. If the group interaction is not a transitory affair, but lasts for some time, a *more or less* stable group structure takes shape, with established, though by no means immutable, *statuses* and *roles* for individual members, from the leader on down. Groups are necessarily hierarchical affairs. The smooth functioning of group activities requires a hierarchi-

cal organization and more or less stabilized roles, which imply more or less stabilized relationships in terms of reciprocal expectations, etc.

With the stabilization of the group structure with relative statuses, which I repeat are not immutable and frozen, corresponding relative weights of *power* arise among the individual members. These *power* relationships are among the topics that are sorely neglected by the majority of social psychologists today. In view of the overstressed emphasis on getting the *leaders* of various groups into a conference room and settling all the points of conflict by discussions there, it should be pointed out that the status and power of the leaders, even though greater than that of others, are not unlimited. The leadership position, too, is a position within the hierarchical scale of the group. If the leader steps out *beyond certain bounds* in his group or in conference with the leaders of other groups, he also is subject to the correctives of the group (drop in his position, loss of prestige, repudiation, being dropped out altogether, and even severely punished).

From the point of view of inter-group relations, the most important consequence of group structuring is the delineation of *in-group* from *out-groups*. The development of in-group and "we-experience" is accompanied by the demarcation and setting of boundaries from out-groups. All these in-group delineations and the setting of boundaries from out-groups are reflected through self-justifying, self-glorifying, and self-righteous attitudes about the in-group and gradations of friendly or hostile attitudes concerning the out-groups thus marked off. The possibilities suggested by the fact of in-group and out-group delineation provide us with a sound basis for the formulation of hypotheses concerning inter-group relations.

4. The *fourth* feature of these groups is the rise of a set of standards, values, or *norms*. In groups in which no standardized norms exist, such norms arise in the course of group interaction. The major *ego-attitudes* of the individual member are formed as a result of his membership in the group and his other reference groups. As this point is expanded elsewhere, I shall not take time now to elaborate it.

The above features concerning intra- and inter-group relations unmistakably point the directions for an adequate program of a coördinated series of experiments in this vital area. Also, they warn us against drawing conclusions concerning inter-group relations on the basis of the properties of in-group relations only. To date, experimental studies of group relations have concentrated mainly on intra-group relations. Kurt Lewin and his associates have demonstrated the differential effects on individual members of different group situations created by three different types of leadership—namely, democratic, autocratic, and laissez-faire. Yet the democratic, autocratic, and laissez-faire character of *in-group relations* thus produced do not necessarily determine the character of *inter-group relations*. For example, in Lewin's experiment friction occurred between the democratic and laissez-faire groups and a "war" broke out. The democratic group did not stop to think of a democratic way to settle the affair: democratic procedure was something to be practiced within the group. The fight that developed was hardly a democratic method of solution. In short, in-group democracy does not necessarily imply democracy toward out-groups, even though we may preach it.

Therefore, it becomes imperative to consider the consequence of in-group formation in relation to other groups. This will give us more promising leads in handling inter-group problems such as group tension and group prejudice.

As we noted in citing the main features of in-groups, one of the products of group formation is a delineation of *"we"* and *"they"*—the *"we"* including the members of the in-group. The *"we"* thus delineated comes to embody a whole host of qualities and values to be upheld, defended, and cherished. Offenses from without or deviations from within are promptly reacted to with appropriate corrective, defensive, and, at times, offensive measures. A set of values, "traits," or stereotypes are attributed to all those groups and individuals who comprise the *"they"* group from the point of view of the *"we"* group. Such attributed traits may be favorable, unfavorable, or both, depending upon the nature of the relations between the groups in question. If the interests, directions, or goals of the inter-group relationship in question are integrated or harmonious, the *"they"* group is pictured in a positive or favorable light. However, if the activities and functional views of the two interacting groups clash, then the characteristics attributed to the out-group are negative and derogatory. If one group takes the position that another group is in its way, that for some reason the other group interferes with the goals or interests of the *"we"* group, or that it should be working in the interest of the *"we"* group, all sorts of stereotypes develop to justify this position. All race-superiority doctrines are deliberate or unconscious justifications for this kind of relationship.

This fact, in favor of which ample evidence can be piled up from the sociological studies of small groups as well as from race-relations studies, comes out also in experiments which are *not* primarily designed to study in-group and out-group delineation. For example, in the study of Sears, Hovland, and Miller (3) of the effects of frustration caused primarily by sleep deprivation, it was observed that an in-group formation was in the making. Jokes and unflattering adjectives were bestowed not only against the experimenters in question, but against psychologists in general. Likewise, in the Minnesota starvation study during World War II, the men sharing semistarvation "built up a tremendous in-group feeling that tended to exclude both their non-starving friends and administrative and technical staff" (4). In short, the world was delineated into "haves" and "have-nots," with appropriate attitudes.

A PRELIMINARY STUDY OF INTER-GROUP RELATIONS

The indications of the converging lines achieved by the experimental work of psychologists, and the rich sociological findings on small groups, show us the way to formulate more fruitful problems, hypotheses, and experimental designs concerning the vital topic of inter-group relations. The study reported in broad outline in this paper stems from the above considerations.

This study of group relations was conducted in a camp in Northern Connecticut during the summer of 1949 with the active and generous backing of Professor Carl I. Hovland, chairman of the Department of Psychology, Yale University.[2] It was carried out in the conviction that experimental study of the essential variables underlying group tension will contribute effectively to a more realistic approach to problems of inter-group tensions in actual life situations. The study represents an attempt to include within a single experimental design the study of in-group properties and of inter-group relations. The dominant idea in its conception was to create controlled situations which would make

---

[2] The study was financed by a grant to Yale University from the research division of the American Jewish Committee, N. Y. I am deeply grateful to the Committee and its director of the research division, Dr. Samuel Flowerman, for the grant.

possible (1) the formation and functioning of in-groups, and (2) inter-group relations between these experimentally produced in-groups.

On the basis of lessons learned from the sociological and psychological study of the properties of small in-groups and functional relationships between in-groups, the following hypotheses were formulated:

1. When individuals having no established relationships are brought together in a group situation to interact in group activities with common goals, they produce a group structure with hierarchical positions and roles within it. The group structure tends in time to generate by-products or *norms* peculiar to the group, such as common attitudes, positive in-group identifications, nicknames, catchwords, etc.

2. The second part of the hypothesis is related directly to inter-group relations. If two in-groups thus formed are brought into functional relationship, positive or negative out-group attitudes and appropriate friendly or hostile actions in relation to the out-group and its members will arise, depending upon the harmony or friction between the goals of the two groups. The testing of this hypothesis also involves in prototype form the process of the rise of group stereotypes.

The *third part of the hypothesis* is related to individual achievements and strivings for position within the in-groups as determined by more or less unique individual factors. Since this aspect of the study will be presented elsewhere, we need not deal with it in this broad presentation.[3]

Subjects

In order to test these hypotheses, it was necessary to eliminate, insofar as possible, group formation and positive or negative relations between groups on the basis of background factors such as ethnic differences and differences in class, religion, education, age, sex, etc. In short, the subject had to be *homogeneous* in as many background and individual respects as possible.

Interviews were held with parents of prospective subjects in their homes and with the ministers of their church groups. Information sheets were filled in for each subject, including the relevant background material as well as the subject's interests, play-group activities, school experiences, etc.

---

[3] A complete report of the study will be incorporated in a book being prepared for Harper and Brothers under the title, *Group Relations.*

The possibility of grouping together on the basis of previous acquaintance was minimized by selecting subjects from different neighborhoods and towns of the New Haven area, such as West Haven and Hamden. There were thus no definitely established friendship bonds among the subjects.

Prior to the experiment, several tests were administered to the subjects by Professor Richard Wittenborn and Dr. Elmer Potter at the Yale Psychology Department. The tests were deliberately administered prior to the appearance of the subjects at the experimental situation. In order to prevent any suspicion on the part of the subjects that these tests would be related to observations of their behavior in the main experimental situation, the test administrators never appeared on the scene while the experiment was in progress. The tests given included an intelligence test, the Rosenzweig Picture-Frustration test, and selected pictures of the TAT.

In attempting to satisfy this criterion of *homogeneity* of subjects, we selected 24 boys of about twelve years of age, all coming from settled American families of the lower middle-class income group in the New Haven area. All of the boys were Protestants. In fact, 19 came from the same denomination, and the other 5 from highly similar denominations. The educational opportunities and backgrounds of the boys were similar. The group had a mean I.Q. of 104.8. All the boys might be called more or less "normal"; none were "behavior problems."

With these factors equated as much as possible, the kind of groupings, statuses within groups, and attitudes which were to be produced between groups could not be attributed to such cultural and social background factors as ethnic, religious, or class differences, or to existing friendship bonds.

The possibility remained that the formation of a particular in-group might be determined chiefly by personal preferences or attractions among the boys, or by their common personal interests. It was necessary, therefore, to plan the experiment in such a way that the weight of personal preferences and interests and personality factors between the experimental groups could be neutralized.

Design and Procedure

Stage I was planned as the period of spontaneous groupings on the basis of personal inclinations and interests. All activities were camp-wide, with a maximum of freedom and "mixing up" of the boys in various games and camp duties. Thus, it became possible to ascertain budding friendship groups and, more or less, to equate the weight of personal factors in the two experimental groups of Stage II.

Stage II was designed as the *stage of in-group formation* of two experimental groups as similar in composition as possible. Each experimental group would participate separately in activities involving all of the members of the group. Activities were chosen on the basis of their motivational appeal and their involvement of the whole group. Different activities afforded varied situations in which all members of a group could find opportunity to participate and "shine." All rewards given in this stage were made on a group-unit basis, not to particular individuals.

Stage III was planned to study *inter-group relations* between the two experimental in-groups thus produced when brought into contact (a) in a series of competitive activities and situations, and (b) in mildly frustrating situations caused by one group to the other. The frustrating situations were arranged in such a way that the blame or responsibility for the frustration would be placed on the experimental groups and not on the adults in the situation.

The particular activities chosen in the three stages were selected from those for which the boys themselves expressed preference. They were timed in terms of the demands of the three stages of the study. Thus the activity and situations in which the boys participated had the motivational value of life situations and were not simply situations prescribed by adults. They will be described in more detail later.

The experiment was conducted at an isolated camp site near the Massachusetts state line and lasted for eighteen days. The nearest town was eight miles away, and there was no bus service in the neighborhood; consequently there were no distractions from neighborhood soda fountains, movies, townspeople, etc. Neither boys nor staff members were permitted to have any visitors during the course of the study.

The site consisted of about 125 acres of land, largely hills and timber, with a stream suitable for swimming and fishing running through it. There were two bunkhouses, a mess hall, kitchen, infirmary, administration building, latrines, etc., and broad level areas for athletic events.

Before giving a more detailed description of the three stages of the experiment and the main results, it is necessary to emphasize the techniques of observation and the role of adults in the camp. Of course, it is well known that individuals behave differently when they know they are being observed or studied, especially by psychologists. The consideration cannot be "allowed for" or explained away. Therefore, all those associated with the study were strongly urged to prevent the boys' suspecting that their behavior was being observed or that various periods of camp activities were planned. The parents and boys were simply told that new methods in camping were being tried out.

The bulk of observational data was obtained by two participant observers who were graduate students. They acted as counselors to the two experimental groups. Each participant observer had the assistance of a junior counselor who was under his direct control and was instructed to follow his lead. Since the junior counselors were experienced in camping activities, the participant observers were comparatively free to observe their groups and to stay with them throughout the camp period. However, the participant observers were instructed not to make notes in the boys' presence unless the situation clearly called for writing something, such as a cabin discussion in which "minutes" could be taken down. Otherwise, the participant observers withdrew or surreptitiously jotted down short notes which they expanded each evening after their boys were asleep.

The other staff members, including an official camp director, activities director, and nurse, were instructed to perform their duties in the camp in strict accordance with the planned activities and stages. The specific demands of the experiment for the next day were discussed in detail each night after the boys' bedtime and after the main observations for the day were obtained from the participant observers.

As far as the boys were concerned, therefore, the situation was as natural and attractive as the usual summer-camp situation. For this reason, and to satisfy the criterion of homogeneity among subjects and staff members, the author appeared on the premises as a caretaker with the name of "Mr. Mussee." This gave me freedom to be at crucial places at crucial times doing odd jobs without attracting the boys' attention. In addition, it was sometimes possible to make naïve statements to the boys and ask naïve questions about matters which every other staff member was expected to know as a matter of course. For example, I usually pretended not to know what group a particular boy belonged to, and I was sometimes able to elicit information that might not have been easily available otherwise.

According to the participant observers and other staff members, who were instructed to watch carefully for any sign to the contrary, this role of caretaker was never suspected. Some typical examples of the boys' reactions to Mr. Mussee will illustrate the role. For example, the rather patronizing attitude accorded a caretaker is seen in one boy's reaction when Mr. Mussee was following his group to a cook-out. The boy yelled: "Hey, Mr. Mussee, hurry up. We can't wait for you!"

On the last day, when the whole camp was breaking up and the premises were being cleaned, the caretaker was busy putting data in order and did not appear. Several boys, not seeing him at his job, complained, one of them remarking, "Where the hell is Mr. Mussee? This is his job."

In addition to observational data, charts of seating arrangements at meals, of bunk choices, of athletic teams chosen, of partners or buddies in various activities and situations were made for each day throughout the camp. A record was kept of all outgoing and incoming mail. Postcards were recorded.

One more point related to group technique is fundamental in understanding the results which will follow. This point concerns the counselors and other members of the staff. The counselors (i.e., participant observers) were in the camp primarily to observe. They and other staff members were *not* to be leaders in the usual sense at boys' camps. They were instructed, rather, to look after the safety of the boys, and to set things right if behavior went too far out of bounds. Neither the counselors nor the boy leaders were asked to exercise any particular kind of leadership technique, democratic or authoritarian. Nor was authority to be delegated or suggested to the boys by the staff members. The tendency to depart from the observance of these instructions on the part of any staff member was forcefully called to his attention so that it might be corrected. The boy leaders and their lieutenants emerged from the ranks of the two experimental groups in the course of group interaction, especially during the stage of in-group formation (i.e., Stage II).

As mentioned earlier, the daily camp program was made up of the activities for which the boys themselves expressed preference. If a hike was scheduled, the boys were left to their own devices in organizing it.

Of course, they were given tents, canteens, food, equipment, etc. as they asked for them and were given any necessary help. The boys were not preached to or organized from above to discuss among themselves the manner in which they would execute their activities. It was their affair and their discussion and their action. On the whole, the demands of the situations, not adult leadership, led the groups to discuss their affairs collectively. For example, the participant observer at one time gave his group a whole watermelon, leaving the division strictly to them. On another occasion, four large chocolate bars were given to each group of 12 boys as a reward in their collective Treasure Hunts. The ways in which the watermelon and chocolate were distributed were up to the boys.

Results

From this study, several types of data were obtained:

1. The main data related to group relations, that is, to in-group formation; the rise of group structure with relative positions and leader-follower relations; the development of in-group products, including in-group and out-group attitudes; and the development of inter-group tension, with rudimentary stereotypes and attitudes of prejudice.

2. Data were also collected concerning individual factors determining particular statuses and roles within the group. Groups are necessarily hierarchical, and it is such individual factors which largely determine the position which each member occupies. For example, when we classify our data, it will be possible to relate intelligence and certain measures from the TAT and Rosenzweig Picture-Frustration test to statuses attained and behavior in the actual group situations.

3. Finally, a special study was made of two boys in the camp, one in each experimental group, who were lowest in their groups in participation in group activities and inconsistent in their identifications. From these data, we will develop some valuable hints for the study of *marginality* and *social isolates.*

Since the principal problem of the study concerns inter-group relations, our concern here will be only with those results most directly related to group relations. Within the limitations of this paper, we shall have to concentrate on the main trend in formation of in-group and inter-group relations without going into details other than those necessary to make this trend clear.

Stage I, which lasted three days, was the stage of "natural" group-ings based on personal likes and dislikes and common interests. As mentioned before, the main purpose of Stage I was to rule out, or at least to minimize, the possibility of interpreting results of the exper-imentally induced in-group formations and inter-group relations of later stages on the basis of personal inclinations of the individual mem-bers for one another. Therefore, during Stage I, all of the 24 boys were put in one large bunkhouse.

It should be emphasized that the boys were free to select their own bunks, seats at meals, buddies for play activities, athletic teams, etc. All activities were camp-wide, i.e. potentially including all boys.

At this stage, an informal poll of preferred activities was taken with the promise that activities would be scheduled which the boys liked best. The main results of this poll were as follows:

Softball and hiking—20 choices each
Football—14 choices
Swimming—13 choices
Soccer—12 choices
Fishing—9 choices
Ping-pong—7 choices
Horseshoes and volleyball—5 choices each
A number of other activities were given choices of 4 or less.

At the end of Stage I, popularity ratings (sociograms) were obtained during informal interviews held on the pretext of getting suggestions for favored activities and for improving the camp. As other such stud-ies have found, the sociograms showed the boys clustering in budding friendship groups of two, three, or four boys. These sociograms served as the most important criterion in assigning the boys to the two experi-mental groups for the period of experimental in-group formation of Stage II. In addition, the two experimental groups were equated in other respects insofar as possible without violating the requirements of the sociogram results. Chief among these other characteristics were size, strength, ability in games, intelligence and personality ratings pre-viously made on the basis of the tests by Professor Wittenborn and Dr. Potter.

The division of the subjects into the two experimental groups was deliberately done to split the budding friendship groups which had developed. For example, if two boys showed preference for one another, one was put in one group and the other boy in the second group. If more than one friendship choice was made, we attempted to put the boy in that group holding the *fewest* of his friendship choices. Therefore, at the start of Stage II—the stage of experimental in-group formation—the number of friendship choices given to members of the experimental in-group was fewer than the number of friendship choices given to members of the experimental out-group.

TABLE I. TOTAL CHOICES OF FRIENDS, END OF STAGE I

| | Choices Received by: | |
Choices Made by:	Eventual Red Devils	Eventual Bull Dogs
Eventual Red Devils	35.1%	64.9%
Eventual Bull Dogs	65.0%	35.0%

One of these experimental groups came to be known as the Red Devils, the other as the Bull Dogs. Therefore, it will be helpful to refer to them by these names although at this point in the experiment the groups had existence only on paper. As Table I shows, of the total friendship choices made by boys who were to become Red Devils, only 35.1 percent were choices of other boys assigned to their group. The remainder, almost two-thirds, of the friendship choices made by future Red Devils were directed to boys who were placed in the Bull Dog group, that is, the out-group.

Similarly, only 35 percent of the total friendship preferences of boys who were to become Bull Dogs were for other future Bull Dogs. Sixty-five percent of their friendship choices were for boys who were placed in the Red Devil group.

Stage II, which lasted five days, was the stage of experimental in-group formation. The subjects were divided into two groups as described. The groups lived in separate bunkhouses. As it happened, the Red Devils, as they were to be known, voted to remain in the old bunkhouse, while the Bull Dogs voted to move to the new bunkhouse.

It had been anticipated that this split into two groups might not be taken easily by some of the boys. In fact, one boy cried for ten minutes at his separation from another camper with whom he had struck up a friendship in the preceding days at camp. For this reason, immediately after the bunkhouse change was made, cars took each group separately from the camp for a hike and cook-out. It will be recalled that hiking had shared first place on the boys' preferred activities, being chosen by 20 boys. The cook-out supplies were particularly sumptuous, including steak for broiling over an open fire.

During Stage II, the two experimental groups were separated as much as possible. They lived separately, ate at separate tables, served on K.P. on alternate days, and engaged separately in frequent hikes, overnight camping trips, etc. Swimming was scheduled separately for the two groups, and each very soon found their own special places some distance apart. One of these swimming places, the Bull Dogs', was secret from the other group.

Each group chose its own special hide-out in the woods in opposite directions from each other. When leaving their hide-out, one group devised an elaborate plan of departure in groups of 2 or 3 designed to camouflage the direction of their hide-out.

The activities of Stage II required that members of each group cooperate collectively in achieving their ends. In addition to hiking, overnight camping trips, and swimming, each group had a "Treasure Hunt" and engaged in group games such as fox and hounds, or bean toss, in which each member had to collect a certain number of beans to win a group reward. A small sum of money ($10.00) was given to each group to spend as they chose. Considerable group effort went to improving their cabins, stenciling insignia on T-shirts, making standards, etc. In addition, one of the groups sometimes chose to engage in craftwork, collecting wildlife, and the like. These varied activities afforded *ample opportunity for each boy to show his worth in some line of pursuit.*

One of the major findings of the study in line with the hypothesis was the formation of a well-defined in-group organization or structure. By in-group structure is meant simply the development of relative hierarchical positions within the group unit ranging from highest to lowest position. In addition to evidence from the sociograms, the hierarchical roles were manifested in terms of successful or unsuccessful initiation of group activities, the greater or lesser responsibility taken in their planning and execution, the degree of adherence to the line of activity taken by the group, the source and effectiveness of group sanctions, etc.[4]

---

[4] The specific behavorial events revealing these hierarchical positions for those subjects who attained leadership and other high positions will be presented in the more

The accompanying sociograms reveal the hierarchical positions of boys within each experimental group in terms of *popularity* (see Figs. 1 and 2). They can be considered as a measure of *one* index of group structure. The important factor which such sociograms do not adequately reflect is *power relationships* within the group. For example, in the Red Devil group, L. is revealed as receiving one more friendship choice than S. However, S. acquired and maintained power over L. and other members high in status and, partly through these boys, over the Red Devil group (see below). In the Bull Dog group, the boy H. exerted greater direction over the group than the popularity rating alone indicates, by virtue of his ability and acknowledged leadership in athletic events, even though he yielded to the overall leadership of C., the Bull Dog leader.

In the Bull Dog group, a boy named C. rose to leadership by his greater contribution in the planning and execution of common activities and by regulating and integrating the tasks and roles of the group members. At the outset, this boy successfully swung the vote to move to the new bunkhouse. His suggestions on improving the bunkhouse, for example, by putting the letter "B" on the door and by building a chinning bar, were, from the first, almost always adopted as good ones. He proved to be very effective in leading the group on their first hike. He was the boy who most frequently helped another in his group: for example, once by bandaging a blister, another time by fixing a belt. It was C. who mapped out the devious route designed to conceal their hide-out in the woods. He frequently praised other group members and instigated group praise. An instance of the latter occurred after the group had worked long and hard on a project to improve their secret swimming pool. C. said, "We did a good job, boys. We should be proud of ourselves." This was followed by cheers for the group effort and C.'s suggestion that they give the pool a name.

The Bull Dog group was, then, focalized around C.'s leadership. However, he did not lead in every situation. For example, he was not as good in athletic events or those requiring muscular skill as a boy named H. H. took over the lead in such situations with C.'s approval.

---

detailed account of the study. Such manifestations can be classified as initiation of group activities and the acceptance or rejection of such initiative by other group members, assuming responsibility in the planning and execution of group activities, degree of adherence to the group plans, the initiation and effectiveness of sanctions within the group, etc.

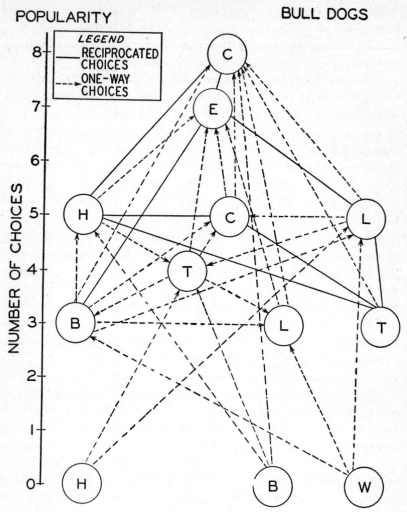

FIGURE 1.   End of stage II, in-group formation.

However, C. would occasionally overrule a decision of H.'s in such a situation, telling him, for example, not to put in a substitute player in a game; and H. would comply. A third popular boy, E., was delegated authority by C. in other tasks, such as camping or hiking.

In some contrast to the Bull Dog group, the boy who became recognized as leader of the Red Devils, S., won his position chiefly by virtue of his daring, athletic skill, and "toughness." He is noted as success-

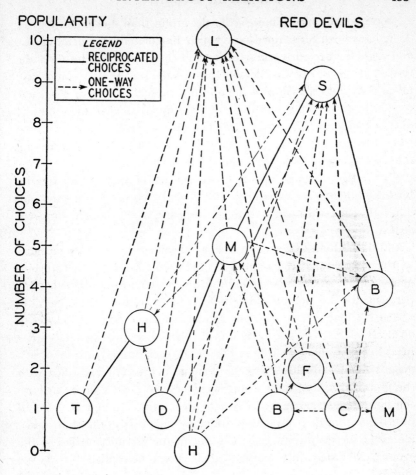

FIGURE 2. End of stage II, in-group formation.

fully leading the group in games and in daring expeditions. He was overtly recognized as "the captain" by other Red Devils. Yet S. tended to be "cliquish," confining his favors and most of his attention on the whole to a few other boys high in status, and preferring to be with them. He sometimes enforced his decisions by threats or actual physical encounters. On some later occasion, he even encouraged and participated in an attack on two members low in status in his own group. For this reason, S.'s leadership position was sometimes shaky. In fact, on the basis of popularity ratings at the end of Stage II, another boy,

L., received one more choice from the group than did S. (see Fig. 2). As it happened, S. retained power over his lieutenants, including L., and these boys in turn had effective and consistent influence over the rest of the group. It was the consensus of the staff that L. could have taken over the leadership of the group if he had wished to. For some reason, he remained subordinate to S. personally and in the group. S. once announced to the group: "My first successor is L." Later, at a time when his leadership was very shaky, he referred to L. as "the co-captain." Actually L. at no time asserted leadership over S.

S.'s prestige in his group was revealed when he spoke of his coming birthday and the boys found that he would be only twelve years old. They all expressed surprise with such remarks as, "I thought you were at least fifteen!"

Within both groups, there was competition for status as exemplified by the struggle between L. and H. of the Bull Dogs. L. tried to compete with H. in athletic events. But all the boys recognized that his performance did not measure up to H.'s. As a result, L. openly resented H's higher status, making remarks such as "Why does H. get to do everything?" On one occasion, H. physically squelched L.'s strivings. In this conflict, C. (the leader) tried to placate L. In spite of L.'s dissatisfaction with his status, he became increasingly identified with the group. One day, some group members expressed a desire to have the horseshoe stakes moved closer to their cabin. L. and H. tried to pull them from their present location. As the others in the group came along, L. successfully tugged them out of the ground and fell to the ground exhausted. In response to their cheers, he replied, "It was me and H."

Along with the formation of a more or less definite group structure, with which we have dealt only sketchily here, each group developed strong in-group feelings of *loyalty* and *solidarity* within the group and of identification of varying degrees with its activities and products. This in-group identification is illustrated by the reaction of the in-groups to those members who continued to mingle with boys in the experimental out-groups several days after the division into two groups at the end of Stage I. For example, three members of the Red Devil group, all low in the status hierarchy, were branded as "traitors" and even threatened with beatings until they saw less of the boys with whom they had been friendly in Stage I and who became Bull Dogs.

When one of the counselors returned from a necessary trip to the cabin of the other group, he was greeted with cries of "Traitor!"

Even the most retiring and ambivalent members were *at times* caught in the in-group. For example, one boy who was lowest in the Bull Dog group for participation, and was caught between loyalty to the group and waves of homesickness, was observed driving a long stick into a piece of red paper, saying, "That's what we'd do to the Red Devils."

An example of in-group identification is a boy's reference to his cabin as "home." He asked the boy leader if he had some equipment "at home." The leader asked, "Which home?" and the boy replied, "Our cabin, I mean."

Along with the group structure, products were standardized by the group, which in turn served to further solidify the in-groups. Obviously one example of such standardization was the names for the groups. The choice of these names was without doubt influenced by the larger setting—Bull Dogs, for example, being a symbol of Yale. Most of the boys were quickly given nicknames in their group: in the Bull Dog group, the boy named Emerson was dubbed "Radio," Luden was called "Cough-drop," and other nicknames clearly referred to the individual characteristics of the boys. H., the boy athletic leader, was admiringly called "Horrible H," another lad was named "Screwball." Interestingly enough, the leader of this group, C., was the only boy in this group respectfully called by his own first name—Lee. The leader of the Red Devils was tagged to typify his toughness and attractive blond appearance as "Baby Face." Other nicknames in this group were "Bones" for a thin boy and "Lemonhead" for L., a boy with a rather long skull.

Each group came to prefer certain songs. In some of them they inserted their own group's name in a glorifying fashion and the names of the other group in a less complimentary way.

Both groups standardized methods of punishment. In the case of the Red Devils, as we have mentioned, sanctions were imposed by S., the leader, through threats or actual encounters. Wayward Bull Dogs, on the other hand, were kept in line with a system of sanctions suggested and always imposed by C., the leader. Although he once was observed verbally threatening a boy, C. relied on the method of sanctions rather consistently. A Bull Dog who got out of line, had to remove a certain number of heavy stones, usually ten, from the Bull Dog Pond. This method started when the boys were improving their secret swimming place by damming it and removing rocks. They actually succeeded in raising the water level six inches.

One of the *crucial tests* of the study was whether or not these experimentally introduced in-group relationships would bring shifts or reversals in the friendship ties which began to form in Stage I on the basis of personal likes or affinities. At the end of Stage II, sociograms were obtained through informal talks with each boy. In obtaining these sociograms, it should be emphasized that the boys were free to mention those boys they liked to be with best *in the whole camp*, i.e., from the other group as well as their own.

The results indicating that such reversals were indeed found can be summarized as shown in the following table:

TABLE II. TOTAL CHOICES OF FRIENDS, END OF STAGE II

| Choices Made by: | Choices Received by: | |
	Red Devils	Bull Dogs
Red Devils	95.0%	5.0%
Bull Dogs	12.3%	87.7%

For comparison purposes the reversals of friendship choices obtained at the end of Stage I, the stage of natural groupings, and at the end of Stage II, the stage of experimental in-group formation, are presented together in Table III. It becomes sharply evident from this comparison that the friendship preferences of these boys were at first predominantly for members of the experimental out-groups. During Stage II, shifts in friendship choices occurred which were definitely in the direction of the members of the developing in-groups.

TABLE III (COMPOSITE TABLE). TOTAL CHOICES OF FRIENDS AT THE END OF STAGE I AND END OF STAGE II (NOTE THE REVERSALS)

| | Choices Made by: | Choices Received by: | |
		Eventual In-Group	Eventual Out-Group
End of Stage I	Eventual Red Devils	35.1%	64.9%
	Eventual Bull Dogs	35.0%	65.0%
		In-Group	Out-Group
End of Stage II	Red Devils	95.0%	5.0%
	Bull Dogs	87.7%	12.3%

It is evident from these tables that after the stage of in-group formation was completed, the members of each experimental group predominantly preferred to associate with members of their own in-group.

Very briefly, we will summarize the results of Stage II. In line with the first part of our hypothesis, it was found that when the two experimentally produced groups were brought together in situations and activities calling for group coöperation toward common goals, an unmistakable in-group structure developed with hierarchical positions and roles within it. The structure was not static, changing with situations within certain limits. As the group formed, the members achieved positive in-group identifications and common attitudes toward the group. By-products or *norms* peculiar to the group were standardized—nicknames, catchwords, ways of doing things, sanctions, preferred songs, etc.

Before going on to the results of Stage III, the period of inter-group relations, it is necessary to emphasize one more finding of Stage II which is related to in-group formation and *specifically related to the cultural background of the subjects*. Along with the delineation of the "we" or in-group, the two experimental groups referred to the "they" or out-group frequently and in a clear-cut way, even though there was comparatively little functional contact between the groups.

More than this, these groups of boys immediately and spontaneously began to make *comparisons,* not just in terms of "what *we* have or do, and what *they* have or do," but in terms of "their lousy cabin," "our pond is better," and even "those low kind." They began to express a desire to each other and to the staff to compete with the other group in games, with considerable assurance that their own group would win. In fact, on the second day of Stage II which followed the rather strenuous hike and cook-out for each group separately on the first day, signs of competitive attitudes between the two groups were mounting. The groups devoted a good share of this second day to the more leisurely activity of improving their respective bunkhouses and surroundings with the help of their counselors. During this activity, comparisons between the efforts of the groups cropped up and boundaries were drawn around the bunkhouse areas. The boundary questions led to disputes between some members of the two groups and some raiding of each other's cabins. This raiding was carried on in a rather playful and adventurous spirit and had the effect of intensifying the developing in-group demarcations. Since the main aim of Stage II was to produce in-group formations through coöperative group interaction rather than through opposition or competition in relation to an out-group, possible contact between the two experimental groups was further reduced during the following days of Stage II by keeping their activities farther apart through overnight hiking, swimming separately, and cook-outs in their respective hide-outs.

This rather strong desire to compete and the spontaneous derogation of the other group in *specific* respects probably *stems from the cultural background and specific socialization of these boys in a competitive society.* However, these instances of competitive feelings and, in some cases, of derogation, were *not* at this stage *standardized* in the sense that they were consistent modes of response to the out-group and its members. They were confined chiefly to the urgent desire to participate in the most attractive of all pastimes for American boys of this age—competition in sports. There was no consistent day-to-day tension or hostility between the groups at this stage.

In Stage III, the stage of inter-group relations which formally lasted nearly five days, the two experimental groups—each with varying degrees of in-group structure and strengthening friendships within the in-group—were brought into functional relationship with each other in competitive and mildly frustrating situations. The frustrating situations were planned in such a way that *on the whole* they seemed to one group to have been caused by the other.

At the beginning of Stage III, a series of competitive games was announced as though giving in to the boys' requests. The plan was for each group to receive a certain number of points or credits for winning athletic events during the coming days and for the excellence of performance in camp duties, such as cabin cleaning, K.P., etc. This point system, which was explained and given to each group orally and on typed sheets, was simple and clear. However, it allowed for some manipulation by the staff in the points given at cabin inspection, K.P., etc. It was possible, therefore, to keep the number of points attained by each group within a surmountable range until near the end of the contest, thus keeping up the strivings of both groups to win. For example, victory in athletic events brought about 15 points, whereas 1 to 10 points could be given for K.P. duties. Since such duties were performed separately, this manipulation did not arouse too much suspicion. The staff agreed that both sides were evenly matched in sports in terms of the size and skill of individual members.

A poster with two thermometers was placed on the bulletin board and the rising score of each group filled in. This poster became a center of attention for the competing groups. The prize to the winning group, which was displayed and much admired, was twelve four-bladed knives—one knife for each member of the winning group.

The effects of competitive games were not immediate. Observers all noted considerable "good sportsmanship" on the part of the two groups at the start. For example, after the first contest, the winning group spontaneously gave a cheer for the losers; and the losers, though still scattered around the field, responded as a group with a cheer for the winners. However, as the contest series progressed, this cheer changed. It started out as "2–4–6–8, who do we appreciate," followed by the name of the other team. It changed to "2–4–6–8, who do we apprecihate."

Each day of Stage III began with a Tug of War between the two groups (see Fig. 3). In this contest, the group members organized themselves and exhorted each other in the intense common effort. As it happened, the Red Devils lost the first contest. Their reaction to the loss represents one of many *perceptual distortions occurring in the group situations.* (We mentioned previously the group's exaggeration of their leader's age by three years.) All Red Devils were convinced that the "ground was against us." They spent most of the morning discussing this and their strategy for the next Tug of War. The following day, this group was on the verge of winning the Tug of War when the Bull Dogs' leader began a series of shouts and encouragement to his boys. This apparently made possible a "second wind" in which the Bull Dogs regained their lost ground and finally defeated the Red Devils again. This time, the Red Devils rationalized their defeat by agreeing that the Bull Dogs "must have done something to the rope."

The series of games also included softball, soccer and touch football. These contests tended to solidify further the in-group structure and loyalty. For example, one of the Bull Dogs became ill and was unable to participate in one of the games. He and other members of his group cried. The boy who was ill said that if the Bull Dogs won the series, he would not accept a knife because he had "let them down." But the other boys shouted down this sacrifice, gave him a cheer, and loudly proclaimed that he was "one of them."

In the Red Devil group, one of the members low in status, a boy named F., revealed increasing identification with the group during this period. When the Red Devils were trailing the Bull Dogs with two outs, and no one on the bases, F. came to bat and was tagged out with a ground ball. He sobbed for some time and went off by himself, saying to a counselor, "I lost the game for us." He was almost afraid to show his face in the Red Devil cabin; but his group never mentioned the incident and were, in fact, kind to him. This incident typifies the manner in which *group efforts and goals* became intensely *personal* ones for the individual members.

As mentioned earlier, inter-group rivalry and hostility increased rapidly during the days of the competitive contest. During one game when the boys were becoming overheated, a staff member cautioned a Red Devil not to drink too much water, because he might get sick. At this, a Bull Dog called out in a nasty tone, "Let him drink all he can. He's a Red Devil." Such expressions of hostility became increasingly frequent.

As the contest progressed, the Bull Dog group pulled out in the lead, probably because of their highly effective organization directed by C. and, in athletic events, led by H. The Red Devils responded to their increasingly apparent losing position by labeling the Bull Dogs as "dirty players." They were sure that they could win if the Bull Dogs were not "such cheaters." They said, "At least we play fair." By the contest's end, the words "dirty players" and "cheats" were almost synonymous with Bull Dogs as far as the Red Devils were concerned. Of course, the Bull Dogs denied such charges and even recognized the role of their more integrated group structure in their performance with such remarks as "We win because we have an organization."

The cumulative effect of the competitive games caused considerable group friction and, to the Red Devils, considerable frustration. The common expression of the winning Bull Dogs and the losing Red Devils in pictures taken immediately following the victory of the Bull Dogs in the athletic series convey an objective glimpse of this fact.

The winning Bull Dogs were tremendously elated at their victory. The reward of knives was distributed by C.'s suggested method—each

FIGURE 3.

boy was blindfolded and chose a knife from a bucket. Thus, not even the high-status members had advantage in choosing preferred colors, etc.

The losing group, the Red Devils, was by this time weakened. In their case, the group failure was conducive to disintegration. S., the leader and athletic captain, was bitter and began blaming and ridiculing members of his own group. At the same time he retired more and more to the company of his lieutenants. This was resented by Red Devils lower in status. Until the Red Devil group experienced an attack from the Bull Dogs and even fought with them at a later time, there was considerable disorganization.

In addition to this competition in Stage III, there were also arranged situations in which it seemed that one group interfered with or frustrated the other. Several such incidents were planned by the staff, but they could not all be carried out because of the extreme effectiveness of the first ones. The examples given were carefully recorded and, with the background of the two crystallized but hostile in-groups, constitute a little experiment in themselves. Unfortunately, many fascinating details must be omitted in this presentation.

On the evening of the victory of the Bull Dogs over the Red Devils in the athletic series and camp competition, both groups were asked to attend a party in the mess hall. By careful timing and by indirectly interesting one group in something else momentarily, the participant observers were able to see to it that the Red Devils got to the mess hall a short time before the Bull Dogs. None of the subjects in either group suspected that this timing was deliberate.

The refreshments of ice cream, cake, etc. were on a table. Half of them had been battered, broken, or crushed; the other half remained whole and delectable. When the first group (the Red Devils) arrived, they were told to go ahead and take their share of the refreshments, leaving half of it for the Bull Dogs, who were late. As we know, the Red Devils were the defeated group and had expressed in no uncertain terms their frustration and envy of the Bull Dogs for winning the prize.

Faced with the refreshments, half fresh and appetizing and half broken and crushed, the Red Devils chose the good portion and carried it to their own table. At this point the Bull Dogs arrived. Upon seeing the sorry-looking refreshments left for them, and the feasting Red

Devils, they immediately protested by sulking and by remarks of hostility against the Red Devils. The Red Devils were quick to justify their actions in terms of "first come, first served," which became the standardized justification for all Red Devil members.

The Bull Dogs discussed the possibility of throwing their beaten-up cake at the Red Devils, but decided against it on the grounds that, after all, it would taste good. They went to the far corner of the mess hall and proceeded to hurl insults and names at the Red Devils. The names were by now standardized, among them being "dirty bums," "rotten jerks," "pukes," and several more objectionable terms.

The Red Devils ate their refreshments in righteous indignation, referring to the Bull Dogs as "dirty players," "cheats," etc. The most vociferous Red Devils were four boys at the bottom status level in their group. The leaders remained more sullen and resentful of the "unjustified" attack. L., the leader's chief lieutenant, told the group to "ignore it."

When they finished, the Red Devils left the mess hall, but one of the stragglers caught sight of the Bull Dogs dumping their dirty plates and ice cream cartons on the Red Devil table. He became involved in a physical altercation which was stopped by the counselor when one Bull Dog pulled out his knife, opened the blade, and had to be restrained from brandishing it.

This event, which the Bull Dogs saw as the doings of the Red Devils, set off a series of raids and fights which soon had to be stopped by all means. The next morning, the Red Devils deliberately dirtied up their table at breakfast to make the clean-up work hard for the Bull Dogs, who were on K.P. that day. When the Bull Dogs saw the messy table, they decided to mess up the table further and leave it. C., their leader, was against this action, but the group went ahead and he joined in. They smeared the table with cocoa, sugar, syrup, etc., and left it. It was soon alive with bees and wasps. The group hung the walls with threatening and derogatory posters against the Red Devils.

The upshot of this was that at lunch that day the two groups lined up across the mess hall from each other and began to fight—shouting, throwing knives, cups, etc., and becoming so excited that intervention became necessary.

No one of either group knew who started the fight. Each was sure it was someone in the other group.

As this point, it was quickly decided by the staff to stop Stage III of the experiment immediately and to concentrate on breaking down the in-groups. The decision was to stop the intense inter-group conflict by any means necessary and then to initiate a camp program in which all boys would participate on a camp-wide basis. The experiment, from the point of view of controlling the situation, was over at this point. There was no systematic attempt at integration after Stage III. The instructions to all the staff members were to do away with the hostility as much as possible in order to send everyone home feeling good. In this period, a great deal of information and significant leads were gained for the future study of integration of hostile groups and elimination of hostility, which is certainly the pressing problem to be tackled.

In spite of the genuine efforts of the participant observers and junior counselors to stop the fighting, the acts and words of hostility continued. The Bull Dogs raided the Red Devil bunkhouse to regain a supply of green apples which they had stored as ammunition "just in case," and which the Red Devils had taken from them.

At the instigation of a counselor, the Bull Dogs decided to send H. on a "peace mission" to the furious Red Devils. H. was chosen because his athletic prowess was admired by all the camp and because during the athletic series he had remained on somewhat better terms with the Red Devil leader than had any other Bull Dog. However, the formerly temperate Red Devil leaders, S. and L., who had advised the group to "ignore" the Bull Dogs, turned down H.'s efforts. In spite of their counselor's argument, the Red Devils declined to settle with the Bull Dogs until they had had a chance to "get even." H.'s "peace mission" ended in inglorious failure: he was chased from the Red Devil bunkhouse in a hail of green apples.

The Red Devils were observed going on unauthorized expeditions to collect green apples and were later instructed that there was to be no more fighting. Pictures were taken of this secret expedition.

In spite of the fact that the Red Devils were dead-tired from the activities of the day, these youngsters succeeded in awakening and dressing at 2 A.M. with the intention of raiding the Bull Dogs. This attempted raid was an "upper-crust" affair, led by S. and his lieutenants. The raid was stopped by the participant observer and junior counselor, who were asleep in the cabin, when one of the would-be raiders kicked over a barrel of green apples which were to be used as ammunition. Since it was dark, no one could be sure who did this. The boys were in general agreement on a culprit who himself vigorously denied the charge, saying that S., the leader, made the noise. After going back to bed, the Red Devils were stopped from raiding again at 6 A.M. the same morning. Both groups were made to dump the ammunition they had hoarded.

The degree of hostility between the two groups can be clearly seen in the posters which were made by the boys and hung in the mess hall and in each others' cabins. These posters were made in every case by boys low in status in their respective groups. This, along with other evidence which has been touched upon, suggests that manifestations of inter-group hostility and rivalry of group members low in status may at times be more intense than the manifestations of members higher in status. It seems likely that the members low in status, having greater strivings for status within the group, may go to greater lengths in trying to gain recognition by showing their identification and loyalty to the in-group (Figs. 4–5 are examples of these posters).

In brief, the consequences of the inter-group relations in competitive situations and in frustrating situations which members of one group perceived as coming from the other group were: (1) to solidify the in-group belongingness and solidarity, to enhance in-group democracy, and to strengthen in-group friendships; (2) to generate and increase out-group hostility, to produce derogatory *name-calling* which came close to standardizing of negative stereotypes in relation to the out-group (i.e., *rudiments of prejudice*).

Thus we see in a concrete way that in-group democracy and coöperation does not necessarily mean democracy and coöperation with the out-group and its member, if the directions and interests of the groups are in conflict.

In dealing with inter-group relations, the vital interests and directions of the groups in their day-to-day living have to be given their due weights. The attempts to bring people into contact in a group situation and to change their perceptions and attitudes without giving proper weight to the *vital interests* of group members is hardly more than playing with shadows. *The facts of structuring and re-structuring perceptions and attitudes are not arbitrary affairs.* They are organi-

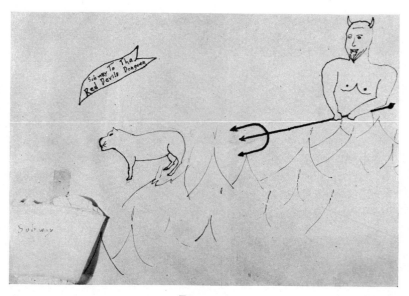

FIGURE 4.

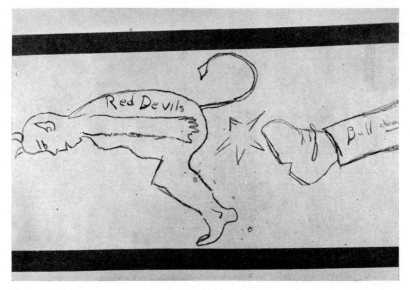

FIGURE 5.

cally related to the motives sanctioned and regulated by actual group memberships.

It is not possible here to deal at any length with other aftermaths of this experiment. After Stage III, the boys were brought together once more. Their tables were separated so that all boys would "mix up," and they were encouraged to do so by the counselors. With some persuasion, the groups attended birthday parties, camp fires, and other activities together. Individual competitions, track meets, a stunt night, etc. were held.

Probably the most effective event for the breaking up of the in-groups was a camp-wide softball game in which a team chosen by the boys from the entire camp competed with an outside group of boys from the neighboring town. In this, the boys participated *as campers*, not as in-group members. However, it should be recognized that any future experiment designed to study the process of integration between two such hostile in-groups should hardly be started by uniting the in-groups against still another in-group.

The postexperimental period did relieve a good deal of the generated tension, in that there were no more collective fights. However, the evidences of the in-group lines developed during the experimental period were observed on subsequent days. Seating arrangements, friendship preferences, etc. continued to follow group lines on the whole. On the last night of camp, the boys of the two experimental groups insisted that they wanted separate campfires because they wanted to be "by themselves" for the last time. In spite of their mixing, the old names and songs for the opposite group cropped up occasionally at these gatherings.

Before closing this general report of our study, I would like to emphasize one theoretical and methodological point that has served as the guiding principle in the conception and execution of our investigation. This guiding principle, as has been pointed out earlier (p. 389 ff.), has been that the reactions (perceptual, judgmental, etc.) of the individual take place within their appropriate reference frames. Following the implications of this principle, it is becoming more and more evident that perceptual, judgmental, motivational, and other reactions of the individual member in a group situation can be adequately understood only by placing him in the group setting of which he is a part. And this, in turn, implies that *the effects of group situations and participation as a group member will be reflected even in the relatively simple discriminations (judgments), perceptions, and other reactions of the individual.* This being the case, the effects of the group situation, and the changes brought about in attitudes toward the in-group and the out-group and their respective members, can be studied in terms of precise laboratory experiments, such as the currently accumulating judgment and perception studies. This will constitute a significant advance in method over observation of actual behavioral events alone. The actual behavioral events are more difficult to observe with precision and present baffling problems in their ordering along definite dimensions. If the psychological significance of the actual behavioral events can be epitomized and measured in terms of representative judgmental and perceptual situations, we shall be achieving a methodological gain close to the laboratory level.

In the observational data, we have concrete leads for reducing the gross behavioral trends to clear-cut perceptual and judgmental situations. For example, in competitive games, the members of the opposing teams were very keen in catching even the slightest errors or fouls committed or supposedly committed by their opponents. Such errors or alleged errors instantaneously brought forth shouts of protest from the group concerned, almost to a man. Correspondingly, any success exhibited by their in-group players brought forth almost unanimous cries of elation. In instances of dispute where errors or fouls were not so clear-cut, both groups invariably lined up against each other and the referees to prove that their opponents were in the wrong, citing all kinds of "observations" to substantiate their point. Following this lead, after in-group and out-group delineation is experimentally produced and tension is mounting between groups, members of opposing teams can be brought into controlled situations to study their perceptual selectivity and distortion. For example, a series of pictures can be designed in which the face of the player committing an error or achieving a success is not clear. These pictures can be shown to members of each of the groups for a suitably short time, and the groups' identifications obtained for the individuals in the pictures who are in error or are achieving success. In line with the findings concerning perceptual selectivity and shifts brought about by motivational factors, it can be predicted that picture identifications will significantly follow group lines—the number of identified heroes being greater on the in-group side and the number of culprits being greater on the antagonistic out-group side.

Another good possibility is the use of the autokinetic situation, which can be employed in different ways to produce significant trends along group lines. For example, one such possibility is to get the scale of distribution and the norm of judgments first *individually* from the members of opposing groups. The members could then be paired, with one member of the pair from each of the opposing groups. Also, the individuals would be paired with other members of their in-group. It can be stated as a plausible hypothesis that the departure from the individual norms of the first individual session in the direction of a common norm in a subsequent group situation will be greater in the case of the in-group pairs than with the pairs composed of in-group and out-group members.

The above are two of several possible judgmental and perceptual situations which can be utilized to measure group effects. Such controlled study of the effects of experimentally produced group situations could be made in relation to other functions as well. Rote learning and selective forgetting could be studied easily by presentation of simple verbal stimuli, such as lists of adjectives. It would be interesting, for example, to compare the rate of learning and retention by in-group members of uncomplimentary adjectives when these adjectives are applied to their in-group and when applied to the out-group and its members.

Through such an approach, judgmental, perceptual, learning, motivational processes can be studied in a unified experimental design in a group setting *which is itself experimentally produced.*

This study was not carried out in a sadistic spirit to generate group tensions. It was carried out with the conviction that we must attain a clear understanding of the underlying factors producing friction and tensions among human groupings if we are to deal with them effectively. Otherwise, our efforts in the direction of their elimination will continue to be wasteful. The real advances in medical sciences have been achieved, I believe, by going at the outset to the causation of disease.

Our next step will be the study of integration in inter-group relations. We have already learned a few lessons from the present study which are in line with the more empirical data of men in the social sciences. These may serve as the basis for further hypotheses and experimentation.

REFERENCES

1. Freud, S. *Group Psychology and the Analysis of the Ego.* London: International Psychology Press, 1922.
2. Sherif, M. *An Outline of Social Psychology.* New York: Harper, 1948. Chap. 5.
3. Sears, R. R., C. I. Hovland, and N. E. Miller. *Minor Studies of Aggression:* 1. Measurement of Aggressive Behavior, *J. Psychol.,* 1940, *9,* 277–281.
4. Guetzkow, H. S., and P. H. Bowman. *Men and Hunger.* Elgin, Ill.: Brethren Publishing House, 1946. P. 31.

Indexes

Name Index

The italicized numbers indicate the pages on which the author's own selection appears in this book.

Subject Index